7th Edition

PRAXIS I® PPST®
PRE-PROFESSIONAL SKILLS TEST

Julie O'Connell, D.Litt.
Seton Hall University
West Orange, New Jersey

Laura Meiselman, M.S.
Former New York Teacher
Cold Springs, New York

Research & Education Association

Visit our Educator Support Center: www.rea.com/teacher
Updates to the test and this book: www.rea.com/praxis/ppst.htm

Research & Education Association
61 Ethel Road West
Piscataway, New Jersey 08854
E-mail: info@rea.com

PRAXIS I PPST (Pre-Professional Skills Test)
7th Edition

Library of Congress Control Number 2010931554

ISBN-13: 978-0-7386-0880-8
ISBN-10: 0-7386-0880-7

About Research & Education Association

Founded in 1959, Research & Education Association is dedicated to publishing the finest and most effective educational materials—including software, study guides, and test preps—for students in middle school, high school, college, graduate school, and beyond.

REA's Test Preparation series includes books and software for all academic levels in almost all disciplines. Research & Education Association publishes test preps for students who have not yet entered high school, as well as for high school students preparing to enter college. Students from countries around the world seeking to attend college in the United States will find the assistance they need in REA's publications. For college students seeking advanced degrees, REA publishes test preps for many major graduate school admission examinations in a wide variety of disciplines, including engineering, law, and medicine. Students at every level, in every field, with every ambition can find what they are looking for among REA's publications.

REA's practice tests are always based upon the most recently administered exams and include every type of question that you can expect on the actual exams.

REA's publications and educational materials are highly regarded and continually receive an unprecedented amount of praise from professionals, instructors, librarians, parents, and students. Our authors are as diverse as the fields represented in the books we publish. They are well-known in their respective disciplines and serve on the faculties of prestigious high schools, colleges, and universities throughout the United States and Canada.

Today, REA's wide-ranging catalog is a leading resource for teachers, students, and professionals.

We invite you to visit us at *www.rea.com* to find out how REA is making the world smarter.

Acknowledgments

We would like to thank Larry Kling, Vice President, Editorial, for his editorial direction; Pam Weston, Publisher, for setting the quality standards for production integrity and managing the publication to completion; John Cording, Vice President, Technology, for coordinating the design, development, and testing of REA's TestWare® ; Diane Goldschmidt, Senior Editor, and Alice Leonard, Senior Editor, for pre-flight editorial review; Kathleen Casey, Senior Editor, for project management; Mel Friedman, Lead Mathematics Editor; Heena Patel, Technology Project Manager, for software testing; Christine Saul, Senior Graphic Artist, for cover design; and Rachel DiMatteo, Graphic Artist, for post-production file mapping.

We also gratefully acknowledge Wallie Hammond for copyediting; DataStream Content Solutions, LLC, for typesetting; and the Editors of REA for proofreading.

About the Authors

Julie O'Connell, D. Litt., teaches English at Seton Hall University. A doctoral candidate at Drew University, she is currently writing her dissertation entitled "Narrative Self-Representations by Writers with Asperger's Syndrome." Ms. O'Connell holds a master's degree from Brown University and a bachelor's degree in English from Georgetown University. For ten years, she served as the Director of the Felician College Writing Lab where she initiated and oversaw an interdisciplinary college writing center which used a Writing Across the Curriculum philosophy. Ms. O'Connell also developed and taught a ten-week Praxis II Elementary Education preparation course for teacher education students.

Ms. O'Connell, has taught college courses in developmental writing, rhetoric and composition, literature, reading, ESL, and Business Communications. She has worked as a Learning Specialist at a large public university, and taught high school English. She's given numerous presentations on learning styles, study strategies, time management, test preparation, test taking, note taking, and reading skills for undergraduate students. She has a special interest in working with students who have learning disabilities and who face other kinds of academic challenges. She has been honored in *Who's Who Among America's Teachers*.

Laura Meiselman, M.S., has taught math to both regular and special education students in public and independent schools in New York for moret than 15 years. She has two master's degrees from Bank Street College of Education, one in Special Education and one in Math Leadership. She is the author of two books: *Tic Tac Math: Grades 5–8* and *What's Your Angle? And 9 More Math Games*, published by Scholastic, Inc. She lives in New York's Hudson Valley with her daughter. When she's not doing curriculum writing or test preparation work, Laura can be found doing yoga, taking cooking classes, or reading.

Contents

PRACTICE TESTS

CHAPTER 1

Introduction

ABOUT THIS BOOK

REA's *Praxis I: Pre-Professional Skills Test (PPST)* test prep is a comprehensive study package designed to assist you in preparing to take the PPST test. To help you to succeed in this important step toward your teaching career, this book features:

- An accurate and complete overview of the three sections of the PPST

- The information you need to know about how the exam works

- A targeted review of each section of the exam

- Tips and strategies for successfully completing standardized tests

- Diagnostic tools to identify areas of strength and weakness

- Four full-length practice tests that replicate the PPST question format and level of difficulty

- Detailed explanations for each answer on the practice tests. Designed specifically to clarify the material, the explanations not only provide the correct answers, but also explain why the other answer choices are incorrect.

Test-takers should note that the computer-delivered version of the PPST (known as the Computerized PPST) and the paper-delivered version of the exam differ in the number of multiple-choice questions and the length of time permitted to take the test. This chapter will explain the format and concepts tested for *both* versions of the PPST.

You should also be aware that every time the PPST is administered, multiple versions of the exam are created and distributed to each testing center. These versions may contain a mix of different questions with different answers. This test versioning can add a greater level of uncertainty for the test-taker. This book is designed to prepare you for every possible version of the PPST. All the information you need to succeed is right here in this book.

HOW TO PREPARE FOR THE PPST

By reviewing and studying from this book, you can achieve a top score on the PPST. The PPST evaluates knowledge you have gained throughout your academic career. Most of the material tested by the PPST is covered in your college or university teacher preparation programs or through other classes. While the test does not measure aspects of teaching such as dedication, rapport with students, and motivation, it does assess the basic skills that are relevant to the teaching profession.

The best way to prepare for the PPST is to replicate the PPST test-taking experience. This test prep includes four full-length practice exams—two paper-delivered and two computer-delivered that accurately reflect the PPST in terms of format, content, and degree of difficulty. Our practice exams mirror the latest PPST and include every type of question that you can expect to encounter on test day. Each practice exam comes with detailed explanations of every test answer.

By completing the practice exams and studying the explanations that follow, you will pinpoint your strengths and weaknesses in each area. This will allow you to concentrate your study on sections of the exam you find to be more difficult.

ABOUT THE PPST

Who Takes the PPST, and What Is it Used For?

The PPST is used as a gateway test for teacher certification and is part of Educational Testing Service's Praxis Series. The Praxis Series of exams are taken by individuals entering the teaching profession as part of the certification process required by professional licensing organizations and many states. Besides licensure, the PPST is often used by colleges and universities to screen candidates seeking entry into teacher education programs. Each state or agency that uses the Praxis exams sets its own requirements for which tests you must take and the associated passing scores. To find out which teacher certification exams are required in your state, visit: http://www.ets.org/praxis.

Who Administers the PPST?

Like all of the Praxis Series tests, the PPST is administered by ETS and involves the assistance of educators throughout the country. The test development process is designed and implemented to ensure that the content and difficulty level of the test are appropriate.

When and Where Is the Test Given?

The Praxis I PPST is available in computer-delivered and paper-delivered formats. The computer-delivered tests are administered year-round by appointment. The paper-delivered tests are administered on pre-scheduled dates throughout the school year. To learn more about test center locations and test dates, visit: http://www.ets.org/praxis/register/centers_dates/.

When you register for the PPST, your registration bulletin will contain test dates, administration sites, and other important information. You may obtain a registration bulletin by contacting:

ETS – The Praxis Series
P.O. Box 6051
Princeton, NJ 08541-6051
Phone: (800) 772-9476

The official PPST bulletin, registration booklets, and forms are available online at: http://www.ets.org/praxis/about/bulletin/.

How Do I Register for the PPST, and Is There a Registration Fee?

You can register for the computer-delivered PPST by telephone. Call Prometric Candidate Services at 1-800-853-6773 or 1-443-751-4859, Monday through Friday, 8 a.m.–8 p.m., Eastern Time (excluding holidays). Details on payment options are available at: http://www.ets.org/praxis/register/computer/.

You can register for the paper-delivered PPST by mail or via a form on the ETS website. Internet registration is offered Monday–Friday, 7 a.m.–1 a.m., Saturday, 7 a.m. to Sunday, 8 p.m., Eastern Time. A registration form and details about payment options are available at: http://www.ets.org/praxis/register/paper/.

The official PPST bulletin, registration booklets, and forms are available online at: http://www.ets.org/praxis/about/bulletin/.

Registration fees are required and vary for the paper-delivered and computer-delivered exams. A complete list of registration fees is listed at http://www.ets.org/praxis/about/fees/.

Fee waivers are available for qualified candidates who are unable to afford registration. Visit http://www.ets.org/praxis/about/bulletin/fees/fee_waivers/ to learn more about eligibility criteria and how to apply for a fee waiver.

What if I Need to Cancel or Change My Registration?

If you need to cancel or reschedule a computer-delivered test, call Prometric candidate services at 1-800-853-6773 or 1-443-751-4859. If you cancel a test, you may be eligible for a partial refund.

To change or reschedule a paper-delivered test, you must complete a Change Request form and submit it to ETS. There is a $45 fee for this service.

The Praxis registration bulletin and forms are available online at: http://www.ets.org/praxis/about/bulletin/.

Can I Retake the Test?

Yes. Because the PPST is usually taken before the completion of a teacher certification program at a college or university, this gives teacher candidates enough time to retake the test if they are not pleased with their score. If you do not achieve a passing score on the PPST, don't panic. You can take the test again. Note that you may only take the computer-delivered test once per month and no more than 6 times within a 12-month period. There is no limit to how many times you can take a paper-delivered test. However, you should contact your state or licensing agency to confirm its retest policies.

FORMAT OF THE PPST

The PPST is divided into three sections: Reading Comprehension, Mathematics, and Writing. The test is made up of multiple-choice questions and one essay question. Each multiple-choice question presents five choices (A through E).

The number of questions and length of the PPST tests vary based on which version of the test you take. The formats and score requirements for the computer-delivered and paper-delivered tests are comparable; however, state score requirements are slightly different.

PPST Test Content and Structure

The content of the PPST computer-delivered and paper-delivered exams is the same. However, the number of questions differs depending on which test you take. The chart on page 5 shows a breakdown on the type of questions, number of questions, and time allowed for each version of the PPST.

Subject	Name and Test Code	Number of Questions and Type	Time Length of Test	Content Areas	Number of Questions	Percentage of Total
Reading	Computerized Pre-Professional Skills Test: Reading (5710)	46 multiple-choice	75 minutes	I. Literal Comprehension	21	45
				II. Critical and Inferential Comprehension	25	55
	Paper-Delivered Pre-Professional Skills Test: Reading (0710)	40 multiple-choice	60 minutes	I. Literal Comprehension	18	45
				II. Critical and Inferential Comprehension	22	55
Mathematics	Computerized Pre-Professional Skills Test: Mathematics (5730)	46 multiple-choice	75 minutes	I. Numbers and Operations	15	32.5
				II. Algebra	9	20
				III. Geometry and Measurement	10	22.5
				IV. Data Analysis and Probability	12	25
	Paper-Delivered Pre-Professional Skills Test: Mathematics (0730)	40 multiple-choice	60 minutes	I. Numbers and Operations	13	32.5
				II. Algebra	8	20
				III. Geometry and Measurement	9	22.5
				IV. Data Analysis and Probability	10	25
Writing	Computerized Pre-Professional Skills Test: Writing (5720)	44 multiple-choice and 1 essay	68 min. (38 min multiple-choice; 30 min essay)	I. Grammatical Relationships	15	17
				II. Structural Relationships	16	18.5
				III. Word Choice and Mechanics	13	14.5
				IV. Essay	1	50
	Paper-Delivered Pre-Professional Skills Test: Writing (0720)	38 multiple-choice and 1 essay	60 min. (30 min. multiple-choice; 30 min. essay)	I. Grammatical Relationships	13	17
				II. Structural Relationships	14	18.5
				III. Word Choice and Mechanics	11	14.5
				IV. Essay	1	50

Format of the Computer-delivered Tests

The computer-delivered PPST tests may be taken either as three separate tests on separate days, or as one combined test. Individual scores will be reported for Reading, Mathematics, and Writing on both the individual and the combined tests.

If you take the PPST computer-delivered tests separately, each session lasts 2 hours. If you take the combined test, the entire session lasts 4½ hours. Each session includes time for tutorials and the collection of background information. The combined test includes time for an optional 15-minute break.

The computer-delivered reading test (test code 5710) and the computer-delivered mathematics test (test code 5730) each contain 46 multiple-choice questions. You will have 75 minutes to take each test.

The computer-delivered writing test (test code 5720) contains 44 multiple-choice questions and one essay. You will have 38 minutes to answer the multiple-choice questions and 30 minutes to write your essay.

Format of the Paper-delivered Tests

Each PPST paper-delivered test (Reading, Mathematics, and Writing) is one hour long and may be taken as 3 separate tests on different days or on the same day.

The paper-delivered reading test (test code 0710) and the paper-delivered mathematics test (test code 0730) each contain 40 multiple-choice questions. You will have 60 minutes to take each test.

The paper-delivered writing test (test code 0720) contains 38 multiple-choice questions and one essay. You will have 30 minutes to answer the multiple-choice questions and 30 minutes to write your essay.

How Do I Score My Practice Tests?

Educational Testing Service does not set the passing scores for the PPST, but if you answer 75% of the questions correctly, you've probably achieved a passing score. Passing scores vary by state, therefore it is best to check with your credentially authority to verify that you passed.

The multiple-choice section of the PPST Writing Test is scored very much the same as the other sections. However, the essay portion of the exam is read and rated by two writing experts. The essays are scored on a six-point scale, with "6" being an exceptional essay and "1" being an unsatisfactory essay. A score of "0" is used for essays that are completely off-topic. Therefore, provided that you respond to the topic, your score will be between 2 and 12. You may use the conversion table to determine your scaled score by locating the number of questions you've answered correctly in the first column, and following that to the row represented by your essay score.

When Will I Receive My Score Report?

All test takers receive a score, regardless of the number of questions answered or the type of test. Your score is based on the number of questions you answer correctly, with no penalty or subtraction for answering a question incorrectly. It is to your advantage to pace yourself so that you have enough time to carefully consider every question.

Your PPST test scores will be available to you online approximately four weeks after your test date. For more information on score reporting dates, accessing your scores, and understanding your test scores, visit: http://www.ets.org/praxis/scores/.

HOW TO USE THIS BOOK

When Should I Start Studying?

It is never too early to start studying for the PPST. The earlier you begin, the more time you will have to sharpen your skills. Do not procrastinate! Cramming is not an effective way to study because it does not allow you the time you need to think about the content, review the material, and take the practice tests. Make the best use of your time by following our study schedule on pages 11 and 12. The schedule is based on an eight-week program, but it can be shortened to 4 weeks if you are starting late.

What Should I Study First?

We strongly recommend that you begin your PPST preparation with Practice Test 1. This test is a full-length model test designed to help you determine your strengths and weaknesses on the material the PPST will cover. For maximum benefit, simulate actual testing conditions by taking the test where you will not be interrupted. After you've taken the practice test, review the detailed explanations of answers to determine what areas you need to study further.

What Do the Review Sections Cover?

The targeted review chapters in this book were designed to help you sharpen the skills you need to succeed on the PPST, as well as provide strategies for answering the questions.

This test prep includes detailed Reading, Mathematics, and Writing review chapters, which correspond to the subject areas on the PPST. Supplementing your studies with our review material will provide focus and structure and will allow you to choose a particular subject or subtopic to study. The reviews are set up to give you exactly what you need to do well on the exam.

Reading Comprehension:

The Reading Test measures your ability to understand and analyze written information. Our Reading Comprehension Review is designed to enhance the reading comprehension skills necessary to achieve a high score on the PPST. Strategies for attacking reading comprehension questions are thoroughly explained, and a four-step approach to answering the test questions is completely outlined. In addition, a vocabulary enhancer is included to help you better understand the passages on the test.

Mathematics:

The Mathematics Test measures competency in mathematical skills that an educated adult will require, including numbers and operations, algebra, geometry and measurement, and data analysis and probability.

Several problems involve the integration of several skills into one problem-solving situation. The Mathematics Review in this test prep will help you reinforce the arithmetic, algebraic, and geometric concepts that will be tested on the PPST. Drill questions are included that will help you sharpen your mathematical skills. A valuable reference table offers quick access to important formulae and an index of mathematical symbols. Careful review of this section should give you all the information you need to pass this section of the PPST.

Writing:

The Writing Test section includes multiple-choice questions and an essay. The multiple-choice questions test the examinees' knowledge of grammatical relationships, structural relationships, and word choices and mechanics. Test-takers will be presented with a topic and must write an original essay within the allotted time.

Our Writing Skills Review contains a wealth of information concerning the structure, content, and format of the PPST essay. Regardless of the topic you are assigned on the exam, a concise, well-constructed essay is essential to achieve a passing score. Careful study of the Essay Writing Review will hone your essay-writing abilities, so that you will be able to write your essay with confidence. The review also covers the material tested on the multiple-choice questions, so you'll be ready to tackle the Writing Section with confidence.

STUDYING FOR THE PPST

You may be wondering how you will find time to work, take care of family obligations, and prepare for the PPST. But don't worry, our helpful test-taking tips and flexible study schedule will show you how to make the most of your valuable time.

Choose a time and place for studying that works best for you. Some people set aside a certain number of hours every morning to study, while others prefer to study at night after work (or school) or before going to sleep. Other people study off and on during the day—for instance, while waiting for a bus or during a lunch break. Only you can determine when and where your study time will be most effective. Be consistent and use your time efficiently. Work out a study routine and stick to it.

Remember, repeated study of the review material helps build and reinforce your skills. After you have reviewed sufficiently, take the practice tests to familiarize yourself with the format of the PPST.

When you take the practice tests, simulate the conditions of the actual exam as closely as possible. Turn off your television, radio, and cell phone, and sit down at a table in a quiet room, free from distraction. After completing a practice test, score it and thoroughly review the explanations to the questions you answered incorrectly; however, do not review too much in one study session. Concentrate on one problem area at a time by reviewing the question and detailed answer explanation, and then study the related review chapters until you are confident that you have mastered the material. Many have found the use of study or note cards very helpful for reviewing "problem" areas.

Keep track of your practice test scores so you can gauge your progress and discover general weaknesses in particular sections. Give extra attention to the reviews that cover your areas of difficulty, so you can build your skills in those areas.

After completing the Writing section of a practice exam, ask a friend, colleague, or family member to read your essay and offer feedback. Each practice test includes sample essays, explains the point system used for grading essays, and offers criticism based on the official scoring criteria. Be sure you understand what is expected of you and carefully study the Writing review chapter.

If you know other people who are studying for the PPST, why not arrange a study group? Study groups make preparing for the exam more enjoyable, and allow you to share knowledge and obtain feedback from other members of your group.

I Started Studying Too Late. What Do I Do Now?

Last-minute cramming is not the best way to prepare for any exam, but if you concentrate your study efforts during the days before the PPST, you can still get a good score.

First, take Practice Test 1 to pinpoint your strengths and weaknesses. Next, review the subject areas where you are weak. Review the test-taking tips in this chapter; then take Practice Test 2. See where you did well and where you need to improve. Review your weak areas again, paying close attention to the detailed answer explanations for the questions you answered wrong. Take Practice Test 3, then study the review sections for any areas you need to improve. If time permits, take Practice Test 4.

While this "crash course" method requires extra energy and focus, we realize that not everyone has the luxury of the time they'd really like put into it. Of course, if you score poorly, you can always register for the next PPST test administration. Just remember to plan ahead and schedule your study time wisely for the next exam, so you can get a great score.

How Can I Use My Study Time Efficiently?

This study schedule will help you become thoroughly prepared for the PPST. Although the schedule is designed as an 8-week study program, it can be compressed into a 4-week plan by combining two weeks of study into one. If you choose the 8-week schedule, you should plan to study for *at least* one hour a day. PPST examinees who are following a 4-week program need to set aside at least two hours for studying every day. The more time you devote to studying, the more prepared and confident you will be on the day of the test.

Study Schedule

REA's *Praxis I: Pre-Professional Skills Test (PPST)* test prep offers you all the practice and information you need to pass the PPST and start teaching. Four full-length practice exams are included in the book and come complete with detailed explanations of answers to help you master what you need to know for test day.

Week	Activity
1.	Acquaint yourself with the PPST by reading the introduction of this book. Be sure you understand the format of the PPST and know exactly what is tested on the exam. Now would be a good time to plan a study schedule. When and where will you study? Are you interested in joining a study group? How will you balance your everyday responsibilities with studying? Decide when and where you study best, and get ready to tackle the PPST!
2.	Start your study routine by taking Practice Test 1 to determine your strengths and weaknesses. Make sure you give yourself several hours after work, on a weekend, or at another convenient time to take the exam. You will need to concentrate, so take the practice test at a time and place where you will not be disturbed. When you take the test, read the instructions carefully and make certain you're sure about a test answer before you go on to the next question. Although the practice exam is given in a timed format, don't rush through the test. Try to do your best, even on sections where you may be confused.
	After you've finished the exam, read the detailed explanations of answers to any questions you answered wrong and try to see where you made an error. If you score low in any subject area, thoroughly review the relevant chapters. For example, if you answered several questions in the Math section incorrectly, you should carefully study the Mathematics Review chapter. Later in the week, study the detailed explanations for the questions you answered incorrectly. Take notes and pay attention to sections where you missed a lot of questions. You will need to spend more time reviewing the related material.
3.	Make a firm commitment to study for *at least* an hour a day, every day for the next few weeks. It may seem hard to find time in your busy schedule, but remember: the more you study, the better prepared you will be for the PPST. This week, study the Reading Review. Complete the practice questions and check your answers. Be sure you are comfortable with the material you've just covered before continuing to next week's study agenda. Give yourself more time to review areas in which you feel you need improvement. After reviewing this section completely, retake only the section that covers Reading on Practice Test 1 to see how your score improves.
4.	Study the Mathematics Review chapter. Study the sample problems and solutions for each section of the review and make sure you understand the concepts completely before moving on to a new section. Complete the practice problems at the end of the review chapter. If you missed a lot of questions in one section (algebra, for example), go back and re-read the algebra section of the review, and check your answers for each drill question that you answered incorrectly. Retake the math section of Practice Test 1 and note any improvement.

Week	Activity
5.	This week, study the Writing Review. Focus on the topics and writing examples provided, and make sure you understand how the essays will be graded. Now is also a good time to review any supplemental materials (such as a writing and/or grammar handbook) that will aid you in writing clearer, better-focused essays. Try a few practice essays on your own and ask a co-worker, spouse, or friend to give you feedback. Later this week, take Practice Test 2.
6.	Now it's time to go back and study any areas of the Reading Skills, Math, or Writing reviews in which you feel you need improvement. Read through the detailed answer explanations for any questions you got wrong on Practice Test 2. Later this week, take Practice Test 3. After you've finished the exam, go back and study the detailed explanations of answers to any questions you answered incorrectly. How much have your scores improved since you took the first test?
7.	Start off Week 7 by taking Practice Test 4. By now you should be familiar with the format of the PPST, so take your time and think about each question as you answer it. Review the detailed answers for any questions you answered incorrectly, then focus your concentration on those section(s) of the relevant review chapter(s).
8.	This is your last week to make the most of your study time. Re-read the review chapters (or sections) for any topics that still give you trouble. Study the answer explanations to all the practice test questions you answered incorrectly, so you can boost your skills before the exam. If you are satisfied with your scores and the time it takes you to complete the three sections of the exams, you have completed your studying and are ready to take the PPST with confidence! Good luck on the PPST!

PPST TEST-TAKING STRATEGIES

Although you may not be familiar with standardized tests like the PPST, our proven test-taking tips will show you how to prepare for the exam and alleviate any test-taking anxieties. By following the suggestions listed here, you can become more relaxed about taking the PPST, as well as other tests.

- Become comfortable with the format of the PPST. When you take our practice tests, simulate the conditions of the actual test. Pace yourself and stay calm. After repeating this process a few times, you will boost your confidence and improve your chances of performing well on test day.

- Read all the possible answers. Just because you think you have found the correct response, do not automatically assume that it is the best answer. Read through each answer choice to be sure that you are not making a mistake by jumping to conclusions.

- If you are uncertain about a question, guess at the answer rather than skipping it. You will not be penalized for answering incorrectly, since wrong answers are not counted toward your final score. This means that you should never leave a blank space on your answer sheet. Even if you do not have time to narrow down the choices, be sure to fill in every space on the answer sheet. You can only gain by this, since you will receive credit for any questions answered correctly—even if purely by luck.

- Use the process of elimination. Go through each answer to a question and eliminate as many incorrect answer choices as possible. If you can eliminate two or three answer choices, you have given yourself a better chance of getting the item correct. Do not leave an answer blank. It is better to guess than not to answer a question on the PPST because there is no penalty for wrong answers.

- Place a question mark in your answer booklet next to the answers you guessed, and then recheck them later if you have time.

- Work quickly and steadily. Do not spend too much time on any one question. If, after a few minutes, you cannot answer a particular question, make a note of it and continue on. You can go back to it after you have completed easier questions first. Taking the practice tests in this book will help you learn to budget your precious time.

- Learn the directions and format of the test. This will not only save time but also will help you avoid anxiety (and the mistakes caused by being anxious).

- When taking the multiple-choice portion of the test, be sure that the answer oval you fill in corresponds to the number of the question in the test booklet. The multiple-choice test is graded by machine, and marking one wrong answer can throw off your answer key and your score. Be extremely careful.

- When writing your essay, write legibly. Remember, your essay will be scored by two people—not a machine—so write neatly. No points will be deducted for poor penmanship, but illegible handwriting impairs communication. Be sure to re-read your essay for content and proofread it to catch any spelling or grammatical errors.

THE DAY OF THE TEST

Before the Test

The night before the test, make sure you have everything you need for test day organized and in one place. (You don't want to forget anything or be rushing around in the morning.) Here are a few important things you should do:

Verify the time and location of the exam: make sure you know when and where you need to report to take the PPST. It's a good idea to get directions to the test center and be sure you know where you're going before test day. (You don't want to risk being late for the exam because you got lost.) You can verify your test information by logging on to your "My Praxis Account" at: https://www.ets.org.

When you sign up for an account, you can register online for paper-delivered tests, access your admission ticket, view scores, and order additional score reports.

Print your admission ticket: If you are taking a paper-delivered test, print a copy of your admission ticket and bring it with you to the test center. If you are taking a computer-delivered test, bring your authorization voucher with you.

Gather your identification documents: You must have acceptable and valid ID with your name, signature and photograph to be admitted to a test center. ID requirements are strictly enforced. (More about proper ID appears in the next section.)

On the morning of the PPST, dress comfortably so you are not distracted by being too hot or too cold while taking the exam. Check your Registration Bulletin or visit http://www.ets.org/praxis/register/centers_dates/ to find out what time to arrive at the testing center. It's always a good idea to arrive at the test center early. Reporting early will allow you to collect your thoughts and relax before the test and will also spare you the anguish that comes with being late.

Procedures for Test Day

For computer-delivered tests: be sure to arrive at your test center location at least 30 minutes before your reporting time. When you arrive, an administrator or supervisor will check you in and assign your seat.

You will be given 30 minutes of practice time for the tutorial and other untimed sections prior to the test. This allows you to become familiar with the computer functions and will help make your computer-delivered testing experience go smoothly.

For paper-delivered tests: Arrive at the testing center by 7:30 a.m. for Session 1 tests, or at 10:45 a.m. for Session 2 tests. When you arrive, an administrator or supervisor will check you in and assign your seat. You may not bring mechanical pencils or paper into the testing room.

For more information on testing procedures, visit: http://www.ets.org/praxis/test_day/procedures.

What to Bring on Test Day

For paper-delivered testing, you MUST bring the following with you to the test site:

- Admission ticket/authorization voucher and acceptable ID

- Several sharpened, soft-lead (No. 2 or HB) pencils with erasers for paper-delivered tests. Pencils are not supplied at paper-delivered testing centers, but <u>are</u> supplied at computer-delivered testing centers. (Note: Mechanical pencils are not allowed.)

- A blue or black pen for paper-delivered tests. Pens are not supplied at the test center.

- A calculator if allowed for your test (Visit: http://www.ets.org/praxis/test_day/policies/calculators for the procedures and policies regarding calculators.)

For computer-delivered testing, you MUST bring the following with you to the test site:

- Your admission ticket
- Proper identification

Test Site Rules

Keep in mind that when you register for the PPST, you are agreeing to comply with all the rules in the current registration bulletin. Violation of test site rules may result in the voiding of your scores.

The following are not permitted at the test site:

- Cell phones, BlackBerry devices, PDAs and/or any other electronic or photographic devices. (If you bring these devices to the test center, you will be dismissed from the test, your registration and test fees will be forfeited and your scores will be canceled. Test center staff members are not permitted to collect and/or store devices.)

- Watches with alarms or other time-keeping devices that make noise

- Smoking and the use of all tobacco products

- Visitors, including relatives, children, and friends

- Pets

- Weapons of any kind

- Handwritten or printed materials, such as dictionaries, notebooks, scratch paper, or textbooks

- Personal items, such as packages and bags of any kind, such as backpacks, briefcases, etc.

- Hats or headwear, except those being worn for religious or medical purposes
- Food and drink
- Unauthorized aids, such as slide rules, rulers, translation aids, highlighters, etc.

For more information on what to bring (or not bring) to the test, visit: http://www.ets.org/praxis/test_day/bring.

Acceptable Identification Documents

Acceptable primary ID includes:

- Passport with name, photograph, and signature
- Valid driver's license with name, photograph, and signature
- State or province ID issued by a motor vehicle agency with name, photograph, and signature
- National ID with name, photograph, and signature
- Military ID with name, photograph, and signature

Supplemental ID may be required if the test center administrator has concerns about the primary ID. If your primary ID does not contain your signature, sign the document or present an acceptable supplemental ID document.

For general questions about acceptable ID, call: 1-800-205-2626 (U.S., U.S. Territories and Canada) or 1-609-771-7393 (all other locations). or more information about acceptable ID and other ID procedures visit: http://www.ets.org/praxis/test_day/id/.

Absentee Policy

If you are absent from the test, you will not receive a refund or a credit. However, you can request a transfer of your registration to a future test date in the same testing year up to 3 days prior to the test date. You may not transfer your registration from the previous testing year to the current testing year. There is a $45 fee for this service.

Refund Policies

Computer-delivered Tests: You are eligible for a refund of $20 per test ($60 for combined test) if you cancel your testing appointment at least three full days prior to your test date.

Paper-delivered Tests: You are eligible for a refund of the test fee(s) and any state surcharges if you cancel your paper-delivered test no later than three full days prior to your test.

Please note that if you are absent from or arrive too late to take the test at the test administration for which you registered, you are not entitled to a refund.

For more information on refunds, visit: http://www.ets.org/praxis/about/fees/refund_policies/.

During the Test

Once you enter the test center, follow all the rules and instructions given by the test supervisor. If you do not, you risk being dismissed from the test and having your score canceled.

When all the materials have been distributed, the test instructor will give you directions for completing the informational portion of your answer sheet. Fill out the sheet carefully, because the information you provide will be printed on your score report.

During testing, you may take restroom breaks. Keep in mind that any time you take for restroom breaks is considered part of the available testing time. You may not leave the testing room in which you have been seated for any purpose (other than to use the restroom) until your test materials have been collected and a test administrator has officially dismissed you. During the test, you may not communicate with other examinees or any unauthorized persons in any way, either in person or by using any communication device.

After the Test

After your test materials have been collected, you will be dismissed. Then your day is free. Celebrate completing the PPST by doing something fun. Go shopping, see a movie, visit with friends, or go home and relax. The good news is that the hard part is over. Now you just have to sit back and wait for the test results.

CHAPTER 2

Reading Comprehension Review

The questions in the Reading Section of the PPST are divided into four content categories that contribute to the total score in the following approximate percentages:

Reading	Code: 0710	60 minutes/ 40 multiple-choice questions based on passages	<u>Literal Comprehension</u> 18 questions—45% (Find main ideas, supporting ideas, organization, vocabulary in context) <u>Critical and Inferential Comprehension</u> 22 questions—55% (Evaluating, inferring, and generalizing)
Computerized Reading	Code: 5710	75 minutes/ 46 multiple-choice questions	<u>Literal Comprehension</u> 21 questions—45% <u>Critical and Inferential Comprehension</u> 25 questions—55% (However, only 40 questions are scored—six are omitted).

In this section of the exam, you will encounter both long and short passages are used. Long passages consist of approximately 200 words and are accompanied by 4–7 questions, while shorter passages are composed of approximately 100 words and have 2–3 questions. Passages are taken from newspapers, magazines, journals, non-fiction books, and fictional pieces.

Strategies for the Reading Section:
1. A Four-Step Approach
2. Additional Tips
3. Vocabulary Enhancer

This review was developed to prepare you for the Reading Section of the PPST. You will be guided through a step-by-step approach to attacking reading passages and answering the questions. We also include tips to help you quickly and accurately answer the questions which will appear in this section of the exam. By studying our review, you will greatly increase your chances of achieving a passing score on the Reading Section of the PPST.

Remember, the more you know about the skills tested, the better you will perform on the test. In this section, the skills you will be tested on are:

Literal Comprehension *(approximately 45% of examination)*

- Determining the main idea or the purpose of the passage or statement.
- Identifying supporting ideas or details.
- Identifying the organization of the passage.
- Comprehending the meaning and structure of the language used.

Critical and Inferential Comprehension *(approximately 55% of examination)*

- Identifying the author's assumptions.
- Discerning the author's attitude toward the subject.
- Developing inferences from the given material.
- Identifying strengths, weaknesses, and validity of the author's argument.
- Gauging the relevance of supporting evidence to the argument.
- Applying ideas presented in the passage to other situations.

To help you master these skills, we present examples of the types of questions you will encounter and explanations of how to answer them. A drill section is also provided for further practice. Even if you are sure you will perform well on this section, make sure to complete the drills, as they will help sharpen your skills.

The Passages

The eight reading passages in the Reading Section are specially designed to be on the level of the types of material that you encounter in college textbooks. They will present you with very diverse subjects. Although you will not be expected to have prior knowledge of the information presented in the passages, you will be expected to know the fundamental reading comprehension techniques presented in this chapter. Only your ability to read and comprehend material will be tested.

The Questions

Each passage will be followed by a number of questions, with the total number appearing in the section being forty questions. The questions will ask you to make determinations based on what you have read. You will encounter 9 main types of questions in this test. These questions will ask you to:

1. determine which of the given answer choices best expresses the main idea of the passage;

2. determine the author's purpose in writing the passage;

3. determine which fact best supports the writer's main idea;

4. know the difference between fact and opinion in a statement;

5. organize the information in the passage;

6. determine which of the answer choices best summarizes the information presented in the passage;

7. recall information from the passage;

8. analyze cause-and-effect relationships based on information in the passage;

9. determine the definition of a word as it is used in the passage.

Before the Test

You should study our review to build your reading skills. Also, make sure to study and learn the directions to save yourself time during the actual test. The directions will be similar to the following:

DIRECTIONS: You will encounter eight passages in this section of the test, each followed by a number of questions. Only ONE answer to each question is the best answer, although more than one answer may appear to be correct. There are 40 multiple-choice questions in this section. Choose your answers carefully and mark them on your answer sheet. Make sure that the space you are marking corresponds to the answer you have chosen.

In addition, you should *practice* prior to the test by working through passages and different types of questions contained in this book.

1. Strategies for the Reading Section: A Four-Step Approach

When you take the Reading Section of the PPST, you will have two tasks:

1. to read the passage and
2. to answer the questions.

Of the two, carefully reading the passage is the more important; answering the questions is based on an understanding of the passage. Here is a four-step approach to reading:

Step 1 Skim through the questions.

Step 2 Read the passage quickly by previewing it.

Step 3 Read actively by marking up the passage.

Step 4 Answer the questions.

In the following section, consider the following exercises and use these four steps when you complete the Reading Section of the PPST.

Step 1: Skim Through the Questions

Read through and underline or circle key words in the question. Don't read the answers—just get a sense of the kinds of questions being asked. Remember: some questions are literal and others are inferential. Practice this step by reading through the questions for the following passage.

Practice <u>skimming through the questions</u> that accompany the following passage. Keep in mind that you should look at the stem of the question. Don't spend time reading the answers to each question in your preview.

─────── **PASSAGE** ───────

1   That the area of obscenity and pornography is a difficult one for the Supreme Court is well documented. The Court's numerous attempts to define obscenity have proven unworkable and left the decision to the subjective preferences of the justices. Perhaps Justice Stewart put it best when, after refusing to

5   define obscenity, he declared, "But I know it when I see it." Does the Court literally have to see it to know it? Specifically, what role does the fact-pattern, including the materials' medium, play in the Court's decision?

Several recent studies employ fact-pattern analysis in modeling the Court's decision making. These studies examine the fact-pattern or case characteristics, often with ideological and attitudinal factors, as a determinant of the decision reached by the Court. In broad terms, these studies owe their theoretical underpinnings to attitude theory. As the name suggests, attitude theory views the Court's attitudes as an explanation of its decisions.

These attitudes, however, do not operate in a vacuum. As Spaeth explains, "the activation of an attitude involves both an object and the situation in which that object is encountered." The objects to which the court directs its attitudes are litigants. The situation—the subject matter of the case—can be defined in broad or narrow terms. One may define the situation as an entire area of the law (e.g., civil liberties issues). On an even broader scale the situation may be defined as the decision to grant certiorari or whether to defect from a minimum-winning coalition.

Defining the situation with such broad strokes, however, does not allow one to control for case content. In many specific issue areas, the cases present strikingly similar patterns. In examining the Court's search and seizure decisions, Segal found a relatively small number of situational and case characteristic variables explain a high proportion of the Court's decisions.

Despite Segal's success, efforts to verify the applicability of fact-pattern analysis in other issue areas and using broad-based factors have been slow in forthcoming. Renewed interest in obscenity and pornography by federal and state governments, the academic community, and numerous antipornography interest groups indicates the Court's decisions in this area deserve closer examination.

The Court's obscenity and pornography decisions also present an opportunity to study the Court's behavior in an area where the Court has granted significant decision-making authority to the states. In *Miller vs. California* (1973) the Court announced the importance of local community standards in obscenity determinations. The Court's subsequent behavior may suggest how the Court will react in other areas where it has chosen to defer to the states (e.g., abortion).

Questions

1. The main idea of the passage is best stated by which of the following?

   (A) The Supreme Court has difficulty convicting those who violate obscenity laws.

   (B) The current definitions for obscenity and pornography provided by the Supreme Court are unworkable.

(C) Fact-pattern analysis is insufficient for determining the attitude of the Court toward the issues of obscenity and pornography.

(D) Despite the difficulties presented by fact-pattern analysis, Justice Segal found the solution in the patterns of search and seizure decisions.

(E) The Supreme Court's habit of frequently returning decisions to the jurisdiction of the state courts.

2. The main purpose of the writer in this passage is to

(A) convince the reader that the Supreme Court is making decisions about obscenity based on their subjective views only

(B) explain to the reader how fact-pattern analysis works with respect to cases of obscenity and pornography

(C) define obscenity and pornography for the layperson

(D) demonstrate the role fact-pattern analysis plays in determining the Supreme Court's attitude about cases in obscenity and pornography

(E) convey a concern of the future decisions of the court regarding abortion.

3. Of the following, which fact best supports the writer's contention that the Court's decisions in the areas of obscenity and pornography deserve closer scrutiny?

(A) The fact that a Supreme Court Justice said, "I know it when I see it."

(B) Recent studies that employ fact-pattern analysis in modeling the Court's decision-making process.

(C) The fact that attitudes do not operate in a vacuum.

(D) The fact that federal and state governments, interest groups, and the academic community show renewed interest in the obscenity and pornography decisions by the Supreme Court.

(E) The fact that a justice would freely say about a serious national issue: "I know it when I see it."

4. Among the following statements, which states an opinion expressed by the writer rather than a fact?

(A) That the area of obscenity and pornography is a difficult one for the Supreme Court is well documented.

(B) The objects to which a court directs its attitudes are the litigants.

(C) In many specific issue areas, the cases present strikingly similar patterns.

(D) The Court's subsequent behavior may suggest how the Court will react in other legal areas.

(E) Several recent studies employ fact-pattern analysis in modeling the Court's decision making.

5. The list of topics below that best reflects the organization of the topics of the passage is

(A) I.   The difficulties of the Supreme Court

     II.   Several recent studies

     III. Spaeth's definition of "attitude"

     IV.   The similar patterns of cases

     V.   Other issue areas

     VI.   The case of *Miller vs. California*

(B) I.   The Supreme Court, obscenity, and fact-pattern analysis

     II.   Fact-pattern analyses and attitude theory

     III. The definition of "attitude" for the Court

     IV.   The definition of "situation"

     V.   The breakdown in fact-pattern analysis

     VI.   Studying Court behavior

(C) I.   Justice Stewart's view of pornography

     II.   Theoretical underpinnings

     III. A minimum-winning coalition

     IV.   Search and seizure decisions

     V.   Renewed interest in obscenity and pornography

     VI.   The importance of local community standards

(D) I.   The Court's numerous attempts to define obscenity

     II.   Case characteristics

     III. The subject matter of cases

     IV.   The Court's proportion of decisions

     V.   Broad-based factors

     VI.   Obscenity determination

(E) I.   Case characteristics

     II.   The Court's search and seizure decisions

III. The history of the Court's decisions

IV. Abortion decisions

V. Several monumental decisions

VI. The variety of cases

6. Which paragraph below is the best summary of the passage?

(A) The Supreme Court's decision-making process with respect to obscenity and pornography has become too subjective. Fact-pattern analyses, used to determine the overall attitude of the Court, reveal only broad-based attitudes on the part of the Court toward the situations of obscenity cases. But these patterns cannot fully account for the Court's attitudes toward case content. Research is not conclusive that fact-pattern analyses work when applied to legal areas. Renewed public and local interest suggests continued study and close examination of how the Court makes decisions. Delegating authority to the states may reflect patterns for Court decisions in other socially sensitive areas.

(B) Though subjective, the Supreme Court decisions are well documented. Fact-pattern analyses reveal the attitude of the Supreme Court toward its decisions in cases. Spaeth explains that an attitude involves both an object and a situation. For the Court, the situation may be defined as the decision to grant certiorari. Cases present strikingly similar patterns, and a small number of variables explain a high proportion of the Court's decisions. Segal has made an effort to verify the applicability of fact-pattern analysis with some success. The Court's decisions on obscenity and pornography suggest weak Court behavior, such as in *Miller vs. California.*

(C) To determine what obscenity and pornography mean to the Supreme Court, we must use fact-pattern analysis. Fact-pattern analysis reveals the ideas that the Court uses to operate in a vacuum. The litigants and the subject matter of cases is defined in broad terms (such as an entire area of law) to reveal the Court's decision-making process. Search and seizure cases reveal strikingly similar patterns, leaving the Court open to grant certiorari effectively. Renewed public interest in the Court's decisions proves how the Court will react in the future.

(D) Supreme Court decisions about pornography and obscenity are under examination and are out of control. The Court has to see the case to know it. Fact-pattern analyses reveal that the Court can only define cases in narrow terms, thus revealing individual egotism on the part of the Justices. As a result of strikingly similar patterns in search and seizure cases, the Court should be studied further for its weakness in delegating authority to state courts, as in the case of *Miller vs. California.*

(E) As seen in the case of *Miller vs. California*, the Supreme Court is uncomfortable taking on high-visibility cases. It has been its history to return difficult cases to the states' higher courts. We need to be very concerned moving forward. We must be watchful to be sure that the Court does not shirk from its duty toward the country. This would result in serious damage to the balance of power so ably conceived by the writers of the U.S. Constitution.

7. Based on the passage, the rationale for fact-pattern analyses arises out of what theoretical groundwork?

(A) Subjectivity theory

(B) The study of cultural norms

(C) Attitude theory

(D) Cybernetics

(E) Fact patterns

8. Based on data in the passage, what would most likely be the major cause for the difficulty in pinning down the Supreme Court's attitude toward cases of obscenity and pornography?

(A) The personal opinions of the Court Justices

(B) The broad nature of the situations of the cases

(C) The ineffective logistics of certiorari

(D) The inability of the Court to resolve the variables presented by individual case content

(E) The narrow nature of the cases being presented

9. In the context of the passage, *subjective* might be most nearly defined as

(A) personal

(B) wrong

(C) focused

(D) objective

(E) communal

If you previewed the stems, you will realize that they can tell you the kind of question being asked. The questions are:

1. main idea of the passage

2. main purpose of the writer in the passage

3. detail question ("Of the following, which fact best supports the writer's contention that the Court's decisions in the areas of obscenity and pornography deserve closer scrutiny?")

4. finding opinion expressed by the writer

5. organization

6. summary of the passage

7. detail question ("Based on the passage, the rationale for fact-pattern analyses arises out of what theoretical groundwork?")

8. cause and effect ("Based on data in the passage, what would most likely be the major cause for the difficulty in pinning down the Supreme Court's attitude toward cases of obscenity and pornography?")

9. Vocabulary in context ("In the context of the passage, *subjective* might be most nearly defined as")

Remember, once you get a sense of the kinds of questions you will be answering, it is easier to spot those answers in the passage itself.

As you begin to examine the passage, you should first determine the main idea of the passage and underline it, so that you can easily refer back to it if a question requires you to do so (see question 1). The main idea should be found in the first paragraph of the passage, and may even be the first sentence. From what you have read thus far, you now know that the main idea of this passage is that the Supreme Court has difficulty in making obscenity and pornography decisions.

In addition, you also know that recent studies have used fact-pattern analysis in modeling the Court's decision. You have learned also that attitudes do not operate independently and that case content is important. The feasibility of using fact-pattern analysis in other areas and broad-based factors have not been quickly verified. To study the behavior of the Court in an area in which they have granted significant decision-making authority to the states, one has only to consider the obscenity and pornography decisions. In summary, the author suggests that the Court's subsequent behavior may suggest how the Court will react in those other areas in which decision-making authority has previously been granted to the states. As you can see, having this information will make the reading of the passage much easier.

Step 2: Read the Passage Quickly by Previewing It

Before closely reading the passage, you should take about 30 seconds to look over the passage. An effective way to preview the passage is to read quickly the first sentence of each paragraph, the concluding sentence of the passage, and the questions—not all the answers—following the passage

Practice previewing each of the following paragraphs to see if you can decide what the primary purpose might be.

Read these examples and see if you can decide what the primary purpose of the following statements might be.

(A) Jogging too late in life can cause more health problems than it solves. I will allow that the benefits of jogging are many: lowered blood pressure, increased vitality, better cardiovascular health, and better muscle tone. However, an older person may have a history of injury or chronic ailments that makes jogging counterproductive. For example, the elderly jogger may have hardening of the arteries, emphysema, or undiscovered aneurysms just waiting to burst and cause stroke or death. Chronic arthritis in the joints will only be aggravated by persistent irritation and use. Moreover, for those of us with injuries sustained in our youth—such as torn Achilles' tendons or torn knee cartilage—jogging might just make a painful life more painful, cancelling out the benefits the exercise is intended to produce.

(B) Jogging is a sporting activity that exercises all the main muscle groups of the body. That the voluntary muscles of the arms, legs, buttock, and torso are engaged goes without question. Running down a path makes you move your upper body muscles as well as your lower body muscles. People do not often take into account, however, how the involuntary muscle system is also put through its paces. The heart, diaphragm, even the eye and face muscles, take part as we hurl our bodies through space at speeds up to five miles per hour over distances as long as 26 miles.

(C) It seems to me that jogging styles are as identifying as fingerprints! People seem to be as individual in the way they run as they are in personality. Here comes the Duck, waddling down the track, little wings going twice as fast as the feet in an effort to stay upright. At about the quarter-mile mark, I see the Penguin, quite natty in the latest jogging suit, body stiff as a board from neck to ankles and the ankles flexing a mile a minute to cover the yards. And down there at the half-mile post—there comes the Giraffe—a tall fellow in a spotted electric yellow outfit, whose long strides cover about a dozen yards each, and whose neck waves around under some old army camouflage hat that probably served its time in a surplus store in the Bronx rather than in Desert Storm. Once you see the animals in the jogger woods once, you can identify them from miles away just by seeing their gait. And by the way, be careful whose hoof you're stepping on, it may be mine!

In choice (A), the writer makes a statement that a number of people would debate and that isn't clearly demonstrated in science or common knowledge. In fact, common wisdom usually maintains the opposite thesis. Many would say that jogging improves the health of the aging—even slows down the aging process. As soon as you see a writer point to or identify *an issue open to debate* and standing in need of proof, the writer is setting out to persuade you of one side or the other. You'll notice, too, that the writer in this case takes a stand, here. It's almost as if the writer is saying, "I have concluded that . . ." But a thesis or arguable idea is only a *hypothesis* until evidence is summoned by the writer to prove it. Effective arguments are based on serious, factual, or demonstrable evidence, not opinion.

In choice (B), the writer is just stating a fact. This is not a matter for debate. From here, the writer's evidence is to *explain* and *describe* what is meant by the fact. The writer proceeds to *analyze* (break down into its elements) the way the different muscle groups come into play or do work when jogging, thus explaining the fact stated as a main point in the opening sentence. That jogging exercises all the muscle groups is not in question or a matter of debate. Besides taking the form of explaining how something works, what parts it is made of (for example, the basic parts of a bicycle are...), writers may show how the idea, object, or event functions. A writer may use this information to prove something. But if the writer doesn't argue to prove a debatable point, then the purpose must be either to inform (as here) or to entertain.

In choice (C), the writer is taking a stand, but the writer is not attempting to prove anything, merely pointing to a lighthearted observation. Moreover, all of the examples the writer uses to support the statement are either fanciful, funny, odd, or peculiar to the writer's particular vision. Joggers aren't really animals, after all.

Make sure to examine all of the facts that the author uses to support the main idea. This will allow you to decide whether or not the writer has made a case, and what sort of purpose the writer supports. Look for supporting details—facts, examples, illustrations, the testimony or research of experts, that are about the topic in question and *show* what the writer *says* is so. In fact, paragraphs and theses consist of *show* and *tell*. The writer *tells* you something is so or not so and then *shows* you facts, illustrations, expert testimony, or experience to back up what the writer says is or is not so. As you determine where the author's supporting details are, you may want to label them with an "S" so that you can refer back to them easily when answering questions (see question 3).

It is also important for you to be able to recognize the difference between the statements of fact presented and statements of the author's opinion. You will be tested on this skill in this section of the test (see question 4). Let's look at the following examples. In each case ask yourself if you are reading a fact or an opinion.

1. Some roses are red.
2. Roses are the most beautiful flower on earth.
3. After humans smell roses, they fall in love.
4. Roses are the worst plants to grow in your backyard.

Number 1 is a fact. All you have to do is go look at the evidence. Go to a florist. You will see that number 1 is true. A fact is anything which can be demonstrated to be true in reality or which has been demonstrated to be true in reality and is documented by others. For example, the moon is in orbit about 250,000 miles from the earth.

Number 2 is an opinion. The writer claims this as truth, but since it is an abstract quality (beauty), it remains to be seen. Others will hold different opinions. This is a matter of taste, not fact.

Number 3 is an opinion. There is probably some time-related coincidence between these two, but there is no verifiable or repeatable and observable evidence that this is always true—at least not the way it is true that if you throw a ball into the air, it will always come back down to earth if left on its own without interference. Opinions have a way of sounding absolute, are held by the writer with confidence, but are not backed up by factual evidence.

Number 4, though perhaps sometimes true, is a matter of opinion. Many variables contribute to the health of a plant in a garden: soil, temperature range, amount of moisture, number, and kinds of bugs. This is a debatable point that the writer would have to prove.

As you read, you should note the structure of the passage. There are several common structures for the passages. Some of these structures are described below.

Main Types of Paragraph Structures

1. The structure is a main idea plus supporting arguments.
2. The structure is a main idea plus examples.
3. The structure includes comparisons or contrasts.
4. There is a pro and a con structure.
5. The structure is chronological.
6. The structure has several different aspects of one idea. For example, a passage on education in the United States in the 1600s and 1700s might first define education, then describe colonial education, then give information about separation of church and state, and then outline the tax opposition and support arguments. Being able to recognize these structures will help you recognize how the author has organized the passage.

Examining the structure of the passage will help you answer questions that ask you to organize (see question 5) the information in the passage, or to summarize (see question 6) the information presented in that passage.

For example, if you see a writer using a transitional pattern that reflects a sequence moving forward in time, such as "In 1982 . . . Then, in the next five years . . . A decade later, in 1997, the trains will . . ." chances are the writer is telling a story, history, or the like. Writers often use transitions of classification to analyze an idea, object, or event. They may say something like, "The first part . . . Secondly . . . Thirdly . . . Finally." You may then ask yourself what the analysis is for. To explain or to persuade me of something? These transitional patterns may also help reveal the relationship of one part of a passage to another. For example, a writer may be writing "on the one hand, . . . on the other hand . . ." This should alert you to the fact that the writer is comparing two things or contrasting them. What for? Is one better than the other? Worse?

By understanding the *relationship* among the main point, transitions, and supporting information, you may more readily determine the pattern of organization as well as the writer's purpose in a given piece of writing.

As with the paragraph examples above showing the difference among possible purposes, you must look at the relationship between the facts or information presented (that's the *show* part) and what the writer is trying to point out to you (that's the *tell* part) with that data. For example, in the data given in number 6 above, the discussion presented about education in the 1600s might be used:

- to prove that it was a failure (a form of argument),
- to show that it consisted of these elements (an analysis of the status of education during that time), or
- to show that education during that time was silly.

To understand the author's purpose, the main point and the evidence that supports it must be considered together to be understood. In number 6, no statement appears that controls these disparate areas of information. To be meaningful, a controlling main point is needed. You need to know that that main point is missing. You need to be able to distinguish between the writer showing data and the writer telling or making a point.

In the two paragraphs below, consider the different relationship between the same data above and the controlling statement, and how that controlling statement changes the discussion from explanation to argument:

(A) Colonial education was different than today's and consisted of several elements. Education in those days meant primarily studying the three "R's" (reading, writing, and arithmetic) and the Bible. The church and state were more closely aligned with one another—education was, after all, for the purpose of serving God better, not to make more money.

(B) Colonial "education" was really just a way to create a captive audience for the Church. Education in those days meant studying the three "R's" in order to learn God's word—the Bible—not commerce. The Church and state were closely aligned with one another, and what was good for the Church was good for the state—or else you were excommunicated, which kept you out of Heaven for sure.

The same information areas are brought up in both cases, but in (A) the writer treats it analytically (. . ."consisted of several elements" . . .), not taking any real debatable stand on the issue. What is, is. However, the controlling statement in (B) puts forth a volatile hypothesis, and then uses the same information to support that hypothesis.

After your preview, you are now ready to read actively. This means that as you read, you will be engaged in such things as underlining important words, topic sentences, main ideas, and words denoting tone of the passage. If you think underlining can help you save time and help you remember the main ideas, feel free to use your pencil.

Carefully read the first sentence of each paragraph since this often contains the topic of the paragraph. You may wish to underline each topic sentence.

During this stage, you should also determine the writer's purpose in writing the passage (see question 2), as this will help you focus on the main points and the writer's key points in the organization of a passage. You can determine the author's purpose by asking yourself, Does *the relationship* between the writer's main idea plus evidence the writer uses answer one of four questions?

- What is the writer's overall primary goal or objective?

- Is the writer trying primarily to persuade you by proving or using facts to make a case for an idea? (P)

- Is the writer trying only primarily to inform and enlighten you about an idea, object, or event? (I)

- Is the writer attempting primarily to amuse you? To keep you fascinated? To keep you laughing? (A)

Step 3: Read Actively

Mark up the passage by identifying the main idea or theme (many times, it is contained within the first few lines of the passage). Don't forget to circle key words or phrases including *as, but, on the other hand, although, however, yet,* and *except.*

Step 4: Answer the Questions

When answering the question, you should

- Approach each question one at a time.
- Read it carefully.
- Identify the type of question being asked.

Main Idea Questions

Looking back at the questions which follow the passage (see pages 22–27), you see that question 1 is a "main idea" question:

1. The main idea of the passage is best stated in which of the following?

   (A) The Supreme Court has difficulty convicting those who violate obscenity laws.

   (B) The current definitions for obscenity and pornography provided by the Supreme Court are unworkable.

   (C) Fact-pattern analysis is insufficient for determining the attitude of the Court toward the issues of obscenity and pornography.

   (D) Despite the difficulties presented by fact-pattern analysis, Justice Segal found the solution in the patterns of search and seizure decisions.

   (E) The Supreme Court has a habit of frequently returning decisions to the jurisdiction of the state courts.

Answer choice (C) is correct. The writer uses the second, third, fourth, and fifth paragraphs to show how fact-pattern analysis is an ineffective determinant of Court attitude toward obscenity and pornography.

Answer choice (A) is incorrect. Nothing is ever said directly about "convicting" persons accused of obscenity, only that the Court has difficulty defining it.

Choice (B) is also incorrect. Though it is stated as a fact by the writer, it is only used as an effect that leads the writer to examine how fact-pattern analysis does or does not work to reveal the "cause" or attitude of the Court toward obscenity and pornography.

Answer choice (D) is incorrect. The statement is contrary to what Segal found when he examined search and seizure cases.

Finally, answer choice (E) is inconclusive.

Purpose Questions

In examining question 2, you see that you must determine the author's purpose in writing the passage:

2. The main purpose of the writer in this passage is to

    (A) convince the reader that the Supreme Court is making decisions about obscenity based on their subjective views only

    (B) explain to the reader how fact-pattern analysis works with respect to cases of obscenity and pornography

    (C) define obscenity and pornography for the layperson

    (D) demonstrate the role fact-pattern analysis plays in determining the Supreme Court's attitude about cases in obscenity and pornography

    (E) convey a concern of the future decisions of the court regarding abortion

Looking at the answer choices, you see that choice (D) is correct. Though the writer never states it directly, s/he summons data consistently to show that fact-pattern analysis only gives us part of the picture, or "broad strokes" about the Court's attitude, but cannot account for the attitude toward individual cases.

Choice (A) is incorrect. The writer doesn't try to convince us of this fact, but merely states it as an opinion resulting from the evidence derived from the "well-documented" background to the problem.

Choice (B) is also incorrect. The writer does more than just explain the role of fact-pattern analysis, but rather shows how it cannot fully apply.

The passage is about the Court's difficulty in defining these terms, not the man or woman in the street. Nowhere do definitions for these terms appear. Therefore, choice (C) is incorrect.

Answer choice (E) is incorrect. The topic is barely considered.

Support Questions

Question 3 requires you to analyze the author's supporting details:

3. Of the following, which fact best supports the writer's contention that the Court's decisions in the areas of obscenity and pornography deserve closer scrutiny?

    (A) The fact that a Supreme Court Justice said, "I know it when I see it."

    (B) Recent studies that employ fact-pattern analysis in modeling the Court's decision-making process.

(C) The fact that attitudes do not operate in a vacuum.

(D) The fact that federal and state governments, interest groups, and the academic community show renewed interest in the obscenity and pornography decisions by the Supreme Court.

(E) Defining a situation with broad strokes does not allow for case content controll.

To answer this question, let's look at the answer choices. Choice (D) must be correct. In the fifth paragraph, the writer states that the "renewed interest"—a real and observable fact—from these groups "indicates the Court's decisions . . . deserve closer examination," another way of saying scrutiny.

Answer choice (A) is incorrect. The writer uses this remark to show how the Court cannot effectively define obscenity and pornography, relying on "subjective preferences" to resolve issues.

In addition, choice (B) is incorrect because the writer points to the data in choice (D), not fact-pattern analyses, to prove this.

Choice (C), too, is incorrect. Although it is true, the writer makes this point to show how fact-pattern analysis doesn't help clear up the real-world "situation" in which the Court must make its decisions.

Answer choice (E) is also incorrect. It is words lifted out of context.

Fact vs. Opinion Questions

By examining question 4, you can see that you are required to know the difference between fact and opinion:

4. Among the following statements, which states an opinion expressed by the writer rather than a fact?

(A) That the area of obscenity and pornography is a difficult one for the Supreme Court is well documented.

(B) The objects to which a court directs its attitudes are the litigants.

(C) In many specific issue areas, the cases present strikingly similar patterns.

(D) The Court's subsequent behavior may suggest how the Court will react in other legal areas.

(E) Several recent studies employ fact-pattern analysis in modeling the Court's decision making.

Keeping in mind that an opinion is something that cannot be proven to hold true in all circumstances, you can determine that choice (D) is correct. It is the only statement among the four for which the evidence is yet to be gathered. It is the writer's opinion that this may be a way to predict the Court's attitudes.

Choices (A), (B), (C) and (E) are all taken from data or documentation in existence already in the world, and are, therefore, incorrect.

Organization Questions

Question 5 asks you to organize given topics to reflect the organization of the passage:

5. The list of topics below that best reflects the organization of the topics of the passage is

   (A) I. The difficulties of the Supreme Court

   II. Several recent studies

   III. Spaeth's definition of "attitude"

   IV. The similar patterns of cases

   V. Other issue areas

   VI. The case of *Miller vs. California*

   (B) I. The Supreme Court, obscenity, and fact-pattern analysis

   II. Fact-pattern analyses and attitude theory

   III. The definition of "attitude" for the Court

   IV. The definition of "situation"

   V. The breakdown in fact-pattern analysis

   VI. Studying Court behavior

   (C) I. Justice Stewart's view of pornography

   II. Theoretical underpinnings

   III. A minimum-winning coalition

   IV. Search and seizure decisions

   V. Renewed interest in obscenity and pornography

   VI. The importance of local community standards

   (D) I. The Court's numerous attempts to define obscenity

   II. Case characteristics

   III. The subject matter of cases

   IV. The Court's proportion of decisions

          V.   Broad-based factors

          VI.   Obscenity determination

(E) I.   Case characteristics

       II.   The Court's search and seizure decisions

       III.   The history of the Court's decisions

       IV.   Abortion decisions

       V.   Several monumental decisions

       VI.   The variety of cases

After examining all of the choices, you will determine that choice (B) is the correct response. These topical areas lead directly to the implied thesis that the role of fact-pattern analysis is insufficient for determining the attitude of the Supreme Court in the areas of obscenity and pornography. (See question 1.)

Answer choice (A) is incorrect because the first topic stated in the list is not the topic of the first paragraph. It is too global. The first paragraph is about the difficulties the Court has with defining obscenity and how fact-pattern analysis might be used to determine the Court's attitude and clear up the problem.

Choice (C) is incorrect because each of the items listed in this topic list are supporting evidence or data for the real topic of each paragraph. (See the list in (B) for correct topics.) For example, Justice Stewart's statement about pornography is only cited to indicate the nature of the problem with obscenity for the Court. It is not the focus of the paragraph itself.

Finally, choices (D) and (E) are incorrect. As with choice (C) these are all incidental pieces of information or data used to make broader points.

Summarization Questions

To answer question 6, you must be able to summarize the passage:

6. Which paragraph below is the best summary of the passage?

(A) The Supreme Court's decision-making process with respect to obscenity and pornography has become too subjective. Fact-pattern analyses, used to determine the overall attitude of the Court, reveal only broad-based attitudes on the part of the Court toward the situations of obscenity cases. But these patterns cannot fully account for the Court's attitudes toward case content. Research is not conclusive that fact-pattern analyses work when applied to legal areas. Renewed public and local interest suggests continued study and close examination of how the Court makes decisions. Delegating authority to the states may reflect patterns for Court decisions in other socially sensitive areas.

(B) Though subjective, the Supreme Court decisions are well documented. Fact-pattern analyses reveal the attitude of the Supreme Court toward its decisions in cases. Spaeth explains that an attitude involves both an object and a situation. For the Court, the situation may be defined as the decision to grant certiorari. Cases present strikingly similar patterns, and a small number of variables explain a high proportion of the Court's decisions. Segal has made an effort to verify the applicability of fact-pattern analysis with some success. The Court's decisions on obscenity and pornography suggest weak Court behavior, such as in *Miller vs. California*.

(C) To determine what obscenity and pornography mean to the Supreme Court, we must use fact-pattern analysis. Fact-pattern analysis reveals the ideas that the Court uses to operate in a vacuum. The litigants and the subject matter of cases is defined in broad terms (such as an entire area of law) to reveal the Court's decision-making process. Search and seizure cases reveal strikingly similar patterns, leaving the Court open to grant certiorari effectively. Renewed public interest in the Court's decisions proves how the Court will react in the future.

(D) Supreme Court decisions about pornography and obscenity are under examination and are out of control. The Court has to see the case to know it. Fact-pattern analyses reveal that the Court can only define cases in narrow terms, thus revealing individual egotism on the part of the Justices. As a result of strikingly similar patterns in search and seizure cases, the Court should be studied further for its weakness in delegating authority to state courts, as in the case of *Miller vs. California*.

(E) As seen in the case of *Miller vs. California*, the Supreme Court is uncomfortable taking on high visibility cases. It has been its history to return difficult cases to the states' higher courts. We need to be very concerned moving forward. We must be watchful to be sure that the Court does not shirk from its duty toward the country. This would result in serious damage to the balance of power so ably conceived by the writers of the U.S. Constitution.

The paragraph that best and most accurately reports what the writer demonstrated based on the implied thesis (see question 1) is answer choice (C), which is correct.

Choice (A) is incorrect. While it reflects some of the evidence presented in the passage, the passage does not imply that all Court decisions are subjective, just the ones about pornography and obscenity. Similarly, the writer does not suggest that delegating authority to the states as in *Miller vs. California* is a sign of some weakness, but merely that it is worthy of study as a tool for predicting or identifying the Court attitude.

Choice (B) is also incorrect. The writer summons information over and over to show how fact-pattern analysis cannot pin down the Court's attitude toward case content.

Choice (D) is incorrect. Nowhere does the writer say or suggest that the justice system is "out of control" or that the justices are "egotists," only that they are liable to be reduced to being "subjective" rather than based on an identifiable shared standard.

Answer choice (E) is incorrect as it is clearly off topic.

At this point, the four remaining question types must be discussed: recall questions (see question 7), cause/effect questions (see question 8), and definition questions (question 9). They are as follows:

Recall Questions

To answer question 7, you must be able to recall information from the passage:

7. Based on the passage, the rationale for fact-pattern analyses arises out of what theoretical groundwork?

   (A) Subjectivity theory
   (B) The study of cultural norms
   (C) Attitude theory
   (D) Cybernetics
   (E) Fact patterns

The easiest way to answer this question is to refer back to the passage. In the second paragraph, the writer states that recent studies using fact-pattern analyses, "owe their theoretical underpinnings to attitude theory." Therefore, we can conclude that choice (C) is correct.

Answer choices (A), (B), (D) and (E) are incorrect, as they are never discussed or mentioned by the writer.

Cause/Effect Questions

Question 8 requires you to analyze a cause-and-effect relationship:

8. Based on data in the passage, what would most likely be the major cause for the difficulty in pinning down the Supreme Court's attitude toward cases of obscenity and pornography?

    (A) The personal opinions of the Court Justices

    (B) The broad nature of the situations of the cases

    (C) The ineffective logistics of certiorari

    (D) The inability of the Court to resolve the variables presented by individual case content

    (E) The narrow nature of the cases being presented

    Choice (D) is correct, as it is precisely what fact-pattern analyses cannot resolve.

    Choice (A) is incorrect because no evidence is presented for this, only that they do make personal decisions.

    Answer choice (B) is incorrect because this is one way in which fact-pattern analysis can be helpful.

    Finally, choice (C) is only a statement about certiorari being difficult to administer, and this was never claimed about them by the writer in the first place.

    Answer choice (E) is incorrect as it is not adequately explained to be recognized as a major cause.

Definition Questions

Returning to question 9, we can now determine an answer:

9. In the context of the passage, *subjective* might be most nearly defined as

    (A) personal

    (B) wrong

    (C) focused

    (D) objective

    (E) communal

Choice (A) is best. By taking note of the example of Justice Stewart provided by the writer, we can see that Justice Stewart's comment is an example not of right or wrong. (He doesn't talk about right or wrong. He uses the verb "know"—whose root points primarily to *know*ledge, understanding, and insight, *not* ethical considerations.) He probably doesn't mean "focused by" since the focus is provided by the appearance or instance of the case itself. By noting the same word ending and the appearance of the root "object"—meaning an observable thing existing outside of ourselves in time and space, and comparing it with the root of subjective, "subject"—often pointing to something personally studied, we can begin to rule out "objective" as the opposite of "subjective." Usually when we talk about people's "preferences," we are referring to matters of taste or quality; preferences don't usually result from scientific study or reasoning but instead arise out of a combination of personal taste and idiosyncratic intuitions. Thus, choice (A) becomes the most likely choice.

Choice (C) is incorrect because the Court's focus is already in place—obscenity and pornography.

Answer choice (B) is incorrect. Nothing is implied or stated about the rightness or wrongness of the decisions themselves. Rather, it is the definition of obscenity that seems "unworkable."

Choice (D) is also incorrect. "Objective" is the direct opposite of "subjective." To reason based on the object of study is the opposite of reasoning based upon the beliefs, opinions, or ideas of the one viewing the object, rather than consideration of the evidence presented by the object itself *independent* of the observer.

Answer choice (E) is incorrect as the definition of the word *communal* is the opposite of *subjective*.

You may not have been familiar with the word "subjective," but from your understanding of the writer's intent, you should have been able to figure out what the writer was after. Surrounding words and phrases almost always provide clues in determining a word's meaning. In addition, any examples that appear in the text may also provide some hints.

2. Additional Tips

In addition to the four-step approach, you should consider the following:

- Use the context of the sentence to find the meaning of an unfamiliar word.
- Identify what sentences are example sentences and label them with an "E."

- Make your final response and move on. Don't dawdle or get frustrated by the really troubling passages. If you haven't gotten answers after two attempts, answer as best you can, mark the passage so you can return to it later (if time permits), and move on.

- If you have time at the end, go back to the passages that were difficult and review them again.

3. Vocabulary Enhancer

It is important to understand the meanings of all words—not just the ones you are asked to define. A good vocabulary is a strength that can help you perform well on all sections of this test. The following information will build your skills in determining the meanings of words.

Similar Forms and Sounds

The complex nature of language sometimes makes reading difficult. Words often become confusing when they have similar forms and sounds. Indeed the author may have a correct meaning in mind, but an incorrect word choice can alter the meaning of the sentence or even make it totally illogical.

No: Martha was always part of that *cliché*.
Yes: Martha was always part of that *clique*.
(A *cliché* is a trite or hackneyed expression; a *clique* is an exclusive group of people.)

No: The minister spoke of the soul's *immorality*.
Yes: The minister spoke of the soul's *immortality*.
(*Immorality* means wickedness; *immortality* means imperishable or unending life.)

No: Where is the nearest *stationary* store?
Yes: Where is the nearest *stationery* store?
(*Stationary* means immovable; *stationery* is paper used for writing.)

Below are groups of words that are often confused because of their similar forms and sounds.

Confusing Word	Definition
accent	*v.* – to stress or emphasize (You must *accent* the last syllable.)
ascent	*n.* – a climb or rise (John's *ascent* of the mountain was dangerous.)
assent	*n.* – consent; compliance (We need your *assent* before we can go ahead with the plans.)
accept	*v.* – to take something offered (She *accepted* the gift.)
except	*prep.* – other than; but (Everyone was included in the plans *except* him.)
advice	*n.* –opinion given as to what to do or how to handle a situation (Her sister gave her *advice* on what to say at the interview.)
advise	*v.* – to counsel (John's guidance counselor *advised* him on which colleges to apply to.)
affect	*v.* – to influence (Mary's suggestion did not *affect* me.)
effect	1. *v.*– to cause to happen (The plan was *effected* with great success.); 2. *n.* – result (The *effect* of the medicine is excellent.)
allusion	*n.* – indirect reference (In the poem, there are many biblical *allusions*.)
illusion	*n.* – false idea or conception; belief or opinion not in accord with the facts (Greg was under the *illusion* that he could win the race after missing three weeks of practice.)
already	*adv.* – previously (I had *already* read that novel.)
all ready	*adv. + adj.* – prepared (The family was *all ready* to leave on vacation.)
altar	*n.* – table or stand used in religious rites (The priest stood at the *altar*.)
alter	*v.* – to change (Their plans were *altered* during the strike.)
capital	1. *n.* – a city where the government meets (The senators had a meeting in Albany, the *capital* of New York.); 2. money used in business (They had enough *capital* to develop the industry.)
capitol	*n.* – building in which the legislature meets (Senator Brown gave a speech at the *capitol* in Washington.)

Confusing Word	Definition
choose	*v.* – to select (Which camera did you *choose*?)
chose	(past tense, *choose* (Susan *chose* to stay home.)
cite	*v.* – to quote (The student *cited* evidence from the text.)
site	*n.* – location (They chose the *site* where the house would be built.)
clothes	*n.* – garments (Because she got caught in the rain, her *clothes* were wet.)
cloths	*n.* – pieces of material (The *cloths* were used to wash the windows.)
coarse	*adj.* – rough; unrefined (Sandpaper is *coarse*.)
course	1. *n.* – path of action (She did not know what *course* would solve the problem.); 2. passage (We took the long *course* to the lake.); 3. series of studies (We both enrolled in the physics *course*.); 4. part of a meal (She served a five *course* meal.)
consul	*n.* – a person appointed by the government to live in a foreign city and represent the citizenry and business interests of his native country there (The *consul* was appointed to Naples, Italy.)
council	*n.* – a group used for discussion, advisement (The *council* decided to accept his letter of resignation.)
counsel	*v.* – to advise (Tom *counsels* Jerry on tax matters.)
decent	*adj.* – proper; respectable (He was very *decent* about the entire matter.)
descent	1. *n.* – moving down (In Dante's *Inferno*, the *descent* into Hell was depicted graphically.); 2. ancestry (He is of Irish *descent*.)
device	1. *n.* – plan; scheme (The *device* helped her win the race.); 2. invention (We bought a *device* that opens the garage door automatically.)
devise	*v.* – to contrive (He *devised* a plan so John could not win.)
emigrate	*v.* – to go away from a country (Many Japanese *emigrated* from Japan in the late 1800s.)
immigrate	*v.* – to come into a country (Her relatives *immigrated* to the United States after World War I.)
eminent	*n.* – prominent (He is an *eminent* member of the community.)
imminent	*adj.* – impending (The decision is *imminent*.)
immanent	*adj.* – existing within (Maggie believed that religious spirit is *immanent* in human beings.)

(continued on next page)

Confusing Word	Definition
fair	1. *adj.* – beautiful (She was a *fair* maiden.); 2. just (She tried to be *fair*.); 3. *n.* – festival (There were many games at the *fair*.)
fare	*n.* – amount of money paid for transportation (The city proposed that the subway *fare* be raised.)
forth	*adv.* – onward (The soldiers moved *forth* in the blinding snow.)
fourth	*n., adj.* – 4th (She was the *fourth* runner-up in the beauty contest.)
its	possessive form of *it* (Our town must improve *its* roads.)
it's	contraction of it is (*It's* time to leave the party.)
later	*adj., adv.* – at a subsequent date (We will take a vacation *later* this year.)
latter	*n.* – second of the two (Susan can visit Monday or Tuesday. The *latter*, however, is preferable.)
lead	1. *n.* – (led) a metal (The handgun was made of *lead*.); 2. *v.t.* – (leed) to show the way (The camp counselor *leads* the way to the picnic grounds.)
led	past tense of *lead* (#2 above) (The dog *led* the way.)
loose	*adj.* – free; unrestricted (The dog was let *loose* by accident.)
lose	*v.* – to suffer the loss of (He was afraid he would *lose* the race.)
moral	1. *adj.* – virtuous (She is a *moral* woman with high ethical standards.); 2. *n.* – lesson taught by a story, incident, etc. (Most fables end with a *moral*.)
morale	*n.* – mental condition (After the team lost the game, their *morale* was low.)
of	*prep.* – from (She is *of* French descent.)
off	*adj.* – away; at a distance (The television fell *off* the table.)
passed	*v.* – having satisfied some requirement (He *passed* the test.)
past	1. *adj.* – gone by or elapsed in time (His *past* deeds got him in trouble.); 2. *n.* – a period of time gone by (His *past* was shady.); 3. *prep.* – beyond (She ran *past* the house.)
personal	*adj.* – private (Jack was unwilling to discuss his childhood; it was too *personal*.)
personnel	*n.* – staff (The *personnel* at the department store were very helpful.)

Confusing Word	Definition
principal	*n.* – head of a school (The *principal* addressed the graduating class.)
principle	*n.* – the ultimate source, origin, or cause of something; a law, truth (The *principles* of physics were reviewed in class today.)
prophecy	*n.* – prediction of the future (His *prophecy* that he would become a doctor came true.)
prophesy	*v.* – to declare or predict (He *prophesied* that we would win the lottery.)
quiet	*adj.* – still; calm (At night all is *quiet*.)
quite	*adv.* – really; truly (She is *quite* a good singer.)
quit	*v.* – to free oneself (Peter had little time to spare so he *quit* the chorus.)
respectfully	*adv.* – with respect, honor, esteem (He declined the offer *respectfully*.)
respectively	*adv.* – in the order mentioned (Jack, Susan and Jim, who are members of the club, were elected president, vice-president, and secretary *respectively*.)
stationary	*adj.* – immovable (The park bench is *stationary*.)
stationery	*n.* – paper used for writing (The invitations were printed on yellow *stationery*.)
straight	*adj.* – not curved (The road was *straight*.)
strait	1. *adj.* – restricted; narrow; confined (The patient was put in a *strait* jacket.); 2. *n.* – narrow waterway (He sailed through the *Straits* of Magellan.)
than	*conj.* – used most commonly in comparisons (Maggie is older *than* I.)
then	*adv.* – soon afterward (We lived in Boston, *then* we moved to New York.)
their	possessive form of they (That is *their* house on Tenafly Drive.)
they're	contraction of they are (*They're* leaving for California next week.)
there	*adv.* – at that place (Who is standing *there* under the tree?)
to	*prep.* – in the direction of; toward; as (She made a turn *to* the right on Norman Street.)
too	1. *adv.* – more than enough (She served *too* much for dinner.); 2. also (He is going to Maine *too*.)
two	*n.* – 2; one and one (We have *two* pet rabbits.)
weather	*n.* – the general condition of the atmosphere (The *weather* is expected to be clear on Sunday.)
whether	*conj.* – if it be a case or fact (We don't know *whether* the trains are late.)

(continued on next page)

Confusing Word	Definition
who's	contraction of who is or who has (*Who's* willing to volunteer for the night shift?)
whose	possessive form of *who* (*Whose* book is this?)
your	possessive form of *you* (Is this *your* seat?)
you're	contraction of you and are (I know *you're* going to do well on the test.)

Multiple Meanings

In addition to words that sound alike, you must be careful when dealing with words that have multiple meanings. For example:

The boy was thrilled that his mother gave him a piece of chewing *gum*.
Dentists advise people to floss their teeth to help prevent *gum* disease.

As you can see, one word can have different meanings depending on the context in which it is used.

Connotation and Denotation

Language can become even more complicated. Not only can a single word have numerous definitions and subtle meanings, it may also take on added meanings through implication. The **connotation** is the idea suggested by its place near or association with other words or phrases. The **denotation** of a word is the direct explicit meaning.

Connotation

Sometimes, you will be asked to tell the meaning of a word in the context of the paragraph. You may not have seen the word before, but from your understanding of the writer's intent, you should be able to figure out what it is s/he's after. For example, read the following paragraph:

Paris is a beautiful city, perhaps the most beautiful on earth. Long, broad avenues are lined with seventeenth and eighteenth century apartments, office buildings, and cafes. Flowers give the city a rich and varied look. The bridges and the river lend an air of lightness and grace to the whole urban landscape.

1. In this paragraph, "rich" most nearly means

(A) wealthy

(B) polluted

(C) colorful

(D) dull

(E) flavorful

If you chose "colorful" you would be right. Although "rich" literally means "wealthy" (that is its *denotation*, its literal meaning), here the writer means more than the word's literal meaning, and seems to be highlighting the variety and color that the flowers add to the avenues, that is, richness in a figurative sense.

The writer is using a non-literal meaning, or *connotation* that we associate with the word "rich" to show what s/he means. When we think of something "rich," we usually also think of abundance, variety, color, and not merely numbers.

Denotation

Determining the denotation of a word is different from determining a word's connotation. Read this paragraph:

> Many soporifics are on the market to help people sleep. Take a glass of water and two *Sleepeze* and you get the "zzzzz" you need. *Sominall* supposedly helps you get the sleep you need so you can go on working. With *Morpho*, your head hits the pillow and you're asleep before the light goes out.

1. From this paragraph, a "soporific" is probably a

   (A) drug that stimulates you to stay awake

   (B) kind of sleeping bag

   (C) kind of bed

   (D) drug that helps you sleep

   (E) a fruit flavored candy that contains caffeine

What is a soporific? You can figure out what it means by looking at what is said around it. People take these "soporifics" to go to sleep, not to wake up. So it can't be (A). You can't take two beds and a glass of water to go to sleep, either. So, it can't be (C). Anyway, you might be able to identify what a soporific is because you recognize the brand names used as examples. So, it must be some sort of pill that you take to sleep. Well, pills are usually drugs of some kind. Therefore, the answer is (D).

Vocabulary Builder

Although the context in which a word appears can help you determine the meaning of the word, one sure-fire way to know a definition is to learn it. By studying the following lists of words and memorizing their definition(s), you will be better equipped to answer Reading Section questions that deal with word meanings.

To benefit most from this vocabulary list, study the words and their definitions, then answer all of the drill questions making sure to check your answers with the answer key that appears at the end of the review.

Group 1

abstract	*adj.* – not easy to understand; theoretical
acclaim	*n.* – loud approval; applause
acquiesce	*v.* – agree or consent to an opinion
adamant	*adj.* – not yielding; firm
adversary	*n.* – an enemy; foe
advocate	1. *v.* – to plead in favor of; 2. *n.* – supporter; defender
aesthetic	*adj.* – showing good taste; artistic
alleviate	*v.* – to lessen or make easier
aloof	*adj.* – distant in interest; reserved; cool
altercation	*n.* – controversy; dispute
altruistic	*adj.* – unselfish
amass	*v.* – to collect together; accumulate
ambiguous	*adj.* – not clear; uncertain; vague
ambivalent	*adj.* – undecided
ameliorate	*v.* – to make better; to improve
amiable	*adj.* – friendly
amorphous	*adj.* – having no determinate form
anarchist	*n.* – one who believes that a formal government is unnecessary
antagonism	*n.* – hostility; opposition
apathy	*n.* – lack of emotion or interest
appease	*v.* – to make quiet; to calm
apprehensive	*adj.* – fearful; aware; conscious

arbitrary	*adj.* – based on one's preference or whim
arrogant	*adj.* – acting superior to others; conceited
articulate	1. *v.* – to speak distinctly; 2. *adj.* – eloquent; fluent; 3. *adj.* – capable of speech; 4. *v.* – to hinge; to connect; 5. *v.* – to convey; to express effectively

■ Drill 1 ■

DIRECTIONS: Match each word in the left column with the word in the right column that is most opposite in meaning.

WORD

1. _____ articulate
2. _____ apathy
3. _____ amiable
4. _____ altruistic
5. _____ ambivalent
6. _____ abstract
7. _____ acquiesce
8. _____ arbitrary
9. _____ amass
10. _____ adversary

MATCH

A. hostile
B. concrete
C. selfish
D. reasoned
E. ally
F. disperse
G. enthusiasm
H. certain
I. resist
J. incoherent

DIRECTIONS: Match each word in the left column with the word in the right column that is most similar in meaning.

WORD

11. _____ adamant
12. _____ aesthetic
13. _____ apprehensive
14. _____ antagonism
15. _____ altercation

MATCH

A. afraid
B. disagreement
C. tasteful
D. insistent
E. hostility

Group 2

assess	*v.* – to estimate the value of
astute	*adj.* – cunning; sly; crafty
atrophy	*v.* – to waste away through lack of nutrition
audacious	*adj.* – fearless; bold
augment	*v.* – to increase or add to; to make larger
austere	*adj.* – harsh; severe; strict

(continued on next page)

authentic	*adj.* – real; genuine; trustworthy
authoritarian	*adj.* – acting as a dictator; demanding obedience
banal	*adj.* – common; petty; ordinary
belittle	*v.* – to make small; to think lightly of
benefactor	*n.* – one who helps others; a donor
benevolent	*adj.* – kind; generous
benign	*adj.* – mild; harmless
biased	*adj.* – prejudiced; influenced; not neutral
blasphemous	*adj.* – irreligious; away from acceptable standards
blithe	*adj.* – happy; cheery; merry
brevity	*n.* – briefness; shortness
candid	*adj.* – honest; truthful; sincere
capricious	*adj.* – changeable; fickle
caustic	*adj.* – burning; sarcastic; harsh
censor	*v.* – to examine and delete objectionable material
censure	*v.* – to criticize or disapprove of
charlatan	*n.* – an imposter; fake
coalesce	*v.* – to combine; come together
collaborate	*v.* – to work together; cooperate

■ Drill 2 ■

DIRECTIONS: Match each word in the left column with the word in the right column that is most opposite in meaning.

WORD

1. ____ augment
2. ____ biased
3. ____ banal
4. ____ benevolent
5. ____ censor

6. ____ authentic
7. ____ candid
8. ____ belittle
9. ____ blasphemous
10. ____ blithe

MATCH

A. permit
B. religious
C. praise
D. diminish
E. dishonest

F. malicious
G. neutral
H. mournful
I. unusual
J. ersatz

DIRECTIONS: Match each word in the left column with the word in the right column that is most similar in meaning.

	WORD				MATCH		
11. ____ collaborate		14. ____ censure		A. harmless		D. cooperate	
12. ____ benign		15. ____ capricious		B. cunning		E. criticize	
13. ____ astute				C. changeable			

Group 3

compatible	*adj.* – in agreement; harmonious
complacent	*adj.* – content; self-satisfied; smug
compliant	*adj.* – yielding; obedient
comprehensive	*adj.* – all-inclusive; complete; thorough
compromise	*v.* – to settle by mutual adjustment
concede	1. *v.* – to acknowledge; admit; 2. to surrender; to abandon one's position
concise	*adj.* – in few words; brief; condensed
condescend	*v.* – to come down from one's position or dignity
condone	*v.* – to overlook; to forgive
conspicuous	*adj.* – easy to see; noticeable
consternation	*n.* – amazement or terror that causes confusion
consummation	*n.* – the completion; finish
contemporary	*adj.* – living or happening at the same time; modern
contempt	*n.* – scorn; disrespect
contrite	*adj.* – regretful; sorrowful
conventional	*adj.* – traditional; common; routine
cower	*v.* – crouch down in fear or shame
defamation	*n.* – any harm to a name or reputation; slander
deference	*n.* – a yielding to the opinion of another
deliberate	1. *v.* – to consider carefully; weigh in the mind; 2. *adj.* – intentional

(continued on next page)

denounce	*v.* – to speak out against; condemn
depict	*v.* – to portray in words; present a visual image
deplete	*v.* – to reduce; to empty
depravity	*n.* – moral corruption; badness
deride	*v.* – to ridicule; laugh at with scorn

■ Drill 3 ■

DIRECTIONS: Match each word in the left column with the word in the right column that is most opposite in meaning.

WORD

1. ____ deplete	6. ____ condone	A. unintentional	F. support
2. ____ contemporary	7. ____ conspicuous	B. disapprove	G. beginning
3. ____ concise	8. ____ consummation	C. invisible	H. ancient
4. ____ deliberate	9. ____ denounce	D. respect	I. virtue
5. ____ depravity	10. ____ contempt	E. fill	J. verbose

MATCH

DIRECTIONS: Match each word in the left column with the word in the right column that is most similar in meaning.

WORD

11. ____ compatible	14. ____ comprehensive	A. portray	D. thorough
12. ____ depict	15. ____ complacent	B. content	E. common
13. ____ conventional		C. harmonious	

MATCH

Group 4

desecrate	*v.* – to violate a holy place or sanctuary
detached	*adj.* – separated; not interested; standing alone
deter	*v.* – to prevent; to discourage; hinder
didactic	1. *adj.* – instructive; 2. dogmatic; preachy
digress	*v.* – stray from the subject; wander from topic
diligence	*n.* – hard work

discerning	*adj.* – distinguishing one thing from another
discord	*n.* – disagreement; lack of harmony
discriminating	1. *v.* – distinguishing one thing from another; 2. *v.* – demonstrating bias; 3. *adj.* – able to distinguish
disdain	1. *n.* – intense dislike; 2. *v.* – look down upon; scorn
disparage	*v.* – to belittle; undervalue
disparity	*n.* – difference in form, character, or degree
dispassionate	*adj.* – lack of feeling; impartial
disperse	*v.* – to scatter; separate
disseminate	*v.* – to circulate; scatter
dissent	*v.* – to disagree; differ in opinion
dissonance	*n.* – harsh contradiction
diverse	*adj.* – different; dissimilar
document	1. *n.* – official paper containing information; 2. *v.* – to support; substantiate; verify
dogmatic	*adj.* – stubborn; biased; opinionated
dubious	*adj.* – doubtful; uncertain; skeptical; suspicious
eccentric	*adj.* – odd; peculiar; strange
efface	*v.* – wipe out; erase
effervescence	1. *n.* – liveliness; spirit; enthusiasm; 2. bubbliness
egocentric	*adj.* – self-centered

▪ Drill 4 ▪

DIRECTIONS: Match each word in the left column with the word in the right column that is most opposite in meaning.

WORD			MATCH		
1. ____ detached	6. ____ dubious		A. agree	F. respect
2. ____ deter	7. ____ diligence		B. certain	G. compliment
3. ____ dissent	8. ____ disdain		C. lethargy	H. sanctify
4. ____ discord	9. ____ desecrate		D. connected	I. harmony
5. ____ efface	10. ____ disparage		E. assist	J. restore

DIRECTIONS: Match each word in the left column with the word in the right column that is most similar in meaning.

	WORD			MATCH	
11.____ effervescence	14.____ document		A. stubborn	D. liveliness
12.____ dogmatic	15.____ eccentric		B. distribute	E. odd
13.____ disseminate			C. substantiate	

Group 5

elaboration	*n.* – the act of clarifying or adding details
eloquence	*n.* – the ability to speak well
elusive	*adj.* – hard to catch; difficult to understand
emulate	*v.* – to imitate; copy; mimic
endorse	*v.* – support; to approve of; recommend
engender	*v.* – to create; bring about
enhance	*v.* – to improve; compliment; make more attractive
enigma	*n.* – mystery; secret; perplexity
ephemeral	*adj.* – temporary; brief; short-lived
equivocal	*adj.* – doubtful; uncertain
erratic	*adj.* – unpredictable; strange
erroneous	*adj.* – untrue; inaccurate; not correct
esoteric	*adj.* – incomprehensible; obscure
euphony	*n.* – pleasant sound
execute	1. *v.* – put to death; kill; 2. to carry out; fulfill
exemplary	*adj.* – serving as an example; outstanding
exhaustive	*adj.* – thorough; complete
expedient	*adj.* – helpful; practical; worthwhile
expedite	*v.* – speed up
explicit	*adj.* – specific; definite
extol	*v.* – praise; commend

extraneous	*adj.* – irrelevant; not related; not essential
facilitate	*v.* – make easier; simplify
fallacious	*adj.* – misleading
fanatic	*n.* – enthusiast; extremist

■ Drill 5 ■

DIRECTIONS: Match each word in the left column with the word in the right column that is most opposite in meaning.

WORD

1. ____ extraneous	6. ____ erratic
2. ____ ephemeral	7. ____ explicit
3. ____ exhaustive	8. ____ euphony
4. ____ expedite	9. ____ elusive
5. ____ erroneous	10. ____ extol

MATCH

A. incomplete	F. eternal
B. delay	G. condemn
C. dependable	H. relevant
D. comprehensible	I. indefinite
E. dissonance	J. accurate

DIRECTIONS: Match each word in the left column with the word in the right column that is most similar in meaning.

WORD

11. ____ endorse	14. ____ fallacious
12. ____ expedient	15. ____ engender
13. ____ facilitate	

MATCH

A. enable	D. worthwhile
B. recommend	E. deceptive
C. create	

Group 6

fastidious	*adj.* – fussy; hard to please
fervor	*n.* – passion; intensity
fickle	*adj.* – changeable; unpredictable
fortuitous	*adj.* – accidental; happening by chance; lucky
frivolity	*n.* – giddiness; lack of seriousness
fundamental	*adj.* – basic; necessary

(continued on next page)

furtive	*adj.* – secretive; sly
futile	*adj.* – worthless; unprofitable
glutton	*n.* – overeater
grandiose	*adj.* – extravagant; flamboyant
gravity	*n.* – seriousness
guile	*n.* – slyness; deceit
gullible	*adj.* – easily fooled
hackneyed	*adj.* – commonplace; trite
hamper	*v.* – interfere with; hinder
haphazard	*adj.* – disorganized; random
hedonistic	*adj.* – pleasure seeking
heed	*v.* – obey; yield to
heresy	*n.* – opinion contrary to popular belief
hindrance	*n.* – blockage; obstacle
humility	*n.* – lack of pride; modesty
hypocritical	*adj.* – two-faced; deceptive
hypothetical	*adj.* – assumed; uncertain
illuminate	*v.* – make understandable
illusory	*adj.* – unreal; false; deceptive

■ Drill 6 ■

DIRECTIONS: Match each word in the left column with the word in the right column that is most opposite in meaning.

WORD		MATCH	
1. ____ heresy	6. ____ fervent	A. predictable	F. beneficial
2. ____ fickle	7. ____ fundamental	B. dispassionate	G. orthodoxy
3. ____ illusory	8. ____ furtive	C. simple	H. organized
4. ____ frivolity	9. ____ futile	D. extraneous	I. candid
5. ____ grandiose	10. ____ haphazard	E. real	J. seriousness

DIRECTIONS: Match each word in the left column with the word in the right column that is most similar in meaning.

WORD		MATCH	
11. ____ glutton	14. ____ hackneyed	A. hinder	D. overeater
12. ____ heed	15. ____ hindrance	B. obstacle	E. obey
13. ____ hamper		C. trite	

Group 7

immune	*adj.* – protected; unthreatened by
immutable	*adj.* – unchangeable; permanent
impartial	*adj.* – unbiased; fair
impetuous	1. *adj.* – rash; impulsive; 2. forcible; violent
implication	*n.* – suggestion; inference
inadvertent	*adj.* – not on purpose; unintentional
incessant	*adj.* – constant; continual
incidental	*adj.* – extraneous; unexpected
inclined	1. *adj.* – apt to; likely to; 2. angled
incoherent	*adj.* – illogical; rambling
incompatible	*adj.* – disagreeing; disharmonious
incredulous	*adj.* – unwilling to believe; skeptical
indifferent	*adj.* – unconcerned
indolent	*adj.* – lazy; inactive
indulgent	*adj.* – lenient; extravagant
inevitable	*adj.* – sure to happen; unavoidable
infamous	*adj.* – having a bad reputation; notorious
infer	*v.* – form an opinion; conclude
initiate	1. *v.* – begin; admit into a group; 2. *n.* – a person who is in the process of being admitted into a group
innate	*adj.* – natural; inborn

(continued on next page)

innocuous	*adj.* – harmless; innocent
innovate	*v.* – introduce a change; depart from the old
insipid	*adj.* – uninteresting; bland
instigate	*v.* – start; provoke
intangible	*adj.* – incapable of being touched; immaterial

■ Drill 7 ■

DIRECTIONS: Match each word in the left column with the word in the right column that is most opposite in meaning.

WORD		MATCH	
1. ____ immutable	6. ____ innate	A. intentional	F. changeable
2. ____ impartial	7. ____ incredulous	B. articulate	G. avoidable
3. ____ inadvertent	8. ____ inevitable	C. gullible	H. harmonious
4. ____ incoherent	9. ____ intangible	D. material	I. learned
5. ____ incompatible	10. ____ indolent	E. biased	J. energetic

DIRECTIONS: Match each word in the left column with the word in the right column that is most similar in meaning.

WORD		MATCH	
11. ____ impetuous	14. ____ instigate	A. lenient	D. conclude
12. ____ incidental	15. ____ indulgent	B. impulsive	E. extraneous
13. ____ infer		C. provoke	

Group 8

ironic	*adj.* – contradictory; inconsistent; sarcastic
irrational	*adj.* – not logical
jeopardy	*n.* – danger
kindle	*v.* – ignite; arouse
languid	*adj.* – weak; fatigued

laud	*v.* – to praise
lax	*adj.* – careless; irresponsible
lethargic	*adj.* – lazy; passive
levity	*n.* – silliness; lack of seriousness
lucid	1. *adj.* – shining; 2. easily understood
magnanimous	*adj.* – forgiving; unselfish
malicious	*adj.* – spiteful; vindictive
marred	*adj.* – damaged
meander	*v.* – wind on a course; go aimlessly
melancholy	*n.* – depression; gloom
meticulous	*adj.* – exacting; precise
minute	*adj.* – extremely small; tiny
miser	*n.* – penny pincher; stingy person
mitigate	*v.* – alleviate; lessen; soothe
morose	*adj.* – moody; despondent
negligence	*n.* – carelessness
neutral	*adj.* – impartial; unbiased
nostalgic	*adj.* – longing for the past; filled with bittersweet memories
novel	*adj.* – new

■ Drill 8 ■

DIRECTIONS: Match each word in the left column with the word in the right column that is most opposite in meaning.

WORD

1. ____ irrational 6. ____ magnanimous
2. ____ kindle 7. ____ levity
3. ____ meticulous 8. ____ minute
4. ____ malicious 9. ____ laud
5. ____ morose 10. ____ novel

MATCH

A. extinguish F. ridicule
B. jovial G. kindly
C. selfish H. sloppy
D. logical I. huge
E. seriousness J. stale

DIRECTIONS: Match each word in the left column with the word in the right column that is most similar in meaning.

WORD

		MATCH	
11. ____ ironic	14. ____ jeopardy	A. lessen	D. carelessness
12. ____ marred	15. ____ negligence	B. damaged	E. danger
13. ____ mitigate		C. sarcastic	

Group 9

nullify	*v.* – cancel; invalidate
objective	1. *adj.* – open-minded; impartial; 2. *n.* – goal
obscure	*adj.* – not easily understood; dark
obsolete	*adj.* – out of date; passe
ominous	*adj.* – threatening
optimist	*n.* – person who hopes for the best; sees the good side
orthodox	*adj.* – traditional; accepted
pagan	1. *n.* – polytheist; 2. *adj.* – polytheistic
partisan	1. *n.* – supporter; follower; 2. *adj.* – biased; one sided
perceptive	*adj.* – full of insight; aware
peripheral	*adj.* – marginal; outer
pernicious	*adj.* – dangerous; harmful
pessimism	*n.* – seeing only the gloomy side; hopelessness
phenomenon	1. *n.* – miracle; 2. occurrence
philanthropy	*n.* – charity; unselfishness
pious	*adj.* – religious; devout; dedicated
placate	*v.* – pacify
plausible	*adj.* – probable; feasible
pragmatic	*adj.* – matter-of-fact; practical
preclude	*v.* – inhibit; make impossible
predecessor	*n.* – one who has occupied an office before another

prodigal	*adj.* – wasteful; lavish
prodigious	*adj.* – exceptional; tremendous
profound	*adj.* – deep; knowledgeable; thorough
profusion	*n.* – great amount; abundance

■ Drill 9 ■

DIRECTIONS: Match each word in the left column with the word in the right column that is most opposite in meaning.

WORD

1. ____ objective
2. ____ obsolete
3. ____ placate
4. ____ profusion
5. ____ peripheral
6. ____ plausible
7. ____ preclude
8. ____ prodigious
9. ____ profound
10. ____ optimism

MATCH

A. scantiness
B. assist
C. mundane
D. biased
E. improbable
F. minute
G. anger
H. pessimism
I. modern
J. central

DIRECTIONS: Match each word in the left column with the word in the right column that is most similar in meaning.

WORD

11. ____ nullify
12. ____ ominous
13. ____ partisan
14. ____ pernicious
15. ____ prodigal

MATCH

A. invalidate
B. follower
C. lavish
D. threatening
E. harmful

Group 10

prosaic	*adj.* – tiresome; ordinary
provincial	*adj.* – regional; unsophisticated
provocative	1. *adj.* – tempting; 2. irritating
prudent	*adj.* – wise; careful; prepared
qualified	*adj.* – experienced; indefinite
rectify	*v.* – correct

(continued on next page)

redundant	*adj.* – repetitious; unnecessary
refute	*v.* – challenge; disprove
relegate	*v.* – banish; put to a lower position
relevant	*adj.* – of concern; significant
remorse	*n.* – guilt; sorrow
reprehensible	*adj.* – wicked; disgraceful
repudiate	*v.* – reject; cancel
rescind	*v.* – retract; discard
resignation	1. *n.* – quitting; 2. submission
resolution	*n.* – proposal; promise; determination
respite	*n.* – recess; rest period
reticent	*adj.* – silent; reserved; shy
reverent	*adj.* – respectful
rhetorical	*adj.* – having to do with verbal communication
rigor	*n.* – severity
sagacious	*adj.* – wise; cunning
sanguine	1. *adj.* – optimistic; cheerful; 2. red
saturate	*v.* – soak thoroughly; drench
scanty	*adj.* – inadequate; sparse

■ Drill 10 ■

DIRECTIONS: Match each word in the left column with the word in the right column that is most opposite in meaning.

WORD		MATCH	
1. ____ provincial	6. ____ remorse	A. inexperienced	F. affirm
2. ____ reticent	7. ____ repudiate	B. joy	G. extraordinary
3. ____ prudent	8. ____ sanguine	C. pessimistic	H. sophisticated
4. ____ qualified	9. ____ relevant	D. unrelated	I. forward
5. ____ relegate	10. ____ prosaic	E. careless	J. promote

DIRECTIONS: Match each word in the left column with the word in the right column that is most similar in meaning.

WORD		MATCH	
11. ____ provocative	14. ____ rescind	A. drench	D. severity
12. ____ rigor	15. ____ reprehensible	B. tempting	E. blameworthy
13. ____ saturate		C. retract	

Group 11

scrupulous	*adj.* – honorable; exact
scrutinize	*v.* – examine closely; study
servile	*adj.* – slavish; groveling
skeptic	*n.* – doubter
slander	*v.* – defame; maliciously misrepresent
solemnity	*n.* – seriousness
solicit	*v.* – ask; seek
stagnant	*adj.* – motionless; uncirculating
stanza	*n.* – group of lines in a poem having a definite pattern
static	*adj.* – inactive; changeless
stoic	*adj.* – detached; unruffled; calm
subtlety	1. *n.* – understatement; 2. propensity for understatement; 3. sophistication; 4. cunning
superficial	*adj.* – on the surface; narrow-minded; lacking depth
superfluous	*adj.* – unnecessary; extra
surpass	*v.* – go beyond; outdo
sycophant	*n.* – servile or self-seeking flatterer
symmetry	*n.* – correspondence of parts; harmony
taciturn	*adj.* – reserved; quiet; secretive
tedious	*adj.* – time-consuming; burdensome; uninteresting

(continued on next page)

temper	v. – soften; pacify; compose
tentative	adj. – not confirmed; indefinite
thrifty	adj. – economical; pennywise
tranquility	n. – peace; stillness; harmony
trepidation	n. – apprehension; uneasiness
trivial	adj. – unimportant; small; worthless

■ Drill 11 ■

DIRECTIONS: Match each word in the left column with the word in the right column that is most opposite in meaning.

WORD		MATCH	
1. _____ scrutinize	6. _____ tentative	A. frivolity	F. skim
2. _____ skeptic	7. _____ thrifty	B. enjoyable	G. turbulent
3. _____ solemnity	8. _____ tranquility	C. prodigal	H. active
4. _____ static	9. _____ solicit	D. chaos	I. believer
5. _____ tedious	10. _____ stagnant	E. give	J. confirmed

DIRECTIONS: Match each word in the left column with the word in the right column that is most similar in meaning.

WORD		MATCH	
11. _____ symmetry	14. _____ subtle	A. understated	D. fear
12. _____ superfluous	15. _____ trepidation	B. unnecessary	E. flatterer
13. _____ sycophant		C. balance	

Group 12

tumid	adj. – swollen; inflated
undermine	v. – weaken; ruin
uniform	adj. – consistent; unvaried; unchanging
universal	adj. – concerning everyone; existing everywhere
unobtrusive	adj. – inconspicuous; reserved
unprecedented	adj. – unheard of; exceptional

unpretentious	*adj.* – simple; plain; modest
vacillation	*n.* – fluctuation
valid	*adj.* – acceptable; legal
vehement	*adj.* – intense; excited; enthusiastic
venerate	*v.* – revere
verbose	*adj.* – wordy; talkative
viable	1. *adj.* – capable of maintaining life; 2. possible; attainable
vigor	*n.* – energy; forcefulness
vilify	*v.* – slander
virtuoso	*n.* – highly skilled artist
virulent	*adj.* – deadly; harmful; malicious
vital	*adj.* – important; spirited
volatile	*adj.* – changeable; undependable
vulnerable	*adj.* – open to attack; unprotected
wane	*v.* – grow gradually smaller
whimsical	*adj.* – fanciful; amusing
wither	*v.* – wilt; shrivel; humiliate; cut down
zealot	*n.* – believer; enthusiast; fan
zenith	*n.* – point directly overhead in the sky; acme

■ Drill 12 ■

DIRECTIONS: Match each word in the left column with the word in the right column that is most opposite in meaning.

WORD		MATCH	
1. ____ uniform	6. ____ vigorous	A. amateur	F. support
2. ____ virtuoso	7. ____ volatile	B. trivial	G. constancy
3. ____ vital	8. ____ vacillation	C. visible	H. lethargic
4. ____ wane	9. ____ undermine	D. placid	I. wax
5. ____ unobtrusive	10. ____ valid	E. unacceptable	J. varied

DIRECTIONS: Match each word in the left column with the word in the right column that is most similar in meaning.

WORD		MATCH	
11. ____ wither	14. ____ vehement	A. intense	D. possible
12. ____ whimsical	15. ____ virulent	B. deadly	E. shrivel
13. ____ viable		C. amusing	

Additional Vocabulary

The following words comprise additional vocabulary terms that may be found on the PPST.

abandon	1. *v.* – to leave behind; 2. *v.* – to give something up; 3. *n.* – freedom; enthusiasm; impetuosity
abase	*v.* – to degrade; humiliate; disgrace
abbreviate	*v.* – to shorten; compress; diminish
aberrant	*adj.* – abnormal
abhor	*v.* – to hate
abominate	*v.* – to loathe; to hate
abridge	1. *v.* – to shorten; 2. to limit; to take away
absolve	*v.* – to forgive; to acquit
abstinence	*n.* – self-control; abstention; chastity
accede	*v.* – to comply with; to consent to
accomplice	*n.* – co-conspirator; partner; partner-in-crime
accrue	*v.* – collect; build up
acrid	*adj.* – sharp; bitter; foul smelling
adept	*adj.* – skilled; practiced
adverse	*adj.* – negative; hostile; antagonistic; inimical
affable	*adj.* – friendly; amiable; good-natured
aghast	1. *adj.* – astonished; amazed; 2. horrified; terrified; appalled
alacrity	1. *n.* – enthusiasm; fervor; 2. liveliness; sprightliness

allocate	*v.* – set aside; designate; assign
allure	1. *v.* – to attract; entice; 2. *n.* attraction; temptation; glamour
amiss	1. *adj.* wrong; awry; 2. *adv.* – wrongly; mistakenly
analogy	*n.* – similarity; correlation; parallelism; simile; metaphor
anoint	1. *v.* – to crown; ordain; 2. to smear with oil
anonymous	*adj.* – nameless; unidentified
arduous	*adj.* – difficult; burdensome
awry	1. *adj., adv.* – crooked(ly); uneven(ly); 2. wrong; askew
baleful	*adj.* – sinister; threatening; evil; deadly
baroque	*adj.* – extravagant; ornate
behoove	*v.* – to be advantageous; to be necessary
berate	*v.* – scold; reprove; reproach; criticize
bereft	*adj.* – hurt by someone's death
biennial	1. *adj.* – happening every two years; 2. *n.* – a plant which blooms every two years
blatant	1. *adj.* – obvious; unmistakable; 2. crude; vulgar
bombastic	*adj.* – pompous; wordy; turgid
burly	*adj.* – strong; bulky; stocky
cache	1. *n.* – stockpile; store; heap; 2. hiding place for goods
calamity	*n.* – disaster
cascade	1. *n.* – waterfall; 2. *v.* – pour; rush; fall
catalyst	*n.* – anything which creates a situation in which change can occur
chagrin	*n.* – distress; shame
charisma	*n.* – appeal; magnetism; presence
chastise	*v.* – punish; discipline; admonish; rebuke
choleric	*adj.* – cranky; cantankerous
cohesion	*n.* – the act of holding together
colloquial	*adj.* – casual; common; conversational; idiomatic

(continued on next page)

conglomeration	*n.* – mixture; collection
connoisseur	*n.* – expert; authority (usually refers to a wine or food expert)
consecrate	*v.* – sanctify; make sacred; immortalize
craven	*adj.* – cowardly; fearful
dearth	*n.* – scarcity; shortage
debilitate	*v.* – deprive of strength
deign	*v.* – condescend; stoop
delineate	*v.* – to outline; to describe
demur	1. *v.* – to object; 2. *n.* – objection; misgiving
derision	*n.* – ridicule; mockery
derogatory	*adj.* – belittling; uncomplimentary
destitute	*adj.* – poor; poverty-stricken
devoid	*adj.* – lacking; empty
dichotomy	*n.* – branching into two parts
disheartened	*adj.* – discouraged; depressed
diverge	*v.* – separate; split
docile	*adj.* – manageable; obedient
duress	*n.* – force; constraint
ebullient	*adj.* – showing excitement
educe	*v.* – draw forth
effervescence	*n.* – bubbliness; enthusiasm; animation
emulate	*v.* – to follow the example of
ennui	*n.* – boredom; apathy
epitome	*n.* – model; typification; representation
errant	*adj.* – wandering
ersatz	*adj.* – artificial
ethnic	*adj.* – native; racial; cultural

evoke	*v.* – call forth; provoke
exotic	*adj.* – unusual; striking
facade	*n.* – front view; false appearance
facsimile	*n.* – copy; reproduction; replica
fathom	*v.* – comprehend; uncover
ferret	*v.* – drive or hunt out of hiding
figment	*n.* – product; creation
finite	*adj.* – measurable; limited; not everlasting
fledgling	*n.* inexperienced person; beginner
flinch	*v.* – wince; draw back; retreat
fluency	*n.* – smoothness of speech
flux	*n.* – current; continuous change
forbearance	*n.* – patience; self-restraint
foster	*v.* – encourage; nurture; support
frivolity	*n.* – lightness; folly; fun
frugality	*n.* – thrift
garbled	*adj.* – mixed up
generic	*adj.* – common; general; universal
germane	*adj.* – pertinent; related; to the point
gibber	*v.* – speak foolishly
gloat	*v.* – brag; glory over
guile	*n.* – slyness; fraud
haggard	*adj.* – tired looking; fatigued
hiatus	*n.* – interval; break; period of rest
hierarchy	*n.* – body of people, things, or concepts divided into ranks
homage	*n.* – honor; respect
hubris	*n.* – arrogance

(continued on next page)

ideology	*n.* – set of beliefs; principles
ignoble	*adj.* – shameful; dishonorable
imbue	*v.* – inspire; arouse
impale	*v.* – fix on a stake; stick; pierce
implement	*v.* – begin; enact
impromptu	*adj.* – without preparation
inarticulate	*adj.* – speechless; unable to speak clearly
incessant	*adj.* – uninterrupted
incognito	*adj.* – unidentified; disguised; concealed
indict	*v.* – charge with a crime
inept	*adj.* – incompetent; unskilled
innuendo	*n.* – hint; insinuation
intermittent	*adj.* – periodic; occasional
invoke	*v.* – ask for; call upon
itinerary	*n.* – travel plan; schedule; course
jovial	*adj.* – cheery; jolly; playful
juncture	*n.* – critical point; meeting
juxtapose	*v.* – place side by side
knavery	*n.* – rascality; trickery
knead	*v.* – mix; massage
labyrinth	*n.* – maze
laggard	*n.* – a lazy person; one who lags behind
larceny	*n.* – theft; stealing
lascivious	*adj.* – indecent; immoral
lecherous	*adj.* – impure in thought and act
lethal	*adj.* – deadly
liaison	*n.* – connection; link

limber	*adj.* – flexible; pliant
livid	1. *adj.* – black-and-blue; discolored; 2. enraged; irate
lucrative	*adj.* – profitable; gainful
lustrous	*adj.* – bright; radiant
malediction	*n.* – curse; evil spell
mandate	*n.* – order; charge
manifest	*adj.* – obvious; clear
mentor	*n.* – teacher
mesmerize	*v.* – hypnotize
metamorphosis	*n.* – change of form
mimicry	*n.* – imitation
molten	*adj.* – melted
motif	*n.* – theme
mundane	*adj.* – ordinary; commonplace
myriad	*adj.* – innumerable; countless
narcissistic	*adj.* – egotistical; self-centered
nautical	*adj.* – of the sea
neophyte	*n.* – beginner; newcomer
nettle	*v.* – annoy; irritate
notorious	*adj.* – infamous; renowned
obdurate	*adj.* – stubborn; inflexible
obligatory	*adj.* – mandatory; necessary
obliterate	*v.* – destroy completely
obsequious	*adj.* – slavishly attentive; servile
obstinate	*adj.* – stubborn
occult	*adj.* – mystical; mysterious
opaque	*adj.* – dull; cloudy; nontransparent

(continued on next page)

opulence	*n.* – wealth; fortune
ornate	*adj.* – elaborate; lavish; decorated
oust	*v.* – drive out; eject
painstaking	*adj.* – thorough; careful; precise
pallid	*adj.* – sallow; colorless
palpable	*adj.* – tangible; apparent
paradigm	*n.* – model; example
paraphernalia	*n.* – equipment; accessories
parochial	*adj.* – pertaining to a parish; narrow-minded
passive	*adj.* – submissive; unassertive
pedestrian	*adj.* – mediocre; ordinary
pensive	*adj.* – reflective; contemplative
percussion	*n.* – the striking of one object against another
perjury	*n.* – the practice of lying
permeable	*adj.* – porous; allowing to pass through
perpetual	*adj.* – enduring for all time
pertinent	*adj.* – related to the matter at hand
pervade	*v.* – to occupy the whole of
petty	*adj.* – unimportant; of subordinate standing
phlegmatic	*adj.* – without emotion or interest
phobia	*n.* – morbid fear
pittance	*n.* – small allowance
plethora	*n.* – condition of going beyond what is needed; excess; overabundance
potent	*adj.* – having great power or physical strength
privy	*adj.* – private; confidential
progeny	*n.* – children; offspring
provoke	*v.* – to stir action or feeling; arouse

pungent	*adj.* – sharp; stinging
quaint	*adj.* – old-fashioned; unusual; odd
quandary	*n.* – dilemma
quarantine	*n.* – isolation of a person to prevent spread of disease
quiescent	*adj.* – inactive; at rest
quirk	*n.* – peculiar behavior; startling twist
rabid	*adj.* – furious; with extreme anger
rancid	*adj.* – having a bad odor
rant	*v.* – to speak in a loud, pompous manner; rave
ratify	*v.* – to make valid; confirm
rationalize	*v.* – to offer reasons for; account for
raucous	*adj.* – disagreeable to the sense of hearing; harsh
realm	*n.* – an area; sphere of activity
rebuttal	*n.* – refutation
recession	*n.* – withdrawal; depression
reciprocal	*n.* – mutual; having the same relationship to each other
recluse	*n.* – solitary and shut off from society
refurbish	*v.* – to make new
regal	*adj.* – royal; grand
reiterate	*v.* – repeat; to state again
relinquish	*v.* – to let go; abandon
render	*v.* – deliver; provide; to give up a possession
replica	*n.* – copy; representation
resilient	*adj.* – flexible; capable of withstanding stress
retroaction	*n.* – an action elicited by a stimulus
reverie	*n.* – the condition of being unaware of one's surroundings; trance
rummage	*v.* – search thoroughly

(continued on next page)

rustic	*adj.* – plain and unsophisticated; homely
saga	*n.* – a legend; story
salient	*adj.* – noticeable; prominent
salvage	*v.* – rescue from loss
sarcasm	*n.* – ironic, bitter humor designed to wound
satire	*n.* – a novel or play that uses humor or irony to expose folly
saunter	*v.* – walk at a leisurely pace; stroll
savor	*v.* – to receive pleasure from; enjoy
seethe	*v.* – to be in a state of emotional turmoil; to become angry
serrated	*adj.* – having a sawtoothed edge
shoddy	*adj.* – of inferior quality; cheap
skulk	*v.* – to move secretly
sojourn	*n.* – temporary stay; visit
solace	*n.* – hope; comfort during a time of grief
soliloquy	*n.* – a talk one has with oneself (esp. on stage)
somber	*adj.* – dark and depressing; gloomy
sordid	*adj.* – filthy; base; vile
sporadic	*adj.* – rarely occurring or appearing; intermittent
stamina	*n.* – endurance
steadfast	*adj.* – loyal
stigma	*n.* – a mark of disgrace
stipend	*n.* – payment for work done
stupor	*n.* – a stunned or bewildered condition
suave	*adj.* – effortlessly gracious
subsidiary	*adj.* – subordinate
succinct	*adj.* – consisting of few words; concise
succumb	*v.* – give in; yield; collapse

sunder	*v.* – break; split in two
suppress	*v.* – to bring to an end; hold back
surmise	*v.* – draw an inference; guess
susceptible	*adj.* – easily imposed; inclined
tacit	*adj.* – not voiced or expressed
tantalize	*v.* – to tempt; to torment
tarry	*v.* – to go or move slowly; delay
taut	*adj.* – stretch tightly
tenacious	*adj.* – persistently holding to something
tepid	*adj.* – lacking warmth, interest, enthusiasm; lukewarm
terse	*adj.* – concise; abrupt
thwar	*v.* – prevent from accomplishing a purpose; frustrate
timorous	*adj.* – fearful
torpid	*adj.* – lacking alertness and activity; lethargic
toxic	*adj.* – poisonous
transpire	*v.* – to take place; come about
traumatic	*adj.* – causing a violent injury
trek	*v.* – to make a journey
tribute	*n.* – expression of admiration
trite	*adj.* – commonplace; overused
truculent	*adj.* – aggressive; eager to fight
turbulence	*n.* – condition of being physically agitated; disturbance
turmoil	*n.* – unrest; agitation
tycoon	*n.* – wealthy leader
tyranny	*n.* – absolute power; autocracy
ubiquitous	*adj.* – ever present in all places; universal
ulterior	*adj.* – buried; concealed

(continued on next page)

uncanny	*adj.* – of a strange nature; weird
unequivocal	*adj.* – clear; definite
unique	*adj.* – without equal; incomparable
unruly	*adj.* – not submitting to discipline; disobedient
unwonted	*adj.* – not ordinary; unusual
urbane	*adj.* – cultured; suave
usurpation	*n.* – act of taking something for oneself; seizure
usury	*n.* – the act of lending money at illegal rates of interest
utopia	*n.* – imaginary land with perfect social and political systems
vacuous	*adj.* – containing nothing; empty
vagabond	*n.* – wanderer; one without a fixed place
vagrant	1. *n.* – homeless person; 2. *adj.* – rambling; wandering; transient
valance	*n.* – short drapery hanging over a window frame
valor	*n.* – bravery
vantage	*n.* – position giving an advantage
vaunted	*adj.* – boasted of
velocity	*n.* – speed
vendetta	*n.* – feud
venue	*n.* – location
veracious	*adj.* – conforming to fact; accurate
verbatim	*adj.* – employing the same words as another; literal
versatile	*adj.* – having many uses; multifaceted
vertigo	*n.* – dizziness
vex	*v.* – to trouble the nerves; annoy
vindicate	*v.* – to free from charge; clear
vivacious	*adj.* – animated; gay
vogue	*n.* – modern fashion

voluble	*adj.* – fluent
waft	*v.* – move gently by wind or breeze
waive	*v.* – to give up possession or right
wanton	*adj.* – unruly; excessive
warrant	*v.* – justify; authorize
wheedle	*v.* – try to persuade; coax
whet	*v.* – sharpen
wrath	*n.* – violent or unrestrained anger; fury
wry	*adj.* – mocking; cynical
xenophobia	*n.* – fear of foreigners
yoke	*n.* – harness; collar; bond
yore	*n.* – former period of time
zephyr	*n.* – a gentle wind; breeze

■ Drill 13 ■

DIRECTIONS: Each of the following questions provides a given word in **bold** followed by five word choices. Choose the word which is opposite in meaning to the given word.

1. **Authentic:**

   (A) cheap   (B) competitive   (C) false

   (D) biased   (E) irrational

2. **Miserly:**

   (A) unhappy   (B) generous   (C) optimistic

   (D) reticent   (E) golden

3. **Diligent:**

   (A) lethargic   (B) morose   (C) silly

   (D) nostalgic   (E) poor

4. **Preclude:**

   (A) commence   (B) include   (C) produce

   (D) perpetuate   (E) enable

5. **Extol:**

   (A) criticize   (B) expedite   (C) pay

   (D) deport   (E) defer

6. **Diverse:**

   (A) solo   (B) furtive   (C) jovial

   (D) wrinkled   (E) similar

7. **Disperse:**

   (A) despair   (B) belittle   (C) renew

   (D) renege   (E) amass

8. **Enduring:**

   (A) fallacious   (B) temporal   (C) dismal

   (D) minute   (E) disseminating

9. **Brevity:**

   (A) gravity   (B) gluttony   (C) cowardice

   (D) authenticity (E) verbosity

10. **Demur:**

    (A) assemble   (B) bereave   (C) approve

    (D) add   (E) ascribe

11. **Unwonted:**

    (A) perceptive   (B) ordinary   (C) tepid

    (D) desirable   (E) qualified

12. **Chastise:**

    (A) repudiate   (B) immortalize (C) endorse

    (D) virility   (E) congratulate

13. **Infamous:**

   (A) revered   (B) resolute   (C) obscure
   (D) contiguous   (E) unknown

14. **Dispassionate:**

   (A) resigned   (B) profound   (C) fanatical
   (D) torrid   (E) prudent

15. **Scanty:**

   (A) redundant   (B) mediocre   (C) calming
   (D) profuse   (E) partisan

16. **Prosaic:**

   (A) poetic   (B) unique   (C) rabid
   (D) disdainful   (E) condescending

17. **Didactic:**

   (A) dubious   (B) imbecilic   (C) punctual
   (D) rhetorical   (E) reverent

18. **Colloquial:**

   (A) poetic   (B) separate   (C) formal
   (D) analogical   (E) anonymous

19. **Cohesive:**

   (A) adhesive   (B) opposed   (C) smooth
   (D) adverse   (E) fragmented

20. **Obligatory:**

   (A) promising   (B) permissible   (C) heaven
   (D) optional   (E) responsible

21. **Opaque:**

   (A) permeable   (B) similar   (C) visible
   (D) opulent   (E) translucent

22. **Sunder:**

    (A) unite   (B) create noise   (C) oust
    (D) rise above   (E) freeze

23. **Narcissistic:**

    (A) flowery   (B) detrimental   (C) gentle
    (D) modest   (E) polite

24. **Foster:**

    (A) destroy   (B) relate   (C) parent
    (D) abort   (E) revere

25. **Livid:**

    (A) homeless   (B) bright   (C) calm
    (D) elusive   (E) opulent

26. **Suppress:**

    (A) justify   (B) advocate   (C) free
    (D) level   (E) immunize

27. **Destitute:**

    (A) organized   (B) ornate   (C) moral
    (D) wealthy   (E) obsequious

28. **Painstaking:**

    (A) healthful   (B) sordid   (C) careless
    (D) sadistic   (E) lethal

29. **Parochial:**

    (A) melancholy   (B) blasphemous   (C) sporting
    (D) irreligious   (E) broad-minded

30. **Mandate:**

    (A) emphasis   (B) sophism   (C) pinnacle
    (D) request   (E) meander

31. **Lucid:**

   (A) obscure   (B) tedious   (C) calm

   (D) frightening   (E) intelligent

32. **Ignoble:**

   (A) brave   (B) honorable   (C) royal

   (D) attentive   (E) informal

33. **Pertinent:**

   (A) respectful   (B) detailed   (C) dreary

   (D) blatant   (E) irrelevant

34. **Abstinence:**

   (A) indulgence   (B) concurrence   (C) hedonism

   (D) diligence   (E) alcoholism

35. **Frugal:**

   (A) unplanned   (B) tempermental   (C) regal

   (D) ethical   (E) extravagant

36. **Fortuitous:**

   (A) lethargic   (B) unprotected   (C) weak

   (D) unlucky   (E) antagonistic

37. **Unequivocal:**

   (A) versatile   (B) equal   (C) noisy

   (D) unclear   (E) truthful

38. **Contempt:**

   (A) respect   (B) pettiness   (C) politeness

   (D) resistance   (E) compliance

39. **Gravity:**

   (A) antipathy   (B) derision   (C) buoyancy

   (D) eloquence   (E) effervescence

40. **Austere:**

   (A) measurable   (B) resilient   (C) indulgent
   (D) indirect   (E) destitute

41. **Passive:**

   (A) thoughtless   (B) supportive   (C) retentive
   (D) contemporary (E) assertive

42. **Stagnant:**

   (A) celibate   (B) active   (C) effluent
   (D) feminine   (E) polluted

43. **Adverse:**

   (A) friendly   (B) quiescent   (C) poetic
   (D) burly   (E) petty

44. **Craven:**

   (A) difficult   (B) reptilian   (C) pungent
   (D) birdlike   (E) courageous

45. **Heed:**

   (A) adjust   (B) resist   (C) attend
   (D) encourage   (E) order

46. **Impartial:**

   (A) biased   (B) complete   (C) eternal
   (D) articulate   (E) raucous

47. **Vindicate:**

   (A) remove   (B) absolve   (C) evoke
   (D) accuse   (E) ferret

48. **Derision:**

   (A) elimination   (B) attention   (C) praise
   (D) entrance   (E) recession

49. **Reprehensible:**

    (A) released   (B) aghast   (C) awry

    (D) incidental   (E) commendable

50. **Relegate:**

    (A) promote   (B) nullify   (C) include

    (D) obliterate   (E) placate

51. **Vain:**

    (A) addicted   (B) modest   (C) unscented

    (D) abasin   (E) choleric

52. **Laggard:**

    (A) haggard   (B) lustrous   (C) haphazard

    (D) advanced   (E) industrious

53. **Labyrinthine:**

    (A) inconsistent   (B) amazing   (C) direct

    (D) incredulous   (E) mythological

54. **Slander:**

    (A) praise   (B) comfort   (C) discipline

    (D) risk   (E) digress

55. **Pittance:**

    (A) mound   (B) plethora   (C) quirk

    (D) grandeur   (E) phlegm

56. **Solace:**

    (A) lunation   (B) turmoil   (C) distress

    (D) valance   (E) spontaneity

57. **Deferent:**

    (A) current   (B) constructive   (C) erratic

    (D) unyielding   (E) applicant

58. **Fickle:**

   (A) bland   (B) cascading   (C) caustic

   (D) dubious   (E) faithful

59. **Exotic:**

   (A) ethnic   (B) diverse   (C) realistic

   (D) mundane   (E) enigmatic

60. **Thwart:**

   (A) imprison   (B) mystify   (C) assist

   (D) fluctuate   (E) saturate

Knowing Your Word Parts

Memorization and practice are not the only ways to learn the meanings of new words. While taking this test, you will have nothing but your own knowledge and context clues to refer to when you come into contact with unfamiliar words. Even though we have provided you with a comprehensive list of words, there is a very good chance that you will come across words that you still do not know. Therefore, you will need to study our list of prefixes, roots, and suffixes in order to be prepared. Learning the meanings of these prefixes, roots, and suffixes is essential to a strong vocabulary and, therefore, to performing well on the Reading Section, as well as the entire PPST exam.

Prefix

Prefix	Meaning	Example
ab-, a-, abs-	away, from	absent – away, not present abstain – keep from doing, refrain
ad-	to, toward	adjacent – next to address – to direct towards
ante-	before	antecedent – going before in time anterior – occurring before
anti-	against	antidote – remedy to act against an evil antibiotic – substance that fights against bacteria
be-	over, thoroughly	bemoan – to mourn over belabor – to exert much labor upon
bi-	two	bisect – to divide biennial – happening every two years

Prefix	Meaning	Example
cata-, cat-, cath-	down	catacombs – underground passage ways catalogue – descriptive list
circum-	around	circumscribe – to draw a circle around circumspect – watchful on all sides
com-	with	combine – join together communication – to have dealing with
contra-	against	contrary – opposed contrast – to stand in opposition
de-	down, from, away	decline – to slope downward decontrol – to remove control from
di-	two	dichotomy – process of dividing into two groups or entities diarchy – system of government with two authorities
dis-, di-	apart, away	discern – to distinguish as separate digress – to turn away from the subject of attention
epi-, ep-, eph-	upon, among	epidemic – happening among a disproportionately large number of individuals epicycle – circle whose center moves round in the circumference of a greater circle
ex-, e-	from, out	exceed – go beyond the limit emit – to send forth
extra-	outside, beyond	extraordinary – beyond or outside conventional means extrasensory – beyond the ordinary senses
hyper-	beyond, over	hyperactive – over the normal activity level hypercritic – one who is critical beyond measure
hypo-	beneath, down	hypodermic – beneath the skin hypoglycemia – abnormally low glucose level in the blood
in-, il-, im-, ir-	not	inactive – not active irreversible – not reversible
in-, il-, im-, ir-	in, on, into	instill – to put in slowly impose – to lay on
inter-	among, between	intercom – to exchange conversations between people interlude – performance given between parts in a play

(continued on next page)

Prefix	Meaning	Example
intra-	within	intravenous – within a vein intramural – being or happening within the confines of a community, group, or institution
meta-	beyond, over, along with	metamorphosis – change over in form or nature metatarsus – part of foot beyond the flat of the foot
mis-	badly, wrongly	misconstrue – to interpret wrongly misappropriate – to use wrongly
mono-	one	monogamy – to be married to one person at a time monotone – a single, unvaried tone
multi-	many	multiple – of many parts multitude – a great number
non-	no, not	nonsense – lack of sense nonentity – not existing
ob-	against	obscene – offensive to modesty obstruct – to hinder the passage of
para-, par-	beside	parallel – continuously at equal distance apart parenthesis – sentence inserted within a passage
per-	through	persevere – to maintain an effort permeate – to pass through
poly-	many	polygon – a plane figure with many sides or angles polytheism – belief in existence of many gods
post-	after	posterior – coming after postpone – to put off till a future time
pre-	before	premature – ready before the proper time premonition – a previous warning
pro-	in favor of, forward	prolific – bringing forth offspring project – throw or cast forward
re-	back, against	reimburse – pay back retract – to draw back
semi-	half	semicircle – half a circle semiannual – half-yearly
sub-	under	subdue – to bring under one's power submarine – travel under the surface of the sea
super-	above	supersonic – above the speed of sound superior – higher in place or position

Prefix	Meaning	Example
tele-, tel-	across	telecast – transmit across a distance telepathy – communication between mind and mind at a distance
trans-	across	transpose – to change the position of two things transmit – to send from one person to another
ultra-	beyond	ultraviolet – beyond the limit of visibility ultramarine – beyond the sea
un-	not	undeclared – not declared unbelievable – not believable
uni-	one	unity – state of oneness unison – sounding together
with-	away, against	withhold – to hold back withdraw – to take away

Root

Root	Meaning	Example
act, ag	do, act, drive	activate – to make active agile – having quick motion
alt	high	altitude – height alto – highest male singing voice
alter, altr	other, change	alternative – choice between two or more things of which just one may be picked altruism – living for the good of others
am, ami	love, friend	amiable – worthy of affection amity – friendship
anim	mind, spirit	animated – spirited animosity – intense hostility
annu, enni	year	annual – occurring every year centennial – a 100-year anniversary
aqua	water	aquarium – tank for water animals and plants aquacade – swimming or diving exhibition
arch	principal, first	archenemy – principal enemy archetype – original pattern from which things are copied
aud, audit	hear	audible – capable of being heard audience – assembly of listeners or spectators

(continued on next page)

Root	Meaning	Example
auto	self	automatic – self-acting autobiography – a story whose subject and author are one and the same
bell	war	belligerent – a nation or state waging war bellicose – favoring or inclined toward hostility
ben, bene	good	benign – kindly disposition beneficial – advantageous
bio	life	biotic – relating to life biology – the science of life
brev	short	abbreviate – make shorter brevity – shortness
cad, cas	fall	cadence – fall in voice casualty – loss caused by death
capit, cap	head	captain – the head or chief decapitate – to cut off the head
cede, ceed, cess	to go, to yield	recede – to move or fall back proceed – to move onward
cent	hundred	century – hundred years centipede – insect with a hundred legs
chron	time	chronology – science dealing with historical dates chronicle – register of events in order of time
cide, cis	to kill, to cut	homicide – a killing of one person by another; the killer of another person incision – a cut
clam, claim	to shout	acclaim – receive with applause proclamation – announce publicly
cogn	to know	recognize – to know again cognition – awareness
corp	body	incorporate – combine into one body corpse – dead body
cred	to trust, to believe	incredible – unbelievable credulous – too prone to believe
cur, curr, curs	to run	current – flowing body of air or water excursion – short trip

Root	Meaning	Example
dem	people	democracy – government formed for the people epidemic – affecting all people
dic, dict	to say	dictate – to read aloud for another to transcribe verdict – decision of a jury
doc, doct	to teach	docile – easily instructed indoctrinate – to instruct
domin	to rule	dominate – to rule dominion – territory of rule
duc, duct	to lead	conduct – act of guiding induce – to overcome by persuasion
eu	well, good	eulogy – speech or writing in praise euphony – pleasantness or smoothness of sound
fac, fact, fect, fic	to do, to make	factory – location of production fiction – something invented or imagined
fer	to bear, to carry	transfer – to move from one place to another refer – to direct to
fin	end, limit	infinity – unlimited finite – limited in quantity
flect, flex	to bend	flexible – easily bent reflect – to throw back
fort	luck	fortunate – lucky fortuitous – happening by chance
fort	strong	fortify – strengthen fortress – stronghold
frag, fract	break	fragile – easily broken fracture – break
fug	flee	fugitive – fleeing refugee – one who flees to a place of safety
gen	class, race	engender – to breed generic – of a general nature in regard to all members
grad, gress	to go, to step	regress – to go back graduate – to divide into regular steps

(continued on next page)

Root	Meaning	Example
gram, graph	writing	telegram – message sent by telegraph autograph – person's handwriting or signature
ject	to throw	projectile – capable of being thrown reject – to throw away
leg	law	legitimate – lawful legal – defined by law
leg, lig, lect	to choose, gather, read	illegible – incapable of being read election – the act of choosing
liber	free	liberal – favoring freedom of ideals liberty – freedom from restraint
log	study, speech	archaeology – study of human antiquities prologue – address spoken before a performance
luc, lum	light	translucent – slightly transparent illuminate – to light up
magn	large, great	magnify – to make larger magnificent – great
mal, male	bad, wrong	malfunction – to operate incorrectly malevolent – evil
mar	sea	marine – pertaining to the sea submarine – below the surface of the sea
mater, matr	mother	maternal – motherly matriarch – government exercised by a mother
mit, miss	to send	transmit – to send from one person or place to another mission – the act of sending
morph	shape	metamorphosis – a changing in shape anthropomorphic – having a human shape
mut	change	mutable – subject to change mutate – to change a vowel
nat	born	innate – inborn native – a person born in a place
neg	deny	negative – expressing denial renege – to deny
nom	name	nominate – to put forward a name anonymous – no name given

Root	Meaning	Example
nov	new	novel – new
		renovate – to make as good as new
omni	all	omnipotent – all powerful
		omnipresent – all present
oper	to work	operate – to work on something
		cooperate – to work with others
pass, path	to feel	pathetic – affecting the tender emotions
		passionate – moved by strong emotion
pater, patr	father	paternal – fatherly
		patriarch – government exercised by a father
ped, pod	foot	pedestrian – one who travels on foot
		podiatrist – foot doctor
pel, puls	to drive, to push	impel – to drive forward
		compulsion – irresistible force
phil	love	philharmonic – loving harmony or music
		philanthropist – one who loves and seeks to do good for others
port	carry	export – to carry out of the country
		portable – able to be carried
psych	mind	psychology – study of the mind
		psychiatrist – specialist in mental disorders
quer, ques, quir, quis	to ask	inquiry – to ask about
		question – that which is asked
rid, ris	to laugh	ridiculous – laughable
		derision – to mock
rupt	to break	interrupt – to break in upon
		erupt – to break through
sci	to know	science – systematic knowledge of physical or natural phenomena
		conscious – having inward knowledge
scrib, script	to write	transcribe – to write over again
		script – text of words
sent, sens	to feel, to think	sentimental – feel great emotion
		sensitive – easily affected by changes
sequ, secut	to follow	sequence – connected series
		consecutive – following one another in unbroken order

(continued on next page)

Root	Meaning	Example
solv, solu, solut	to loosen	dissolve – to break up absolute – without restraint
spect	to look at	spectator – one who watches inspect – to look at closely
spir	to breathe	inspire – to breathe in respiration – process of breathing
string, strict	to bind	stringent – binding strongly restrict – to restrain within bounds
stru, struct	to build	misconstrue – to interpret wrongly construct – to build
tang, ting, tact, tig	to touch	tangent – touching, but not intersecting contact – touching
ten, tent, tain	to hold	tenure – holding of office contain – to hold
term	to end	terminate – to end terminal – having an end
terr	earth	terrain – tract of land terrestrial – existing on earth
therm	heat	thermal – pertaining to heat thermometer – instrument for measuring temperature
tort, tors	to twist	contortionist – one who twists violently torsion – act of turning or twisting
tract	to pull, to draw	attract – draw toward distract – to draw away
vac	empty	vacant – empty evacuate – to empty out
ven, vent	to come	prevent – to stop from coming intervene – to come between
ver	true	verify – to prove to be true veracious – truthful
verb	word	verbose – use of excess words verbatim – word for word
vid, vis	to see	video – picture phase of television vision – act of seeing external objects

Root	Meaning	Example
vinc, vict, vang	to conquer	invincible – unconquerable victory – defeat of enemy
viv, vit	life	vital – necessary to life vivacious – lively
voc	to call	provocative – serving to excite or stimulate to action vocal – uttered by voice
vol	to wish, to will	involuntary – outside the control of will volition – the act of willing or choosing

Suffix

Suffix	Meaning	Example
-able, -ble	capable of	believable – capable of being believed legible – capable of being read
-acious, -icious, -ous	full of	vivacious – full of life wondrous – full of wonder
-ant, -ent	full of	eloquent – full of eloquence expectant – full of expectation
-ary	connected with	honorary – for the sake of honor disciplinary – enforcing instruction
-ate	to make	ventilate – to make public consecrate – to make sacred
-fy	to make	magnify – to make larger testify – to make witness
-ile	pertaining to, capable of	docile – capable of being managed easily civil – pertaining to a city or state
-ism	principle or practice	conservatism – interest in preserving or restoring idiotism – foolish conduct or action
-ist	doer	artist – one who creates art pianist – one who plays the piano
-ose	full of	verbose – full of words grandiose – striking, imposing
-osis	condition	neurosis – nervous condition psychosis – psychological condition
-tude	state	magnitude – state of greatness multitude – state of quantity

Figures of Speech

Figurative language helps to create imaginative and detailed writing. A figure of speech is used in the imaginative rather than the literal sense. It helps the reader to make connections between the writer's thoughts and the external world. Knowing the different types of figures of speech can help you determine the context in which a word is being used and, thereby, help you determine the meaning of that word. The following are some commonly used figures of speech.

Simile

A simile is an explicit comparison between two things. The comparison is made by using *like* or *as*.

> Her hair was *like* straw.
> The blanket was *as* white as snow.

Metaphor

Like the simile, the metaphor likens two things. However, *like* or *as* are not used in the comparison.

> "All the world's a stage." Shakespeare
> Grass is nature's blanket.

A common error is the mixed metaphor. This occurs when a writer uses two inconsistent metaphors in a single expression.

> The blanket of snow clutched the earth with icy fingers.

Hyperbole

A hyperbole is a deliberate overstatement or exaggeration used to express an idea.

> I have told you a thousand times not to play with matches.

Personification

Personification is the attribution of human qualities to an object, animal, or idea.

> The wind laughed at their attempts to catch the flying papers.

■ Drill 14 ■

Reading Comprehension

DIRECTIONS: Read the passage and answer the questions that follow.

——— WATER ———

The most important source of sediment is earth and rock material carried to the sea by rivers and streams; the same materials may also have been transported by glaciers and winds. Other sources are volcanic ash and lava, shells and skeletons of organisms, chemical precipitates formed in seawater, and particles
5 from outer space.

Water is a most unusual substance because it exists on the surface of the earth in its three physical states: ice, water, and water vapor. There are other substances that might exist in a solid and liquid or gaseous state at temperatures normally found at the earth's surface, but there are fewer substances
10 which occur in all three states.

Water is odorless, tasteless, and colorless. It is the only substance known to exist in a natural state as a solid, liquid, or gas on the surface of the earth. It is a universal solvent. Water does not corrode, rust, burn, or separate into its components easily. It is chemically indestructible. It can corrode almost any metal and
15 erode the most solid rock. A unique property of water is that it expands and floats on water when frozen or in the solid state. Water has a freezing point of 0°C and a boiling point of 100°C. Water has the capacity for absorbing great quantities of heat with relatively little increase in temperature. When **distilled**, water is a poor conductor of electricity but when salt is added, it is a good conductor of electricity.

20 Sunlight is the source of energy for temperature change, evaporation, and currents for water movement through the atmosphere. Sunlight controls the rate of photosynthesis for all marine plants, which are directly or indirectly the source of food for all marine animals. Migration, breeding, and other behaviors of marine animals are affected by light.

25 Water, as the ocean or sea, is blue because of the molecular scattering of the sunlight. Blue light, being of short wavelength, is scattered more effectively than light of longer wavelengths. Variations in color may be caused by particles suspended in the water, water depth, cloud cover, temperature, and other variable factors. Heavy concentrations of dissolved materials cause a yellowish hue, while
30 algae will cause the water to look green. Heavy populations of plant and animal materials will cause the water to look brown.

1. Which of the following lists of topics best organizes the information in the selection?

   (A) I.   Water as vapor

        II.   Water as ice

        III. Water as solid

   (B) I.   Properties of seawater

        II.   Freezing and boiling points of water

        III. Photosynthesis

        IV.   Oceans and seas

   (C) I.   Water as substance

        II.   Water's corrosion

        III. Water and plants

        IV.   Water and algae coloration

   (D) I.   Water's physical states

        II.   Properties of water

        III. Effects of the sun on water

        IV.   Reasons for color variation in water

   (E) I.   Water and plants

        II.   Brown water

        III. Water absorption

        IV.   Good conductor of electricity

2. According to the passage, what is the most unique property of water?

   (A) Water is odorless, tasteless, and colorless.

   (B) Water exists on the surface of the earth in three physical states.

   (C) Water is chemically indestructible.

   (D) Water is a poor conductor of electricity.

   (E) Sunlight causes currents for water movement.

3. Which of the following best defines the word *distilled* as it is used in line 18.?

   (A) Free of salt content

   (B) Free of electrical energy

   (C) Dehydrated

   (D) Containing wine

   (E) Chemically indestructible

4. The writer's main purpose in this selection is to

   (A) explain the colors of water

   (B) examine the effects of the sun on water

   (C) define the properties of water

   (D) describe the three physical states of all liquids

   (E) describe the surface of the Earth

5. The writer of this selection would most likely agree with which of the following statements?

   (A) The properties of water are found in most other liquids on this planet.

   (B) Water should not be consumed in its most natural state.

   (C) Water might be used to serve many different functions.

   (D) Water is too unpredictable for most scientists.

   (E) The color of water never changes.

DIRECTIONS: Read the passage and answer the questions that follow.

THE BEGINNINGS OF THE SUBMARINE

A submarine was first used as an offensive weapon during the American Revolutionary War. The Turtle, a one-man submersible designed by an American inventor named David Bushnell and hand-operated by a screw propeller, attempted to sink a British man-of-war in New York Harbor. The plan was to attach a charge

5   of gunpowder to the ship's bottom with screws and explode it with a time fuse. After repeated failures to force the screws through the copper sheathing of the hull of H.M.S. *Eagle*, the submarine gave up and withdrew, exploding its powder a short distance from the *Eagle*. Although the attack was unsuccessful, it caused the British to move their blockading ships from the harbor to the outer bay.

10   On 17 February 1864, a Confederate craft, a hand-propelled submersible, carrying a crew of eight men, sank a Federal corvette that was blockading Charleston Harbor. The hit was accomplished by a torpedo suspended ahead of the Confederate Hunley as she rammed the Union frigate *Housatonic*, and is the first recorded instance of a submarine sinking a warship.

15   The submarine first became a major component in naval warfare during World War I, when Germany demonstrated its full potential. Wholesale sinking of Allied shipping by the German U-boats almost swung the war in favor of the Central Powers. Then, as now, the submarine's greatest advantage was that it could oper-

20   ate beneath the ocean surface where detection was difficult. Sinking a submarine was comparatively easy, once it was found—but finding it before it could attack was another matter.

During the closing months of World War I, the Allied Submarine Devices Investigation Committee was formed to obtain from science and technology more effective underwater detection equipment. The committee developed a reasonably

25   accurate device for locating a submerged submarine. This device was a trainable hydrophone, which was attached to the bottom of the ASW ship, and used to detect screw noises and other sounds that came from a submarine. Although the committee disbanded after World War I, the British made improvements on the locating device during the interval between then and World War II, and named it

30   ASDIC after the committee.

American scientists further improved on the device, calling it SONAR, a name derived from the underlined initials of the words <u>so</u>und <u>na</u>vigation and <u>r</u>anging.

At the end of World War II, the United States improved the snorkel (a device

35   for bringing air to the crew and engines when operating submerged on diesels) and developed the Guppy (short for greater underwater propulsion power), a conversion of the fleet-type submarine of World War II fame. The superstructure was changed by reducing the surface area, streamlining every protruding object, and enclosing the periscope shears in a streamlined metal fairing. Performance in-

40   creased greatly with improved electronic equipment, additional battery capacity, and the addition of the snorkel.

6. The passage implies that one of the most pressing modifications needed for the submarine was to

   (A) streamline its shape
   (B) enlarge the submarine for accommodating more torpedoes and men
   (C) reduce the noise caused by the submarine
   (D) add a snorkel
   (E) reduce its size so that it would be more difficult to find

7. It is inferred that

   (A) ASDIC was formed to obtain technology for underwater detection.
   (B) ASDIC developed an accurate device for locating submarines.
   (C) the hydrophone was attached to the bottom of the ship.

(D) ASDIC was formed to develop technology to defend U.S. shipping.

(E) near the end of World War I, the British were developing a submarine that was quieter than that of the Germans.

8. SONAR not only picked up the sound of submarines moving through the water but also

(A) indicated the speed at which the sub was moving

(B) gave the location of the submarine

(C) indicated the speed of the torpedo

(D) placed the submarine within a specified range

(E) gave the size and classification of the sub

9. According to the passage, the submarine's success was due in part to its ability to

(A) strike and escape undetected

(B) move swifter than other vessels

(C) submerge to great depths while being hunted

(D) run silently

(E) hit a number of vessels before being detected

10. From the passage, one can infer

(A) David Bushnell was indirectly responsible for the sinking of the Federal corvette in Charlestown Harbor.

(B) David Bushnell invented the Turtle

(C) the Turtle was a one-man submarine

(D) the Turtle sank the *Eagle* on February 17, 1864

(E) the British sailors heard the clanging of the screws on the hull of their ship

READING DRILLS

Drill 1

1.	(J)	9.	(F)
2.	(G)	10.	(E)
3.	(A)	11.	(D)
4.	(C)	12.	(C)
5.	(H)	13.	(A)
6.	(B)	14.	(E)
7.	(I)	15.	(B)
8.	(D)		

Drill 2

1.	(D)	9.	(B)
2.	(G)	10.	(H)
3.	(I)	11.	(D)
4.	(F)	12.	(A)
5.	(A)	13.	(B)
6.	(J)	14.	(E)
7.	(E)	15.	(C)
8.	(C)		

Drill 3

1.	(E)	9.	(F)
2.	(H)	10.	(D)
3.	(J)	11.	(C)
4.	(A)	12.	(A)
5.	(I)	13.	(E)
6.	(B)	14.	(D)
7.	(C)	15.	(B)
8.	(G)		

Drill 4

1.	(D)	9.	(H)
2.	(E)	10.	(G)
3.	(A)	11.	(D)
4.	(I)	12.	(A)
5.	(J)	13.	(B)
6.	(B)	14.	(C)
7.	(C)	15.	(E)
8.	(F)		

Drill 5

1.	(H)	9.	(D)
2.	(F)	10.	(G)
3.	(A)	11.	(B)
4.	(B)	12.	(D)
5.	(J)	13.	(A)
6.	(C)	14.	(E)
7.	(I)	15.	(C)
8.	(E)		

Drill 6

1.	(G)	9.	(F)
2.	(A)	10.	(H)
3.	(E)	11.	(D)
4.	(J)	12.	(E)
5.	(C)	13.	(A)
6.	(B)	14.	(C)
7.	(D)	15.	(B)
8.	(I)		

Drill 7

1.	(F)	9.	(D)
2.	(E)	10.	(J)
3.	(A)	11.	(B)
4.	(B)	12.	(E)
5.	(H)	13.	(D)
6.	(I)	14.	(C)
7.	(C)	15.	(A)
8.	(G)		

Drill 8

1.	(D)	9.	(F)
2.	(A)	10.	(J)
3.	(H)	11.	(C)
4.	(G)	12.	(B)
5.	(B)	13.	(A)
6.	(C)	14.	(E)
7.	(E)	15.	(D)
8.	(I)		

Drill 9

1.	(D)	9.	(C)
2.	(I)	10.	(H)
3.	(G)	11.	(A)
4.	(A)	12.	(D)
5.	(J)	13.	(B)
6.	(E)	14.	(E)
7.	(B)	15.	(C)
8.	(F)		

Drill 10

1.	(H)	9.	(D)
2.	(I)	10.	(G)
3.	(E)	11.	(B)
4.	(A)	12.	(D)
5.	(J)	13.	(A)
6.	(B)	14.	(C)
7.	(F)	15.	(E)
8.	(C)		

Drill 11

1.	(F)	9.	(E)
2.	(I)	10.	(G)
3.	(A)	11.	(C)
4.	(H)	12.	(B)
5.	(B)	13.	(E)
6.	(J)	14.	(A)
7.	(C)	15.	(D)
8.	(D)		

Drill 12

1.	(J)	9.	(F)
2.	(A)	10.	(E)
3.	(B)	11.	(E)
4.	(I)	12.	(C)
5.	(C)	13.	(D)
6.	(H)	14.	(A)
7.	(D)	15.	(B)
8.	(G)		

Drill 13

1.	(C)	16.	(B)	31.	(A)	46.	(A)
2.	(B)	17.	(B)	32.	(B)	47.	(D)
3.	(A)	18.	(C)	33.	(E)	48.	(C)
4.	(E)	19.	(E)	34.	(A)	49.	(E)
5.	(A)	20.	(D)	35.	(E)	50.	(A)
6.	(E)	21.	(E)	36.	(D)	51.	(B)
7.	(E)	22.	(A)	37.	(D)	52.	(E)
8.	(B)	23.	(D)	38.	(A)	53.	(C)
9.	(E)	24.	(A)	39.	(E)	54.	(A)
10.	(C)	25.	(C)	40.	(C)	55.	(B)
11.	(B)	26.	(B)	41.	(E)	56.	(C)
12.	(E)	27.	(D)	42.	(B)	57.	(D)
13.	(A)	28.	(C)	43.	(A)	58.	(E)
14.	(C)	29.	(E)	44.	(E)	59.	(D)
15.	(D)	30.	(D)	45.	(B)	60.	(C)

■ Drill 14 ■

Reading Comprehension—Detailed Explanations of Answers

1. **(D)**

    The correct choice is (D) because its precepts are summations of each of the composition's main paragraphs. Choice (A) only mentions points made in the second paragraph. Choices (B), (C), and (E) only mention scattered points made throughout the passage, each of which does not represent a larger body of information within the passage.

2. **(B)**

    The second paragraph states that this is the reason that water is a most unusual substance. Choices (A), (C), and (E) list unusual properties of water, but are not developed in the same manner as the property stated in choice (B). Choice (D) is not even correct under all circumstances.

3. **(A)**

    The sentence contrasts distilled water to that which contains salt, so choice (A) is correct. Choices (B), (C), and (D) are not implied by the passage. Choice (E) is incorrect.

4. **(C)**

    The writer's didactic summary of water's properties is the only perspective found in the passage. Choices (A), (B), and (E) are the subjects of individual paragraphs within the passage, but hardly represent the entire passage itself. An in-depth discussion of the physical states of liquids choice (D) is not offered within the passage.

5. **(C)**

    The correct choice is (C) because of the many properties of water ascribed to it in the passage, each of which might serve one practical purpose or another. Choices (A), (D), and (E) are contradicted within the passage, while choice (B) is not implied at all by the passage.

6. **(A)**

    Answer choice (A) is correct because of the importance of streamlining mentioned in the final paragraph. Choices (B), (C), and (E) are not suggested in the paragraph, and (D) is secondary in importance to choice (A).

7. **(D)**

Since it may be inferred from the general purpose of underwater detection equipment, Choice (D) is correct. While choices (A) and (B) are true statements, they are not inferences. Choices (C) and (E) is not implied in the passage.

8. **(D)**

Answer choice (D) is correct because the "R" in SONAR stands for "Ranging." Choices (A), (B), (C) and (E) are neither mentioned nor implied by the passage.

9. **(A)**

As was mentioned in the third sentence of the third paragraph, Choice (A) is correct. Choices (B), (C), (D), and (E) are not mentioned in the passage.

10. **(A)**

It may be inferred that Bushnell's invention led to the success of the later version of the submarine. Choices (B) and (C) are true, but are not inferences because they are directly stated in the first paragraph. Choice (D) is not a true statement; the Turtle had no direct link to the 1864 incident. Choice (E) is improbable. Action would have been taken against the Turtle.

CHAPTER 3

Basic Math Skills Review

1.	Number and Operations
2.	Algebra
3.	Geometry and Measurement
4.	Data Analysis and Probability

1. Number and Operations

(A) Order

Demonstrate an understanding of order among integers, fractions, and decimals

The numbers used in basic mathematics courses are called the *real numbers*. Real numbers are comprised of rational and irrational numbers. *Rational numbers* are numbers that can be written as a ratio of two integers. Rational numbers include integers, fractions, and decimals. *Integers* are the whole numbers and their opposites: $\{...-3, -2, -1, 0, 1, 2, 3...\}$. Whole numbers and counting numbers are subsets of integers. *Whole numbers* are all the positive integers and 0: $\{0, 1, 2, 3...\}$. *Counting numbers* are the positive integers beginning with 1: $\{1, 2, 3, 4...\}$. A *decimal number* is a number represented by the digits 0 to 9 and may include a decimal point. Examples of decimal numbers are 4.5, .003, and 367. *Fractions* are numbers used to express numbers that include parts of a whole. A fraction has a numerator and a denominator. The *denominator* is the number on the bottom, and it shows how many pieces the fraction is broken up into. The *numerator* shows how many parts of the fraction you have. An *irrational number* is a number that cannot be expressed as the ratio of two integers. Decimals that never end and do not repeat are irrational. Square roots of numbers that are not perfect squares are irrational numbers. The ratio of a circle's circumference to its diameter, π, is an irrational number.

PROBLEM

Which number below shows an integer that is NOT a whole number?

(A) −10   (D) 3

(B) −4.5   (E) 7.7

(C) 0

APPROACH TO SOLUTION

This problem taps into your knowledge of vocabulary. Ask yourself, "What integers are not whole numbers?" Whole numbers start with 0. Integers include all whole numbers and their opposites. Therefore, negative integers are not whole numbers. The first negative integer is −1. So, any integer that is −1 or less will be a solution to this problem. The only negative integer in the answer choices is −10, choice (A).

Each number has a specific value and may be written in a number of different forms, such as a fraction, decimal, percent, or integer. All real numbers can be placed on a number line to show how they compare to other numbers. A number line is actually infinite, continuing in both directions forever. In order to make a physical representation of a number line, however, we are only able to draw a finite portion of it. Below is an example of a number line that shows the integers from −10 to +10. Although only the integers are marked, there are an infinite number of numbers that can be represented on the number line. For example, between 0 and 1, you could place .3, .45, .8, $\sqrt[3]{7}$, and − because they are numbers greater than 0 and less than 1.

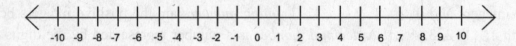

As you move to the right on a number line, numbers get larger. As you move to the left on a number line, numbers get smaller. You can choose to show as many or as few numbers as you wish on a number line. In addition, you can divide the number line into whatever divisions suit the situation. If you wanted to compare numbers between 0 and 1, for example, you could show just the portion of a number line between 0 and 1, divided up into tenths, if you wanted.

PROBLEM

On the number line below, between which two points would you place –.85?

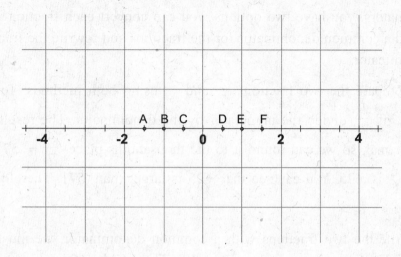

(A) A and B

(B) B and C

(C) C and D

(D) D and E

(E) E and F

APPROACH TO SOLUTION

To solve this problem correctly, you must be able to read a number line correctly. In addition, you need to be able to understand place value. Looking closely at the number line, you can see that each tick mark is ½ a unit or .5. (A) is at –1.5, B is at –1.0, and (C) is at –.5. The number –.85 is less than –.5, but greater than –1.0. Therefore, it would lie between (B) and (C) on the number line. The correct answer is (B).

Comparing fractions involves knowing which fraction is larger and which is smaller. If fractions are shown on a number line, the fraction to the right is the larger one. However, fractions are not always shown on a number line. Comparing fractions is simple when the fractions have the same denominator. The same denominator means that the fractions are broken up into the same number of pieces. All you have to do is compare the numerators to see which fraction is larger. For example, which is larger, $\frac{9}{15}$ or $\frac{7}{15}$? Since 9 is larger than 7, you know that $\frac{9}{15}$ is larger than $\frac{7}{15}$. If you want to compare two fractions that have different denominators, you have two options. You can convert each fraction into a decimal, or you can find a common denominator for the fractions and rewrite the fractions with that common denominator.

Let's compare the two fractions $\frac{4}{7}$ and $\frac{5}{8}$ using both methods. To find the decimal equivalent of $\frac{4}{7}$, divide the numerator by the denominator. The resulting decimal is a repeating decimal, so we can round it to the thousandths place. $\frac{4}{7} \approx .571$. The decimal equivalent of $\frac{5}{8}$ is .625. You can see that .625 is larger than .571. Therefore, $\frac{5}{8}$ is larger than $\frac{4}{7}$.

To rewrite the two fractions with a common denominator, we must find the least common multiply of the denominators, 7 and 8. The LCM is 56. Then, we rewrite each fraction as an equivalent fraction with the denominator of 56. The fraction $\frac{4}{7}$ will be multiplied by $\frac{8}{8}$ and the fraction $\frac{5}{8}$ will be multiplied by $\frac{7}{7}$. Equivalent fractions have the same value; also, equivalent fractions both simplify to the same fraction when they are in lowest terms. See below:

$$\frac{4}{7} \times \frac{8}{8} = \frac{32}{56}$$

$$\frac{5}{8} \times \frac{7}{7} = \frac{35}{56}$$

$\frac{35}{56}$ is greater than $\frac{32}{56}$. Therefore, $\frac{5}{8}$ is greater than $\frac{4}{7}$.

PROBLEM

Which list below shows the fractions $\frac{4}{6}, \frac{1}{2}, \frac{4}{5}$ in order from least to greatest?

(A) $\frac{4}{6}, \frac{1}{2}, \frac{4}{5}$

(B) $\frac{4}{6}, \frac{4}{5}, \frac{1}{2}$

(C) $\frac{1}{2}, \frac{4}{6}, \frac{4}{5}$

(D) $\frac{1}{2}, \frac{4}{5}, \frac{4}{6}$

(E) $\frac{4}{5}, \frac{4}{6}, \frac{1}{2}$

APPROACH TO SOLUTION

When you first look at a problem like this, you might think that you need to find a common denominator for all of the fractions to put them in order. However, save yourself time by noticing that both $\frac{4}{5}$ and $\frac{4}{6}$ are greater than ½. Therefore, you already know that the first fraction in your answer choice will be ½. The only two possible answer choices with ½ first are (C) and (D). To determine which fraction comes next, $\frac{4}{5}$ or $\frac{4}{6}$, you do not need to find a common denominator. Use your skills of logic and estimation to help you. Notice that both numerators are the same. Both fractions have 4 pieces. The question you should ask yourself is, "Which 4 pieces are larger?" The two denominators are 6 and 5; so ask yourself, "Which pieces are larger, sixths or fifths?" The larger the denominator, the smaller the pieces, so fifths are larger than sixths. So, without doing any mathematical figuring, you know that $\frac{4}{5}$ is larger than $\frac{4}{6}$. Since $\frac{4}{5}$ is larger than $\frac{4}{6}$, the correct order of the fractions from least to greatest is $\frac{1}{2}, \frac{4}{6}, \frac{4}{5}$, answer choice (C).

(B) Equivalence

Demonstrate an understanding that a number can be represented in more than one way

Quantities can be presented in a variety of ways—as decimals, percents, or fractions. Depending on the situation, it may be appropriate to use one form rather than another. Therefore, it is beneficial to know how to convert among the three forms.

Writing a fraction as a decimal is simple if the denominator of the fraction is a power of 10, such as 10, 100, or 1000. For example, $\frac{2}{10} = .2$, $\frac{17}{100} = .17$, and $\frac{45}{1000} = .045$. All you have to do is put the digits in their correct places. If the denominator is not a power of 10, then divide the numerator by the denominator as shown in the example below.

Example:

What is $\frac{4}{5}$ as a decimal?

When you divide 4 by 5, you need to add a decimal point and a 0 after the 4, so you are dividing 4.0 by 5. Completing this division gives you .8; therefore, $\frac{4}{5}$ and .8 are equivalent.

To write a decimal as a fraction, write the numbers of the decimal in the numerator of a fraction without the decimal point. Locate the digit that is farthest to the right in the number and write its place value as the denominator. If the fraction needs to be simplified, then rewrite it in lowest terms.

Example:

Write .55 as a fraction.

1. Write 55 in the numerator and 100 in the denominator: $\dfrac{55}{100}$
2. Simplify the fraction: $\dfrac{11}{20}$.

Example:

Write 4.2 as a fraction.

1. Write 42 in the numerator and 10 in the denominator: $\dfrac{42}{10}$
2. Rewrite as a mixed number in lowest terms: $4\dfrac{1}{5}$.

There are two steps to write a decimal as a percent. First move the decimal point two places to the right (this may result in the decimal point being at the end of the number; in that case, you can leave it off). The next step is to add the percent sign. Here's an example: Write .09 as a percent. Move the decimal point two places to the right and add the percent sign to get 9% (notice how the decimal point at the end of the number is not included because it is not necessary).

There are also two steps to write a percent as a decimal. First, move the decimal point in the number two places to the left. If there is no decimal point, it means that the number in front of the percent sign is a whole number. The decimal point in a whole number is actually at the end of the number. In the number 19, for example, the decimal point (not written) would be at the end of the number: 19. is the same as 19 without the decimal point. After moving the decimal point two places to the left, take away the percent sign.

Example:

Write 14% as a decimal.

Since we do not see the decimal point, it is after the 14, so we can write 14.%. Move the decimal point two places to the left and drop the percent sign. You get .14.

To write a percent as a fraction, write the number in front of the percent sign in the numerator of a fraction. Since we are working with percents, put 100 in the denominator. Remember to simplify the fraction, if necessary.

Let's look at the following: Write 91% as a fraction. $\frac{91}{100}$. And another: Write 8% as a fraction. $\frac{8}{100}$ which simplifies to $\frac{2}{25}$.

To write a fraction as a percent, follow the steps for writing a fraction as a decimal. Then follow the steps for writing a decimal as a percent. Example: Write $\frac{1}{8}$ as a percent. First $\frac{1}{8}$ = .125. Then .125 = 12.5%.

If you are asked to compare numbers to each other and they are presented in a variety of forms, it is helpful to put them all in the same form—whichever is easiest for you, or whichever form makes most sense in the problem. If you have to put the following numbers in order from least to greatest, .18, $\frac{1}{8}$, 15%, and 10%, you could rewrite $\frac{1}{8}$, 15%, and 10% as decimals. Then it would be easy to see how to order them. $\frac{1}{8}$ = .125; 15% = .15; and 10% = .10. So, the numbers in order are 10%, $\frac{1}{8}$, 15%, and .18.

PROBLEM

Danielle and Francesca took the same Geometry test. Danielle earned 77% on the test, and Francesca got 16 of the 20 problems correct. How much better did Francesca do on the test than Danielle?

(A) .003

(B) .3

(C) 3%

(D) 9%

(E) 80%

APPROACH TO SOLUTION

You are trying to find how much better Francesca scored on the test than Danielle. However, notice that Danielle's score is given in a percent, while Francesca's score is given as a ratio. Ask yourself, "What would be the easiest way to compare those two values?" One value is already a percent. You can rewrite $\frac{16}{20}$ as a percent. This will be easy because 20 is a factor of 100 ($20 \times 5 = 100$). Multiply both 16 and 20 by 5 to get the equivalent fraction, $\frac{80}{100} \cdot \frac{80}{100} = 80\%$. Now that both values are in the same form, you can answer the question. "How much better" implies the difference between the two values. $80\% - 77\% = 3\%$. Notice that some of the answers are in decimal form; however, none of them is equivalent to 3%. 3% as a decimal would be .03. Answer choice (C) is correct.

It is also helpful to know how to convert between mixed numbers and improper fractions. To explain how to rewrite a mixed number as an improper fraction, let's look at an example.

Write $5\frac{3}{8}$ as an improper fraction. Multiply the denominator of the fraction by the whole number, $8 \times 5 = 40$. Then, add that answer to the numerator of the fraction, $40 + 3 = 43$. That answer, 43, is the numerator of the equivalent improper fraction. The denominator remains the same; in this example, it is 8. Therefore, $5\frac{3}{8}$ is equivalent to $\frac{43}{8}$.

To write an improper fraction as a mixed number, you follow the opposite process as changing a mixed number into an improper fraction. Let's write $\frac{27}{4}$ as a mixed number. Divide the denominator into the numerator. See how many times it divides into the numerator without going over the numerator. In this case, 4 divides into 27 six times because $4 \times 6 = 24$. The number 6 becomes the whole number of the mixed number. As you can see, the numerator 27 is 3 more than 24. Therefore, 3 is the remainder, which will be the numerator of the fraction. The denominator remains 4. Therefore, $\frac{27}{4} = 6\frac{3}{4}$.

It is common to write all fractions in lowest terms. A fraction is in lowest terms if the largest factor that the numerator and denominator share is 1. For example, $\frac{8}{15}$, $\frac{14}{19}$, and $\frac{25}{54}$ are all in lowest terms because the only factor that the numerator and denominator of each fraction share is 1. If a fraction can be written in lowest terms, do so. When you rewrite a fraction to lowest terms, you are dividing the numerator and denominator by the same value; what you are doing, in fact, is dividing the fraction by a form of 1. Since 1 is the identity element for multiplication (and division), dividing by 1 will not change the value. To write a fraction in lowest terms, find the greatest factor that the numerator and denominator have in common. Then divide both numerator and denominator by that number.

Equivalent fractions are two fractions that are equal to each other, but have different denominators; equivalent fractions both simplify to the same fraction when they are written in lowest terms. Some examples of equivalent fractions are: $\frac{1}{8}$ and $\frac{2}{16}$; $\frac{4}{12}$ and $\frac{12}{36}$; and $\frac{11}{22}$ and $\frac{1}{2}$.

It is helpful to find the equivalent fraction with the following setup:

$$\frac{3}{5} \times \frac{?}{?} = \frac{?}{10}$$

You are looking for the number that multiplies by 5 to get 10. That number is 2. So, you also multiply the numerator, which is 3, by 2 to get 6. Since $\frac{2}{2} = 1$, you are multiplying $\frac{3}{5}$ by 1, which does not change its value $\frac{6}{10}$ is equivalent to $\frac{3}{5}$. Now that you have the same denominators, you can add $\frac{1}{10}$ and $\frac{6}{10}$, which is $\frac{7}{10}$.

Let's look at another example: $\frac{11}{12} - \frac{3}{8}$. In this example, 8 is not a factor of 12, so we cannot use 12 as our LCM. In cases like this where the smaller denominator is not a factor of the larger one, it is a good idea to list the multiples of each denominator until you find one that they share. Multiples of a number are found by multiplying that number by the counting numbers, starting with 1. The first four multiples of 12 are 12, 24, 36, 48. The first four multiples of 8 are 8, 16, 24, 32. As you can see, both numbers share the multiple 24, so that is the LCM.

$$\frac{11}{12} \times \frac{?}{?} = \frac{?}{24} \quad \text{and} \quad \frac{3}{8} \times \frac{?}{?} = \frac{?}{24}$$

Use the set-up described above to find the number that when you multiply it by 12 gives you 24 to find an equivalent fraction for $\frac{11}{12}$ with a denominator of 24. That number is 2. So multiply 11 by 2 to get 22 for the numerator. In the second fraction, to get 24, you must multiply 8 by 3. Multiply 3 by 3 to get 9 in the numerator. $\frac{9}{24}$ is equivalent to $\frac{3}{8}$. Now that we have rewritten both fractions with a common denominator, we can do the subtraction. $\frac{22}{24} - \frac{9}{24} = \frac{13}{24}$.

If you find that you need to multiply a number by itself a number of times, you may need to use exponents as a more efficient way to write the problem. If, for example, you would like to write $10 \times 10 \times 10 \times 10$, you can do that in a shorthand way by writing 10^4. 10, the large number on the bottom, is the base and 4, the small raised number, is the exponent. The exponent tells you how many times you must multiply the base as a factor. When computing the value of an expression presented in exponential form, it is often a good idea to write the expression out to make sure that you arrive at the correct answer. If you have 2^5, a common error is to multiply 2 by 5 and get 10. This is incorrect. Writing the expression out in expanded form ensures that you do not make this mistake. In this case, 2^5 is the same as $2 \times 2 \times 2 \times 2 \times 2$, which is 32.

Perfect square numbers are numbers that result from multiplying an integer by itself. The following chart shows some square numbers.

Side of square (x)	x^2	Expanded form of x^2	Area of square/square number
1	1^2	1×1	1
2	2^2	2×2	4
3	3^2	3×3	9
4	4^2	4×4	16
5	5^2	5×5	25

As you can see, the first perfect square number is 1. There are an infinite number of square numbers, and it is helpful to be able to recognize them when you see them. The reason they are called square numbers is because if you start with a positive integer, you can imagine that it is the side length of a square. When you multiply that number by itself, the answer you get can represent the area of a square. See the diagrams below representing the first six square numbers.

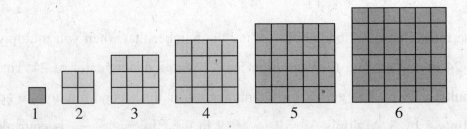

You can square any number by multiplying it by itself; however, if you do not square an integer, you will not get a perfect square number.

Just as you can square a number, you can also find the square root of a number. The *square root* of a number is the number that you get when you multiply it by itself. The square root of 1 is 1. The square root of 4 is 2. The square root of 9 is 3, etc. If you are finding the square root of a perfect square number, then you will get an integer. If, however, you are finding the square root of a non-perfect square number, the square root will be an irrational number. That is, you can find the square root of numbers like 6, 15, and 30; however, they will be non-terminating, non-repeating decimal numbers.

A *radical* is a root sign. If you wanted to find the square root of 100, you could write, $\sqrt{100}$. Sometimes you will need to rewrite an expression with a radical in a different or simpler form. Therefore, it is important to be able to rewrite radicals in simplest form. If the number under a radical has a perfect square factor greater than 1, you should take that factor out. For example, $\sqrt{75}$ can be rewritten as $\sqrt{25} \times \sqrt{3}$. The square root of 25 is 5, so you can write $\sqrt{75}$ in simplest form as $5\sqrt{3}$.

(C) Numeration and Place Value
Demonstrate an understanding of place value, how numbers are named, and order of magnitude of numbers

The value of a digit depends on where it shows up in the number, called its *place value*. That is, the 3 in 73 is equal to 3, while the 3 in 38 is equal to 30. One way to clearly see the value of each digit in a number is to look at the number in expanded form. *Expanded form* is a way to write a number to show the value of each digit.

The number 1,234,567 in **expanded form** would be:

$$(1 \times 1,000,000) + (2 \times 100,000) + (3 \times 10,000) + (4 \times 1,000)$$
$$+ (5 \times 100) + (6 \times 10) + (7 \times 1)$$

As you can see, expanded form allows you to look at each digit's value individually. The 4, for example, is equal to 4,000 because the 4 is in the thousands place.

The number .34567 in expanded form would be:

$$(3 \times .1) + (4 \times .01) + (5 \times .001) + (6 \times .0001) + (7 \times .00001)$$

As you can see, the 6 is not equal to 6, but is equal to .0006 because of where the 6 is located in the number. Hence, the name, "place value."

To compare decimal numbers, you must place the numbers so that the same place values line up underneath each other. In such a way, you can find which number is larger by comparing the digits in the corresponding places.

Example:

Which number is larger, .408 or .41?

Line up the numbers underneath each other:

.408
.41

Compare the digits. Both numbers have a 4 in the tenths place. The top number has a 0 in the hundredths place. The bottom number has a 1 in the hundredths place. Which is larger, 0 or 1? Since 1 is larger, .41 is larger than .408. Even though .408 has more digits, it is a smaller value than .41.

Decimal Numbers: The numbers we use are made up of the digits 0 to 9. All numbers have one or more of those digits. Numbers that are greater than 1 are found to the left of the decimal point. Numbers that are less than 1 are found after the decimal point. A number that is greater than 1 could also have a portion of a number that is less than 1. In that case, there will be digits to the left and to the right of the decimal point. A digit's value is determined by its place in the number. The place value chart below shows values from the millions to the thousandths; however, this is just a part of the place-value chart. Numbers continue infinitely in either direction of the decimal point. The first number to the left of the decimal point is the ones place. Every place value to the left is ten times larger than the place on its right. The first number to the right of the decimal point is the tenths place. Each place value to the right of that is ten times smaller. That is the hundredths are ten times smaller than the tenths, and the thousandths are ten times smaller than the hundredths.

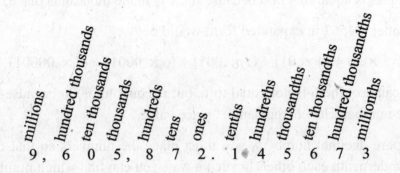

There are different types of decimal numbers. Some are *terminating*, which means they end. Some examples are .5, .49, or 6.78. Some decimals are *repeating*. Repeating decimals that have a pattern are *rational numbers*. A bar is written over the repeating digits to indicate which digits are repeating. For example, to indicate .666…, you would write $.\overline{6}$.

To indicate the decimal .636363…you would write $.\overline{63}$. Notice that in this decimal number: .5444…only the 4 repeats. Therefore, the bar will only be over the 4, like so: $.5\overline{4}$. Repeating decimals that do not have a pattern are *irrational*. They cannot be written as a ratio of two integers.

PROBLEM

How do you write .935 in expanded form?

    (A) $(9 \times .1) + (3 \times .01) + (5 \times .001)$

    (B) $(9 \times 1) + (3 \times 10) + (5 \times 1000)$

    (C) $(9 \times 1) + (3 \times .1) + (5 \times .01)$

    (D) $(.9 \times .1) + (.03 \times .01) + (.005 \times .001)$

    (E) $(9 \times .01) + (3 \times .001) + (5 \times .0001)$

APPROACH TO SOLUTION

You have to know what expanded form is in order to answer this question correctly. Using expanded form with decimal numbers requires knowledge of the place values after the decimal point. The number .935 has a 9 in the tenths place, a 3 in the hundredths place, and a 5 in the thousandths place. Therefore, the correct answer is (A).

(D) Number Properties

Demonstrate an understanding of the properties of whole numbers without necessarily knowing the names of the properties

Factors are the numbers that you multiply to get another number. For example, 8 and 2 are factors of 16 because $8 \times 2 = 16$. Factors must divide evenly into a number with no remainder. That is, 5 is not a factor of 12 because even though 5 divides into 12 two times, there is a remainder of 2. To find the greatest common factor of two numbers, the GCF, you must find the largest factor that both numbers have in common. If you wanted to find the GCF of 8 and 12, list the factors of each number, and then select the largest one that both numbers have in common. Factors of 8 are: 1, 2, 4, 8. Factors of 12 are: 1, 2, 3, 4, 6, 12. The common factors are 1, 2, and 4. The greatest common factor is 4. Finding the GCF of two numbers is useful when you want to simplify fractions. To simplify $\frac{25}{30}$, divide the numerator and denominator by the GCF of 5. Therefore, $\frac{25}{30} = \frac{5}{6}$ when simplified.

There are times you will want to know what numbers are factors of other numbers. In this case, you are looking for numbers that divide evenly into another number. Familiarity with divisibility rules will help you recognize factors quickly.

How can you tell if a number is evenly divisible by another? Here are some divisibility rules you can follow.

- Divisible by 1: All whole numbers are divisible by 1.

- Divisible by 2 (also called even): If a number ends in 0, 2, 4, 6, or 8, it is an even number.

- Divisible by 3: Add up the digits of the number; if that sum is divisible by 3, then the number is divisible by 3.

- Divisible by 5: A number is divisible by 5 if it ends in 5 or 0.

- Divisible by 9: A number is divisible by 9 if the sum of its digits is divisible by 9.

- Divisible by 10: If a number ends in 0 it is divisible by 10.

Every whole number is divisible by 1 and itself. If a number is only divisible by 1 and itself and has no other factors (therefore having only 2 factors), it is a *prime number*. The prime numbers less than 20 are 2, 3, 5, 7, 11, 13, 17, and 19. There are an infinite number of prime numbers. If a number has more than two factors, it is a *composite number*. The number 1 has only one factor, the number 1; therefore, it is neither prime nor composite.

To find the multiple of a number, multiply that number by any integer. That is, some multiples of 4 are: −8, 0, 12, and 20 because $4 \times -2 = -8$, $4 \times 0 = 0$, $4 \times 3 = 12$, and $4 \times 5 = 20$. The least common multiple, or LCM, of two numbers is the smallest number that is a multiple of both numbers. To find the LCM of 6 and 9, you will need to list the non-zero multiples of each until you find a common one. The first five non-zero multiples of 6 are: 6, 12, 18, 24, and 30, and the first five non-zero multiples of 9 are: 9, 18, 27, 36, and 45. The LCM is 18.

PROBLEM

A school ordered some notebooks and some pencils. Notebooks come 6 to a box, and pencils come 20 to a box. The school received the same number of each item. How many boxes of each item did they receive if they received between 200 and 250 of each item?

(A) 10 boxes of notebooks and 3 boxes of pencils

(B) 20 boxes of notebooks and 6 boxes of pencils

(C) 40 boxes of notebooks and 12 boxes of pencils

(D) 60 boxes of notebooks and 18 boxes of pencils

(E) 80 boxes of notebooks and 24 boxes of pencils

APPROACH TO SOLUTION

This problem requires reading several times to make sure you understand what it is asking. Since the number of notebooks and pencils received is the same, you are looking for a common multiple of 6 and 20. The LCM of 6 and 20 is 60. All multiples of 60 are multiples of both 6 and 20. The problem states that the school received between 200 and 250 of each item. Ask yourself, "What common multiple of 6 and 20 is between 200 and 250?" The answer is 240. Now, you have to find how many boxes of each item were ordered. Since there are 6 notebooks to a box, divide 240 by 6 to get 40 boxes of notebooks. Since there are 20 pencils to a box, divide 240 by 20 to get 12 boxes of pencils. The correct answer is (C).

Even numbers end in 0, 2, 4, 6, or 8. Odd numbers end in 1, 3, 5, 7, or 9. A number is either even or odd. The following laws are true about even and odd numbers:

Addition and Subtraction

- even $\pm$ even = even
- even $\pm$ odd = odd
- odd $\pm$ odd = even

Multiplication

- even $\times$ even = even
- even $\times$ odd = even
- odd $\times$ odd = odd

Division

When you divide two integers, you do not always get an integer. Sometimes you do, as in the example, $8 \div 2 = 4$, but other times you do not, as in the example, $2 \div 8 = \frac{1}{4}$. The concept of even and odd only applies to integers.

Properties of 0 and 1: *Zero* is the identity element for addition (and subtraction). What that means is if you add (or subtract) 0 to a number, it will not change the value. For example, $7 + 0 = 7$. Adding 0 does not change the value of 7. The *number 1* is the identity element for multiplication (and division). If you multiply (or divide) a number by 1, it will not change the value. For example, $8 \times 1 = 8$. Multiplying by 1 does not change the value of 8.

Examples:

What value of the variable makes each equation true?

a) $7y = 7$

b) $z + 45.6 = 45.6$

c) $3.9 - p = 3.9$

d) $12 \div x = 12$

Solutions:

a) $y = 1$ b) $z = 0$ c) $p = 0$ d) $x = 1$

(E) Operation Properties

Demonstrate an understanding of the properties—Commutative, Associative, and Distributive—of the basic operations of addition, subtraction, multiplication, and division

The Commutative Property works for addition and multiplication only. The *Commutative Property* of Addition states that if you add two terms (they may be numbers or variables), the order does not affect the sum. That is, $4 + 3 = 3 + 4$. In this example, you can see that the answers on both sides of the equal sign are the same even though the order of the two numbers is different. This property works with variables as well. $12 + y = y + 12$. Even though we do not know the value of y, we can be certain that both sides of the equation are equal because the same two terms are being added on each side. The Commutative Property also works for multiplication. $9 \times 5 = 5 \times 9$ illustrates the Commutative Property of multiplication. Both sides of the equation equal 45. If there are variables involved, such as in the example, $ab = ba$, we know both sides are equal because we are multiplying the same two numbers, just in a different order.

The *Associative Property* is a grouping property and it works for both addition and multiplication. The order of operations tells us that the first thing we must do when simplifying expressions is to simplify operations within grouping symbols. Therefore, if given the following expression, $(4 + 6) + 2$, you would add 4 and 6 together before adding 2. However, let's compare the following expressions: $(4 + 6) + 2$ and $4 + (6 + 2)$. Notice that both have only addition, the same three numbers, and a set of parentheses. What is different is that the first expression groups 4 and 6 together while the second expression groups 6 and 2 together. How do the answers compare?

$$(4 + 6) + 2 = \qquad 4 + (6 + 2) =$$
$$10 + 2 = \qquad 4 + 8 =$$
$$12 \qquad\qquad 12$$

Notice that both expressions yield the same answer. The Associative Property changes the numbers that are grouped together, but it does not change the answer.

To see how the Associative Property of multiplication works, we can compare the following two expressions that contain only multiplication, the same three numbers, and one set of grouping symbols. The only difference is which numbers are grouped together.

$$(5 \times 8) \times 6 = \qquad 5 \times (8 \times 6) =$$
$$40 \times 6 = \qquad 5 \times 48 =$$
$$240 \qquad\qquad 240$$

As you can see, both answers are the same even though in one expression, we multiplied 5 and 8 before multiplying by 6, and in the other expression, we multiplied 8 by 6 before multiplying by 5.

The Distributive Property of multiplication over addition shows that $a(b + c)$ is equal to $ab + ac$. You can prove this yourself by substituting in some numbers.

Example:

Does $4(30 + 6) = (4 \times 30) + (4 \times 6)$?

Original Problem	4(30 + 6)	(4 × 30) + 4 × 6)
Step #1	4(36)	(120) + (24)
Step #2	144	144

As you can see, the two expressions are equal to each other. When dealing with numbers only, it does not make sense to use the Distributive Property; that is, it is not more efficient. However, when working with variables, using the Distributive Property is necessary to simplify an expression, which involves removing parentheses. For example, $5(x + 3)$ can be rewritten as $5x + 15$. There is no other way to simplify the expression except for using the Distributive Property.

PROBLEM

Which of the expressions below is equivalent to 35y + 60?

(A) 95y

(B) (35 + y + 60)

(C) 5(7y + 12)

(D) 5 + (7y + 12)

(E) (35)(y)(60)

APPROACH TO SOLUTION

This problem requires being able to work with the Distributive Property. The two terms in the given expression have a GCF of 5. Therefore, you can divide both terms by 5. Write the 5 on the outside of a set of parentheses. Inside the parentheses write 7y and 12 because those are the two terms that result when you divide 35y and 60 by 5. (C) is the correct answer. To check that it is correct, use the Distributive Property: Multiply 5 by both 7y and 12. You will get 35y + 60; this checks your answer.

In mathematics, there are four operations—addition, subtraction, multiplication, and division. When adding two whole numbers together, you arrive at a *sum* (the answer to an addition problem) that is greater than either number. For example, if you have $75 in your wallet and you add a $20 bill, you will have 75 + 20 = 95, which is $95. However, when working with negative numbers, as well as positive ones, it is possible to have a sum that is less than one or both of the addends. When adding –8 to 3, for example, the sum is –5, which is less than 3. When adding –2 and –5, the sum is –7, which is less than both addends separately.

Subtracting means taking one amount from another. When working with whole numbers, the *difference* (the answer to a subtraction problem) is less than the first number you start with. For instance, if you have $20 and spend $8, how much money would you have left? This problem is an example of a subtraction problem. 20 – 8 = 12; you would have $12 left. If you are working with negative numbers as well as positive ones, the difference may not be smaller than the two numbers you are subtracting. For example, –9 – (–3) = –6. The difference is smaller than –3, but it is larger than –9.

Multiplication is a shortcut to adding the same number many times. It is a more efficient way of completing repeated addition. If you wanted to know the number of tires there are on 5 cars, for example, you could certainly add $4 + 4 + 4 + 4 + 4$, which would show there are 20 tires all together. However, when you have a problem that asks you to add the same number many times, you can use multiplication; using multiplication is often more efficient than doing repeated addition. The answer to a multiplication problem is called a *product*. In the example above, instead of the addition problem presented, you could find 5×4, which can be translated as 5 groups of 4. 5×4 gives the same answer as $4 + 4 + 4 + 4 + 4$. Facility with the multiplication facts from 2–12 is important; math can be accomplished more quickly when you can produce the answers to multiplication problems immediately.

Dividing means putting a number into groups of the same size. For instance, if a child baked 35 brownies, and he wants to put them into 7 different bags with the same number of brownies in each bag, how many brownies will be in each bag? This problem requires dividing 35 into 7 groups—one group for each bag. $35 \div 7 = 5$. That means there will be 5 brownies in each bag. Just as multiplication is a shortcut way to do repeated addition, division is a shortcut way to do repeated subtraction. Let's look at the example that follows: If you baked 36 cookies and plan to put 4 cookies in each bag to give as gifts, how many bags will you need? You could certainly solve this problem with subtraction. That is, put 4 cookies in the first bag, and you have 32 left (because $36 - 4 = 32$). Put another 4 in the next bag, and you have 28 cookies left (because $32 - 4 = 28$). If you continue in this way, you will discover you need exactly 9 bags for your cookies. Although you will arrive at the correct answer, it is more efficient to solve this problem with division; the corresponding division problem for the example above would be $36 \div 4 = 9$. If you want to know how many weeks there are in 56 days, you could solve the problem $56 \div 7$. What this problem is asking is, how many groups of 7 are there in 56? The answer is 8. There are 8 weeks in 56 days. The answer to a division problem is called the *quotient*. Therefore, the quotient of 56 and 7 is 8.

Mathematics follows rules and procedures. If you encounter a problem with different operations, or one that also has parentheses and exponents in it, you must know in what order to simplify the problem. Without being given any instruction on this topic, you might think that you would simplify from left to right; however, this is not always correct. To make sure that everyone who completes the same problem gets the same answer, there is an order of operations to follow. The order of operations is as follows:

1) Simplify everything inside grouping symbols.

2) Simplify exponents.

3) Do multiplication and division from left to right.

4) Do addition and subtraction from left to right.

People often use the mnemonic, "Please Excuse My Dear Aunt Sally" to remember the order of operations, PEMDAS.

Let's start by looking at problems that contain only the four operations of addition, subtraction, multiplication, and division. By following the rules of the order of operations, do multiplication and division from left to right before addition and subtraction, which you also do from left to right. Therefore, in the following problem: $4 + 7 \times 2$, multiply 7 by 2 first, then add that answer to 4. The answer is 18.

Let's look at this problem: $12 \div 3 \times 5$. This problem has both multiplication and division. Neither multiplication nor division comes *before* the other; they are to be done as they occur from left to right. In this problem, do 12 divided by 3 and then multiply that answer by 5. You get 4×5, which is 20.

If, in addition to any of the four operations, a problem has parentheses or exponents, you must do what's inside the parentheses first, what's in parentheses before exponents.

Let's look at a problem that has parentheses, exponents, and several operations. $6 \times (8 + 2) \div 5 - 3^2$.

Follow the order of operations to complete the problem in the following order:

1) Add 8 and 2 (10)

2) Simplify 3^2 (9)

3) Multiply 6 by 10 (60)

4) Divide 60 by 5 (12)

5) Subtract 9 from 12.

6) The answer is 3.

Recognize equivalent computational procedures

Addition and subtraction are opposites of each other, and multiplication and division are opposites of each other. Therefore, it is possible to rewrite an equation using one operation to an equivalent one using another. Can you rewrite a problem that is equivalent to $12 + 3 = 15$ using subtraction? Yes. There are two equations you could write. 1) $15 - 3 = 12$, and

2) 15 − 12 = 3. Here's another example: Can you rewrite a problem that is equivalent to 6 × 8 = 48 using division? Yes. There are two equations you could write. 1) 48 ÷ 8 = 6, and 2) 48 ÷ 6 = 8.

(F) Computation
Perform computations

Every integer has an absolute value. The *absolute value* of a number is its distance from 0 on the number line. The absolute value of 11 is 11. The absolute value of −11 is also 11. The reason both 11 and −11 have the same absolute value is that both numbers are 11 units from 0. *Some like to think that the absolute value of a number is the number without a sign.*

When adding two positive integers, the answer is positive: 8 + 2 = 10. When adding two negative integers, the answer is negative. Add the absolute values of the numbers (8 + 2 = 10), and then add the negative sign. −8 + −2 = −10. When adding one positive and one negative number, there are two steps to follow.

Let's look at the following problem as an illustration: **−7 + 2**

The first step is to subtract the number whose absolute value is smaller from the number whose absolute value is larger (ignoring the signs of the numbers). In this example, subtract 2 from 7 to get 5.

The second step is to take the sign of the number with the larger absolute value and attach it to your answer. In this example, −7 has the larger absolute value (because it is farther from 0 than 2), so put a negative sign in front of the 5. So, −7 + 2 = −5.

Let's look at another example: **10 + (−3)**

Subtract 3 from 10 to get 7. Take the sign of the 10 (which is positive); your answer is 7.

Subtracting integers is best accomplished by rewriting the subtraction problem as an equivalent addition one. Rewriting a subtraction problem as an addition one requires leaving the first integer alone, changing the subtraction to addition, and then changing the second integer to its opposite. Once the problem is an addition one, you can follow the rules of adding integers described above.

For example: **−4 − −3**

Rewrite as −4 + 3. The answer is −1.

Another example: **2 − 6**

Rewrite as 2 + −6. The answer is −4.

Both multiplying and dividing integers follow the same rules. If both numbers have the same sign, the answer is positive. $4 \times 5 = 20$, $-4 \times -5 = 20$, $16 \div 8 = 2$, and $-90 \div -9 = 10$. If the numbers have different signs, then the answer is negative. It does not matter whether the first or second integer is negative; the answer is negative. For example, $-3 \times 7 = -21$ and $18 \div -9 = -2$.

When adding mixed numbers with like or unlike denominators, you may find that your answer contains a whole number along with an improper fraction. When you get such an answer, there is an extra step needed to complete the problem. Let's look at the example of adding $3\frac{3}{5}$ and $4\frac{4}{5}$ to make the explanation more clear.

$$
\begin{array}{r}
3\frac{3}{5} \\
+4\frac{4}{5} \\
\hline
7\frac{7}{5}
\end{array}
$$

As you can see, your answer has a whole number and an improper fraction. You cannot leave the answer in that form. You need to rewrite $\frac{7}{5}$ as a mixed number (you will get $1\frac{2}{5}$), and then combine that mixed number with the whole number (7). You will get $7 + 1\frac{2}{5}$, which equals $8\frac{2}{5}$. If the two mixed numbers you are adding have different denominators, the process is the same, although you must first find a common denominator before combining the mixed numbers.

When subtracting mixed numbers with like or unlike denominators, you may find that you need to borrow from the whole number in order to do the subtraction. Let's look at the example $7\frac{1}{8} - 3\frac{7}{8}$.

$$
\begin{array}{r}
7\frac{1}{8} \\
-3\frac{7}{8} \\
\hline
\end{array}
$$

As you can see, you cannot subtract $\frac{7}{8}$ from $\frac{1}{8}$ because $\frac{1}{8}$ is smaller than $\frac{7}{8}$. What you need to do is borrow from the whole number—in this case, it's a 7. If you take 1 away from the 7, it becomes a 6. Now you need to add that 1 to $\frac{1}{8}$. Since you are working in eighths, 1 whole equals $\frac{8}{8}$. Therefore, add $\frac{8}{8}$ to $\frac{1}{8}$, which gives you $\frac{9}{8}$. See the rewritten (and equivalent problem) below.

$$6\frac{9}{8}$$

$$-3\frac{7}{8}$$

Now do the subtraction. The answer is $3\frac{2}{8}$, which in lowest terms is $3\frac{1}{4}$.

To multiply simple fractions, just multiply the numerators together and multiply the denominators together as in the example: $\frac{3}{4} \times \frac{2}{5} = \frac{3 \times 2}{4 \times 5} = \frac{6}{20}$. Remember to simplify the fraction $\frac{6}{20}$ by dividing both the numerator and denominator by the GCF of 2. This will give you $\frac{3}{10}$. If one or both of the fractions that you are multiplying is a mixed number, rewrite them as improper fractions, then multiply the numerators together and multiply the denominators together.

Let's look at $3\frac{1}{4} \times \frac{2}{7}$. Rewrite $3\frac{1}{4}$ as $\frac{13}{4}$, then follow the procedure described above. $\frac{13}{4} \times \frac{2}{7} = \frac{26}{28}$. Simplify the fraction by dividing both numerator and denominator by their GCF, which is 2. This gets you $\frac{13}{14}$.

When you are multiplying fractions, you can simplify before you multiply, if you would like. This is sometimes helpful because you avoid having to multiply large numbers. Simplifying before multiplying is similar to simplifying fractions. However, not only can you simplify within one fraction, but you can also simplify using the numerator of one fraction and the denominator of the other fraction. Let's use the following problem to illustrate how to simplify before multiplying: $\frac{8}{9} \times \frac{3}{16}$. As you can see, 8 and 16 have a GCF of 8. Divide 8 by 8 to get 1 and divide 16 by 8 to get 2. Put a slash through the 8 and replace it with the 1. Also, put a slash through the 16 and replace it with the 2. Now look at the 3 and 9. They have a GCF of 3. Divide the 9 by 3 to get 3. Divide 3 by 3 to get 1. Put a slash through the 9 and replace it with the 3. Put a slash through the 3 and replace it with the 1. Now the simplified (and important to remember—equivalent) problem is: $\frac{1}{3} \times \frac{1}{2}$. The answer is $\frac{1}{6}$. Simplifying first is easier because the numbers we have to multiply are smaller. If we had multiplied first and simplified later, we would have had to multiply 8 by 3 and then 9 by 16, which would have been more work.

In order to divide fractions, you must rewrite the division problem as an equivalent multiplication one, then follow the procedure for multiplying fractions. Let's look at the example $\frac{7}{8} \div \frac{1}{3}$. When you rewrite a division problem as a multiplication one, leave the first fraction as it is. In this case, $\frac{7}{8}$ stays as $\frac{7}{8}$. Rewrite the division as multiplication. Rewrite the second fraction as its reciprocal. The product of a number and its reciprocal is 1. A quick way to find the reciprocal of a number is to switch the numerator and denominator with each other. Hence $\frac{7}{9}$ and $\frac{9}{7}$ are reciprocals. $\frac{4}{5}$ and $\frac{5}{4}$ are reciprocals. So in the problem $\frac{7}{8} \div \frac{1}{3}$, the reciprocal of the second fraction, $\frac{1}{3}$, is $\frac{3}{1}$. Therefore, the equivalent multiplication problem is $\frac{7}{8} \times \frac{3}{1}$. The answer is $\frac{21}{8}$. This improper fraction can be rewritten as a mixed number as $2\frac{5}{8}$. When dividing fractions, rewrite any mixed numbers as improper fractions before rewriting the problem as an equivalent multiplication problem. Remember, too, that you can simplify before multiplying, and you should write your final answer as a simple or mixed number in lowest terms.

Just as you line up the same place values when adding or subtracting whole numbers, you must do the same when adding or subtracting decimal numbers. Line up the same place values below one another. Bring the decimal point straight down in the answer as in the example below

$$
\begin{array}{r}
15.443 \\
- \ 9.121 \\
\hline
6.322
\end{array}
$$

When multiplying decimal numbers, it is not necessary to line up the decimal points. What makes most sense is to line up the digits, not necessarily those with the same place value. If you are multiplying 4.3×8.56, you would set up the problem as shown below: As you can see, the place values are not lined up under each other. You would still get the right answer if you did line up the place values, but it is unnecessary and may result in extra work. Perform the multiplication as if the numbers were whole numbers. Placement of the decimal point comes at the end after you have completed the multiplication.

			8.	5	6
				4.	3
3	6	8	0	.	8

Once you have the digits in the answer, then you have to put the decimal point where it belongs. Look at the two numbers you are multiplying. The number 8.56 has 2 numbers *after* the decimal point. The number 4.3 has 1 number *after* the decimal point. So add 2 + 1 to get 3—that means there will be 3 places after the decimal point in the answer; so the answer is 36.808.

Each number in a division problem has a name. The number you are dividing by is called the *divisor*. The number you are dividing into is called the *dividend*. The answer, as mentioned previously, is the *quotient*. When dividing a decimal number by a whole number divisor, just follow the procedure for dividing whole numbers and put the decimal point in your answer directly above where it is in the dividend.

Dividing a decimal or whole number by a decimal divisor requires a little more work. Since it would be very difficult to figure out how many times a portion of a number such as .4 or .25 goes into a number, it is customary to rewrite the problem so that the divisor is a whole number. It makes sense that if you are going to change the divisor, you will also have to change the dividend; otherwise, you will be solving a different problem than the one that was presented to you. What you want is to solve an equivalent problem. Let's look at an example: In the following division problem: $\frac{3.78}{.2}$, you can see that the divisor is a decimal number. We are going to multiply both the divisor and the dividend by a power of 10 that will result in the divisor becoming a whole number. In this example, we use 10. If you multiply a number by 10, the decimal point moves one place to the right. If you multiply a number by 100, the decimal point moves two places to the right, and so on. Multiplying both 3.78 and .2 by 10 gives us the problem $\frac{37.8}{2}$. Since we have multiplied both numbers by 10, we have multiplied the fraction by 1 because $\frac{10}{10}$ is 1. Therefore, $\frac{37.8}{2}$ is equivalent to the original problem of $\frac{3.78}{.2}$. The answer is 18.9.

Adjust the result of a computation to fit the context of a problem

Sometimes when solving a problem you have to adjust the answer to fit the problem. You may have to convert an answer from one form to another. For example, you have to be at work at 9:00 a.m. It takes you 20 minutes to drive to work, 15 minutes to shower, 15 minutes to have breakfast, and 25 minutes to get dressed. What is the latest time that you can get up in order to get to work on time? First you have to figure out how much time you will need. Add 20 + 15 + 15 + 25, which gives you 75 minutes. You may want to convert 75 minutes into hours and minutes. Since there are 60 minutes in an hour, 75 minutes is equal to 1 hour and 15 minutes. Now, you need to count backwards from 9:00 a.m. to figure out what time you need to get up. Take one hour away from 9:00 and that brings you to 8:00 a.m. Then take another 15 minutes away and that brings you to 7:45 a.m., which is the latest time you can get up to make it to work on time.

PROBLEM

Mr. Thompson is planning a school trip to the zoo. He found out that each bus holds 70 people. Mr. Thompson is expecting 368 students and 12 teachers to attend the trip. How many busses should he get?

APPROACH TO SOLUTION

First you have to find out the total number of people going on the trip. This can be found by adding 368 + 12. This gives a total of 380 people. You know that you can fit 70 people on a bus, so divide 380 by 70 to find out how many busses you will need. Because 70 does not divide evenly into 380, you get an answer of $5\frac{3}{7}$. Even though $5\frac{3}{7}$ is the correct answer to dividing 380 by 70, it does not answer the question. You need to know how many busses are needed. You can only have a whole number of busses; there is no such thing as a fractional part of a bus. Five busses will not be enough, so Mr. Thompson will need 6 busses.

Identify numbers or information or operations needed to solve a problem

Word problems often include information that is not needed in the problem. Sometimes this is called extraneous information. When you are trying to solve a problem, you must read the details in the problem carefully to figure out what information you need and what information you can ignore. It is recommended that you read word problems at least two times before attempting to solve them. Do not think that you must use every number that is in a problem. Sometimes there is information that is included to help clarify the situation, but the numbers are not needed to answer the question. If you find it helpful, you should underline key words such as "how many" or "at what time" to help you focus on what the question is asking.

Another important thing to remember when solving word problems is that they do not tell you what operation to use. You have to figure that out based on the context of the problem. For example, the language, "all together" and "the total" indicate that you will use addition. The language, "how much more" or "how much taller than" indicate subtraction. See the chart below for different vocabulary that you may see for each of the four operations:

Addition	Subtraction	Multiplication	Division
Add	Subtract	Multiply	Divide
And	Minus	Times	Quotient
Plus	Difference	Product	
More than	Less than		
Increased by	Decreased by		
Sum	Take away		
Total	Fewer		

PROBLEM

Derrick bought some sandwiches at the deli, totaling $18.99. He paid for his sandwiches with a $50 bill. He went to another store where he bought a flashlight and batteries for $12.45. He paid with a $20 bill. How much money did Derrick spend in the two stores all together?

APPROACH TO SOLUTION

After reading the problem carefully, you should notice that the information about what bills Derrick paid with are extraneous. In order to answer the question, all you have to do is add $18.99 and $12.45. $31.44 is the answer.

(G) Estimation

Sometimes it is not necessary to get an exact answer to a problem—only an **estimate** is required. When that happens, it is important to be able to round numbers so that they are easier to work with. If you need an **estimate** of how much money you would need to buy 12 packages of crackers when each package costs $2.89, you could round $2.89 up to $3 and then multiply by 12, which would give you $36. You would need about $36 to buy the crackers.

If you needed to estimate the area of a field that was 190 meters by 217 meters, you could round 190 meters up to 200 meters, and you could round 217 meters down to 200 meters. Therefore, the approximate or estimated area would be about 200 × 200, which is 40,000 square meters.

Estimating can sometimes save you time when you have to compare fractions to one another. If, for example, you are asked to list a group of fractions with different denominators in order from least to greatest, you may be able to do so without going through the laborious work of finding a common denominator. Let's look at an example. Put the following fractions in order from least to greatest: $\frac{2}{5}, \frac{7}{8}, \frac{3}{4}, \frac{6}{17}, \frac{13}{14}$. At first glance, this looks like a very time-consuming and difficult problem because all the fractions have different denominators. However, when you look closely, you should notice that you can use your estimation skills to put the fractions in order. Ask yourself if any of the fractions are less than $\frac{1}{2}$. Notice that $\frac{2}{5}$ and $\frac{6}{17}$ are the only fractions that are less than $\frac{1}{2}$. You can tell because the numerators are less than half of the denominators. Therefore, either $\frac{2}{5}$ or $\frac{6}{17}$ will be the smallest fraction. Can you use your estimating skills again to figure out which of the two fractions is smallest? Notice that $\frac{2}{5}$ is very close to $\frac{1}{2}$. $\frac{2.5}{5}$ would be exactly $\frac{1}{2}$. What about $\frac{6}{17}$? Notice that $\frac{6}{18}$ would be exactly $\frac{1}{3}$ and $\frac{6}{17}$ is very close to that. $\frac{1}{3}$ is smaller than $\frac{1}{2}$. Therefore, $\frac{6}{17}$ is smaller than $\frac{2}{5}$. Now, you have two of the five fractions in order: $\frac{6}{17}$ and $\frac{2}{5}$. Now examine the other three fractions: $\frac{7}{8}, \frac{3}{4}$, and $\frac{13}{14}$. Notice that $\frac{3}{4}$ can be easily rewritten as $\frac{6}{8}$. Which is smaller, $\frac{6}{8}$ or $\frac{7}{8}$? $\frac{6}{8}$ is smaller, so you know thatt $\frac{3}{4}$ comes before $\frac{7}{8}$. The final fraction, $\frac{13}{14}$, is very close to one whole, which would be $\frac{14}{14}$. Therefore, you can order all five fractions from least to greatest as follows: $\frac{6}{17}, \frac{2}{5}, \frac{3}{4}, \frac{7}{8}, \frac{13}{14}$. Be sure to see if you can use estimation rather than exact computation. If you can, it will often be more efficient than performing tedious calculations.

Estimate the result of a calculation

Sometimes it is necessary to estimate the result of a calculation. You may wish to estimate before doing a calculation to be sure that your answer is reasonable. You may also choose to estimate an answer when you do not need an exact answer. If you want to know how long it will take you to complete some errands before meeting a friend, you probably will not need an exact answer. Sometimes an estimate is good enough. Estimating the result of a calculation may involve rounding. If you bought a package of 8 cookies for $1.99 and wanted to know what the price per cookie is, you would divide 1.99 by 8. When you do so, you get .24875. That is the exact answer. However, when talking about price, we usually go to the nearest cent. So, in this example, each cookie costs approximately 25 cents.

PROBLEM

What is 4.584 rounded to the nearest tenth?

(A) .6   (D) 4.58

(B) 4.5   (E) 4.6

(C) 4.57

APPROACH TO SOLUTION

To solve this problem, you need to know place value and how to round numbers. To round to the nearest tenth, look at the digit in the hundredths place, which is 8. Because 8 is 5 or greater, you will round the tenths digits up. The tenths digit goes from 5 to 6. The correct answer is 4.6, answer choice (E).

Determine the reasonableness of an estimate

Estimating before calculating can be helpful. But it's important to be sure that your estimate makes sense.

PROBLEM

Harry wanted to buy 19 books that each cost $4.32. Which expression below could he use to estimate how much money he would need for the books?

(A) 10×4 (D) 20×5

(B) 15×4 (E) 30×5

(C) 20×4

APPROACH TO SOLUTION

When estimating the answer to a problem, it is helpful to use numbers that are easier to work with. Because 19 is very close to 20, that would be a good estimate for 19. $4.32 is between $4 and $5, but is closer to $4, so 4 is a good estimate for $4.32. The expression that gives the best estimate for the answer is 20×4, answer choice (C).

(H) Ratio, Proportion, and Percent

Solve problems involving ratio, proportion, and percent

A *ratio* is a comparison of two quantities. There was once a commercial, which stated 4 out of 5 dentists prefer a particular brand of toothpaste; that is a ratio. Ratios can be written three different ways:

- With the word "to": 4 to 5

- With a colon: 4:5

- As a fraction: $\dfrac{4}{5}$

Ratios are used frequently in daily life. A teacher might say, "Eight of the twenty-five students are out sick." A bakery owner could say, "We sold 56 of the 200 croissants." When two ratios are equal to each other, that is called a *proportion*. An example of a proportion is $\dfrac{12}{36} = \dfrac{9}{27}$. An easy way to see if two ratios are equivalent is to simplify them into lowest terms. A fraction is in lowest terms if the only factor the numerator and denominator have in common is 1. If both ratios simplify to the same fraction, then the ratios are equivalent and it is a proportion. Oftentimes, we use the principle of a proportion to solve for an unknown quantity.

Here's an example: There are 150 calories in an 8-ounce serving of whole milk. How many calories are in a 12-ounce serving? You can set up the following proportion to answer the question:

$$\frac{8}{150} = \frac{12}{C}$$

The first ratio has an 8 in the numerator; this represents the number of ounces given in the problem. In the denominator of the first ratio is 150. This represents the number of calories in 8 ounces of milk. This information is given in the problem. The other ratio has a 12 in the numerator because 12 represents the number of ounces of milk you are asked about in the problem. Notice how both numbers that represent the number of ounces are in the numerator. Numbers representing the same quantity must be in the same places in the ratios. The second ratio has a C in the denominator. This C represents the unknown number of calories we are trying to find in 12 ounces of milk.

To solve a proportion, you cross-multiply. That means you multiply the numerator in one ratio by the denominator in the other. You set those products equal to each other. Then, you divide both sides by the number that is multiplied by the variable.

- $\dfrac{8}{150} = \dfrac{12}{C}$
- $8C = 1800$
- $C = 225$

Therefore, there are 225 calories in 12 ounces of whole milk.

There are several different types of problems that you may encounter involving percents. If you want to find the percent of a number, the easiest way is to rewrite the percent as its decimal equivalent and multiply.

Example:

What is 25% of 800?

Multiply $.25 \times 800$ to get 200.

However, you can also write a proportion. One of the ratios will be $\dfrac{25}{100}$. The other ratio will have 800 in the denominator because it represents the whole. A variable will go in the numerator. Write the following proportion: $\dfrac{25}{100} = \dfrac{x}{800}$ Cross-multiply and divide to find that x = 200.

If you need to know what percent one number is of another as in the problem, you should set up and solve a proportion. One of the ratios will have 100 as a denominator.

Example:

What percent of 50 is 10?

Write the proportion: $\dfrac{10}{50} = \dfrac{y}{100}$

Cross-multiply, and then divide by the number in front of the variable. You get $y = 20$. Therefore, 10 is 20% of 50.

If you are asked to find the whole when given the part and the percent, you can also write a proportion.

Example:

20% of what number is 12?

Write the proportion: $\dfrac{20}{100} = \dfrac{12}{Z}$. Cross multiply which gives you $20Z = 1200$, then divide both sides by 20 to get $Z = 60$.

PROBLEM

Sophia bought a pink dress for $61.60 at a 30% off sale. What was the original price of the dress?

(A) $18.48

(D) $81.60

(B) $43.12

(E) $88.00

(C) $77.00

APPROACH TO SOLUTION

Many percent problems are straightforward. However, make sure that you understand the problem before attempting to solve it. In this problem, Sophia bought a dress for 30% off. Ask yourself, "What percent of the original price did Sophia pay?" Sophia paid 70% of the original price. Therefore, $61.60 is 70% of the original price. Set up and solve a proportion to find the original price. $\dfrac{61.60}{x} = \dfrac{70}{100}$. Cross-multiply and then divide to find that x = $88. The correct answer is (E).

There are many times when you need to find the percent of increase or decrease. Percent of increase (or decrease) is found by using the following proportion:

$$\frac{amount\ of\ change}{original\ amount} = \frac{x}{100}$$

PROBLEM

Siobhan wanted to buy a scarf priced at $40. The following week she went back to the store and saw that the scarf was now priced at $35. What was the percent of decrease of the price of the scarf?

APPROACH TO SOLUTION

Since this is a percent of decrease problem, you have to find the amount of change and the original amount. The price of the scarf went from $40 to $35, so the amount of change is

$5. The original amount is $40. Therefore, the proportion you should set up and solve is: $\frac{5}{40} = \frac{x}{100}$. Cross-multiply and then divide to find that the percent of decrease is 12.5%.

(I) Numerical Reasoning

Logical connectives and quantifiers: interpret statements that use logical connectives (and, if-then) as well as quantifiers (some, all, none)

Reading problems accurately is one of the most important skills you can have when approaching mathematics, especially word problems.

Consider the following problem: A quadrilateral is drawn on a piece of poster board. None of its sides are congruent. One pair of its sides is parallel. What would be the best name for this shape?

We are told that none of the sides of the quadrilateral are congruent. Therefore, we can eliminate many of the special quadrilaterals we know that have opposite sides congruent. We know that one pair of sides is parallel. The best name for this shape is a trapezoid.

Validity of arguments: use deductive reasoning to determine whether an argument (as series of statements leading to a conclusion) is valid or invalid

Determining whether a statement is valid (true) or invalid (false) often involves using *deductive reasoning*. Deductive reasoning is about going from the general to the specific. It is about applying a characteristic to a class of things, and then, by association, applying that characteristic to a member of that class.

Example:

1. All squares have four right angles.
2. This shape is a square.
3. The square must have four right angles.

Example:

1. The sum of all three angles in a triangle is 180 degrees.
2. The sum of the angles of this shape is 180 degrees.
3. Therefore, this shape must be a triangle.

| PROBLEM |

Statement 1: All multiples of 10 are also multiples of 2.
Statement 2: All multiples of 2 are also multiples of 10.
Statement 3: No multiples of 2 are multiples of 5.

Consider the two statements above. Which answer choice below is correct?

(A) Statement 1, 2, and 3 are true.

(B) Statements 1 and 2 are true, and statement 3 is false.

(C) Statement 1 is true, and statements 2 and 3 are false.

(D) Statements 1 and 2 are false, and statement 3 is true.

(E) Statements 1, 2, and 3 are false.

APPROACH TO SOLUTION

Examine each statement for validity. Pay special attention to the words "all" and "no." Before trying to select the correct answer choice, read through the statements to see which ones are true. Statement 1 is true because all multiples of 10 are also multiples of 2. All multiples of 10 are even, so 2 will divide evenly into all multiples of 10. Statement 2 is false. Some multiples of 2 are multiples of 10, such as 10, 20, and 30. However, many multiples of 2 are not multiples of 10, such as 4, 8, and 28. Statement 3 is false. Some multiples of 2 are also multiples of 5. For example, 10, 20, and 30. Therefore, statement 1 is true, and statements 2 and 3 are false. The correct answer is (C).

2. Algebra

(A) Equations and Inequalities
Solve simple equations and inequalities

Although some algebraic equations can be solved by the guess-and-check method, it is efficient to follow a specific procedure when solving equations. To solve an equation involving one operation, you must apply the inverse operation to the problem to solve it. The *inverse operation* means the opposite operation. The opposite of addition is subtraction and vice versa. The opposite of multiplication is division and vice versa. You must always do the same thing to both sides of an equation to keep it balanced. When you are presented with an equation, the expression on the left is equal to the expression on the right. Therefore, if you manipulate the equation in any way, you must be sure to do the same thing to both expressions. For example, if you subtract 5 from one side of an equation, you must subtract 5 from the other side.

Here are some examples:

$$y - 4 = 12$$
$$ + 4 + 4$$
$$y = 16$$

$$x + 3 = 10$$
$$ - 3 - 3$$
$$x = 7$$

$$12z = 36$$
$$\div 12 \div 12$$
$$z = 3$$

$$\frac{p}{5} = 6$$
$$(5)\frac{p}{5} = 6\,(5)$$
$$p = 30$$

A *two-step equation* is an equation that requires performing two operations to find the solution. A two-step equation has multiplication or division and addition or subtraction. You must perform the inverse operation on the addition or subtraction before you perform the inverse operation on the multiplication or division.

See the examples below:

$$6y - 3 = 27$$
$$ + 3 + 3$$
$$6y = 30$$
$$\div 6 \div 6$$
$$y = 5$$

$$\frac{m}{4} + 7 = 10$$

$$\underline{-7 \quad -7}$$

$$\frac{m}{4} = 3$$

$$(4)\frac{m}{4} = 3\,(4)$$

$$m = 12$$

PROBLEM

Equation: $-3x + 5y = 15$

Which equation below is equivalent to the given equation?

(A) $-3x = -5y - 15$

(B) $3x - 5y = -15$

(C) $15 = 3x - 5y$

(D) $-6x - 10y = -30$

(E) $5y = 3x - 15$

APPROACH TO SOLUTION

A problem like this requires being able to manipulate equations accurately. Remember you can add (or subtract) anything to both sides of an equation, as long as you do the same thing to both sides. If you multiply or divide both sides of an equation by a value, multiply or divide every *term* by that same value. Also, in this kind of problem, you must pay very close attention to the positive and negative signs. Those are the details that make the difference between choosing the correct or incorrect answer. Choice (A) is not correct because 15 should be positive. Choice (C) is not correct because 15 should be negative. Choice (D) is not correct because all terms have not been multiplied by the same value: $-3x$ and $5y$ were multiplied by 2, but 15 was multiplied by -2. Choice (E) is incorrect because 15 should be positive. Choice (B) is the correct answer and results from multiplying each term of the original equation by -1.

Inequalities are solved in a similar manner as solving equations. That is, just as in an equation, an inequality requires that you use the inverse operation of the operation that is in the problem to solve it. Also, both equations and inequalities require that you do the same thing to both sides. The main difference between solving equations and inequalities occurs when you multiply or divide an inequality by a negative number. When you do, you must reverse the inequality symbol to keep the inequality true. Another difference between equations and inequalities is that an equation usually has one solution while an inequality has a range of solutions. For example, if the solution to an inequality is $x > 5$, then any number greater than 5 is a solution. There are an infinite number of numbers that are greater than 5. Remember that in addition to whole numbers, there are fractions and decimals. Because there are often an infinite number of solutions to an inequality, they are sometimes shown on a number line.

The solutions to the inequality $y \geq -2$ are shown on the number line below.

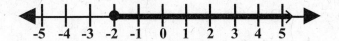

Below is an example of solving an inequality when you have to reverse the inequality symbol:

$-3y > 12$

To solve, divide both sides by –3. Then reverse the inequality symbol.

$-3y > 12$

$\div -3 \div -3$

$y < -4$

Predict the outcome of changing some number or condition in the problem

You may confront problems that ask you to rethink them or change something about them. When this happens, you must be sure to understand the original problem as well as the way in which you are being asked to change the problem.

PROBLEM

On Thursday, Ms. Partridge put her students into groups with 6 students each, she had 7 groups. The following day, 2 students were absent and she made groups with 5 students each. How many groups did Ms. Partridge have?

(A) 5 (D) 8

(B) 6 (E) It cannot be determined from the given information.

(C) 7

APPROACH TO SOLUTION

Read the problem and ask yourself, "How many students are in Ms. Partridge's class on Tuesday?" The answer is 42 because $6 \times 7 = 42$. The following day, two students were absent, so there are 40 students. With 5 students in each group, you know that there will be 8 groups because $40 \div 5 = 8$. (D) is the correct answer.

(B) Algorithmic Thinking

Demonstrate an understanding of the algorithmic point of view; that is, follow a given procedure or flowchart

An *algorithm* is a precise set of rules specifying how to solve a particular type of problem. We follow non-mathematical algorithms all the time. For example, if you find that your lamp does not light, you may check to see if it is plugged in. If it is not plugged in, then you will plug it in. If it is plugged in, you will put in a new bulb and see if that works. If it still does not work, then you will take it to get fixed. These are specific steps to follow to assess why the lamp is not working. In mathematics, there are algorithms for a number of processes. For example, the Distributive Property of multiplication over addition involves multiplying the term on the outside of the parentheses by each term inside the parentheses and separating those terms by an addition sign.

Example:

$$4(y + 5) = 4y + 20$$

Being able to follow an algorithm accurately is an integral part of completing mathematical procedures accurately.

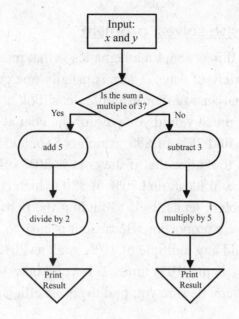

PROBLEM

Input: x and y

Is the sum a multiple of 3?

Yes   No

Add 5   Subtract 3

Divide by 2   Multiply by 5

Print result   Print result

If the result that is printed from the flowchart was 8.5, which two input values for x and y are possible?

(A) $x = 3; y = 10$ (D) $x = 8.5; y = 2.5$

(B) $x = 5; y = 7$ (E) $x = 10; y = 6.5$

(C) $x = 7; y = 8$

APPROACH TO SOLUTION

The best way to approach this problem is to try one of the answer choices and see if it is correct. Working backwards would be too time consuming because there are two possible answers. It will be more efficient to try the answers given. Let's look at (C). If you add 7 and 8, you get 15, which is a multiple of 3. So add 5, which gives you 20, then divide by 2 to get 10. (C) is not correct. Let's try (B) Adding 5 and 7 gives 12, which is a multiple of 3. Add 5 to get 17. Divide by 2 to get 8.5, which is the result that was printed. (B) is the correct answer.

Recognize various ways to solve a problem

One of the most interesting things about mathematics is that most problems you are asked to solve can be solved in a variety of ways. There is usually one correct answer, but there may be several paths to get to that answer. For example, let's look at the following problem: The price of a coat is $80. How much would you pay for the coat at a 20% off sale? One way to approach this problem is to find 20% of $80, which is $16, and then subtract $16 from $80, giving $64. Another way is to realize that if the coat is 20% off the original price, you will pay 80% of the original price. You can find 80% of $80, which is $64. What is also important to point out is that this problem lends itself to finding the percent "in your head"; it is not necessary to set up and solve a proportion. Because it is easy to find 10% of $80 (just divide 80 by 10), you can easily find any multiple of 10%, such as 20%, 30%, or in this case, 80%. If you know 10%, then 20% is just 10% times 2. If you know 10%, then 80% is 10% times 8. Before diving into a problem, be sure you find the most efficient way to solve it.

▌PROBLEM

There was $\frac{3}{5}$ of a cake in a pan and Alexa ate 40% of the cake that was there. Which expression below would NOT find the amount that Alexa ate?

(A) $.6 \times .4$

(B) $\frac{3}{5} \times \frac{4}{10}$

(C) $\frac{3}{5} \times .4$

(D) $\frac{3}{5} \div .40$

(E) $.6 \div 2.5$

APPROACH TO SOLUTION

In this problem Alexa ate part of a part of a cake. It can be helpful to know that the word "of" usually means multiplication. To find the portion of the cake that Alexa ate, you can multiply the two amounts together. You must also be comfortable recognizing different forms of the same number. You can write $\frac{3}{5}$ as its decimal equivalent .6. You can write 40% as its decimal equivalent, .4. Your job is to find the one expression that is not equivalent to $\frac{3}{5} \times .40$. Remember that multiplication and division are inverse operations when examining answer choices (D) and (E). The only expression which does not result in the correct answer of .24 is answer choice (D).

Identify, complete, or analyze a procedure

Mathematics involves using a variety of procedures. First you have to read the problem to figure out what procedure you need to follow to solve it. Then you have to complete the procedure. An important step is analyzing the procedure. Ask yourself, "Did I approach this problem correctly? Did I understand what it was asking? Did I answer the question asked?"

PROBLEM

If 5 * 8 = 41 and 3 * 9 = 28, then what is 2 * 7?

(A) 9 (D) 19

(B) 14 (E) 33

(C) 15

APPROACH TO SOLUTION

Ask yourself, "What procedure is taking place in the two examples given?" What does the * tell you to do with the numbers on either side of it? You will have to play around with different operations to figure out what procedure 8 means. Notice that $5 \times 8 = 40$ and 41 is 1 greater than 40. Notice that $3 \times 9 = 27$ and 28 is 1 greater than 27. Therefore, you can figure out what 2 * 7 will result in. $2 \times 7 = 14$, then $14 + 1 = 15$. The correct answer is (C).

(C) Patterns

Discover patterns in a procedure

Math is full of patterns and seeing those patterns helps math make sense. For example, if you did not know how to find the area of a triangle, but were given the table below showing the base, height, and area of four different triangles, could you figure out the area of a triangle with a base of 9 and a height of 2? By noticing the pattern in the first four triangles, it is possible to find the area. When you multiply the base by the height and then divide by 2, you get the area. As you can see, that is the pattern in the first four rows of the table. Therefore, the area of a triangle with a base of 9 and a height of 2 is 9.

Base	Height	Area
4	8	16
5	10	25
7	6	21
3	12	18
9	2	?

PROBLEM

A box of pens cost $1.89. Which equation shows how to find the total cost, C, of B boxes of pens?

(A) $B = 1.89C$

(D) $B = \dfrac{1.89}{C}$

(B) $C = 1.89B$

(E) $C = 1.89 - B$

(C) $C = \dfrac{1.89}{B}$

APPROACH TO SOLUTION

If you want, you can create a table for this problem. However, what is more efficient is to visualize a table. For every 1 box of pens you have, the cost is $1.89. Therefore, 2 boxes would be 2($1.89). Three boxes would be 3($1.89), etc. So, to find the total cost of B boxes of pens, multiply the price for 1 box ($1.89) by ($B$). The correct answer is B, $C = 1.89(B)$.

Identify and recognize patterns in data

Identifying and recognizing patterns in data is a basic tenet of mathematics. Looking for patterns in data helps you analyze it effectively.

PROBLEM

Which equation shows the relationship between x and y in the table below?

x	y
10	6
12	7
14	8
16	9

(A) $y = x - 1$

(D) $y = \dfrac{x}{2} + 1$

(B) $y = x - 4$

(E) $y = 2x + 1$

(C) $y = \dfrac{x}{2} - 1$

APPROACH TO SOLUTION

When looking for the relationship in a table of values, it is important to remember that the relationship must be the same for each input and output value. Answer choice (B) could be correct for the first (x, y) pair, but it does not hold true for all other pairs in the table. You can choose one of the answer choices and substitute in the values to find the correct one. The relationship in the table is divide the input value by 2, and then add 1. This holds true for all (x, y) pairs in the table. The correct answer is (D).

Demonstrate an understanding of direct, inverse, and other kinds of variation without necessarily knowing the correct term for the relationship

Direct variation and inverse variation are two relationships you may encounter. A mathematical relationship between two variables where one is equal to a constant number times the other is *direct variation*. An example of direct variation is if a package of gum has 5 pieces in it, then you can find the number of pieces in any number of packages of gum by using the equation $y = 5x$, where x equals the number of packages of gum and y equals the total number of pieces of gum. When examining a table of values, you can tell if it shows direct variation. Notice that as one value is increasing, the other value is also increasing.

The mathematical relationship that results when the product of two variables is a constant number is *inverse variation*. An example of inverse variation is the time it takes to drive a set distance as the speed increases. The faster you drive, the less time it will take you. In inverse variation, as one value increases, the other value decreases.

Examine the following table. Does it show direct variation, inverse variation, or neither?

x	y
5	270
10	135
15	90
20	67.5

This table shows inverse variation. If you multiply each x, y pair together, you get the same constant, 1350.

Examine the following table. Does it show direct variation, inverse variation, or neither?

x	y
5	35
10	70
15	105
20	140

This table shows direct variation. If you multiply each *x*-value by 7, you get the *y*-value.

PROBLEM

Which ordered pair satisfies the given equation?

$$y = \frac{10}{x}$$

(A) (10, 100)   (D) (20, .05)

(B) (2, .5)   (E) (1, 1)

(C) (.1, 100)

APPROACH TO SOLUTION

The equation shows an inverse relationship. As the *x*-value increases, the *y*-value decreases. The product of each pair of *x*- and *y*-values is 10. Try the ordered pairs given in the answer choice to find the one that is correct. The only pair that is correct is (.1, 100), answer choice (C).

(D) Algebraic Representations

Explore relationship between verbal or symbolic expressions and graphs

Certain graphs can show a situation. The graph below shows the distance and time it took for a woman to walk from her home to her office. Her office is 160 meters from her home. Even if you are not told specifically about her trip, you can make up a legitimate story of her trip by following the graph. For example, during the first 50 seconds after the woman left her home, she walked at a steady rate toward work. Notice that as the time increased steadily, the distance increased steadily. From 50 seconds to 70 seconds, the woman walked at a steady pace back toward her home. Notice that although the time is increasing, the distance from home is decreasing. What might have happened? Perhaps she thought she forgot something and then headed back toward home, but then found what she was looking for in her pocket. From 70 seconds to 100 seconds, she walked toward her office at a steady pace. Notice that as the time increases, the distance also increases. At 100 seconds, she gets to her office (it is 160 meters from her home). Notice that from 100 seconds until 120 seconds, the distance does not change. What might be going on? Perhaps she ran into a friend in front of her office and talked with her there for 20 seconds. Other "stories" for the graph below are possible, as long as they make sense with the given information in the graph.

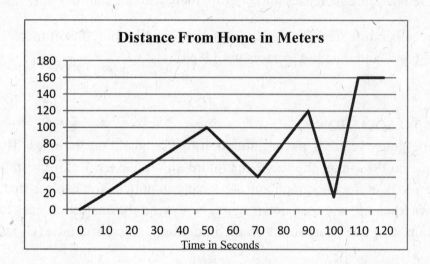

Distance From Home in Meters

Time in Seconds

PROBLEM

Which statement below correctly describes the line graph of air temperature on Wednesday?

Air Temperature on Wednesday

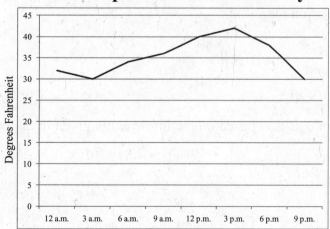

(A) The temperature rises steadily from 12 am until 6 am, then decreases until 6 pm, and then increases until 9 pm.

(B) The temperature decreases after 9 am, increases until 12 pm, decreases until 6 pm, and then holds steady until 9 pm.

(C) The temperature decreases slightly after 12 am, then increases until 3 pm, and then decreases until 9 pm.

(D) The temperature increases until 12 pm, then decreases until 9 pm.

(E) The temperature remains steady from 12 am until 3 pm, then it increases slightly until 6 pm, and then it decreases until 9 pm.

APPROACH TO SOLUTION

Reading a line graph requires paying attention to the labels on the axes. This line graph shows the time on the x-axis and the temperature on the y-axis. Before reading the answer choices, take a look at the line graph and see what you notice. You can see that the temperature goes down, then up, and then down again. Now, read the answer choices to find the one that matches up with the information on the line graph. Answer choice (C) is the only correct answer.

Use symbolic algebra to represent situations and to solve problems

Some problems lend themselves to being solved by using algebra. Let's take a look at one: Jon is 5 years older than Zachary. Ben is twice Jon's age. The sum of all three ages is 39. Find Ben's age. You can certainly solve this problem by using guess-and-check, but you can also solve it algebraically. First start by making a key. A key indicates what each algebraic expression in the equation represents.

z = Zachary's age

$z + 5$ = Jon's age

$2(z + 5)$ = Ben's age

Then, write an equation based on the information given in the problem.

$$z + z + 5 + 2(z + 5) = 39$$

Solve the equation.

$z + z + 5 + 2z + 10 = 39$

$4z + 15 = 39$

$4z = 24$

$z = 6$

Since you know that $z = 6$, you know that Zachary is 6. Jon is 11 and Ben is 22. Check to see that all three ages add up to 39, which they do, so you know you are correct.

PROBLEM

Evan has some quarters and dimes. He has six more dimes than he has quarters. All together he has $1.65. How many dimes does Evan have?

(A) 3   (D) 2

(B) 6   (E) 15

(C) 9

APPROACH TO SOLUTION

You could solve this problem using guess and check or you can use algebra.

You can write the following key to represent the coins in the problem.

x = number of quarters

$x + 6$ = number of dimes

$25x$ = value of quarters

$10(x + 6)$ = value of dimes

Write an equation that shows the value of the quarters and the value of the dimes totaling 165 (165 cents). Then solve the equation for x.

$$25x + 10(x + 6) = 165$$
$$25x + 10x + 60 = 165$$
$$35x + 60 = 165$$
$$35x = 105$$
$$x = 3$$

Therefore, there are 3 quarters and $x + 6$, or 9, dimes. Answer choice (A) is the number of quarters, not the number of dimes. The correct answer is 9 dimes, which is answer choice (C).

(E) Algebraic Reasoning

Logical connectives and quantifiers: interpret statements that use logical connectives (and, if-then) as well as quantifiers (some, all, none)

Following logic is critical in mathematics, and it is important to pay attention to words like *some*, *all*, or *none* as they can make the difference between a statement being true or not true. For example, "All factors of 15 are prime" is not true because 1 is neither prime nor composite; however, "Some factors of 15 are prime" is true because two of the 4 factors of 15 are prime. Also, there are mathematical statements in the "if...then" form. For example, If $x - 3 < 0$, then $x < 3$. Examine the statement to see if it is always true for every value of x. Ask yourself, "What values of x make $x - 3 < 0$ true? Any value less than 3 makes the inequality true. Therefore, x must be less than 3. When x is less than 3, all values of $x - 3$ are less than 0. Therefore, the full statement if $x - 3 < 0$, then $x < 3$ is true for all values of x.

PROBLEM

All values of x are even.

All of the following are consistent with the statement in the box EXCEPT:

(A) Some values of x are divisible by 4.

(B) Some values of x are divisible by 5.

(C) All values of x have an even number in the tens digit.

(D) No values of x have an odd number in the ones digit.

(E) Some values of x are multiples of 10.

APPROACH TO SOLUTION

Questions that use the words, *none*, *some*, or *all* require careful reading to be sure they are completely understood. In this problem, it says "all values of x are even". Ask yourself, "How do I identify an even number?" An even number has a 0, 2, 4, 6, or 8 in the ones digit. Even numbers are divisible by 2. Go through the answer choices to find the one that is NOT consistent with the statement. Answer choice (A) is true because some even numbers are divisible by 4. Answer choice (B) is true because some even numbers are divisible by 5, such as 10, 20, and 30. Answer choice (D) is true because an even number will never have an odd number in the ones place. Answer choice (E) is true because some even numbers are multiples of 10, such as 40, 60, and 70. Answer choice (C) is NOT consistent with the statement given because even numbers can have an odd number in the tens place. For example, 54, 96, and 378 are all even numbers even though they have odd numbers in the tens place.

Validity of arguments: use deductive reasoning to determine whether an argument (a series of statements leading to a conclusion) is valid or invalid

Deductive reasoning takes place when you come to a conclusion using facts, definitions, rules, or properties. Deductive reasoning uses reasoning about a general situation and then applying it to a specific situation. For example, you know that an equation is balanced. In order for an equation to stay balanced, you must be sure to add, subtract, multiply, or divide the same amount on both sides of the equal sign. With that general knowledge, you can solve any equation that you are given.

PROBLEM

Find the measure of ∠DCB in the given diagram.

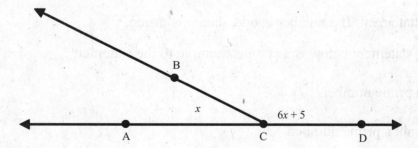

APPROACH TO SOLUTION

The diagram shows two adjacent angles. You can see that both angles together add up to a straight line, which is 180 degrees. Two angles that add up to 180 degrees are called *supplementary* angles. You are using deductive reasoning to solve this problem. What you are saying to yourself is, "Supplementary angles add up to 180 degrees. These are two supplementary angles, so they must add up to 180 degrees." You can write an equation to find the measure of either angle. See below:

$$x + 6x + 5 = 180$$
$$7x + 5 = 180$$
$$7x = 175$$
$$x = 25$$

The measure of $\angle ACB$ is 25 degrees because it is x in the diagram. However, we have to find the measure of $\angle DC(B)$. Substitute 25 for x in the expression $6x + 5$ to find that $\angle DCB$ equals 155 degrees.

Generalization: identify an appropriate generalization, an example that disproves an inappropriate generalization, or a hidden assumption

A *counterexample* is an example that shows that a given statement is false. If you make a statement and you can provide one example that disproves it, then the statement cannot be true. For example, consider the statement: "The square of a positive integer is always greater than the integer itself." Is this statement always true? If you can come up with even one example that shows that this statement is not always true, then you have proven that the statement is false. Such an example is a counterexample. The square of most integers is greater than the integer itself. 32 = 9, and this is greater than 3. 52 = 25, and this is greater than 5. However, 12 = 1, and 1 is not greater than 1. Choosing 1 as the integer in the statement, "The square of a positive integer is always greater than the integer itself" provides a counterexample for the statement.

▮ PROBLEM

Consider the statement: If a number is odd, then it is prime.

Which statement below is a counterexample to the statement?

(A) 7 is a prime number.

(B) 18 is not a prime number.

(C) 33 is a prime number.

(D) 9 is not a prime number.

(E) 2 is a prime number.

APPROACH TO SOLUTION

Ask yourself, "Are all odd numbers prime?" The answer is no. Therefore, you must select the answer choice that is a counterexample to the statement. You must pick an odd number that is not prime. Answer choice (D) disproves the statement, "If a number is odd, then it is prime" and is the correct answer.

Geometry and Measurement

Geometry

(A) Geometric Properties

Understand and apply the characteristics and properties of two-dimensional geometric shapes

Working with two-dimensional geometric shapes involves measures of length, width, height, perimeter, circumference, radius, diameter, and area. Being able to recognize and name two-dimensional shapes is important. Being comfortable working with formulas is important here, although to find many measures, you do not have to use a formula if you know how to find what is being asked for. The perimeter for any shape is found by adding up the measures of all of the sides; however, for some shapes, you may choose to use a formula. For example, the perimeter of a rectangle can be found by the following formula: $P = 2l + 2w$, where l = the length and w = the width. Sometimes using formulas can be more efficient, so it is helpful to know them and be able to work with them.

PROBLEM

A certain parallelogram has a base of 8 cm and an area of 60 cm^2. What is its height?

(A) 7.5 cm   (D) 32 cm

(B) 10 cm   (E) 480 cm

(C) 12.5 cm

APPROACH TO PROBLEM

To answer this question correctly, you have to know the formula for finding the area of a parallelogram. The formula is: $A = bh$. In this problem, you are given the area and the base. To find the height, you must divide the area by the base: $60 \div 8 = 7.5$. So the height is 7.5 cm, answer (A). Incorrect answer (E) results from multiplying 60 and 8.

Use geometric relationships such as the Pythagorean relationship, congruence, and similarity

The *Pythagorean theorem* is used to find the missing side length of a right triangle. If you know two of the three sides, you can find the third using the Pythagorean theorem. The Pythagorean theorem is $a^2 + b^2 = c^2$, where a and b are the legs and c is the hypotenuse of the right triangle. The *legs* are the two sides that make up the right angle (it does not matter which leg is a and which leg is b). The *hypotenuse* is the longest side of the right triangle and is opposite the right angle. There are many situations in real life where you can apply the Pythagorean theorem. Oftentimes, these problems do not explicitly state that you need to use the Pythagorean theorem. You have to notice that the information you are trying to find is a side length of a right triangle. An example might be if you are given the length of a ladder and asked how far its base is from a building. You may be asked how high up the building the top of the ladder is. In the diagram below, if you knew the length of the ladder and the distance of the base of the ladder from the building, you could find how high up the building the top of the ladder is. In this example, the ladder is the hypotenuse and the other two measures are the legs of a right triangle.

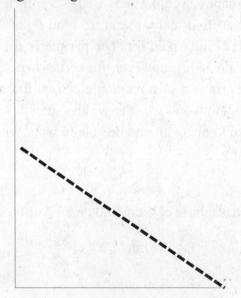

PROBLEM

A rectangle has a perimeter of 26 cm. Its width is 5 cm. Find the length of the diagonal of the rectangle.

(A) $\sqrt{89}$ cm   (D) 16 cm

(B) 12 cm   (E) $\sqrt{466}$ cm

(C) $\sqrt{281}$ cm

APPROACH TO SOLUTION

In order to solve this problem, you have to know that a rectangle has two equal widths and two equal lengths. Since you know one width is 5 cm, you know the other width is 5 cm. Therefore, the two lengths must add up to 16 cm because $26 - (5 + 5) = 16$. If both lengths add up to 16, then one length is 8 cm. When given problems with geometric objects and no diagram is provided, it is advisable to make a sketch. In this case, you see that the diagonal cuts the rectangle into two congruent right triangles. The diagonal is the hypotenuse of the right triangles. So, the sides of the rectangle are the two legs of the right triangle. Therefore, you can use the Pythagorean theorem to find the length of the diagonal. The Pythagorean theorem is $a^2 + b^2 = c^2$, where a and b are the legs and c is the hypotenuse.

Substitute in the values you know to find the hypotenuse of the right triangle, which is also the diagonal of the rectangle.

$$a^2 + b^2 = c^2$$
$$5^2 + 8^2 = c^2$$
$$25 + 64 = c^2$$
$$89 = c^2$$
$$\sqrt{89} = c$$

The correct answer is (A).

When two figures are *congruent* they are the same size and shape. Corresponding parts of congruent figures are congruent. That means corresponding sides and corresponding angles are congruent. If you have two congruent regular pentagons, for example, and you know the length of one side of one of the pentagons, you can find the length of the sides of the other pentagon. Congruent figures are also considered similar. *Similar figures* are figures whose side lengths are proportional. The angles of similar figures are the same. If a figure is scaled up, then the new figure will be larger than the original figure. If a figure is scaled down, then the new figure will be smaller than the original figure. A right triangle with sides 3, 4, and 5 cm would be similar to a right triangle with sides 18, 24, and 30 cm because 18, 24, and 30 are six times larger than 3, 4, and 5.

PROBLEM

Triangle ABC is similar to triangle DEF. BC is 10 cm and EF is 25 cm. If the length of AB is 6 cm, what is the length of DE?

(A) 9.5 cm

(D) 15 cm

(B) 12 cm

(E) 16 cm

(C) 12.5 cm

APPROACH TO SOLUTION

Since you know that the triangles are similar, you know that the ratios of the corresponding sides of the two triangles are proportional. You are given one ratio: BC = 10 and EF = 25. Find the scale factor by dividing 25 by 10. The scale factor is 2.5, which means that each side of triangle DEF is 2.5 times larger than the side lengths in triangle ABC. Multiply the length of AB, which is 6, by 2.5 to find the length of DE. DE is 15, answer choice (D).

Apply transformations or use symmetry to analyze mathematical situations

There are four different types of transformations: translations, reflections, rotations, and dilations. No matter which transformation you apply, the transformed shape is called the *image*. *Translations* are sometimes called slides and result from moving a figure up, down, left, or right. In a translation, the original shape and its translation are the same size and shape and have the same orientation on the page. A *reflection*, sometimes called a flip, results from reflecting a shape over a line of reflection. Often this line of reflection is the x or *y*-axis, although other lines of reflection can be used as well. In a reflection, the original shape and its image are the same size and shape, although the orientation is not the same. A *rotation* results from rotating the original shape about a point of rotation. Rotations of specific number of degrees are common, such as 90 degrees, 180 degrees, and 270 degrees. In a rotation, the original shape and its image are the same size and shape; however, the orientation is not the same. The last transformation is a *dilation*. A dilation is a shrinking or stretching of the original shape. As a result of a dilation, the image remains the same shape as the original figure, but the size is different. The orientation remains the same, however.

PROBLEM

What are the coordinates of C', the image of C, when triangle ABC in the given diagram is reflected over the *y*-axis?

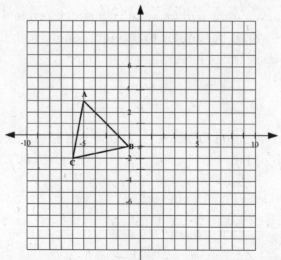

(A) (–6, 2)   (D) (2, –6)

(B) (–2, 6)   (E) (6, 2)

(C) (6, –2)

APPROACH TO SOLUTION

When a point is reflected over the *y*-axis, its *x*-coordinate becomes its opposite while its *y*-coordinate stays the same. In this example, C', the image of C, will fall in Quadrant IV.

The coordinates of C are (–6, –2), so the coordinates of C' are (6, –2), which is answer choice (C).

(B) The *xy*-Coordinate Plane

Use coordinate geometry to represent geometric concepts

The *coordinate plane* is made up of two perpendicular axes. The *x*-axis is horizontal, and the *y*-axis is vertical. Where the two axes intersect is called the *origin*; this point has the coordinates (0, 0). The intersection of the two axes creates four separate areas called *quadrants*. Quadrant I is in the upper right hand corner. Quadrants II, III, and IV are counterclockwise to Quadrant I.

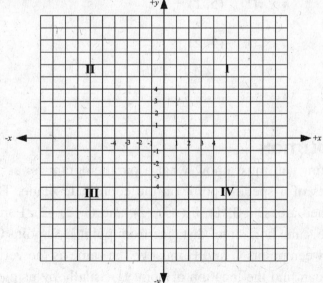

To plot a point on the coordinate plane, you must have both an *x*-coordinate and a *y*-coordinate. The *x*-coordinate tells you how many spaces to move left or right, and the *y*-coordinate tells you how many spaces to move up or down. For example, to plot the point (–3, 4), you would start at the origin. Move three spaces to the left, and then move

4 spaces up. The coordinate plane can be used to show geometric shapes, equations, and transformations.

PROBLEM

What would be the coordinates of point H, which would be the fourth point creating a parallelogram with points E, F, and G?

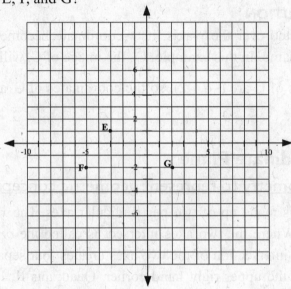

(A) (4, 1)

(B) (3, 1)

(C) (5, 2)

(D) (5, 1)

(E) (4, 2)

APPROACH TO SOLUTION

To solve this problem, you must know what a parallelogram is, as well as know how to name the coordinates of a specific point on the coordinate plane. The coordinates of the points that are graphed are: E (–3, 1), F (–5, –2), and G (2, –2). Point H will be in Quadrant I and will be the same horizontal distance from point E as point G is from point F. The vertical distance between points G and H must be the same as the vertical distance between points E and F. You can find the location of point H visually by using the coordinate plane. You can also find the location of point H by using the coordinates of the points given. The horizontal distance between points F and G is 7 units. This can be found by taking the absolute value of the difference between the x-coordinates $|2 – (–5)| = 7$. We now know that the x-coordinate of H will be 7 more than the x-coordinate of E. The x-coordinate of H is 4 because $–3 + 7 = 4$. The vertical distance between points E and F is 3 units. This can be found by taking the absolute value of the difference between the y-coordinates. $|–2 – 1| = 3$.

We now know that the *y*-coordinate of H will be 4 more than the *y*-coordinate of G. The *y*-coordinate of H is 1 because –2 + 3 = 1. The coordinates of point H will be (4, 1). The correct answer is answer choice (A).

(C) Geometric Reasoning

Logical connectives and quantifiers: interpret statements that use logical connectives (and, if-then) as well as quantifiers (some, all, none)

Logical thinking is necessary for success in mathematics. You need to pay attention to specific words like *some*, *all*, or *none*. For example, "*Some* parallelograms are rectangles" is true because some parallelograms do have four right angles. However, "*All* rectangles are squares" is not true because only some rectangles have four congruent sides, which would make them squares as well as rectangles. Although the words *some*, *all*, or *none* are small, they do make a big difference in the truth of a statement.

Also, there are mathematical statements in the "if…then" form. For example, "if a circle's area is 36π, then its radius is 6" is true because the formula for the area of a circle is $A = \pi r^2$. If the area is 36π, then the radius would be 6.

Let's look at the following example:

If a quadrilateral has 4 equal sides, then it is a square.

Which answer below about the statement is accurate?

I.   The statement is always true.

II. The statement is never true.

III. The statement is sometimes true.

Let's examine each statement for validity. Statement I says that the statement is always true. Ask yourself, "Are all quadrilaterals with 4 equal sides squares?" No. All of them are not. Some quadrilaterals with 4 equal sides are rhombi, while others are squares. Statement II says that the statement is never true. We know this if false because some quadrilaterals with 4 equal sides are squares. Statement III says that the statement is sometimes true. This is true. Some quadrilaterals with 4 equal sides are squares.

PROBLEM

Examine the three statements below and choose the correct answer.

I.   All of the angles in a regular polygon are congruent.

II. Some right triangles are isosceles.

III. Some trapezoids are rectangles.

(A) Statements I, II, and III are true.

(B) Statements I and III are true. Statement II is false.

(C) Statements I and II are true. Statement III is false.

(D) Statements I, II, and III are false.

(E) Statements I and II are false. Statement III is true.

APPROACH TO SOLUTION

Pay special attention to the words *all*, *some*, and *none*. Read each statement carefully to determine if it is true or false. Let's look at statement I. Ask yourself, "Are all the angles in a regular polygon congruent?" A regular polygon is one that has all sides and all angles congruent, so statement I is true. Let's look at statement II. Ask yourself, "Can a right triangle also be isosceles?" Yes, if a right triangle has two congruent legs, then the triangle is both right and isosceles. Statement II is true. Let's look at statement III. Ask yourself, "Can a trapezoid also be a rectangle?" The definition of a trapezoid is a quadrilateral with exactly one pair of parallel sides. Therefore, no trapezoids can be rectangles too. Statement III is false. Now, find the answer choice that matches up with statements I and II being true and statement III being false. The correct answer is (C).

Validity of arguments: use deductive reasoning to determine whether an argument (a series of statements leading to a conclusion) is valid or invalid

Determining whether a statement is true or false often involves using deductive reasoning. *Deductive reasoning* is using a general understanding and applying it to a specific situation. An example could be: The sum of the interior angles of all quadrilaterals is 360 degrees. Here is a quadrilateral. The sum of its interior angles must equal 360 degrees.

Generalization: identify an appropriate generalization, an example that disproves an inappropriate generalization, or a hidden assumption

In mathematics, when you have seen a number of examples that show the same thing, you are able to make a generalization. Your generalization may be accurate; however, it is possible that it is not. It may be impossible to test every possible case. For example, if you are exploring even numbers and you notice that all even numbers end in 0, 2, 4, 6, or 8, you can make a generalization to that effect. However, there is no way you can consider every even number because there is an infinite number of numbers. When you are working with a generalization, if you can find an example that disproves it, then you have proven that the generalization is not correct. An example that disproves a possible generalization is called a *counterexample*.

PROBLEM

Which equation below is a counterexample to the statement: "The sum of two integers is always greater than the larger integer"?

(A) $7 + 3 = 10$ (D) $8 - 1 = 7$

(B) $-2 + 4 = 2$ (E) $-4 - (-8) = 4$

(C) $1 + 5 = 6$

APPROACH TO SOLUTION

To solve this problem, you must know what a counterexample is and you need to know what the word *sum* means. A counterexample disproves a statement. The sum is the answer to an addition problem. You can eliminate answer choices (D) and (E) since they do not include addition. Look for the answer choice that shows the sum is not greater than the larger integer. In answer choice (A), 10 is larger than 7. In answer choice (C), 6 is larger than 5. In answer choice (B), 2 is not larger than 4. So, you have found your counterexample. (B) is the correct answer.

Measurement

(D) Systems of Measurement

Demonstrate basic literacy in both the U.S. customary and metric systems of measurement

The standard unit of measurement in the United States is the foot, which has 12 inches in it. Three feet make up a yard, and there are 5,280 feet in a mile.

The *metric system* is an international system of measurement, which is simpler to work with than standard measurements because all its measures are in base 10. For example, a meter (m) has 100 centimeters (cm) and a centimeter has 10 millimeters (mm). Therefore, a meter has 1000 mm.

Convert from one unit to another within the same system

If you need to convert inches to feet, you need to divide by 12 since there are 12 inches in each foot. For example, if you have 42 inches, how many feet do you have? When you divide 42 by 12, you get 3 with a remainder of 6. Since your divisor is 12, $\frac{6}{12} = \frac{1}{2}$; therefore, you have $3\frac{1}{2}$ feet. Here's another example: If you have 16 inches, how many feet do you have? When you divide 16 by 12, you get 1 with a remainder of 4. Since your divisor is 12, $\frac{4}{12} = \frac{1}{3}$; therefore, you have $1\frac{1}{3}$ feet. If you want to find out how many feet you have in a given number of yards, multiply by 3 because every yard has 3 feet. Let's look at this example: If you have 8 yards, how many feet do you have? Since $8 \times 3 = 24$, you have 24 feet. If you wanted to know how many inches that was, multiply 24 by 12 since each foot has 12 inches. $12 \times 24 = 288$. That means there are 288 inches in 24 feet (and in 8 yards).

Converting within the metric system is straightforward, involving multiplying or dividing by a power of 10. If something is 4 m long, it is 400 cm long because 1 m $\times 100$ cm $= 400$ cm. If an object is 8.4 m long, then it would be 840 cm because 8.4 m $\times 100$ cm $= 840$ cm. How many meters are in 735 cm? Since there are 100 cm in one meter, you must divide 735 by 100, which gives you 7.35. Therefore 735 cm $= 7.35$ m. If you wanted to know how many mm there are in a number of meters, multiply by 1000 because there are 1000 mm in one meter. How many mm are in 5.8 meters? $5.8 \times 1000 = 5800$. So, there are 580 mm in 5.8 meters.

PROBLEM

Melissa is 158 cm tall. How tall is she in meters?

(A) .158 m   (D) 158 m

(B) 1.58 m   (E) 1580 m

(C) 15.8 m

APPROACH TO SOLUTION

To solve this problem you must know that there are 100 cm in one meter. So, to find the number of meters in 158 cm, you must divide by 100. The correct answer is 1.58 m, answer choice (B).

Recognize and use appropriate units of measure

When you measure an object, you want to be as precise as you can be In addition, you want to use the most appropriate unit of measure. If you are measuring the length of a pencil, you would not use meters (because that is too large a unit of measure). You may use centimeters or millimeters. If you want to measure the volume of a swimming pool, you would not use millileters (because that is too small a unit of measure). Choosing the most appropriate unit of measure is important. Also important is knowing how to label your units of measure. Length, width, height, diameter, radius, and circumference are all one dimension, so those units will be to the first power. Area involves two dimensions, so those units will be to the second power. Volume has three dimensions, so those units will be to the third power.

Read a graduated scale

Reading a graduated scale on a cylinder or a beaker requires noticing the way the units are divided. For example, does each line represent 1 ml, 5 ml, or 10 ml? Examine the graduated cylinder below:

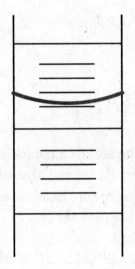

Notice that each line indicates 1 ml. Therefore, the amount of liquid in the cylinder is 16 ml.

Examine the graduated cylinder below and notice that each line represents 2 ml, rather than 1 ml. It is important to pay attention to the scale when measuring.

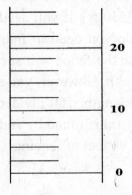

(E) Measurement
Determine the measurements needed to solve a problem

When you are given a problem to solve, you are not necessarily given only the numbers that you need. Sometimes there is extra information that is not necessary to solve the problem. Reading the problem correctly and identifying the measures you need is an important skill.

PROBLEM

A parallelogram has a base of 12 cm and side lengths of 8 cm. Its height is 6 cm. Two of its angle measures are 85 degrees, and the other two angle measures are 105 degrees. What is the area of the parallelogram?

(A) 20 cm²

(D) 96 cm²

(B) 40 cm²

(E) 105 cm²

(C) 72 cm²

APPROACH TO SOLUTION

This problem is asking you to find the area of a parallelogram; however, you are given more information than you need. The formula for the area of a parallelogram is A = bh. Therefore, the side lengths and angle measures are extraneous information. The area is found by multiplying 12 by 6. The area is 72 cm², answer choice (C).

Recognize and use geometric concepts in making linear, area, and volume measurements

Sometimes you have to know what information you need from a given situation. For example, the length of a room is 12 feet and the width is 10 feet. If you need to buy carpeting for the room, what measure do you need to find? Perimeter? Area? Volume? In this case, you need to find the area of the room. Here's another example: A rectangular shaped backyard has a length of 25 feet and an area of 550 ft². If you need to know how much fence to buy to surround the yard, what measure do you need to find? Perimeter? Area? Volume? You will need to find the perimeter because the fence will surround the yard. You are given the length, which is 25 feet, but not the width. However, you are given the area, so you can find the width by dividing the area by the length. 550 divided by 25 equals 22. Therefore, the width is 22 feet. The perimeter of the yard is found by adding both lengths and both widths. 25 + 25 + 22 + 22 = 94. You will need 94 feet of fencing.

PROBLEM

The carton that Helga purchased has a length of 12 inches, a width of 14 inches, and a height of 24 inches. Helga plans to mail the stuffed animal that she bought for her baby cousin, and she hopes it will fit in the carton. Which measures does Helga need to make to see if the stuffed animal will fit in the carton?

(A) $(12 \times 24) + (14 \times 24) + (12 \times 14)$

(B) $2(12 \times 24) + 2(14 \times 24)$

(C) $12 \times 24 \times 14$

(D) $12 + 24 + 14$

(E) $(12 + 24 + 14)2$

APPROACH TO SOLUTION

Helga will need to know the volume of the carton (and, of course, the size of the stuffed animal). To find the volume of a rectangular prism, multiply the length, width, and height together. This is found in answer choice (C).

Solve measurement problems by using a formula, estimating, employing indirect measurement, using rates as measures, making visual comparisons, using scaling or proportional reasoning, or using nonstandard unit

Measurement problems can be solved in a variety of ways. Sometimes you will follow a formula. Other times you may just need to make an estimate or compare two objects visually. You may use *proportional reasoning* if you are comparing two similar objects to one another. Also, measurements can sometimes be done using nonstandard units. One example that you may be familiar with is finding the height of a horse. Rather than use a standard measure or a metric measure, horses are measured in *hands*. A *hand* is equivalent to 4 inches, but it is not a typical "standard" measurement.

PROBLEM

The two laptop computers shown below are different sizes. Which statement best describes the relationship of the laptops to each other?

Black Laptop   White Laptop

(A) The white laptop is about $\frac{1}{8}$ the size of the black laptop.

(B) The white laptop is about $\frac{1}{2}$ the size of the black laptop.

(C) The black laptop is about 7 times the size of the white laptop.

(D) The black laptop is about 4 times larger than the white laptop.

(E) The black laptop is about 5 times larger than the white laptop.

APPROACH TO SOLUTION

Since this problem provides no specific measures, you must use a visual comparison of the two laptops. Ask yourself, "How do the two laptops compare?" You should notice that the white laptop is about $\frac{1}{2}$ the size of the black one. This is choice (B).

PROBLEM

Annalisa wanted to buy the laundry detergent that was the best price. She saw two different brands. Brand A was priced at $6.59 for 64 ounces and Brand B was priced at $3.19 for 24 ounces. What measures would Annalisa need to make to figure out which detergent is the best price?

(A) $6.59 \div 64$ and $3.19 \div 24$

(B) $64 \div 6.59$ and $24 \div 3.19$

(C) 64×6.59 and 24×3.19

(D) $64 + 6.59$ and $24 + 3.19$

(E) $64 \div 6.59 - 24 \div 3.19$

APPROACH TO SOLUTION

To compare these two different sizes of detergent with two different prices, it makes sense to find the price per ounce for Brand A and Brand B, and then find the one that has the lower price per ounce. To find the price per ounce, divide the total price by the number of ounces. This procedure is shown in answer choice (A).

Data Analysis and Probability

(A) Data Interpretation

<u>Read and interpret visual displays of quantitative information, such as bar graphs, line graphs, pie charts, pictographs, tables, stem-and-leaf plots, scatter plots, schedules, and Venn and other diagrams</u>

Information, or data, can be displayed in charts, tables, or a variety of graphs. The main reason that data is collected is so that it can be analyzed. Some data is better suited for being displayed in one form rather than another. For example, data that shows change over time is well suited for a *line graph*. *Scatter plots* are useful for examining trends. *Venn diagrams* help to see where two or more sets of data intersect. When you are given data in a chart, table, or graph, the best thing you can do is take your time reading the information. Some questions you might ask yourself: What is the title? What information is on the *x*-axis and the *y*-axis? What is the scale being used? What is the time period being covered? If you are examining a *pictograph*, don't assume that each picture represents one unit; often the picture represents larger numbers, such as 10, 100, or 1000. When considering a *stem-and-leaf plot*, be sure to notice the stem as well the leaf when observing the data.

In addition to paying attention to the information that is given in the chart, table, or graph, you can often find other information using what is given. For example, the circle graph below shows the percentages consumers spent on different areas in 1992. Notice that the portions of the pie chart are given in percents. It is possible, however, to find the amount of money spent on each category by using the average total expenditure of $29,846 that is given. To find how much money was spent on housing, you could find 32% of $29,846 by completing the following computation: .32 × 29846 = 9550.72. $9,550.72 is spent on housing. So, even though the dollar amounts are not given in the pie graph, they can be found.

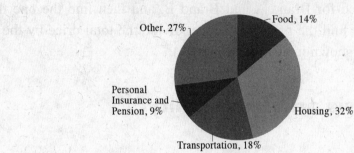

Consumer Expenditures in 1992
Average Total Expenditures: $29,846

Source: 1991 Census Bureau's Statistical Abstract of the U.S.

PROBLEM

Which statement about the given stem-and-leaf plot is true?

Stem	Leaf
5	1
6	
7	
8	4 6 8
9	
10	
11	3 4
12	1 2 4
13	8
14	4 7 8
15	1

$1\frac{1}{3} = 113$

(A) The mode is 114.

(B) The mean is 110.

(C) The median is 117.5.

(D) The range is 202.

(E) There are 18 pieces of data.

APPROACH TO SOLUTION

In order to answer this question correctly, you must understand the vocabulary mean, median, mode, and range. You also have to know how to find those values from a set of data. If you can identify a false answer choice or two, you can narrow down the possible choices for the correct answer. This data has no mode, so (A) is false. Rather than figure out the mean, which will be a time-consuming process, let's take a look at (C): Since there are 16 pieces of data, the median is the average of the 8th and 9th data items. The average of 114 and 121 is 117.5, so (C) is true. There is no need to figure out the mean or the range.

(B) Data Representation

Understand the correspondence between data sets and their graphic representations

After data is collected and then organized, it can be put into a graphic representation. Be careful that you present your data accurately.

PROBLEM

Which answer choice shows the data that is displayed in the bar graph?

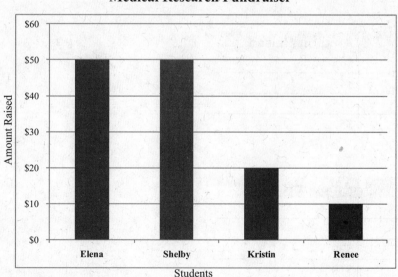

Medical Research Fundraiser

(A)

Student	Amount Raised
Elena	$40
Shelby	$40
Kristin	$10
Renee	$5

(B)

Student	Amount Raised
Elena	$50
Shelby	$50
Kristin	$20
Renee	$10

(C)

Student	Amount Raised
Elena	$500
Shelby	$500
Kristin	$200
Renee	$100

(D)

Student	Amount Raised
Elena	$45
Shelby	$45
Kristin	$15
Renee	$5

(E)

Student	Amount Raised
Elena	$50
Shelby	$50
Kristin	$30
Renee	$10

APPROACH TO SOLUTION

When reading a bar graph, be sure to pay attention to the information on both axes. The data in answer choice (B) represents the data in the graph.

(C) Trends and Inferences

Make observations, comparisons, and predictions or extrapolations from a given data display

Looking at data allows you to make observations, comparison, predictions, or extrapolations. It is important to note that data is collected for a reason. It is collected and organized so that we can make observations from it.

Look at the following bar graph showing students' scores on a math test. There are many observations that can be made from the data. Some possible observations:

- More students scored 80 than any other score (the mode)

- 18 students took the test

- The range on the test was 50

- Almost half of the students scored less than 70 on the test

- No one achieved a perfect score

- The median score was 70

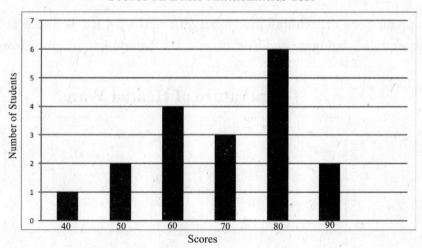

Scores on Basic Mathematics Test

Bar graphs are good for comparing different amounts to each other. For example, in the bar graph below showing students' favorite fruit, you can make many comparisons. Notice that 2 children selected kiwi, mango, and other as their favorite fruit. Notice that four times as many children said that apple was their favorite fruit as said that orange was their favorite fruit. Bar graphs lend themselves to comparing different amounts easily because you can visually compare the height of the bars.

You can also make predictions or extrapolations from a graph. For example, if you were buying fruit for the school cafeteria, and you had the results of the bar graph below, which two types of fruit would you buy most? Apples and bananas are the two most popular fruits in the bar graph, so you would buy more of those two types of fruit. You can predict that more children will choose apples and bananas than will choose mangos and kiwis. As a result, you can prepare accordingly.

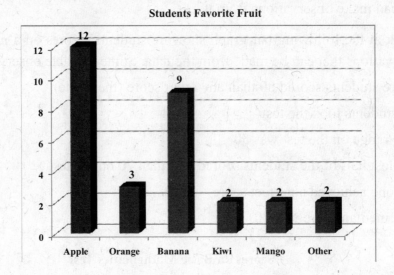

What predictions or extrapolations can you make from the line graph of the temperature of water that is being heated over time, shown in the line graph below?

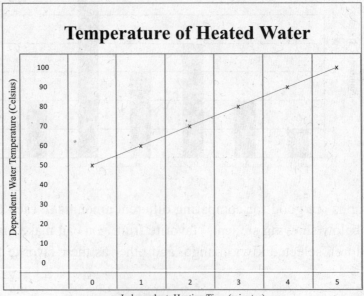

As you can see, the line graph shows a constant increase of about 10 degrees every minute. So even though the graph does not show the temperature of the water after 6 or more minutes, we can extrapolate what the temperature will be based on the information that we are given. What temperature would you expect the water to be after 8 minutes? At 5 minutes, the temperature is 100 degrees; the graph shows that the water increases 10 degrees every minute. You would expect the water to be at 130 degrees after 8 minutes. Although this temperature would follow the pattern of the graph (and it would be a logical extrapolation), it does not make sense in the real world as water boils at 100 degrees. Therefore, it cannot get any hotter than that! Therefore, you must pay attention to the patterns that you see in graphs, but you must also pay attention to what you know to be true in the real world. Using this "real world" knowledge, you can predict that after reaching its highest temperature at 5 minutes, the temperature of the water will remain the same, 100 degrees, as time goes on. So, at 8 minutes the temperature would still be 100 degrees.

Draw conclusions or make inferences from a given data display

▌PROBLEM▐

A class of students made circle graphs of the colors of their eyes. They put the girls' data in one graph and the boys' data in another. Which statement below cannot be concluded from considering the data in the graphs?

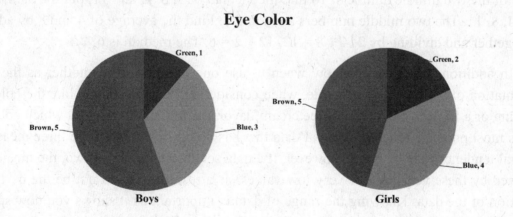

Eye Color

Boys — Green, 1; Brown, 5; Blue, 3

Girls — Green, 2; Brown, 5; Blue, 4

(A) The least common eye color is green.

(B) About one-third of the girls have blue eyes.

(C) Half the boys have brown eyes.

(D) One-fourth of the girls have green eyes.

(E) More students have brown eyes than any other eye color.

APPROACH TO SOLUTION

Interpreting the information that is displayed in a graph is an important skill. To approach this problem, look for the statement that is NOT true. Statement (A) is true. You can tell because the smallest section in each circle graph is green. Statement (B) is true; you must estimate that the blue portion of the circle graph for girls is about one-third of the whole circle. Statement (C) is true. Half the circle graph for boys is brown. Statement (D) is not true. Less than one-fourth of the girls have green eyes. Therefore Statement (D) cannot be concluded from the graphs and is the correct answer choice.

(D) Measures of Center and Spread
Determine mean, median, mode(s), and range

Familiarity with the central tendencies of mean, median, and mode are important. You must know how to find them. The *mean* is found by adding up all the data items and dividing by the total number of data items: The mean of 4, 5, and 12 is found by adding $4 + 5 + 12$, which equals 21, and then dividing by 3. The mean is 7. The *median* is found by putting the data in order from least to greatest, and then finding the middle data item. When there is an odd number of items, this is fairly straightforward. To find the median of 10, 6, 4, 8, and 12, put the data in order from least to greatest: 4, 6, 8, 10, 12. The middle number is 8. The median is 8. If there is an even number of data items, the median is found by finding the average of the two middle numbers. To find the median of 3, 8, 4, and 11, put the data in order: 3, 4, 8, 11. The two middle numbers are 4 and 8. Find the average of 4 and 8 by adding them together and dividing by 2. $4 + 8 = 12$. $12 \div 2 = 6$. The median is 6.

In addition, you need to know when to use one measure over another as the best representation of the data. For example, when considering qualitative data like the color of something or a favorite candy bar or ice cream flavor, the mode will tell you which color or flavor is most popular. When looking at data that has no outliers, any of the three measures of central tendency may be good. However, if a data set has an outlier or two, the mean will be skewed by these very high or very low values; as a result, it would not be the best representation of the data. Knowing the range of data is important as it shows you how spread out the data is. To find the range, subtract the smallest data item from the largest data item.

PROBLEM

For which set of data does the number 10 represent the mean?

(A) 4, 5, 10, 13, 23   (D) 1, 5, 8, 11, 19

(B) 3, 5, 5, 8, 13   (E) 7, 8, 8, 12, 15

(C) 2, 10, 10, 10, 11

APPROACH TO SOLUTION

To answer this question correctly, you need to know how to find the mean of a set of data. (Add up all of the data items and divide by the number of items.) The data in answer choice (A) has a median of 10, but its mean is 11. The data in answer choice (B) has a range of 10, but its mean is 6.8. The data in answer choice (C) has both a median and a mode of 10, but its mean is 8.6. For the data in answer choice (D), the average of the lowest and highest numbers is 10, but the mean for all its data is 8.8. The data in answer choice (E) does have a mean of 10. The correct answer is choice (E).

(E) Trends and Inferences
Interpret numbers used to express simple probability

To find the probability of an event occurring, you need to write a ratio. The *numerator* of the ratio is the number of times the favorable event will occur, and the *denominator* is the total number of events possible. For example, if you want to find the probability of choosing a caramel-filled chocolate out of a box of chocolates, you need to know how many chocolates are caramel-filled and how many chocolates there are total. So, if there are 8 caramel-filled chocolates and there are 24 chocolates in the box, then the probability of choosing a caramel-filled chocolate from the box at random is $\frac{8}{24}$, which can also be written as $\frac{1}{3}$.

PROBLEM

There are 100 tiles in the game of *Scrabble*. The probability of selecting a blank tile from all of the tiles is $\frac{1}{50}$. How many blank tiles are there?

(A) 1

(B) 2

(C) 3

(D) 4

(E) 5

APPROACH TO SOLUTION

In order to answer this question, you need to understand how a probability ratio is written. The numerator is the desired outcome, and the denominator is the total number of outcomes. You are told that the probability of selecting a blank tile is $\frac{1}{50}$, and you know that there are 100 tiles all together. Therefore, you must write and solve a proportion using the ratio you are given. Like so: $\frac{1}{50} = \frac{x}{100}$. As you can see, the numerator for the ratio that has 100 as a denominator must be 2. There are 2 blank tiles in the set.

Assign a probability to a possible outcome

You can use a probability ratio to figure out the number of times of an event occurring. Let's look at the following example: Years ago, cereal boxes had little prizes at the bottom of them. Imagine that a certain cereal manufacturer reports that .30 of the boxes have a puzzle, .20 have a ring, and .50 have a whistle. If one family bought 40 boxes of cereal over the course of a year, what is the best prediction of the number of rings they would have gotten? Since .20 of the boxes have rings in them, if we find 20% of 40, we will have the answer. 20% of 40 is 8, so we would predict the family would get 8 rings that year.

PROBLEM

Officer Russell has found that .15 of the cars that drive through the intersection of Pine and Main fail to stop at the stop sign. If 200 cars pass through that intersection each week, what is the best prediction of the number of cars who will NOT stop at the stop sign?

(A) 15

(D) 30

(B) 19

(E) 35

(C) 20

APPROACH TO SOLUTION

You are told that .15 of the cars do not stop at the stop sign. That means 15 out of 100 cars do not stop. If you want to know how many cars out of 200 do not stop, you could set up the following proportion: $\frac{15}{100} = \frac{x}{200}$. As you can see, you can find the value of x in your head. All you have to do is double 15. Therefore, you would expect 30 cars out of 200 not to stop at the stop sign. Answer (D) is correct.

In addition to finding the probability of one event, you may want to find the probability of two or more independent events occurring. Two events are considered independent if the results of one event occurring does not affect the results of the other one occurring. An example of independent events is tossing two number cubes. The number that one number cube lands on is independent of the number that the other number cube lands on. To find the probability of independent events, find the probability of each event occurring on its own, then multiply those probabilities.

Example:

Tyrone tosses two coins on the table. What is the probability that both coins will land heads up?

Ask yourself, "What is the probability that the first coin lands heads up?" This is $\frac{1}{2}$.

Ask yourself, "What is the probability that the second coin lands heads up?" This is $\frac{1}{2}$.

Multiply those two probabilities together: $\frac{1}{2} \times \frac{1}{2} = \frac{1}{4}$. So, the probability that both coins land heads up is $\frac{1}{4}$.

PROBLEM

Danny throws a 6-sided number cube and a penny. What is the probability that he will get a prime number on the number cube and a tail on the penny?

(A) $\frac{1}{6}$ (D) $\frac{2}{3}$

(B) $\frac{1}{4}$ (E) 1

(C) $\frac{1}{2}$

APPROACH TO SOLUTION:

This is an example of independent probability. First find the probability of getting a prime number. You must be able to identify prime numbers. The number 1 is not a prime number! The only prime numbers on a number cube are 2, 3, and 5; therefore the probability of getting a prime number is $\frac{3}{6}$ or $\frac{1}{2}$. The probability of getting a tail is ½. Multiply those probabilities together to find the probability of both occurring at the same time. $\frac{1}{2} \times \frac{1}{2} = \frac{1}{4}$. The correct answer is (B).

CHAPTER 4

Writing Skills Review

The questions in the Writing Section of the PPST are divided into four content categories that contribute to the total score in the following approximate percentages:

Writing	Code: 0720	30 minutes/ 38 multiple-choice questions 30 min/1 essay	Grammar 13 questions—17% Structure 14 questions—18.5% Word choice/mechanics— 11 questions—14.5% Essay 1 question—50%
Computerized Writing	Code: 5720	38 minutes/ 44 multiple-choice questions 30 min/1 typed essay	Grammar 15 questions—17% Structure 16 questions—18.5% Word choice/mechanics— 13 questions—14.5% Essay 1 question—50%

Essays should be composed for an adult audience and organized logically with a clear thesis, supporting points, examples, and details developed clearly with few if any errors in standard written English.

The PPST does not require that you know grammatical terms such as *gerund*, *subject complement*, or *dependent clause*, although general familiarity with such terms may be helpful to you in determining whether a sentence or part of a sentence is correct or incorrect. In the multiple choice section, you will be asked to identiry errors in grammar, spelling, punctuation, capitalization, sentence structure, and word choice. Remember : this is a test of written language skills in formal academic writing, not what would be appropriate for casual conversation.

QUIZ

This quiz is meant to be diagnostic. In other words, it is intended to help you identify areas of difficulty you may have on the PPST. After taking the test, look at the answers and study the areas within the Writing Skills chapter which are giving you difficulty.

Correct the sentence:

1. He played the guitar good.

2. The newspaper reported that teacher's salaries had gone down.

3. I like to sing so I join the choir.

4. I have a book, a pen, and am going to the library.

5. Now, there is currently no plan for the environmental crisis.

6. In the closet I found a shoe a coat and a container.

7. I like to go to nantucket in the month of august.

8. She cleaned the tables but they're surfaces were still dusty.

9. As markers and crayons slid off the table.

10. Bill is a whiner when problems occur they are always someone else's fault.

QUIZ ANSWERS

1. He played the guitar good. INCORRECT. Correct answer: He played the guitar well. If you got this question wrong, review the section on *Adjectives and Adverbs*.

2. The newspaper reported that teacher's salaries had gone down. INCORRECT. Correct answer: The newspaper reported that teachers' salaries had gone down. If you got this question wrong, review the sections on *Nouns* and *Punctuation*.

3. I like to sing so I join the choir. INCORRECT. Correct answer: I like to sing, so I joined the choir. If you got this question wrong, review the section on *Verbs*.

4. I have a book, a pen, and am going to the library. INCORRECT. Correct answer: I have a book and a pen. In addition, I am going to the library (or some variation thereof). If you got this question wrong, review the sections on *Parallelism*.

5. Now, there is currently no plan for the environmental crisis. INCORRECT. Now and currently are redundant. If you got this question wrong, review the section on *Redundancy*.

6. In the closet I found a shoe a coat and a container. INCORRECT. Correct answer: In the closet, I found a shoe, a coat, and a container. If you got this question wrong, review the section on *Punctuation*.

7. I like to go to nantucket in the month of august. INCORRECT. Correct answer: I like to go to Nantucket in the month of August. If you got this question wrong, review the section on *Capitalization*.

8. She cleaned the tables but they're surfaces were still dusty. INCORRECT. Correct answer: She cleaned the tables but their surfaces were still dusty. If you got this question wrong, review the section on *Commonly Confused Words*.

9. As markers and crayons slid off the table. INCORRECT. This is a sentence fragment. If you got this question wrong, review the section on *Fragments*.

10. Bill is a whiner when problems occur they are always someone else's fault. INCORRECT. This is a run on. Correct answer: Bill is a whiner. When problems occur, they are always someone else's fault. If you got this question wrong, review the section on *Run-Ons*.

GRAMMAR

ETS asks that you be able to identify errors in adjectives, adverbs, nouns (agreement), pronouns (agreement and proper use) and verbs (agreement, form, and tense).

Adjectives and Adverbs

Correct Usage

Adjectives are words that modify nouns or pronouns by defining, describing, limiting, or qualifying those nouns or pronouns.

Adverbs are words that modify verbs, adjectives, or other adverbs and that express such ideas as time, place, manner, cause, and degree. Use adjectives as subject complements with linking verbs; use adverbs with action verbs.

EX:	The old man's speech was *eloquent*.	ADJECTIVE
	Mr. Brown speaks *eloquently*.	ADVERB
	Please be *careful*.	ADJECTIVE
	Please drive *carefully*.	ADVERB

Good or well

Good is an adjective; its use as an adverb is colloquial and nonstandard.

INCORRECT:	He plays *good*.
CORRECT:	He looks *good* to be an octogenarian.
	The quiche tastes very *good*.

Well may be either an adverb or an adjective. As an adjective, *well* means "in good health."

CORRECT:	He plays *well*.	ADVERB
	My mother is not *well*.	ADJECTIVE

Bad or badly

Bad is an adjective used after sense verbs such as *look, smell, taste, feel,* or *sound*, or after linking verbs (*is, am, are, was, were*).

INCORRECT:	I feel *badly* about the delay.
CORRECT:	I feel *bad* about the delay.

Badly is an adverb used after all other verbs.

INCORRECT:	It doesn't hurt very *bad*.
CORRECT:	It doesn't hurt very *badly*.

Real or really

Real is an adjective; its use as an adverb is colloquial and nonstandard. It means "genuine."

INCORRECT:	He writes *real* well.
CORRECT:	This is *real* leather.

Really is an adverb meaning "very."

INCORRECT:	This is *really* diamond.
CORRECT:	Have a *really* nice day.

EX:	This is *real* amethyst.	ADJECTIVE
	This is *really* difficult.	ADVERB

This is a *real* crisis.	ADJECTIVE
This is *really* important.	ADVERB

Sort of and kind of

Sort of and *kind of* are often misused in written English by writers who actually mean *rather* or *somewhat*.

INCORRECT: Jan was *kind of* saddened by the results of the test.

CORRECT: Jan was *somewhat* saddened by the results of the test.

Faulty Comparisons

Sentences containing a faulty comparison often sound correct because their problem is not one of grammar but of logic. Read these sentences closely to make sure that like things are being compared, that the comparisons are complete, and that the comparisons are logical.

When comparing two persons or things, use the comparative, not the superlative form, of an adjective or an adverb. Use the superlative form for comparison of more than two persons or things. Use *any*, *other*, or *else* when comparing one thing or person with a group of which it/he or she is a part.

Most one- and two-syllable words form their comparative and superlative degrees with *-er* and *-est* suffixes. Adjectives and adverbs of more than two syllables form their comparative and superlative degrees with the addition of *more* and *most*.

Positive	Comparative	Superlative
good	better	best
old	older	oldest
friendly	friendlier	friendliest
lonely	lonelier	loneliest
talented	more talented	most talented
beautiful	more beautiful	most beautiful

A double comparison occurs when the degree of the modifier is changed incorrectly by adding both *-er* and *more* or *-est* and *most* to the adjective or adverb.

INCORRECT:	He is the *most nicest* brother.
CORRECT:	He is the *nicest* brother.
INCORRECT:	She is the *more meaner* of the sisters.
CORRECT:	She is the *meaner* sister.

Illogical comparisons occur when there is an implied comparison between two things that are not actually being compared or that cannot be logically compared.

INCORRECT:	The interest at a loan company is higher *than* a bank.
CORRECT:	The interest at a loan company is higher *than* that *at* a bank.
OR	The interest at a loan company is higher *than at* a bank.

Ambiguous comparisons occur when elliptical words (those omitted) create for the reader more than one interpretation of the sentence.

INCORRECT:	I like Mary better than you. (than you *what*?)
CORRECT:	I like Mary better than I like you.
OR	I like Mary better than you do.

Incomplete comparisons occur when the basis of the comparison (the two categories being compared) is not explicitly stated.

INCORRECT:	Skywriting is *more* spectacular.
CORRECT:	Skywriting is *more* spectacular *than* billboard advertising.

Do not omit the words *other, any,* or *else* when comparing one thing or person with a group of which it/he or she is a part.

INCORRECT:	Joan writes better *than any* student in her class.
CORRECT:	Joan writes better *than any other* student in her class.

Do not omit the second *as* of *as...as* when making a point of equal or superior comparison.

INCORRECT:	The University of West Florida is *as large* or larger than the University of North Florida.
CORRECT:	The University of West Florida is *as large as* or larger than the University of Northern Florida.

Do not omit the first category of the comparison, even if the two categories are the same.

INCORRECT: This is one of the best, if not the best, college in the country.

CORRECT: This is one of the best colleges in the country, if not the best.

The problem with the incorrect sentence is that *one of the best* requires the plural word *colleges*, not *college*.

■ Drill: Adjectives and Adverbs ■

DIRECTIONS: Choose the correct option.

1. Although the band performed <u>badly</u>, I feel <u>real bad</u> about missing the concert.

   (A) badly…real badly

   (B) bad…badly

   (C) badly…very bad

   (D) No change is necessary.

2. These reports are <u>relative simple</u> to prepare.

   (A) relatively simple

   (B) relative simply

   (C) relatively simply

   (D) No change is necessary.

3. He did <u>very well</u> on the test although his writing skills are not <u>good</u>.

   (A) real well…good

   (B) very good…good

   (C) good…great

   (D) No change is necessary.

4. Shake the medicine bottle <u>good</u> before you open it.

   (A) very good

   (B) real good

   (C) well

   (D) No change is necessary.

5. Though she speaks <u>fluently</u>, she writes <u>poorly</u> because she doesn't observe <u>closely</u> or think <u>clear</u>.

   (A) fluently…poorly…closely…clearly

   (B) fluent…poor…close…clear

   (C) fluently…poor…closely…clear

   (D) No change is necessary.

> **DIRECTIONS:** Select the sentence that clearly and effectively states the idea and has no structural errors.

6. (A) Los Angeles is larger than any city in California.

   (B) Los Angeles is larger than all the cities in California.

   (C) Los Angeles is larger than any other city in California.

7. (A) Art history is as interesting as, if not more interesting than, music appreciation.

   (B) Art history is as interesting, if not more interesting than, music appreciation.

   (C) Art history is as interesting as, if not more interesting, music appreciation.

8. (A) The baseball team here is as good as any other university.

   (B) The baseball team here is as good as all the other universities.

   (C) The baseball team here is as good as any other university's.

9. (A) I like him better than you.

   (B) I like him better than I like you.

   (C) I like him better.

10. (A) You are the most stingiest person I know.

    (B) You are the most stingier person I know.

    (C) You are the stingiest person I know.

Nouns (Agreement)

A noun refers to a *person*, *place*, *thing*, *event*, *substance*, *quality*, *quantity*, or *idea*.

> The **dog** sat on the **rug**.
>
> Please hand in your **paper** by the **end** of the **week**.
>
> **John Adams** was the second **president** of the **United States of America**.

Nouns have to agree in number—start with plural, end with plural; start with singular, end with singular. But you should be careful. Take this example:

> Catherine and Sue are planning to move to Hawaii in order to become a beach bum.

Two people, *Catherine and Sue*, can't become **one** beach bum:

> Catherine and Sue are planning to move to Hawaii in order to become **beach bums.**

Another commonly tested feature of nouns is **countability**. Look at the following sentences:

> I have many feelings.

> To mature is to transcend much failure.

Both sentences are correct. *Feelings are* something one can count; *they* are discrete entities like rocks. *Failure*, however, cannot be counted; *failure* is an abstract state of being, like *sorrow*, *liberty*, *hatred, love*, and *happiness*. Concrete entities can be **noncountable** as well: *air* and *water*, to name two.

Pronouns

Pronoun Case

Pronoun case questions test your knowledge of the use of nominative and objective case pronouns:

Nominative Case	Objective Case
I	me
he	him
she	her
we	us
they	them
who	whom

This review section answers the most frequently asked grammar questions: when to use *I* and when to use *me*; when to use *who* and when to use *whom*. Some writers avoid *whom* altogether, and instead of distinguishing between *I* and *me*, many writers incorrectly use *myself*.

Use the nominative case (subject pronouns)

for the subject of a sentence:

We students studied until early morning for the final.

Alan and *I* "burned the midnight oil," too.

for pronouns in apposition to the subject:

Only two students, Alex and *I*, were asked to report on the meeting.

for the predicate nominative/subject complement:

The actors nominated for the award were *she* and *I*.

for the subject of an elliptical clause:

Molly is more experienced than *he*.

for the subject of a subordinate clause:

Robert is the driver *who* reported the accident.

for the complement of an infinitive with no expressed subject:

I would not want to be *he*.

Use the objective case (object pronouns)

for the direct object of a sentence:

Mary invited *us* to her party.

for the object of a preposition:

The books that were torn belonged to *her*.

Just between you and *me*, I'm bored.

for the indirect object of a sentence:

Walter gave a dozen red roses to *her*.

for the appositive of a direct object:

The committee elected two delegates, Barbara and *me*.

for the object of an infinitive:

The young boy wanted to help *us* paint the fence.

for the object of a gerund:

Enlisting *him* was surprisingly easy.

for the object of a past participle:

Having called the other students and *us*, the secretary went home for the day.

for a pronoun that precedes an infinitive (the subject of an infinitive):

The supervisor told *him* to work late.

for the complement of an infinitive with an expressed subject:

The fans thought the best player to be *him*.

for the object of an elliptical clause:

Bill tackled Joe harder than *me*.

for the object of a verb in apposition:

Charles invited two extra people, Carmen and *me*, to the party.

When a conjunction connects two pronouns or a pronoun and a noun, remove the "and" and the other pronoun or noun to determine what the correct pronoun form should be:

Mom gave ~~Tom and~~ myself a piece of cake.

Mom gave ~~Tom and~~ I a piece of cake

Mom gave ~~Tom and~~ me a piece of cake.

Removal of these words reveals what the correct pronoun should be:

Mom gave *me* a piece of cake.

The only pronouns that are acceptable after *between* and other prepositions are: *me, her, him, them,* and *whom.* When deciding between *who* and *whom,* try substituting *he* for *who* and *him* for *whom;* then follow these easy transformation steps:

1. Isolate the *who* clause or the *whom* clause:

    whom we can trust

2. Invert the word order, if necessary. Place the words in the clause in the natural order of an English sentence, subject followed by the verb:

    we can trust whom

3. Read the final form with the *he* or *him* inserted:

>   We can trust ~~whom~~ him.

When a pronoun follows a comparative conjunction like *than* or *as*, complete the elliptical construction to help you determine which pronoun is correct.

>   EX: She has more credit hours than me [do].

>   She has more credit hours than I [do].

Pronoun-Antecedent Agreement

These kinds of questions test your knowledge of using an appropriate pronoun to agree with its antecedent in number (singular or plural form) and gender (masculine, feminine, or neuter). An antecedent is a noun or pronoun to which another noun or pronoun refers.

Here are the two basic rules for pronoun reference-antecedent agreement:

1. Every pronoun must have a conspicuous antecedent.

2. Every pronoun must agree with its antecedent in number, gender, and person.

When an antecedent is one of dual gender like *student*, *singer*, *artist*, *person*, *citizen*, etc., use *his* or *her*. Some careful writers change the antecedent to a plural noun to avoid using the sexist, singular masculine pronoun *his*:

>   INCORRECT: Everyone hopes that he will win the lottery.

>   CORRECT: Most people hope that they will win the lottery.

Ordinarily, the relative pronoun *who* is used to refer to people, *which* to refer to things and places, *where* to refer to places, and *that* to refer to places or things. The distinction between *that* and *which* is a grammatical distinction (see the section on Word Choice Skills).

Many writers prefer to use *that* to refer to collective nouns.

>   EX: A family *that* traces its lineage is usually proud of its roots.

Many writers, especially students, are not sure when to use the reflexive case pronoun and when to use the possessive case pronoun. The rules governing the usage of the reflexive case and the possessive case are quite simple.

Use the possessive case

before a noun in a sentence:

Our friend moved during the semester break.

My dog has fleas, but *her* dog doesn't.

before a gerund in a sentence:

Her running helps to relieve stress.

His driving terrified her.

as a noun in a sentence:

Mine was the last test graded that day.

to indicate possession:

Karen never allows anyone else to drive *her* car.

Brad thought the book was *his,* but it was someone else's.

Use the reflexive case

as a direct object to rename the subject:

I kicked *myself.*

as an indirect object to rename the subject:

Henry bought *himself* a tie.

as an object of a prepositional phrase:

Tom and Lillie baked the pie for *themselves.*

as a predicate pronoun:

She hasn't been *herself* lately.

Do not use the reflexive in place of the nominative pronoun:

INCORRECT: Both Randy and *myself* plan to go.

CORRECT: Both Randy and *I* plan to go.

INCORRECT:	*Yourself* will take on the challenges of college.
CORRECT:	*You* will take on the challenges of college.

INCORRECT:	Either James or *yourself* will paint the mural.
CORRECT:	Either James or *you* will paint the mural.

Watch out for careless use of the pronoun form:

INCORRECT:	George *hisself* told me it was true.
CORRECT:	George *himself* told me it was true.

INCORRECT:	They washed the car *theirselves*.
CORRECT:	They washed the car *themselves*.

Notice that reflexive pronouns are not set off by commas:

INCORRECT:	Mary, *herself*, gave him the diploma.
CORRECT:	Mary *herself* gave him the diploma.

INCORRECT:	I will do it, *myself*.
CORRECT:	I will do it *myself*.

Pronoun Reference

Pronoun reference questions require you to determine whether the antecedent is conspicuously written in the sentence or whether it is remote, implied, ambiguous, or vague, none of which results in clear writing. Make sure that every italicized pronoun has a conspicuous antecedent and that one pronoun substitutes only for another noun or pronoun, not for an idea or a sentence.

Pronoun reference problems occur

when a pronoun refers to either of two antecedents:

INCORRECT:	Joanna told Pam that *she* was getting fat.
CORRECT:	Joanna told Pam, "I'm getting fat."

when a pronoun refers to a remote antecedent:

INCORRECT: A strange car followed us closely, and *he* kept blinking his lights at us.

CORRECT: A strange car followed us closely, and its driver kept blinking his lights at us.

when *this*, *that*, and *which* refer to the general idea of the preceding clause or sentence rather than the preceding word:

INCORRECT: The students could not understand the pronoun reference handout, which annoyed them very much.

CORRECT: The students could not understand the pronoun reference handout, a fact which annoyed them very much.

OR   The students were annoyed because they could not understand the pronoun reference handout.

when a pronoun refers to an unexpressed but implied noun:

INCORRECT: My husband wants me to knit a blanket, but I'm not interested in it.

CORRECT: My husband wants me to knit a blanket, but I'm not interested in knitting.

when *it* is used as something other than an expletive to postpone a subject:

INCORRECT: It says in today's paper that the newest shipment of cars from Detroit, Michigan, seems to include outright imitations of European models.

CORRECT: Today's paper says that the newest shipment of cars from Detroit, Michigan, seems to include outright imitations of European models.

INCORRECT: The football game was canceled because it was bad weather.

CORRECT: The football game was canceled because the weather was bad.

when *they* or *it* is used to refer to something or someone indefinitely, and there is no definite antecedent:

INCORRECT:	At the job placement office, they told me to stop wearing ripped jeans to my interviews.
CORRECT:	At the job placement office, I was told to stop wearing ripped jeans to my interviews.

when the pronoun does not agree with its antecedent in number, gender, or person:

INCORRECT:	Any graduate student, if they are interested, may attend the lecture.
CORRECT:	Any graduate student, if he or she is interested, may attend the lecture.
OR	All graduate students, if they are interested, may attend the lecture.
INCORRECT:	Many Americans are concerned that the overuse of slang and colloquialisms is corrupting the language.
CORRECT:	Many Americans are concerned that the overuse of slang and colloquialisms is corrupting their language.
INCORRECT:	The Board of Regents will not make a decision about tuition increase until their March meeting.
CORRECT:	The Board of Regents will not make a decision about tuition increase until its March meeting.

when a noun or pronoun has no expressed antecedent:

INCORRECT:	In the President's address to the union, he promised no more taxes.
CORRECT:	In his address to the union, the President promised no more taxes.

▪ Drill: Pronouns ▪

DIRECTIONS: Choose the correct option.

1. My friend and <u>myself</u> bought tickets for *Cats*.

   (A) I   (C) us

   (B) me   (D) No change is necessary.

2. Alcohol and tobacco are harmful to <u>whomever</u> consumes them.

   (A) whom   (C) whoever

   (B) who   (D) No change is necessary.

3. Everyone is wondering <u>whom</u> her successor will be.

   (A) who   (C) who'll

   (B) whose   (D) No change is necessary.

4. Rosa Lee's parents discovered that it was <u>her who</u> wrecked the family car.

   (A) she who   (C) her whom

   (B) she whom   (D) No change is necessary.

5. A student <u>who</u> wishes to protest <u>his or her</u> grades must file a formal grievance in the Dean's office.

   (A) that...their   (C) whom...their

   (B) which...his   (D) No change is necessary.

6. One of the best things about working for this company is that <u>they pay</u> big bonuses.

   (A) it pays   (C) they paid

   (B) they always pay   (D) No change is necessary.

7. Every car owner should be sure that <u>their</u> automobile insurance is adequate.

   (A) your   (C) its

   (B) his or her   (D) No change is necessary.

8. My mother wants me to become a teacher, but I'm not interested in <u>it</u>.

   (A) this   (C) that

   (B) teaching   (D) No change is necessary.

9. Since I had not paid my electric bill, <u>they</u> sent me a delinquent notice.

   (A) the power company   (C) it

   (B) he   (D) No change is necessary.

10. Margaret seldom wrote to her sister when <u>she</u> was away at college.

    (A) who   (C) her sister

    (B) her   (D) No change is necessary.

Verbs

Verb Forms

This section covers the principal parts of some irregular verbs including troublesome verbs like *lie* and *lay*. The use of regular verbs like *look* and *receive* poses no real problem to most writers since the past and past participle forms end in *-ed*; it is the irregular forms which pose the most serious problems—for example, *seen*, *written*, and *begun*.

Verb Tenses

Tense sequence indicates a logical time sequence.

Use present tense

> in statements of universal truth:

> > I learned that the sun *is* 90 million miles from the earth.

> in statements about the contents of literature and other published works:

> > In this book, Sandy *becomes* a nun and *writes* a book on psychology.

Use past tense

> in statements concerning writing or publication of a book:

> > He *wrote* his first book in 1949, and it *was* published in 1952.

Use present perfect tense

> for an action that began in the past but continues into the future:
>
> > I have *lived* here all my life.

Use past perfect tense

> for an earlier action that is mentioned in a later action:
>
> > Cindy ate the apple that she *had picked*.
>
> (First she picked it, then she ate it.)

Use future perfect tense

> for an action that will have been completed at a specific future time:
>
> > By May, I *shall have graduated*.

Use a present participle

> for action that occurs at the same time as the verb:
>
> > *Speeding* down the interstate, I saw a cop's flashing lights.

Use a perfect participle

> for action that occurred before the main verb:
>
> > *Having read* the directions, I started the test.

Use the subjunctive mood

> to express a wish or state a condition contrary to fact:
>
> > *If it were not raining,* we could have a picnic.

> in *that* clauses after verbs like *request, recommend, suggest, ask, require,* and *insist*; and after such expressions as *it is important* and *it is necessary*:
>
> > It is necessary that all papers *be* submitted on time.

Subject-Verb Agreement

Agreement is the grammatical correspondence between the subject and the verb of a sentence: *I do; we do; they do; he, she, it does.*

> Every English verb has five forms, two of which are the bare form (plural) and the -*s* form (singular). Simply put, singular verb forms end in -*s;* plural forms do not.

Study these rules governing subject-verb agreement:

A verb must agree with its subject, not with any additive phrase in the sentence such as a prepositional or verbal phrase. Ignore such phrases.

> Your *copy* of the rules *is* on the desk.

> Ms. Craig's *record* of community service and outstanding teaching *qualifies* her for a promotion.

In an inverted sentence beginning with a prepositional phrase, the verb still agrees with its subject.

> At the end of the summer come the best *sales*.

> Under the house *are* some old Mason *jars*.

Prepositional phrases beginning with compound prepositions such as *along with, together with, in addition to*, and *as well as* should be ignored, for they do not affect subject-verb agreement.

> *Gladys Knight*, as well as the Pips, *is* riding the midnight train to Georgia.

A verb must agree with its subject, not its subject complement.

> *Taxes are* a problem.

> A *problem is* taxes.

When a sentence begins with an expletive such as *there, here*, or *it*, the verb agrees with the subject, not the expletive.

> Surely, there *are* several *alumni* who would be interested in forming a group.

> There *are* 50 *students* in my English class.

> There *is* a horrifying *study* on child abuse in *Psychology Today*.

Indefinite pronouns such as *each, either, one, everyone, everybody*, and *everything* are singular.

> *Somebody* in Detroit *loves* me.

> *Does either* [one] of you have a pencil?

> *Neither* of my brothers *has* a car.

Indefinite pronouns such as *several, few, both*, and *many* are plural.

> *Both* of my sorority sisters *have* decided to live off campus.

> *Few seek* the enlightenment of transcendental meditation.

Indefinite pronouns such as *all, some, most*, and *none* may be singular or plural depending on their referents.

> *Some* of the food *is* cold.

> *Some* of the vegetables *are* cold.

> I can think of some retorts, but *none* seem appropriate.

> *None* of the children *is* as sweet as Sally.

Fractions such as *one-half* and *one-third* may be singular or plural depending on the referent.

> *Half* of the mail *has* been delivered.

> *Half* of the letters *have* been read.

Subjects joined by *and* take a plural verb unless the subjects are thought to be one item or unit.

> *Jim* and *Tammy were* televangelists.

> *Earth, Wind, and Fire is* my favorite group.

In cases when the subjects are joined by *or, nor, either…or*, or *neither…nor*, the verb must agree with the subject closer to it.

> Either the teacher or the *students are* responsible.

> Neither the students nor the *teacher is* responsible.

Relative pronouns, such as *who, which*, or *that*, which refer to plural antecedents require plural verbs. However, when the relative pronoun refers to a singular subject, the pronoun takes a singular verb.

> She is one of the girls *who cheer* on Friday nights.

> She is the only cheerleader *who has* a broken leg.

Subjects preceded by *every, each*, and *many a* are singular.

> *Every* man, woman, and child *was* given a life preserver.

> *Each* undergraduate *is* required to pass a proficiency exam.

> *Many a* tear *has* to fall before one matures.

A collective noun, such as *audience, faculty, jury,* etc., requires a singular verb when the group is regarded as a whole, and a plural verb when the members of the group are regarded as individuals.

The *jury has* made its decision.

The *faculty are* preparing their grade rosters.

Subjects preceded by *the number of* or *the percentage of* are singular, while subjects preceded by *a number of* or *a percentage of* are plural.

The number of vacationers in Florida *increases* every year.

A number of vacationers are young couples.

Titles of books, companies, name brands, and groups are singular or plural depending on their meaning.

Great Expectations is my favorite novel.

The *Rolling Stones are* performing in the Superdome.

Certain nouns of Latin and Greek origin have unusual singular and plural forms.

Singular	**Plural**
criterion	criteria
alumnus	alumni
datum	data
medium	media

The *data are* available for inspection.

The only *criterion* for membership *is* a high GPA.

Some nouns such as *deer, shrimp,* and *sheep* have the same spellings for both their singular and plural forms. In these cases, the meaning of the sentence will determine whether they are singular or plural.

Deer are beautiful animals.

The spotted *deer is* licking the sugar cube.

Some nouns like *scissors, jeans,* and *wages* have plural forms but no singular counterparts. These nouns almost always take plural verbs.

The *scissors are* on the table.

My new *jeans fit* me like a glove.

Words used as examples, not as grammatical parts of the sentence, require singular verbs.

Can't is the contraction for "cannot."

Cats is the plural form of "cat."

Mathematical expressions of subtraction and division require singular verbs, while expressions of addition and multiplication take either singular or plural verbs.

Ten *divided* by two *equals* five.

Five *times* two *equals* ten.

OR   Five *times* two *equal* ten.

Nouns expressing time, distance, weight, and measurement are singular when they refer to a unit and plural when they refer to separate items.

Fifty yards is a short distance.

Ten years have passed since I finished college.

Expressions of quantity are usually plural.

Nine out of ten dentists *recommend* that their patients floss.

Some nouns ending in *-ics*, such as *economics* and *ethics*, take singular verbs when they refer to principles or a field of study; however, when they refer to individual practices, they usually take plural verbs.

Ethics is being taught in the spring.

His unusual business *ethics are* what got him into trouble.

Some nouns like *measles, news*, and *calculus* appear to be plural but are actually singular in number. These nouns require singular verbs.

Measles is a very contagious disease.

Calculus requires great skill in algebra.

A verbal noun (infinitive or gerund) serving as a subject is treated as singular, even if the object of the verbal phrase is plural.

Hiding your mistakes *does* not make them go away.

To run five miles *is* my goal.

A noun phrase or clause acting as the subject of a sentence requires a singular verb.

What I need is to be loved.

Whether there is any connection between them is unknown.

Clauses beginning with *what* may be singular or plural depending on the meaning, that is, whether *what* means "the thing" or "the things."

What I want for Christmas is a new motorcycle.

What matters are Clinton's ideas.

A plural subject followed by a singular appositive requires a plural verb; similarly, a singular subject followed by a plural appositive requires a singular verb.

When the girls throw a party, *they* each bring a *gift*.

The *board*, all ten members, *is* meeting today.

■ Drill: Verbs ■

DIRECTIONS: Choose the correct option.

1. If you <u>had been concerned</u> about Marilyn, you <u>would have went</u> to greater lengths to ensure her safety.

   (A) had been concern…would have gone

   (B) was concerned…would have gone

   (C) had been concerned…would have gone

   (D) No change is necessary.

2. Susan <u>laid</u> in bed too long and missed her class.

   (A) lays   (C) lied

   (B) lay   (D) No change is necessary.

3. The Great Wall of China <u>is</u> fifteen hundred miles long; it <u>was built</u> in the third century B.C.E.

   (A) was…was built   (C) has been…was built

   (B) is…is built   (D) No change is necessary.

4. Joe stated that the class <u>began</u> at 10:30 a.m.

(A) begins

(B) had begun

(C) was beginning

(D) No change is necessary.

5. The ceiling of the Sistine Chapel <u>was</u> painted by Michelangelo; it <u>depicted</u> scenes from the Creation in the Old Testament.

(A) was...depicts

(B) is...depicts

(C) has been...depicting

(D) No change is necessary.

6. After Christmas <u>comes</u> the best sales.

(A) has come

(B) come

(C) is coming

(D) No change is necessary.

7. The bakery's specialty <u>are</u> wedding cakes.

(A) is

(B) were

(C) be

(D) No change is necessary.

8. Every man, woman, and child <u>were given</u> a life preserver.

(A) have been given

(B) had gave

(C) was given

(D) No change is necessary.

9. Hiding your mistakes <u>don't</u> make them go away.

(A) doesn't

(B) do not

(C) have not

(D) No change is necessary.

10. The Board of Regents <u>has recommended</u> a tuition increase.

(A) have recommended

(B) has recommend

(C) had recommended

(D) No change is necessary.

Sentence Structure

ETS asks that you be able to identify errors in comparison, coordination, correlation, negation, and parallelism.

Comparison

Sometimes, when we need to compare things, we use comparative adjectives such as *new,* *newer,* and *newest.* Consider the following chart:

Positive	Comparative	Superlative
good	better	best
well	better	best
bad	worse	worst
far	farther	farthest
far	further	furthest
little	littler, less(er)	littlest, least
many	more	most

Subordination, Coordination, and Predication

Suppose, for the sake of clarity, you wanted to combine the information in these two sentences to create one statement:

> I studied a foreign language. I found English quite easy.

How you decide to combine this information should be determined by the relationship you'd like to show between the two facts. *I studied a foreign language, and I found English quite easy* seems rather illogical. The **coordination** of the two ideas (connecting them with the coordinating conjunction *and)* is ineffective. Using **subordination** instead (connecting the sentences with a subordinating conjunction) clearly shows the degree of relative importance between the expressed ideas:

> After I studied a foreign language, I found English quite easy.

When using a conjunction, be sure that the sentence parts you are joining are in agreement.

INCORRECT: She loved him dearly but not his dog.

CORRECT: She loved him dearly but she did not love his dog.

A common mistake that is made is to forget that each member of the pair must be followed by the same kind of construction.

INCORRECT: They complimented them for their bravery and they thanked them for their being kind.

CORRECT: They complimented them for their bravery and thanked them for their kindness.

While refers to time and should not be used as a substitute for *although*, *and*, or *but*.

INCORRECT: While I'm usually interested in Fellini movies, I'd rather not go tonight.

CORRECT: Although I'm usually interested in Fellini movies, I'd rather not go tonight.

Where refers to time and should not be used as a substitute for *that*.

INCORRECT: We read in the paper where they are making great strides in DNA research.

CORRECT: We read in the paper that they are making great strides in DNA research.

After words like "reason" and "explanation," use *that*, not *because*.

INCORRECT: His explanation for his tardiness was because his alarm did not go off.

CORRECT: His explanation for his tardiness was that his alarm did not go off.

■ Drill: Sentence Structure Skills ■

DIRECTIONS: Choose the sentence that expresses the thought most clearly and that has no error in structure.

1. (A) Many gases are invisible, odorless, and they have no taste.

   (B) Many gases are invisible, odorless, and have no taste.

   (C) Many gases are invisible, odorless, and tasteless.

2. (A) Everyone agreed that she had neither the voice or the skill to be a speaker.

   (B) Everyone agreed that she had neither the voice nor the skill to be a speaker.

   (C) Everyone agreed that she had either the voice nor the skill to be a speaker.

3. (A) The mayor will be remembered because he kept his campaign promises and because of his refusal to accept political favors.

   (B) The mayor will be remembered because he kept his campaign promises and because he refused to accept political favors.

   (C) The mayor will be remembered because of his refusal to accept political favors and he kept his campaign promises.

4. (A) While taking a shower, the doorbell rang.

   (B) While I was taking a shower, the doorbell rang.

   (C) While taking a shower, someone rang the doorbell.

5. (A) He swung the bat, while the runner stole second base.

   (B) The runner stole second base while he swung the bat.

   (C) While he was swinging the bat, the runner stole second base.

DIRECTIONS: Choose the correct option.

6. Nothing grows as well in Mississippi as <u>cotton. Cotton</u> being the state's principal crop.

   (A) cotton, cotton   (C) cotton cotton

   (B) cotton; cotton   (D) No change is necessary.

7. It was a heartwrenching <u>movie; one</u> that I had never seen before.

   (A) movie and   (C) movie. One

   (B) movie, one   (D) No change is necessary.

8. Traffic was stalled for three miles on the <u>bridge. Because</u> repairs were being made.

   (A) bridge because   (C) bridge, because

   (B) bridge; because   (D) No change is necessary.

9. The ability to write complete sentences comes with <u>practice writing</u> run-on sentences seems to occur naturally.

(A) practice, writing

(B) practice. Writing

(C) practice and

(D) No change is necessary.

10. Even though she had taken French classes, she could not understand native French <u>speakers they</u> all spoke too fast.

(A) speakers, they

(B) speakers. They

(C) speaking

(D) No change is necessary.

Negation

Negation takes many forms. Essentially, it is when you discuss an idea in the negative. Take these examples:

I _am_ tired/ I _am not (I'm not)_ tired.

You _are going_ to be early/ You _are not (aren't)_ going to be late.

We _were_ happy/We _were not_ happy. (_weren't_)

Bill _was waiting_/Bill _was not waiting_. (_wasn't_)

They _will come_.	They _will not come_. (_won't come_)
Bob _can read_.	Bob _cannot read_. (_can't read_)
We _could help_.W	e _could not help_. (_couldn't help_)
You _may go_ now.	You _may not go_ now.

1. present simple:

I _love_ reading.	I _do not love_ reading. (_don't_)
Sue _drives_ a Mini.	Sue _does not drive_ a Mini. (_doesn't_)
He _reads_ a lot.	He _does not read_ a lot. (_doesn't_)
They _do_ their work well.	They _do not do_ their work well. (_don't_)

2. past simple:

They _lived_ on an island.	They _did not live_ on an island. (_didn't_)
I _knew_ the answer.	I _did not know_ the answer. (_didn't_)
She _did_ the washing-up.	She _did not do_ the washing-up. (_didn't_)
We _had_ pasta for lunch.	We _did not have_ pasta for lunch. (_didn't_)

3. present perfect:

He _has finished_ eating.	He _has not finished eating_. (_hasn't_)
They _have called_.	They _have not called_. (_haven't_)
I _have been waiting long_.	I _have not been waiting long_. (_haven't_)
They _have received_ it.	They _have not received_ it. (_haven't_)

4. past perfect:

They had closed.	They had not closed. (_hadn't_)
It had begun.	It had not begun. (_hadn't_)
He had been studying.	He had not been studying. (_hadn't_)
We had worked.	We had not worked. (_hadn't_)

Parallelism

Parallel structure is used to express matching ideas. It refers to the grammatical balance of a series of any of the following:

Phrases:

The squirrel ran along the _fence_, up the _tree_, and into his _burrow_ with a mouthful of acorns.

Adjectives:

The job market is flooded with _very_ talented, _highly_ motivated, and _well-educated_ young people.

Nouns:

You will need a *notebook*, *pencil*, and *dictionary* for the test.

Clauses:

The children were told to decide *which toy they would keep* and *which toy they would give away*.

Verbs:

The farmer plowed, planted, and harvested his corn in record time.

Verbals:

Reading, writing, and calculating are fundamental skills that all of us should possess.

Correlative conjunctions:

Either you will do your homework or you will fail.

Repetition of structural signals:

(such as articles, auxiliaries, prepositions, and conjunctions)

INCORRECT: I have quit my job, enrolled in school, and am looking for a reliable babysitter.

CORRECT: I have quit my job, have enrolled in school, and am looking for a reliable babysitter.

Note: Repetition of prepositions is considered formal and is not necessary.

You can travel by car, by plane, or by train; it's all up to you.

OR

You can travel by car, plane, or train; it's all up to you.

When a sentence contains items in a series, check for both punctuation and sentence balance. When you check for punctuation, make sure the commas are used correctly. When you check for parallelism, make sure that the conjunctions connect similar grammatical constructions, such as all adjectives or all clauses.

Misplaced and Dangling Modifiers

A misplaced modifier is one that is in the wrong place in the sentence. Misplaced modifiers come in all forms—words, phrases, and clauses. Sentences containing misplaced modifiers are often very comical: *Mom made me eat the spinach instead of my brother*. Misplaced modifiers, like the one in this sentence, are usually too far away from the word or words they modify. This sentence should read: *Mom made me, instead of my brother, eat the spinach*.

Modifiers like *only*, *nearly*, and *almost* should be placed next to the word they modify and not in front of some other word, especially a verb, that they are not intended to modify.

A modifier is misplaced if it appears to modify the wrong part of the sentence or if we cannot be certain what part of the sentence the writer intended it to modify. To correct a misplaced modifier, move the modifier next to the word it describes.

INCORRECT: She served hamburgers to the men on paper plates.

CORRECT: She served hamburgers on paper plates to the men.

Split infinitives also result in misplaced modifiers. Infinitives consist of the marker *to* plus the plain form of the verb. The two parts of the infinitive make up a grammatical unit that should not be split. Splitting an infinitive is placing an adverb between the *to* and the verb.

INCORRECT: The weather service expects temperatures to not rise.

CORRECT: The weather service expects temperatures not to rise.

Sometimes a split infinitive may be natural and preferable, though it may still bother some readers.

EX: Several U.S. industries expect to more than triple their use of robots within the next decade.

A squinting modifier is one that may refer to either a preceding or a following word, leaving the reader uncertain about what it is intended to modify. Correct a squinting modifier by moving it next to the word it is intended to modify.

INCORRECT: Snipers who fired on the soldiers often escaped capture.

CORRECT: Snipers who often fired on the soldiers escaped capture.

OR   Snipers who fired on the soldiers escaped capture often.

A dangling modifier is a modifier or verb in search of a subject: the modifying phrase (usually an *-ing* word group, an *-ed* or *-en* word group, or a *to + a verb* word group—participle phrase or infinitive phrase respectively) either appears to modify the wrong word or has nothing to modify. It is literally dangling at the beginning or the end of a sentence. The sentences often look and sound correct: *To be a student government officer, your grades must be above average.* (However, the verbal modifier has nothing to describe. Who is *to be a student government officer*? Your grades?) Questions of this type require you to determine whether a modifier has a headword or whether it is dangling at the beginning or the end of the sentence.

To correct a dangling modifier, reword the sentence by either: 1) changing the modifying phrase to a clause with a subject, or 2) changing the subject of the sentence to the word that should be modified. The following are examples of a dangling gerund, a dangling infinitive, and a dangling participle:

INCORRECT:	Shortly after leaving home, the accident occurred.
	Who is <u>leaving home</u>, the accident?
CORRECT:	Shortly after we left home, the accident occurred.

INCORRECT:	To get up on time, a great effort was needed.
	<u>To get up</u> needs a subject.
CORRECT:	To get up on time, I made a great effort.

Fragments

A fragment is an incomplete construction which may or may not have a subject and a verb. Specifically, a fragment is a group of words pretending to be a sentence. Not all fragments appear as separate sentences, however. Often, fragments are separated by semicolons.

INCORRECT:	Traffic was stalled for ten miles on the freeway. Because repairs were being made on potholes.
CORRECT:	Traffic was stalled for ten miles on the freeway because repairs were being made on potholes.

INCORRECT:	It was a funny story; one that I had never heard before.
CORRECT:	It was a funny story, one that I had never heard before.

Run-on/Fused Sentences

A run-on/fused sentence is not necessarily a long sentence or a sentence that the reader considers too long; in fact, a run-on may be two short sentences: *Dry ice does not melt it evaporates.* A run-on results when the writer fuses or runs together two separate sentences without any correct mark of punctuation separating them.

INCORRECT:	Knowing how to use a dictionary is no problem each dictionary has a section in the front of the book telling how to use it.
CORRECT:	Knowing how to use a dictionary is no problem. Each dictionary has a section in the front of the book telling how to use it.

Even if one or both of the fused sentences contains internal punctuation, the sentence is still a run-on.

INCORRECT:	Bob bought dress shoes, a suit, and a nice shirt he needed them for his sister's wedding.
CORRECT:	Bob bought dress shoes, a suit, and a nice shirt. He needed them for his sister's wedding.

Comma Splices

A comma splice is the unjustifiable use of only a comma to combine what really is two separate sentences.

INCORRECT:	One common error in writing is incorrect spelling, the other is the occasional use of faulty diction.
CORRECT:	One common error in writing is incorrect spelling; the other is the occasional use of faulty diction.

Both run-on sentences and comma splices may be corrected in one of the following ways:

RUN-ON:	Neal won the award he had the highest score.
COMMA SPLICE:	Neal won the award, he had the highest score.

Separate the sentences with a period:

Neal won the award. He had the highest score.

Separate the sentences with a comma and a coordinating conjunction (*and*, *but*, *or*, *nor*, *for*, *yet*, *so*):

Neal won the award for he had the highest score.

Separate the sentences with a semicolon:

Neal won the award; he had the highest score.

Separate the sentences with a subordinating conjunction such as *although*, *because*, *since*, *if*:

Neal won the award because he had the highest score.

WORD CHOICE/MECHANICS

ETS asks that you be able to correct errors in word choice (idioms, commonly confused words, wrong word use, redundancy), mechanics (capitalization, punctuation of commas, semicolons, and apostrophes) as well as sentences free from errors.

Connotative and Denotative Meanings

The denotative meaning of a word is its *literal,* dictionary definition: what the word denotes or "means." The connotative meaning of a word is what the word connotes or "suggests"; it is a meaning apart from what the word literally means. A writer should choose a word based on the tone and context of the sentence; this ensures that a word bears the appropriate connotation while still conveying some exactness in denotation. For example, a gift might be described as "cheap," but the directness of this word has a negative connotation—something cheap is something of little or no value. The word "inexpensive" has a more positive connotation, though "cheap" is a synonym for "inexpensive." Questions of this type require you to make a decision regarding the appropriateness of words and phrases for the context of a sentence.

Wordiness and Conciseness

Effective writing is concise. Wordiness, on the other hand, decreases the clarity of expression by cluttering sentences with unnecessary words.

Wordiness questions test your ability to detect redundancies (unnecessary repetitions), circumlocution (failure to get to the point), and padding with loose synonyms. Wordiness questions require you to choose sentences that use as few words as possible to convey a message clearly, economically, and effectively.

Notice the difference in impact between the first and second sentences in the following pairs:

INCORRECT:	The medical exam that he gave me was entirely complete.
CORRECT:	The medical exam he gave me was complete.
INCORRECT:	Larry asked his friend John, who was a good, old friend, if he would join him and go along with him to see the foreign film made in Japan.
CORRECT:	Larry asked his good, old friend John if he would join him in seeing the Japanese film.
INCORRECT:	I was absolutely, totally happy with the present that my parents gave to me at 7 a.m. on the morning of my birthday.
CORRECT:	I was happy with the present my parents gave me on the morning of my birthday.

■ Drill: Word Choice Skills ■

DIRECTIONS: Choose the correct option.

1. His <u>principal</u> reasons for resigning were his <u>principles</u> of right and wrong.

   (A) principal...principals   (C) principle...principles

   (B) principle...principals   (D) No change is necessary.

2. The book tells about Alzheimer's disease—how it <u>affects</u> the patient and what <u>effect</u> it has on the patient's family.

   (A) effects...affect   (C) effects...effects

   (B) affects...affect   (D) No change is necessary.

3. The <u>amount</u> of homeless children we can help depends on the <u>number</u> of available shelters.

   (A) number…number   (C) number…amount

   (B) amount…amount   (D) No change is necessary.

4. All students are <u>suppose to</u> pass the test before <u>achieving</u> upper-division status.

   (A) suppose to…acheiving

   (B) suppose to…being achieved

   (C) supposed to…achieving

   (D) No change is necessary.

5. The reason he <u>succeeded</u> is <u>because</u> he worked hard.

   (A) succeeded…that   (C) succede…because of

   (B) seceded…that   (D) No change is necessary.

DIRECTIONS: Select the sentence that clearly and effectively states the idea and has no structural errors.

6. (A) South of Richmond, the two roads converge together to form a single highway.

   (B) South of Richmond, the two roads converge together to form an interstate highway.

   (C) South of Richmond, the two roads converge to form an interstate highway.

   (D) South of Richmond, the two roads converge to form a single interstate highway.

7. (A) The student depended on his parents for financial support.

   (B) The student lacked the ways and means to pay for his room and board, so he depended on his parents for this kind of money and support.

   (C) The student lacked the ways and means or the wherewithal to support himself, so his parents provided him with the financial support he needed.

   (D) The student lacked the means to pay for his room and board, so he depended on his parents for financial support.

8. (A) Vincent van Gogh and Paul Gauguin were close personal friends and companions who enjoyed each other's company and frequently worked together on their artwork.

   (B) Vincent van Gogh and Paul Gauguin were friends who frequently painted together.

   (C) Vincent van Gogh was a close personal friend of Paul Gauguin's, and the two of them often worked together on their artwork because they enjoyed each other's company.

   (D) Vincent van Gogh, a close personal friend of Paul Gauguin's, often worked with him on their artwork.

9. (A) A college education often involves putting away childish thoughts, which are characteristic of youngsters, and concentrating on the future, which lies ahead.

   (B) A college education involves putting away childish thoughts, which are characteristic of youngsters, and concentrating on the future.

   (C) A college education involves putting away childish thoughts and concentrating on the future.

   (D) A college education involves putting away childish thoughts and concentrating on the future which lies ahead.

10. (A) I had the occasion to visit an Oriental pagoda while I was a tourist on vacation and visiting in Kyoto, Japan.

    (B) I visited a Japanese pagoda in Kyoto.

    (C) I had occasion to visit a pagoda when I was vacationing in Kyoto, Japan.

    (D) On my vacation, I visited a Japanese pagoda in Kyoto.

Idiomatic expressions

An idiom is a phrase where the words together have a meaning that is different from the dictionary definitions of the individual words. For instance: "a fresh pair of eyes" = A person who is brought in to examine something carefully. It doesn't literally mean a fresh pair of eyes. ESL students in particular need to be on the lookout for idiomatic expressions as they can be confusing for non-native speakers.

Commonly confused words

The following is a list of twenty commonly confused words. These are words that can confuse a writer because they sound alike or are nearly alike.

ACCEPT	to receive She accepts defeat well.
EXCEPT	to take or leave out Please take all the shoes off the shelf except for the red one.
AFFECT	*v.,* to influence Lack of sleep affects the quality of your life.
EFFECT	*n.,* result, The subtle effect of the storm made the room look ominous.
A LOT	(two words)-many.
ALOT	(one word)-Not the correct form.
ALLUSION	an indirect reference The professor made an allusion to John Donne's work.
ILLUSION	a false perception of reality They saw an oasis: that is a type of illusion one sees in the desert.
ASCENT	climb The airplane's ascent made my ears pop.
ASSENT	agreement The alien assented to undergo experiments.
BREATH	noun, air inhaled or exhaled You could see his breath in the cold air.
BREATHE	verb, to inhale or exhale If you don't breathe, then you are dead.
CAPITAL	seat of government. Also financial resources. The capital of New Jersey is Trenton. The company had enough capital to build the new plant.
CAPITOL	the actual building in which the legislative body meets The governor announced his plan in a speech given at the capitol today.
CITE	to quote or document I cited five ideas from the same author in my paper.
SIGHT	vision The sight of the Twin Towers arouses different emotions in different parts of the country.
SITE	position or place The new housing complex was built on the site of a cemetery.

(continued on next page)

COMPLEMENT	noun, something that completes; verb, to complete A red wine complements a meat entree.
COMPLIMENT	noun, praise; verb, to praise The professor complimented Sue on her essay.
CONSCIENCE	sense of right and wrong The boy's conscience kept him from lying.
CONSCIOUS	awake I was conscious when the you got home.
ELICIT	to draw or bring out The professor elicited the correct response from the student.
ILLICIT	illegal The gang leader was arrested for his illicit activities.
ITS	of or belonging to it The puppy will cry as soon as its owner walks out of the room.
IT'S	contraction for it is It's a gorgeous day today.
LEAD	noun, a type of metal Is that pipe made of lead?
LED	verb, past tense of the verb "to lead" She led the them over the mountain.
LIE	to lie down (a person or animal. *hint: people can tell lies*) I feel sick, so I'm going to lie down for a while. *(also lying, lay, has/have lain—The dog has lain in the shade all day; yesterday, the dog lay there for twelve hours).*
LAY	to lay an object down. Lay down that gun. *(also laying, laid, has/have laid—At that point, Pappy laid the shotgun on the ground).*
LOSE	verb, to misplace or not win Dad should not lose the keys.
LOOSE	adjective, to not be tight; verb (rarely used)—to release His pants were so loose that they fell down. The dog was never set loose from his leash.
PASSED	verb, past tense of "to pass," to have moved The hurricane passed through the city quickly, but it caused great damage.
PAST	belonging to a former time or place Who was the past president of this organization?
PRECEDE	to come before Studying precedes graduation.
PROCEED	to go forward He proceeded to pass back the essays.

PRINCIPAL	adjective, most important; noun, a person who has authority The principal element in the job is hard work. The principal of the school reads the school news each morning.
PRINCIPLE	a general or fundamental truth The course was based on the principles of ethics.
THAN	use with comparisons I would rather go out to eat than stay in.
THEN	at that time, or next I studied for my exam for three hours, and then I went to bed.
THEIR	possessive form of they Their house is at the end of the street.
THERE	indicates location (hint: think of "here and there") There goes my chance of dating him!
THEY'RE	contraction for "they are" They're in Australia for the summer—again!
WHO	pronoun, referring to a person or persons I wondered how Sam, who is funny, could be alone at the table.
WHICH	pronoun, replacing a singular or plural thing(s);not used to refer to persons Which section of English did you get into?
THAT	used to refer to things or a group or class of people I lost the book that I bought last week.

Wrong word use

Wrong word use means choosing awkward, confusing, or overly formal words which are poor choices. If you wish to write with clarity and grace, you must be willing to spend some time thinking about the words you use as well as their sounds, rhythms, and connotations. Avoid words that are either too pretentious or too colloquial, and beware of jargon. Try to use language that is vivid and precise; a sentence that relies on vague and abstract language will be difficult to understand.

Redundancy

In his book *The Elements of Style*, William Strunk explains, "Vigorous writing is concise. A sentence should contain no unnecessary words, a paragraph no unnecessary sentences, for the same reason that a drawing should have no unnecessary lines and a machine no unnecessary parts. This requires not that the writer make all his sentences short, or that he avoid all detail and treat his subjects only in outline, but that every word tell." When you write, avoid saying things twice (*12 midnight* as opposed to *midnight*, *exactly the same* as opposed to *the same*, *the end result* vs. *the result*) and be ready to pare down your writing to make it simpler and less wordy.

CAPITALIZATION

When a word is capitalized, it calls attention to itself. This attention should be for a good reason. There are standard uses for capital letters. In general, capitalize (1) all proper nouns, (2) the first word of a sentence, and (3) the first word of a direct quotation.

You should also capitalize

Names of ships, aircraft, spacecraft, and trains:

Apollo 13	*Mariner IV*
DC-10	S.S. United States
Sputnik II	Boeing 707

Names of deities:

God	Jupiter
Allah	Holy Ghost
Buddha	Venus
Jehovah	Shiva

Geological periods:

Neolithic age	Cenozoic era
late Pleistocene times	Ice Age

Names of astronomical bodies:

Mercury	Big Dipper
the Milky Way	Halley's comet
Ursa Major	North Star

Personifications:

Reliable Nature brought her promised Spring.

Bring on Melancholy in his sad might.

She believed that Love was the answer to all her problems.

Historical periods:

the Middle Ages	World War I
Reign of Terror	Great Depression
Christian Era	Roaring Twenties
Age of Louis XIV	Renaissance

Organizations, associations, and institutions:

Girl Scouts	North Atlantic Treaty Organization
Kiwanis Club	League of Women Voters
New York Yankees	Unitarian Church
Smithsonian Institution	Common Market
Library of Congress	Franklin Glen High School
New York Philharmonic	Harvard University

Government and judicial groups:

United States Court of Appeals	Senate
Committee on Foreign Affairs	Parliament
New Jersey City Council	Peace Corps
Arkansas Supreme Court	Census Bureau
House of Representatives	Department of State

A general term that accompanies a specific name is capitalized only if it follows the specific name. If it stands alone or comes before the specific name, it is put in lowercase:

Washington State	the state of Washington
Senator Dixon	the senator from Illinois
Central Park	the park
Golden Gate Bridge	the bridge
President Obama	the president of the United States
Pope Benedict XVI	the pope
Queen Elizabeth II	the queen of England
Tropic of Capricorn	the tropics

Monroe Doctrine	the doctrine of expansion
the Mississippi River	the river
Easter Day	the day
Treaty of Versailles	the treaty
Webster's Dictionary	the dictionary
Equatorial Current	the equator

Use a capital to start a sentence:

Our car would not start.

When will you leave? I need to know right away.

Never!

Let me in! Please!

When a sentence appears within a sentence, start it with a capital letter:

We had only one concern: When would we eat?

My sister said, "I'll find the Monopoly game."

He answered, "We can only stay a few minutes."

The most important words of titles are capitalized. Those words not capitalized are conjunctions (*and, or, but*) and short prepositions (*of, on, by, for*). The first and last word of a title must always be capitalized:

A Man for All Seasons	*Crime and Punishment*
Of Mice and Men	*Rise of the West*
Strange Life of Ivan Osokin	"Sonata in G Minor"
"Let Me In"	"Ode to Billy Joe"
"Rubaiyat of Omar Khayyam"	"All in the Family"

Capitalize newspaper and magazine titles:

U.S. News & World Report

National Geographic

The New York Times

The Washington Post

Capitalize radio and TV station call letters:

ABC	NBC
WNEW	WBOP
CNN	HBO

Do not capitalize compass directions or seasons:

west	north
east	south
spring	winter
autumn	summer

Capitalize regions:

the South	the Northeast
the West	Eastern Europe

BUT: the south of France

the east part of town

Capitalize specific military units:

the U.S. Army

the 7th Fleet

the German Navy

the 1st Infantry Division

Capitalize political groups and philosophies:

Democrat	Communist
Marxist	Nazism
Whig	Federalist
Existentialism	Transcendentalism

BUT do not capitalize systems of government or individual adherents to a philosophy:

democracy	communism
fascist	agnostic

■ Drill: Capitalization ■

DIRECTIONS: Choose the correct option.

1. Mexico is the southernmost country in <u>North America</u>. It borders the United States on the north; it is bordered on the <u>south</u> by Belize and Guatemala.

   (A) north America…South

   (B) North America…South

   (C) North america…south

   (D) No change is necessary.

2. (A) Until 1989, Tom Landry was the only Coach the Dallas cowboys ever had.

   (B) Until 1989, Tom Landry was the only coach the Dallas Cowboys ever had.

   (C) Until 1989, Tom Landry was the only Coach the Dallas Cowboys ever had.

3. The <u>Northern Hemisphere</u> is the half of the <u>earth</u> that lies north of the <u>Equator.</u>

   (A) Northern hemisphere…earth…equator

   (B) Northern hemisphere…Earth…Equator

   (C) Northern Hemisphere…earth…equator

   (D) No change is necessary.

4. (A) My favorite works by Ernest Hemingway are "The Snows of Kilamanjaro," *The Sun Also Rises,* and *For Whom the Bell Tolls.*

   (B) My favorite works by Ernest Hemingway are "The Snows Of Kilamanjaro," *The Sun Also Rises,* and *For Whom The Bell Tolls.*

   (C) My favorite works by Ernest Hemingway are "The Snows of Kilamanjaro," *The Sun also Rises,* and *For whom the Bell Tolls.*

5. Aphrodite (<u>Venus in Roman Mythology</u>) was the <u>Greek</u> goddess of love.

   (A) Venus in Roman mythology…greek

   (B) venus in roman mythology…Greek

(C) Venus in Roman mythology...Greek

(D) No change is necessary.

6. The <u>Koran</u> is considered by <u>Muslims</u> to be the holy word.

(A) koran...muslims

(B) koran...Muslims

(C) Koran...muslims

(D) No change is necessary.

7. (A) The freshman curriculum at the community college includes english, a foreign language, Algebra I, and history.

(B) The freshman curriculum at the community college includes English, a foreign language, Algebra I, and history.

(C) The Freshman curriculum at the Community College includes English, a foreign language, Algebra I, and History.

8. At the <u>spring</u> graduation ceremonies, the university awarded over 2,000 <u>bachelor's</u> degrees.

(A) Spring...Bachelor's

(B) spring...Bachelor's

(C) Spring...bachelor's

(D) No change is necessary.

9. The fall of the <u>Berlin wall</u> was an important symbol of the collapse of <u>Communism</u>.

(A) berlin Wall...communism

(B) Berlin Wall...communism

(C) berlin wall...Communism

(D) No change is necessary.

10. A photograph of <u>mars</u> was printed in <u>the *New York Times*</u>.

(A) Mars...*The New York Times*

(B) mars...*The New York times*

(C) mars...*The New York Times*

(D) No change is necessary.

PUNCTUATION

Commas

Commas should be placed according to standard rules of punctuation for purpose, clarity, and effect. The proper use of commas is explained in the following rules and examples:

In a series:

When more than one adjective describes a noun, use a comma to separate and emphasize each adjective. The comma takes the place of the word *and* in the series.

> the long, dark passageway
>
> another confusing, sleepless night
>
> an elaborate, complex, brilliant plan
>
> the old, grey, crumpled hat

Some adjective-noun combinations are thought of as one word. In these cases, the adjective in front of the adjective-noun combination needs no comma. If you inserted *and* between the adjective-noun combination, it would not make sense.

> a stately oak tree
>
> an exceptional wine glass
>
> my worst report card
>
> a china dinner plate

The comma is also used to separate words, phrases, and whole ideas (clauses); it still takes the place of *and* when used this way.

> an apple, a pear, a fig, and a banana
>
> a lovely lady, an elegant dress, and many admirers
>
> She lowered the shade, closed the curtain, turned off the light, and went to bed.

The only question that exists about the use of commas in a series is whether or not one should be used before the final item. It is standard usage to do so, although many newspapers and magazines have stopped using the final comma. Occasionally, the omission of the comma can be confusing.

INCORRECT: He got on his horse, tracked a rabbit and a deer and rode on to Canton.

We planned the trip with Mary and Harold, Susan, Dick and Joan, Gregory and Jean and Charles.

With a long introductory phrase:

Usually if a phrase of more than five or six words or a dependent clause precedes the subject at the beginning of a sentence, a comma is used to set it off.

After last night's fiasco at the disco, she couldn't bear the thought of looking at him again.

Whenever I try to talk about politics, my wife leaves the room.

Provided you have said nothing, they will never guess who you are.

It is not necessary to use a comma with a short sentence.

In January she will go to Switzerland.

After I rest I'll feel better.

During the day no one is home.

If an introductory phrase includes a verb form that is being used as another part of speech (a *verbal*), it must be followed by a comma.

INCORRECT: When eating Mary never looked up from her plate.

CORRECT: When eating, Mary never looked up from her plate.

INCORRECT: Because of her desire to follow her faith in James wavered.

CORRECT: Because of her desire to follow, her faith in James wavered.

INCORRECT: Having decided to leave Mary James wrote her a letter.

CORRECT: Having decided to leave Mary, James wrote her a letter.

To separate sentences with two main ideas:

To understand this use of the comma, you need to be able to recognize compound sentences. When a sentence contains more than two subjects and verbs (clauses), and the two clauses are joined by a conjunction (*and, but, or, nor, for, yet*), use a comma before the conjunction to show that another clause is coming.

> I thought I knew the poem by heart, but he showed me three lines I had forgotten.

> Are we really interested in helping the children, or are we more concerned with protecting our good names?

> He is supposed to leave tomorrow, but he is not ready to go.

> Jim knows you are disappointed, and he has known it for a long time.

If the two parts of the sentence are short and closely related, it is not necessary to use a comma.

> He threw the ball and the dog ran after it.

> Jane played the piano and Michael danced.

Be careful not to confuse a sentence that has a compound verb and a single subject with a compound sentence. If the subject is the same for both verbs, there is no need for a comma.

INCORRECT:	Charles sent some flowers, and wrote a long letter explaining why he had not been able to attend.
CORRECT:	Charles sent some flowers and wrote a long letter explaining why he had not been able to attend.
INCORRECT:	Last Thursday we went to the concert with Julia, and afterwards dined at an old Italian restaurant.
CORRECT:	Last Thursday we went to the concert with Julia and afterwards dined at an old Italian restaurant.

INCORRECT: For the third time, the teacher explained that the literacy level for high school students was much lower than it had been in previous years, and, this time, wrote the statistics on the board for everyone to see.

CORRECT: For the third time, the teacher explained that the literacy level for high school students was much lower than it had been in previous years and this time wrote the statistics on the board for everyone to see.

In general, words and phrases that stop the flow of the sentence or are unnecessary for the main idea are set off by commas.

Abbreviations after names:

Did you invite John Paul, Jr., and his sister?

Martha Harris, Ph.D., will be the speaker tonight.

Interjections (an exclamation without added grammatical connection):

Oh, I'm so glad to see you.

I tried so hard, alas, to do it.

Hey, let me out of here.

Direct address:

Roy, won't you open the door for the dog?

I can't understand, Mother, what you are trying to say.

May I ask, Mr. President, why you called us together?

Hey, lady, watch out for that car!

Tag questions:

You're really hungry, aren't you?

Jerry looks like his father, doesn't he?

Geographical names and addresses:

The concert will be held in Chicago, Illinois, on August 12.

The letter was addressed to Mrs. Marion Heartwell, 1881 Pine Lane, Palo Alto, CA 95824.

(Note: No comma is needed before the ZIP code, because it is already clearly set off from the state name.)

Transitional words and phrases:

On the other hand, I hope he gets better.

In addition, the phone rang constantly this afternoon.

I'm, nevertheless, going to the beach on Sunday.

You'll find, therefore, that no one is more loyal than I am.

Parenthetical words and phrases:

You will become, I believe, a great statesman.

We know, of course, that this is the only thing to do.

In fact, I planted corn last summer.

The Mannes affair was, to put it mildly, a surprise.

Unusual word order:

The dress, new and crisp, hung in the closet.

Intently, she stared out the window.

With nonrestrictive elements:

Parts of a sentence that modify other parts are sometimes essential to the meaning of the sentence and sometimes not. When a modifying word or group of words is not vital to the meaning of the sentence, it is set off by commas. Since it does not restrict the meaning of the words it modifies, it is called "nonrestrictive." Modifiers that are essential to the meaning of the sentence are called "restrictive" and are not set off by commas.

ESSENTIAL:	The girl *who wrote the story* is my sister.
NONESSENTIAL:	My sister, *the girl who wrote the story*, has always loved to write.

ESSENTIAL:	John Milton's famous poem *Paradise Lost* tells a remarkable story.
NONESSENTIAL:	Dante's greatest work, *The Divine Comedy*, marked the beginning of the Renaissance.

ESSENTIAL:	The cup *that is on the piano* is the one I want.
NONESSENTIAL:	The cup, *which my brother gave me last year*, is on the piano.

ESSENTIAL:	The people *who arrived late* were not seated.
NONESSENTIAL:	George, *who arrived late*, was not seated.

To set off direct quotations:

Most direct quotes or quoted materials are set off from the rest of the sentence by commas.

"Please read your part more loudly," the director insisted.

"I won't know what to do," said Michael, "if you leave me."

The teacher said sternly, "I will not dismiss this class until I have silence."

Who was it who said "Do not ask for whom the bell tolls; it tolls for thee"?

Note: Commas always go inside the closing quotation mark, even if the comma is not part of the material being quoted.

Be careful not to set off indirect quotes or quotes that are used as subjects or complements.

"To be or not to be" is the famous beginning of a soliloquy in Shakespeare's Hamlet. (subject)

She said she would never come back. (indirect quote)

Back then my favorite poem was "Evangeline." (complement)

<u>To set off contrasting elements:</u>

Her intelligence, not her beauty, got her the job.

Your plan will take you a little further from, rather than closer to, your destination.

It was a reasonable, though not appealing, idea.

He wanted glory, but found happiness instead.

<u>In dates:</u>

Both forms of the date are acceptable.

She will arrive on December 6, 2010.

He left on 5 August 2010.

In January 2010, he handed in his resignation.

On October 22, 1992, Frank and Julie were married.

Usually, when a subordinate clause is at the end of a sentence, no comma is necessary preceding the clause. However, when a subordinate clause introduces a sentence, a comma should be used after the clause. Some common subordinating conjunctions are:

after	so that
although	though
as	till
as if	unless
because	until
before	when
even though	whenever
if	while
inasmuch as	since

Semicolons

Questions testing semicolon usage require you to be able to distinguish between the semicolon and the comma, and the semicolon and the colon. This review section covers the basic uses of the semicolon: to separate independent clauses not joined by a coordinating conjunction, to separate independent clauses separated by a conjunctive adverb, and to separate items in a series with internal commas. It is important to be consistent; if you use a semicolon between *any* of the items in the series, you must use semicolons to separate *all* of the items in the series.

Usually, a comma follows the conjunctive adverb. Note also that a period can be used to separate two sentences joined by a conjunctive adverb. Some common conjunctive adverbs are:

accordingly	nevertheless
besides	next
consequently	nonetheless
finally	now
furthermore	on the other hand
however	otherwise
indeed	perhaps
in fact	still
moreover	therefore

Then is also used as a conjunctive adverb, but it is not usually followed by a comma.

Use the semicolon

to separate independent clauses which are not joined by a coordinating conjunction:

I understand how to use commas; the semicolon I have not yet mastered.

to separate two independent clauses connected by a conjunctive adverb:

He took great care with his work; *therefore*, he was very successful.

to combine two independent clauses connected by a coordinating conjunction if either or both of the clauses contain other internal punctuation:

Success in college, some maintain, requires intelligence, industry, and perseverance; *but* others, fewer in number, assert that only personality is important.

to separate items in a series when each item has internal punctuation:

I bought an old, dilapidated chair; an antique table, which was in beautiful condition; and a new, ugly, blue and white rug.

Call our customer service line for assistance: Arizona, 1-800-555-6020; New Mexico, 1-800-555-5050; California, 1-800-555-3140; or Nevada, 1-800-555-3214.

Do not use the semicolon

to separate a dependent and an independent clause:

INCORRECT: You should not make such statements; even though they are correct.

CORRECT: You should not make such statements even though they are correct.

to separate an appositive phrase or clause from a sentence:

INCORRECT: His immediate aim in life is centered on two things; becoming an engineer and learning to fly an airplane.

CORRECT: His immediate aim in life is centered on two things: becoming an engineer and learning to fly an airplane.

to precede an explanation or summary of the first clause:

Note: Although the sentence below is punctuated correctly, the use of the semicolon provides a miscue, suggesting that the second clause is merely an extension, not an explanation, of the first clause. The colon provides a better clue.

WEAK: The first week of camping was wonderful; we lived in cabins instead of tents.

BETTER: The first week of camping was wonderful: we lived in cabins instead of tents.

to substitute for a comma:

INCORRECT: My roommate also likes sports; particularly football, basketball, and baseball.

CORRECT: My roommate also likes sports, particularly football, basketball, and baseball.

to set off other types of phrases or clauses from a sentence:

INCORRECT: Being of a cynical mind; I should ask for a recount of the ballots.

CORRECT: Being of a cynical mind, I should ask for a recount of the ballots.

INCORRECT: The next meeting of the club has been postponed two weeks; inasmuch as both the president and vice-president are out of town.

CORRECT: The next meeting of the club has been postponed two weeks, inasmuch as both the president and vice-president are out of town.

Note: The semicolon is not a terminal mark of punctuation; therefore, it should not be followed by a capital letter unless the first word in the second clause ordinarily requires capitalization.

Colons

While it is true that a colon is used to precede a list, one must also make sure that a complete sentence precedes the colon. The colon signals the reader that a list, explanation, or restatement of the preceding will follow. It is like an arrow, indicating that something is to follow. The difference between the colon and the semicolon and between the colon and the period is that the colon is an introductory mark, not a terminal mark. Look at the following examples:

The Constitution provides for a separation of powers among the three branches of government.

government. The period signals a new sentence.

government; The semicolon signals an interrelated sentence.

government, The comma signals a coordinating conjunction followed by another independent clause.

government: The colon signals a list.

The Constitution provides for a separation of powers among the three branches of government: executive, legislative, and judicial.

Ensuring that a complete sentence precedes a colon means following these rules:

Use the colon to introduce a list (one item may constitute a list):

I hate this one course: English.

Three plays by William Shakespeare will be presented in repertory this summer at the University of Michigan: *Hamlet*, *Macbeth*, and *Othello*.

To introduce a list preceded by *as follows* or *the following*:

> The reasons she cited for her success are as follows: integrity, honesty, industry, and a pleasant disposition.

To separate two independent clauses, when the second clause is a restatement or explanation of the first:

> All of my high school teachers said one thing in particular: college is going to be difficult.

To introduce a word or word group which is a restatement, explanation, or summary of the first sentence:

> These two things he loved: tofu and chick peas.

To introduce a formal appositive:

> I am positive there is one appeal which you can't overlook: money.

To separate the introductory words from a quotation which follows, if the quotation is formal, long, or contained in its own paragraph:

> The actor then stated: "I would rather be able to adequately play the part of Hamlet than to perform a miraculous operation, deliver a great lecture, or build a magnificent skyscraper."

The colon should only be used after statements that are grammatically complete.

Do *not* use a colon after a verb:

INCORRECT: My favorite holidays are: Christmas, New Year's Eve, and Halloween.

CORRECT: My favorite holidays are Christmas, New Year's Eve, and Halloween.

Do *not* use a colon after a preposition:

INCORRECT: I enjoy different ethnic foods such as: Greek, Chinese, and Italian.

CORRECT: I enjoy different ethnic foods such as Greek, Chinese, and Italian.

Do *not* use a colon interchangeably with the dash:

INCORRECT: Mathematics, German, English: These gave me the greatest difficulty of all my studies.

CORRECT: Mathematics, German, English—these gave me the greatest difficulty of all my studies.

Information preceding the colon should be a complete sentence regardless of the explanatory information following the clause.

Do *not* use the colon before the words *for example, namely, that is,* or *for instance* even though these words may be introducing a list.

INCORRECT: We agreed to it: namely, to give him a surprise party.

CORRECT: There are a number of well-known American women writers: for example, Nikki Giovanni, Phillis Wheatley, Emily Dickinson, and Maya Angelou.

Colon usage questions test your knowledge of the colon preceding a list, restatement, or explanation. These questions also require you to be able to distinguish between the colon and the period, the colon and the comma, and the colon and the semicolon.

Apostrophes

Apostrophe questions require you to know when an apostrophe has been used appropriately to make a noun possessive, not plural. Remember the following rules when considering how to show possession.

Add *'s* to singular nouns and indefinite pronouns:

Tiffany's flowers

a dog's bark

everybody's computer

at the owner's expense

today's paper

Add *'s* to singular nouns ending in *s,* unless this distorts the pronunciation:

> Delores's paper
>
> the boss's pen
>
> Dr. Yots' class
>
> for righteousness' sake
>
> Dr. Evans's office OR Dr. Evans' office

Add *an apostrophe* to plural nouns ending in *s* or *es*:

> two cents' worth
>
> ladies' night
>
> thirteen years' experience
>
> two weeks' pay

Add *'s* to plural nouns not ending in *s:*

> men's room
>
> children's toys

Add *'s* to the last word in compound words or groups:

> brother-in-law's car
>
> someone else's paper

Add *'s* to the last name when indicating joint ownership:

> Joe and Edna's home
>
> Julie and Kathy's party
>
> women and children's clinic

Add *'s* to both names if you intend to show ownership by each person:

> Joe's and Edna's trucks
>
> Julie's and Kathy's pies
>
> Ted's and Jane's marriage vows

Possessive pronouns change their forms *without* the addition of an apostrophe:

> her, his, hers
>
> your, yours

their, theirs

it, its

Use the possessive form of a noun preceding a gerund:

His driving annoys me.

My bowling a strike irritated him.

Do you mind our stopping by?

We appreciate your coming.

Add 's to words and initials to show that they are plural:

no if's, and's, or but's

the do's and don't's of dating

three A's

IRA's are available at the bank.

Add s to numbers, symbols, and letters to show that they are plural:

TVs

VCRs

the 1800s

the returning POWs

Quotation Marks and Italics

These kinds of questions test your knowledge of the proper use of quotation marks with other marks of punctuation, with titles, and with dialogue. These kinds of questions also test your knowledge of the correct use of italics and underlining with titles and words used as sample words (for example, *the word _is_ is a common verb).*

The most common use of double quotation marks (") is to set off quoted words, phrases, and sentences.

"If everybody minded their own business," said the Duchess in a hoarse growl, "the world would go round a great deal faster than it does."

"Then you would say what you mean," the March Hare went on.

"I do," Alice hastily replied: "at least—at least I mean what I say—that's the same thing, you know."

—from Lewis Carroll's Alice in Wonderland

Single quotation marks are used to set off quoted material within a quote.

"Shall I bring 'Rime of the Ancient Mariner' along with us?" she asked her brother.

Mrs. Green said, "The doctor told me, 'Go immediately to bed when you get home!'"

"If she said that to me," Katherine insisted, "I would tell her, 'I never intend to speak to you again! Goodbye, Susan!'"

When writing dialogue, begin a new paragraph each time the speaker changes.

"Do you know what time it is?" asked Jane.

"Can't you see I'm busy?" snapped Mary.

"It's easy to see that you're in a bad mood today!" replied Jane.

Use quotation marks to enclose words used as words (sometimes italics are used for this purpose).

"Judgment" has always been a difficult word for me to spell.

Do you know what "abstruse" means?

"Horse and buggy" and "bread and butter" can be used either as adjectives or as nouns.

If slang is used within more formal writing, the slang words or phrases should be set off with quotation marks.

Harrison's decision to leave the conference and to "stick his neck out" by flying to Jamaica was applauded by the rest of the conference attendees.

When words are meant to have an unusual or specific significance to the reader, for instance irony or humor, they are sometimes placed in quotation marks.

For years, women were not allowed to buy real estate in order to "protect" them from unscrupulous dealers.

The "conversation" resulted in one black eye and a broken nose.

To set off titles of TV shows, poems, stories, and book chapters, use quotation marks. (Book, motion picture, newspaper, and magazine titles are underlined when hand-written and italicized when printed.)

The article "Moving South in the Southern Rain," by Jergen Smith in the *Southern News*, attracted the attention of our editor.

The assignment is "Childhood Development," Chapter 18 of *Human Behavior*.

My favorite essay by Montaigne is "On Silence."

"Happy Days" led the TV ratings for years, didn't it?

You will find Keats' "Ode on a Grecian Urn" in Chapter 3, "The Romantic Era," in Lastly's *Selections from Great English Poets*.

Errors to avoid:

Be sure to remember that quotation marks always come in pairs. Do not make the mistake of using only one set.

INCORRECT:	"You'll never convince me to move to the city, said Thurman. I consider it an insane asylum."
CORRECT:	"You'll never convince me to move to the city," said Thurman. "I consider it an insane asylum."

INCORRECT:	"Idleness and pride tax with a heavier hand than kings and parlia-ments," Benjamin Franklin is supposed to have said. If we can get rid of the former, we may easily bear the latter."
CORRECT:	"Idleness and pride tax with a heavier hand than kings and parlia-ments," Benjamin Franklin is supposed to have said. "If we can get rid of the former, we may easily bear the latter."

When a quote consists of several sentences, do not put the quotation marks at the beginning and end of each sentence; put them at the beginning and end of the entire quotation.

INCORRECT:	"It was during his student days in Bonn that Beethoven fastened upon Schiller's poem." "The heady sense of liberation in the verses must have appealed to him." "They appealed to every Ger-man." —John Burke

CORRECT: "It was during his student days in Bonn that Beethoven fastened upon Schiller's poem. The heady sense of liberation in the verses must have appealed to him. They appealed to every German."
—John Burke

Instead of setting off a long quote with quotation marks, if it is longer than five or six lines you may want to indent and single space it. If you do indent, do not use quotation marks.

In his *First Inaugural Address*, Abraham Lincoln appeals to the war-torn American people:

We are not enemies, but friends. We must not be enemies. Though passion may have strained, it must not break, our bonds of affection. The mystic chords of memory, stretching from every battlefield and patriot grave to every living heart and hearthstone all over this broad land, will yet swell the chorus of the Union when again touched, as surely they will be, by the better angels of our nature.

Be careful not to use quotation marks with indirect quotations.

INCORRECT: Mary wondered "if she would get over it."

CORRECT: Mary wondered if she would get over it.

INCORRECT: The nurse asked "how long it had been since we had visited the doctor's office."

CORRECT: The nurse asked how long it had been since we had visited the doctor's office.

When you quote several paragraphs, it is not sufficient to place quotation marks at the beginning and end of the entire quote. Place quotation marks at the *beginning of each paragraph,* but only at the *end of the last paragraph.* Here is an abbreviated quotation for an example:

"Here begins an odyssey through the world of classical mythology, starting with the creation of the world...

"It is true that themes similar to the classical may be found in any corpus of mythology...Even technology is not immune to the influence of Greece and Rome...

"We need hardly mention the extent to which painters and sculptors...have used and adapted classical mythology to illustrate the past, to reveal the human body, to express romantic or antiromantic ideals, or to symbolize any particular point of view."

Remember that commas and periods are *always* placed inside the quotation marks even if they are not actually part of the quote.

INCORRECT:	"Life always gets colder near the summit", Nietzsche is purported to have said, "—the cold increases, responsibility grows".
CORRECT:	"Life always gets colder near the summit," Nietzsche is purported to have said, "—the cold increases, responsibility grows."
INCORRECT:	"Get down here right away", John cried. "You'll miss the sunset if you don't."
CORRECT:	"Get down here right away," John cried. "You'll miss the sunset if you don't."
INCORRECT:	"If my dog could talk", Mary mused, "I'll bet he would say, 'Take me for a walk right this minute'".
CORRECT:	"If my dog could talk," Mary mused, "I'll bet he would say, 'Take me for a walk right this minute'."

Other marks of punctuation, such as question marks, exclamation points, colons, and semicolons, go inside the quotation marks if they are part of the quoted material. If they are not part of the quotation, however, they go outside the quotation marks. Be careful to distinguish between the guidelines for the comma and period, which always go inside the quotation marks, and those for other marks of punctuation.

INCORRECT:	"I'll always love you"! he exclaimed happily.
CORRECT:	"I'll always love you!" he exclaimed happily.
INCORRECT:	Did you hear her say, "He'll be there early?"
CORRECT:	Did you hear her say, "He'll be there early"?

INCORRECT:	She called down the stairs, "When are you going"?
CORRECT:	She called down the stairs, "When are you going?"

INCORRECT:	"Let me out"! he cried. "Don't you have any pity"?
CORRECT:	"Let me out!" he cried. "Don't you have any pity?"

Remember to use only one mark of punctuation at the end of a sentence ending with a quotation mark.

INCORRECT:	She thought out loud, "Will I ever finish this paper in time for that class?".
CORRECT:	She thought out loud, "Will I ever finish this paper in time for that class?"

INCORRECT:	"Not the same thing a bit!", said the Hatter. "Why, you might just as well say that 'I see what I eat' is the same thing as 'I eat what I see'!".
CORRECT:	"Not the same thing a bit!" said the Hatter. "Why, you might just as well say that 'I see what I eat' is the same thing as 'I eat what I see'!"

■ Drill: Punctuation ■

DIRECTIONS: Choose the correct option.

1. Indianola, <u>Mississippi, where B.B. King and my father grew up,</u> has a population of less than 50,000 people.

(A) Mississippi where, B.B. King and my father grew up,

(B) Mississippi where B.B. King and my father grew up,

(C) Mississippi; where B.B. King and my father grew up,

(D) No change is necessary.

2. John Steinbeck's best known novel *The Grapes of Wrath* is the story of the <u>Joads an Oklahoma family</u> who were driven from their dustbowl farm and forced to become migrant workers in California.

   (A) Joads, an Oklahoma family

   (B) Joads, an Oklahoma family,

   (C) Joads; an Oklahoma family

   (D) No change is necessary.

3. All students who are interested in student teaching next <u>semester, must submit an application to the Teacher Education Office.</u>

   (A) semester must submit an application to the Teacher Education Office.

   (B) semester, must submit an application, to the Teacher Education Office.

   (C) semester: must submit an application to the Teacher Education Office.

   (D) No change is necessary.

4. Whenever you travel by <u>car, or plane, you</u> must wear a seatbelt.

   (A) car or plane you   (C) car or plane, you

   (B) car, or plane you   (D) No change is necessary.

5. Wearing a seatbelt is not just a good <u>idea, it's</u> the law.

   (A) idea; it's   (C) idea. It's

   (B) idea it's   (D) No change is necessary.

6. Senators and representatives can be reelected <u>indefinitely; a</u> president can only serve two terms.

   (A) indefinitely but a   (C) indefinitely a

   (B) indefinitely, a   (D) No change is necessary.

7. Students must pay a penalty for overdue library <u>books, however, there</u> is a grace period.

   (A) books; however, there   (C) books: however, there

   (B) books however, there   (D) No change is necessary.

8. Among the states that seceded from the Union to join the Confederacy in 1860-1861 <u>were:</u> Mississippi, Florida, and Alabama.

   (A) were

   (B) were;

   (C) were.

   (D) No change is necessary.

9. The art exhibit displayed works by many famous <u>artists such as:</u> Dali, Picasso, and Michelangelo.

   (A) artists such as;

   (B) artists such as

   (C) artists. Such as

   (D) No change is necessary.

10. The National Shakespeare Company will perform <u>the following plays:</u> *Othello*, *Macbeth*, *Hamlet*, and *As You Like It*.

    (A) the following plays,

    (B) the following plays;

    (C) the following plays

    (D) No change is necessary.

ESSAY

ETS asks that you compose an essay which is organized, has a thesis, uses support, and demonstrates clarity and error-free writing. The essay should be written for an adult audience.

Essay Writing Review

The PPST contains one writing exercise. You will have 30 minutes to plan and write an essay on a given topic. You must write on only that topic. Since you will have only 30 minutes to complete the essay, efficient use of your time is essential.

Writing under pressure can be frustrating, but if you study this review, practice and polish your essay skills, and have a realistic sense of what to expect, you can turn problems into possibilities. The following review will show you how to plan and write a logical, coherent, and interesting essay.

Pre-Writing/Planning

Before you begin to actually write, there are certain preliminary steps you need to take. A few minutes spent planning pays off—your final essay will be more focused, well-developed, and clearer. For a 30-minute essay, you should spend about seven minutes on the pre-writing process.

Understand the Question

Read the essay question very carefully and ask yourself the following questions:

- What is the meaning of the topic statement?
- Is the question asking me to persuade the reader of the validity of a certain opinion?
- Do I agree or disagree with the statement? What will be my thesis (main idea)?
- What kinds of examples can I use to support my thesis? Explore personal experiences, historical evidence, current events, and literary subjects.

Sample Essay Topic

DIRECTIONS: You will have 30 minutes to plan and write an essay on the following topic. Read the topic carefully. Organize your thoughts and then write a response.

Schools should be required to replace beverages in soda machines with healthy alternatives.

Discuss the extent to which you agree or disagree with this opinion. Support your views with specific reasons and examples from your experiences, observations, and readings.

Consider Your Audience

Essays would be pointless without an audience. Why write an essay if no one wants or needs to read it? Why add evidence, organize your ideas, or correct bad grammar? The reason to do any of these things is because someone out there needs to understand what you mean or say.

What does the audience need to know to believe you or to come over to your position? Imagine someone you know listening to you declare your position or opinion and then saying, "Oh, yeah? Prove it!" This is your audience—write to them. Ask yourself the following questions so that you will not be confronted with a person who says, "Prove it!"

- What evidence do I need to prove my idea to this skeptic?
- What would s/he disagree with me about?
- What does he or she share with me as common knowledge? What do I need to tell the reader?

Writing Your Essay

Once you have considered your position on the topic and thought of several examples to support it, you are ready to begin writing.

Organizing Your Essay

Decide how many paragraphs you will write. In a 30-minute exercise, you will probably have time for no more than four or five paragraphs. In such a format, the first paragraph will be the introduction, the next two or three will develop your thesis with specific examples, and the final paragraph should be a strong conclusion.

The Introduction

The focus of your introduction should be the thesis statement. This statement allows your reader to understand the point and direction of your essay. The statement identifies the central idea of your essay and should clearly state your attitude about the subject. It will also dictate the basic content and organization of your essay. If you do not state your thesis clearly, your essay will suffer.

The thesis is the heart of the essay. Without it, readers won't know what your major message or central idea is in the essay.

The thesis must be something that can be argued or needs to be proven, not just an accepted fact. For example, "Animals are used every day in cosmetic and medical testing," is a fact—it needs no proof. But if the writer says, "Using animals for cosmetic and medical testing is cruel and should be stopped," we have a point that must be supported and defended by the writer.

The thesis can be placed in any paragraph of the essay, but in a short essay, especially one written for evaluative exam purposes, the thesis is most effective when placed in the last sentence of the opening paragraph.

Consider the following sample question:

ESSAY TOPIC:

"That government is best which governs least."

ASSIGNMENT: Do you agree or disagree with this statement? Choose a specific example from current events, personal experience, or your reading to support your position.

After reading the topic statement, decide if you agree or disagree. If you agree with this statement, your thesis statement could be the following:

"Government has the right to protect individuals from interference but no right to extend its powers and activities beyond this function."

This statement clearly states the writer's opinion in a direct manner. It also serves as a blueprint for the essay. The remainder of the introduction should give two or three brief examples that support your thesis.

Supporting Paragraphs

The next two or three paragraphs of your essay will elaborate on the supporting examples you gave in your introduction. Each paragraph should discuss only one idea. Like the introduction, each paragraph should be coherently organized, with a topic sentence and supporting details.

The topic sentence is to each paragraph what the thesis statement is to the essay as a whole. It tells the reader what you plan to discuss in that paragraph. It has a specific subject and is neither too broad nor too narrow. It also establishes the author's attitude and gives the reader a sense of the direction in which the writer is going. An effective topic sentence also arouses the reader's interest.

Although it may occur in the middle or at the end of the paragraph, the topic sentence usually appears at the beginning of the paragraph. Placing it at the beginning is advantageous because it helps you stay focused on the main idea.

The remainder of each paragraph should support the topic sentence with examples and illustrations. Each sentence should progress logically from the previous one and be centrally connected to your topic sentence. Do not include any extraneous material that does not serve to develop your thesis.

Conclusion

Your conclusion should briefly restate your thesis and explain how you have shown it to be true. Since you want to end your essay on a strong note, your conclusion should be concise and effective.

Do not introduce any new topics that you cannot support. If you were watching a movie that suddenly shifted plot and characters at the end, you would be disappointed or even angry. Similarly, conclusions must not drift away from the major focus and message of the essay. Make sure your conclusion is clearly on the topic and represents your perspective without any confusion about what you really mean and believe. The reader will respect you for staying true to your intentions.

The conclusion is your last chance to grab and impress the reader. You can even use humor, if appropriate, but a dramatic close will remind the reader you are serious, even passionate, about what you believe.

EFFECTIVE USE OF LANGUAGE

Clear organization, while vitally important, is not the only factor the graders of your essay consider. You must also demonstrate that you can express your ideas clearly, using correct grammar, diction, usage, spelling, and punctuation. For rules on grammar, usage, and mechanics, consult the English Language Skills Review in this book.

Point-of-View

Depending on the audience, essays may be written from one of three points of view:

1. *Subjective/Personal* Point of View:

   "I think . . ."

   "I believe cars are more trouble than they are worth."

   "I feel . . ."

2. *Second Person* Point of View (We . . . You; I . . . You):

   "If you own a car, you will soon find out that it is more trouble than it is worth."

3. *Third Person* Point of View (focuses on the idea, not what "I" think of it):

   "Cars are more trouble than they are worth."

It is very important to maintain a consistent point of view throughout your essay. If you begin writing in the first-person ("I"), do not shift to the second- or third-person in the middle of the essay. Such inconsistency is confusing to your reader and will be penalized by the graders of your essay.

Tone

A writer's tone results from his or her attitude towards the subject and the reader. If the essay question requires you to take a strong stand, the tone of your essay should reflect this.

Your tone should also be appropriate for the subject matter. A serious topic demands a serious tone. For a more light-hearted topic, you may wish to inject some humor into your essay.

Whatever tone you choose, be consistent. Do not make any abrupt shifts in tone in the middle of your essay.

Verb Tense

Make sure to remain in the same verb tense in which you began your essay. If you start in the past, make sure all verbs are past tense. Staying in the same verb tense improves the continuity and flow of ideas. Avoid phrases such as "now was," a confusing blend of present and past. Consistency of time is essential to the reader's understanding.

Connecting Ideas Through Transitional Words and Phrases

Transitions are like the links of a bracelet, holding the beads or major points of your essay together. They help the reader follow the smooth flow of your ideas and show a connection between major and minor ideas. Transitions are used either at the beginning of a paragraph, or to show the connections among ideas within a single paragraph. Without transitions, you will jar the reader and distract him from your true ideas.

Here are some typical transitional words and phrases:

Linking similar ideas

again	for example	likewise
also	for instance	moreover
and	further	nor
another	furthermore	of course
besides	in addition	similarly
equally important	in like manner	too

Linking dissimilar/contradictory ideas

although	however	on the other hand
and yet	in spite of	otherwise
as if	instead	provided that
but	nevertheless	still
conversely	on the contrary	yet

Indicating cause, purpose, or result

as	for	so
as a result	for this reason	then
because	hence	therefore
consequently	since	thus

Indicating time or position

above	before	meanwhile
across	beyond	next
afterwards	eventually	presently
around	finally	second
at once	first	thereafter
at the present time	here	thereupon

Indicating an example or summary

as a result	in any event	in other words
as I have said	in brief	in short
for example	in conclusion	on the whole
for instance	in fact	to sum up

How to Generate a Thesis Statement

Turn the topic into a question. In our example, the topic at hand is the following: Schools should be required to replace beverages in soda machines with healthy alternatives." You can ask yourself, "What are the potential benefits if the school replaces soda with healthy alternatives?"

Q: "What are the potential benefits if the school replaces soda with healthy alternatives?"

A: "The potential benefits of replacing soda with healthy alternatives are . . ."

OR

A: "Healthy alternatives in the vending machine promise to improve . . ."

The answer to the question is the thesis statement for the essay.

Remember, your thesis statement still needs to answer the question about the issue you'd like to explore.

A good thesis statement will usually:

- Narrow the topic
- Assert something about it
- express one main idea
- assert your conclusions about a subject

Let's see how to generate a thesis statement for a social policy paper.

Brainstorm the topic.

Let's say that your class focuses upon the problems posed by changes in the dietary habits of Americans. You find that you are interested in the amount of sugar Americans consume.

You start out with a thesis statement like this:

Sugar consumption.
This fragment isn't a thesis statement. Instead, it simply indicates a general subject. Furthermore, your reader doesn't know what you want to say about sugar consumption.

Narrow the topic.

Your readings about the topic, however, have led you to the conclusion that elementary school children are consuming far more sugar than is healthy.

You change your thesis to look like this:

Reducing sugar consumption by elementary school children.
This fragment not only announces your subject, but it focuses on one segment of the population: elementary school children. Furthermore, it raises a subject upon which reasonable people could disagree, because while most people might agree that children consume more sugar than they used to, not everyone would agree on what should be done or who should do it. You should note that this fragment is not a thesis statement because your reader doesn't know your conclusions on the topic.

Take a position on the topic.

After reflecting on the topic a little while longer, you decide that what you really want to say about this topic is that something should be done to reduce the amount of sugar these children consume.

You revise your thesis statement to look like this:

More attention should be paid to the food and beverage choices available to elementary school children.

This statement asserts your position, but the terms *more attention* and *food and beverage choices* are vague.

Use specific language.

You decide to explain what you mean about *food and beverage choices*, so you write:

Experts estimate that half of elementary school children consume nine times the recommended daily allowance of sugar.

This statement is specific, but it isn't a thesis. It merely reports a statistic instead of making an assertion.

Make an assertion based on clearly stated support.

You finally revise your thesis statement one more time to look like this:

Because half of all American elementary school children consume nine times the recommended daily allowance of sugar, schools should be required to replace the beverages in soda machines with healthy alternatives.

Notice how the thesis answers the question, "What should be done to reduce sugar consumption by children, and who should do it?" When you started thinking about the paper, you may not have had a specific question in mind, but as you became more involved in the topic, your ideas became more specific. Your thesis changed to reflect your new insights.

Variety of Sentence Structures

It is important to vary the types of sentences you use when you write to keep your writing interesting. Make sure to include the following types of sentences when you write:

Simple: Subject and verb.
                         Ex: I ate the sandwich. (i.e., a clause)

Compound: 2 subjects and 2 verbs.
                         Ex: I went to the store, and I found the item. (i.e., 2 clauses)

Complex: 1 independent clause and 1 or more subordinate clauses.

Ex: If you need to, take a limosine home.

(subordinate clause)

Compound-Complex: at least 2 independent clauses (it's compound) and at least one subordinate clause (complex).

Ex: Figure out when you want to leave and I will be there to pick you up and drive you to the store.

Common Writing Errors

The four writing errors most often made by beginning writers are run-ons (also known as fused sentences), fragments, lack of subject-verb agreement, and incorrect use of the object:

1. **Run-ons**: "She swept the floor it was dirty" is a run-on, because the pronoun "it" stands as a noun subject and starts a new sentence. A period or semicolon is needed after "floor."

2. **Fragments**: "Before Jimmy learned how to play baseball" is a fragment, even though it has a subject and verb (Jimmy learned). The word "before" fragmentizes the clause, and the reader needs to know what happened before Jimmy learned how to play baseball.

3. **Problems with subject-verb agreement**: "Either Maria or Robert are going to the game" is incorrect because either Maria is going or Robert is going, but not both. The sentence should say, "Either Maria or Robert is going to the game."

4. **Incorrect object**: Probably the most common offender in this area is saying "between you and I," which sounds correct, but isn't. "Between" is a preposition that takes the objective case "me." The correct usage is "between you and me."

The PPST scorers also cite lack of thought and development, misspellings, incorrect pronouns or antecedents, and lack of development as frequently occurring problems. Finally, keep in mind that clear, coherent handwriting always works to your advantage. Readers will appreciate an essay they can read with ease.

Five Words Weak Writers Overuse

Weak and beginning writers overuse the vague pronouns "you," "we," "they," "this," and "it," often without telling exactly who or what is represented by the pronoun.

1. Beginning writers often shift to second person **"you,"** when the writer means "a person." This shift confuses readers and weakens the flow of the essay. Although "you" is commonly accepted in creative writing, journalism, and other arenas, in a short, formal essay, it is best to avoid "you" altogether.

2. **"We"** is another pronoun that should be avoided. If by "we" the writer means "Americans," "society," or some other group, then he or she should say so.

3. **"They"** is often misused in essay writing, because it is overused in conversation: "I went to the doctor, and they told me to take some medicine." Tell the reader who "they" are.

4. **"This"** is usually used incorrectly without a referent: "She told me she received a present. This sounded good to me." This what? This idea? This news? This present? Be clear—don't make your readers guess what you mean. The word "this" should be followed by a noun or referent.

5. **"It"** is a common problem among weak writers. To what does "it" refer? Your readers don't appreciate vagueness, so take the time to be clear and complete in your expression of ideas.

Use Your Own Vocabulary

Is it a good idea to use big words that sound good in the dictionary or thesaurus, but that you don't really use or understand? No. So whose vocabulary should you use? Your own. You will be most comfortable with your own level of vocabulary.

This "comfort zone" doesn't give you license to be informal in a formal setting or to violate the rules of standard written English, but if you try to write in a style that is not yours, your writing will be awkward and lack a true voice.

You should certainly improve and build your vocabulary at every opportunity, but remember: you should not attempt to change your vocabulary level at this point.

Avoid the Passive Voice

In writing, the active voice is preferable because it is emphatic and direct. A weak passive verb leaves the doer unknown or seemingly unimportant. However, the passive voice is essential when the action of the verb is more important than the doer, when the doer is unknown, or when the writer wishes to place the emphasis on the receiver of the action rather than on the doer.

PROOFREADING

Make sure to leave yourself enough time at the end to read over your essay for errors such as misspellings, omitted words, or incorrect punctuation. You will not have enough time to make large-scale revisions, but take this chance to make any small changes that will make your essay stronger. Consider the following when proofreading your work:

- Are all your sentences really sentences? Have you written any fragments or run-on sentences?

- Are you using vocabulary correctly?

- Did you leave out any punctuation? Did you capitalize correctly?

- Are there any misspellings, especially of difficult words?

If you have time, read your essay backwards from end to beginning. By doing so, you may catch errors that you missed reading forward only.

■ Drill: Essay Writing ■

DIRECTIONS: You have 30 minutes to plan and write an essay on the topic below. You may write only on the assigned topic.

Make sure to give specific examples to support your thesis. Proofread your essay carefully and take care to express your ideas clearly and effectively.

ESSAY TOPIC:

In the last 20 years, the deterioration of the environment has become a growing concern among both scientists and ordinary citizens.

ASSIGNMENT: Choose one pressing environmental problem, explain its negative impact, and discuss possible solutions.

WRITING DRILLS

Answer Key

Drill: Adjectives and Adverbs

1. **(C)**	4. **(C)**	7. **(A)**	10. **(C)**
2. **(A)**	5. **(A)**	8. **(C)**	
3. **(D)**	6. **(C)**	9. **(B)**	

Drill: Pronouns

1. **(A)**	4. **(A)**	7. **(B)**	10. **(C)**
2. **(C)**	5. **(D)**	8. **(B)**	
3. **(A)**	6. **(A)**	9. **(A)**	

Drill: Verbs

1. **(C)**	4. **(A)**	7. **(A)**	10. **(D)**
2. **(B)**	5. **(A)**	8. **(C)**	
3. **(D)**	6. **(B)**	9. **(A)**	

Drill: Sentence Structure Skills

1. **(C)**	4. **(B)**	7. **(B)**	10. **(B)**
2. **(B)**	5. **(A)**	8. **(A)**	
3. **(B)**	6. **(A)**	9. **(B)**	

Drill: Word Choice Skills

1. **(D)**	4. **(C)**	7. **(A)**	10. **(B)**
2. **(D)**	5. **(A)**	8. **(B)**	
3. **(A)**	6. **(C)**	9. **(C)**	

Drill: Capitalization

1.	**(D)**	4.	**(A)**	7.	**(B)**	10.	**(A)**
2.	**(B)**	5.	**(C)**	8.	**(D)**		
3.	**(C)**	6.	**(D)**	9.	**(B)**		

Drill: Punctuation

1.	**(D)**	4.	**(C)**	7.	**(A)**	10.	**(D)**
2.	**(B)**	5.	**(A)**	8.	**(A)**		
3.	**(A)**	6.	**(D)**	9.	**(B)**		

DETAILED EXPLANATIONS OF ANSWERS

Drill: Adjectives and Adverbs

1. **(C)**

   Choice (C) is correct. *Bad* is an adjective; *badly* is an adverb. *Real* is an adjective meaning *genuine* (*a real problem*, *real leather*). To qualify an adverb of degree to express how bad, how excited, how boring, etc., choose *very*.

2. **(A)**

   Choice (A) is correct. Use an adverb as a qualifier for an adjective. *How simple? Relatively simple.*

3. **(D)**

   Choice (D) is correct. *Good* is an adjective; *well* is both an adjective and an adverb. As an adjective, *well* refers to health; it means "not ill."

4. **(C)**

   Choice (C) is correct. All the other choices use *good* incorrectly as an adverb. *Shake* is an action verb that requires an adverb, not an adjective.

5. **(A)**

   Choice (A) is correct. The action verbs *speaks*, *writes*, *observe,* and *think* each require adverbs as modifiers.

6. **(C)**

   Choice (C) is correct. The comparisons in choices (A) and (B) are illogical: these sentences suggest that Los Angeles is not in California because it *is larger than any city in California.*

7. **(A)**

   Choice (A) is correct. Do not omit the second *as* of the correlative pair *as…as* when making a point of equal or superior comparison, as in choice (B). Choice (C) omits *than* from "if not more interesting [than]."

8. **(C)**

   Choice (C) is correct. Choice (A) illogically compares *baseball team* to a *university*, and choice (B) illogically compares *baseball team* to *all the other universities.*

Choice (C) logically compares the baseball team here to the one at any other university, as implied by the possessive ending on university—*university's*.

9. **(B)**

Choice (B) is correct. Choices (A) and (C) are ambiguous; because these sentences are too elliptical, the reader does not know where to place the missing information.

10. **(C)**

Choice (C) is correct. Choice (A) is redundant; there is no need to use *most* with *stingiest*. Choice (B) incorrectly combines the comparative word *more* with the superlative form *stingiest*.

Drill: Pronouns

1. **(A)**

Choice (A) is correct. Do not use the reflexive pronoun *myself* as a substitute for *I*.

2. **(C)**

Choice (C) is correct. In the clause *whoever consumes them*, *whoever* is the subject. *Whomever* is the objective case pronoun and should be used only as the object of a sentence, never as the subject.

3. **(A)**

Choice (A) is correct. Use the nominative case pronoun *who* as the subject complement after the verb *is*.

4. **(A)**

Choice (A) is correct. In this sentence use the nominative case/subject pronouns *she who* as the subject complement after the *be* verb *was*.

5. **(D)**

Choice (D) is correct. *Student* is an indefinite, genderless noun that requires a singular personal pronoun. While *his* is a singular personal pronoun, a genderless noun includes both the masculine and feminine forms and requires *his or her* as the singular personal pronoun.

6. **(A)**

Choice (A) is correct. The antecedent *company* is singular, requiring the singular pronoun *it*, not the plural *they*.

7.   **(B)**

Choice (B) is correct. Choice (A) contains a person shift: *Your* is a second person pronoun, and *his* and *her* are third person pronouns. The original sentence uses the third person plural pronoun *their* to refer to the singular antecedent *every car owner*. Choice (B) correctly provides the masculine and feminine forms *his or her* required by the indefinite, genderless *every car owner*.

8.   **(B)**

Choice (B) is correct. The implied antecedent is *teaching*. Choices (A) and (C) each contain a pronoun with no antecedent. Neither *it* nor *this* are suitable substitutions for *teacher*.

9.   **(A)**

Choice (A) is correct. The pronoun *they* in the original sentence has no conspicuous antecedent. Since the doer of the action is obviously unknown (and therefore genderless), choice (B), *he*, is not the correct choice.

10.   **(C)**

Choice (C) is correct. The original sentence is ambiguous: the pronoun *she* has two possible antecedents; we don't know whether it is Margaret or her sister who is away at college.

Drill: Verbs

1.   **(C)**

Choice (C) is correct. The past participle form of each verb is required because of the auxiliaries (helping verbs) *had been* (concerned) and *would have* (gone).

2.   **(B)**

Choice (B) is correct. The forms of the irregular verb meaning *to rest* are *lie (rest)*, *lies (rests)*, *lay (rested)*, and *has lain (has rested)*. The forms of the verb meaning *to put* are *lay (put), lays (puts), laying (putting), laid (put),* and *have laid (have put)*.

3.   **(D)**

Choice (D) is correct. The present tense is used for universal truths and the past tense is used for historical truths.

4. **(A)**

Choice (A) is correct. The present tense is used for customary happenings. Choice (B), *had begun*, is not a standard verb form. Choice (C), *was beginning*, indicates that 10:30 a.m. is not the regular class time.

5. **(A)**

Choice (A) is correct. The past tense is used for historical statements, and the present tense is used for statements about works of art.

6. **(B)**

Choice (B) is correct. The subject of the sentence is the plural noun *sales*, not the singular noun *Christmas*, which is the object of the prepositional phrase.

7. **(A)**

Choice (A) is correct. The subject *specialty* is singular.

8. **(C)**

Choice (C) is correct. Subjects preceded by *every* are considered singular and therefore require a singular verb form.

9. **(A)**

Choice (A) is correct. The subject of the sentence is the gerund *hiding*, not the object of the gerund phrase *mistakes*. *Hiding* is singular; therefore, the singular verb form *does* should be used.

10. **(D)**

Choice (D) is correct. Though the form of the subject *Board of Regents* is plural, it is singular in meaning.

Drill: Sentence Structure Skills

1. **(C)**

Choice (C) is correct. Each response contains items in a series. In choices (A) and (B), the word group after the conjunction is not an adjective like the first words in the series. Choice (C) contains three adjectives.

2. **(B)**

Choice (B) is correct. Choices (A), (C), and (D) combine conjunctions incorrectly.

3. **(B)**

Choice (B) is correct. Choices (A) and (C) appear to be parallel because the conjunction *and* connects two word groups that both begin with *because*, but the structure on both sides of the conjunction are very different. *Because he kept his campaign promises* is a clause; *because of his refusal to accept political favors* is a prepositional phrase. Choice (B) connects two dependent clauses.

4. **(B)**

Choice (B) is correct. Choices (A) and (C) contain the elliptical clause *While … taking a shower*. It appears that the missing subject in the elliptical clause is the same as that in the independent clause—the *doorbell* in choice (A) and *someone* in choice (C), neither of which is a logical subject for the verbal *taking a shower*. Choice (B) removes the elliptical clause and provides the logical subject.

5. **(A)**

Choice (A) is correct. Who swung the bat? Choices (B) and (C) both imply that it is the runner who swung the bat. Only choice (A) makes it clear that as *he* swung the bat, someone else (the *runner*) stole second base.

6. **(A)**

Choice (A) is correct. The punctuation in the original sentence and in choice (B) creates a fragment. *Cotton being the state's principal crop* is not an independent thought because it lacks a complete verb—*being* is not a complete verb.

7. **(B)**

Choice (B) is correct. The punctuation in the original sentence and in choice (A) creates a fragment. Both the semicolon and the period should be used to separate two independent clauses. The word group *one that I have never seen before* does not express a complete thought and therefore is not an independent clause.

8. **(A)**

Choice (A) is correct. The dependent clause *because repairs were being made* in choices (B) and (C) is punctuated as if it were a sentence. The result is a fragment.

9. **(B)**

Choice (B) is correct. Choices (A) and (C) do not separate the complete thoughts in the independent clauses with the correct punctuation.

10. **(B)**

Choice (B) is correct. Choices (A) and (C) do not separate the independent clauses with the correct punctuation.

Drill: Word Choice Skills

1. **(D)**

Choice (D) is correct. No change is necessary. *Principal* as a noun means "head of a school." *Principle* is a noun meaning "axiom" or "rule of conduct."

2. **(D)**

Choice (D) is correct. No change is necessary. *Affect* is a verb meaning "to influence" or "to change." *Effect* as a noun meaning "result."

3. **(A)**

Choice (A) is correct. Use *amount* with noncountable, mass nouns (*amount* of food, help, money); use *number* with countable, plural nouns (*number* of children, classes, bills).

4. **(C)**

Choice (C) is correct. *Supposed to* and *used to* should be spelled with a final *d*. *Achieving* follows the standard spelling rule—*i* before *e*.

5. **(A)**

Choice (A) is correct. Use *that*, not *because*, to introduce clauses after the word *reason*. Choice (A) is also the only choice that contains the correct spelling of "succeeded."

6. **(C)**

Choice (C) is correct. *Converge together* is redundant, and *single* is not needed to convey the meaning of *a highway*.

7. **(A)**

Choice (A) is correct. It is economical and concise. The other choices contain unnecessary repetition.

8. **(B)**

Choice (B) is correct. Choices (A) and (C) pad the sentences with loose synonyms that are redundant. Choice (D), although a short sentence, does not convey the meaning as clearly as choice (B).

9. **(C)**

    Choice (C) is correct. The other choices all contain unnecessary repetition.

10. **(B)**

    Choice (B) is correct. Choices (A) and (C) contain circumlocution; they fail to get to the point. Choice (D) does not express the meaning of the sentence as concisely as choice (B).

Drill: Capitalization

1. **(D)**

    Choice (D) is correct. *North America*, like other proper names, is capitalized. *North, south, east,* and *west* are only capitalized when they refer to geographic regions (*the Southwest, Eastern Europe*); as compass directions, they are not capitalized.

2. **(B)**

    Choice (B) is correct. Although persons' names are capitalized, a person's title is not (*coach*, not *Coach*). Capitalize the complete name of a team, school, river, etc. (Dallas Cowboys).

3. **(C)**

    Choice (C) is correct. Capitalize all geographic units, and capitalize *earth* only when it is mentioned with other planets. *Equator* is not capitalized.

4. **(A)**

    Choice (A) is correct. Capitalize the first word in a title and all other words in a title except articles, prepositions with fewer than five letters, and conjunctions.

5. **(C)**

    Choice (C) is correct. Capitalize proper adjectives (proper nouns used as adjectives): *Greek* goddess, *Roman* mythology.

6. **(D)**

    Choice (D) is correct. Capitalize all religious groups, books, and names referring to religious deities.

7. **(B)**

    Choice (B) is correct. Do not capitalize courses unless they are languages (English) or course titles followed by a number (Algebra I).

8. **(D)**

Choice (D) is correct. Do not capitalize seasons unless they accompany the name of an event such as *Spring Break*. Do not capitalize types of degrees (*bachelor's degrees*); capitalize only the name of the degree (*Bachelor of Arts degree*).

9. **(B)**

Choice (B) is correct. As a landmark, *Berlin Wall* is capitalized; however, do not capitalize systems of government or individual adherents to a philosophy, such as *communism*.

10. **(A)**

Choice (A) is correct. *Earth* is capitalized when it is mentioned with other planets, and all other planets are always capitalized. Names of newspapers are also capitalized.

Drill: Punctuation

1. **(D)**

Choice (D) is correct. Nonrestrictive clauses, like other nonrestrictive elements, should be set off from the rest of the sentence with commas.

2. **(B)**

Choice (B), which places commas around the phrase *an Oklahoma family* is correct. Use commas where two non-restrictive appositive phrases modify the noun. In this case, both the phrase, *an Oklahoma family,* and the phrase, *who were driven from their dustbowl farm and forced to become migrant workers in California,* modify the noun *Joads*.

3. **(A)**

Choice (A) is correct. Do not use unnecessary commas to separate a subject and verb from their complement. Both choices (B) and (C) use superfluous punctuation.

4. **(C)**

Choice (C) is correct. Do not separate two items in a compound with commas. The original sentence incorrectly separates "car or plane." Choice (A) omits the comma after the introductory clause.

5. **(A)**

Choice (A) is correct. Use a semicolon to separate two independent clauses/sentences that are not joined by a coordinating conjunction, especially when the ideas in the sentences are interrelated.

6. **(D)**

Choice (D) is correct. Use a semicolon to separate two sentences not joined by a coordinating conjunction.

7. **(A)**

Choice (A) is correct. Use a semicolon to separate two sentences joined by a conjunctive adverb.

8. **(A)**

Choice (A) is correct. Do not use a colon after a verb or a preposition. Remember that a complete sentence must precede a colon.

9. **(B)**

Choice (B) is correct. Do not use a colon after a preposition, and do not use a colon to separate a preposition from its objects.

10. **(D)**

Choice (D) is correct. Use a colon preceding a list that is introduced by words such as *the following* and *as follows*.

Drill: Essay Writing

This Answer Key provides three sample essays which represent possible responses to the essay topic. Compare your own response to those given on the next few pages. Allow the strengths and weaknesses of the sample essays help you to critique your own essay and improve your writing skills.

ESSAY I (Score: 5–6)

There are many pressing environmental problems facing both this country and the world today. Pollution, the misuse and squandering of resources, and the cavalier attitude many people express all contribute to the problem. But one of the most pressing problems this country faces is the apathetic attitude many Americans have towards recycling.

Why is recycling so imperative? There are two major reasons. First, recycling previously used materials conserves precious national resources. Many people never stop to think that reserves of metal ores are not unlimited. There is only so much gold, silver, tin, and other metals in the ground. Once it has all been mined, there will never be any more unless we recycle what has already been used.

Second, the United States daily generates more solid waste than any other country on earth. Our disposable consumer culture consumes fast food meals in paper or styrofoam containers, uses disposable diapers with plastic liners that do not biodegrade, receives pounds, if not tons, of unsolicited junk mail every year, and relies more and more on prepackaged rather than fresh food.

No matter how it is accomplished, increased recycling is essential. We have to stop covering our land with garbage, and the best ways to do this are to reduce our dependence on prepackaged goods and to minimize the amount of solid waste disposed of in landfills. The best way to reduce solid waste is to recycle it. Americans need to band together to recycle, to preserve our irreplaceable natural resources, reduce pollution, and preserve our precious environment.

Analysis

This essay presents a clearly defined thesis, and the writer elaborates on this thesis in a thoughtful and sophisticated manner. Various aspects of the problem under consideration are presented and explored, along with possible solutions. The support provided for the writer's argument is convincing and logical. There are few usage or mechanical errors to interfere with the writer's ability to communicate effectively. This writer demonstrates a comprehensive understanding of the rules of written English.

ESSAY II (Score: 3–4)

A pressing environmental problem today is the way we are cutting down too many trees and not planting any replacements for them. Trees are beneficial in many ways, and without them, many environmental problems would be much worse.

One of the ways trees are beneficial is that, like all plants, they take in carbon dioxide and produce oxygen. They can actually help clean the air this way. When too many trees are cut down in a small area, the air in that area is not as good and can be unhealthy to breath.

Another way trees are beneficial is that they provide homes for many types of birds, insects, and animals. When all the trees in an area are cut down, these animals lose their homes and sometimes they can die out and become extinct that way. Like the spotted owls in Oregon, that the loggers wanted to cut down the trees they lived in. If the loggers did cut down all the old timber stands that the spotted owls lived in, the owls would have become extinct.

But the loggers say that if they can't cut the trees down then they will be out of work, and that peoples' jobs are more important than birds. The loggers can do two things—they can either get training so they can do other jobs, or they can do what they should have done all along, and start replanting trees. For every mature tree they cut down, they should have to plant at least one tree seedling.

Cutting down the trees that we need for life, and that lots of other species depend on, is a big environmental problem that has a lot of long term consaquences. Trees are too important for all of us to cut them down without thinking about the future.

Analysis

This essay has a clear thesis, which the author does support with good examples. But the writer shifts between the chosen topic, which is that indiscriminant tree-cutting is a pressing environmental problem, and a list of the ways in which trees are beneficial and a discussion about the logging profession. Also, while there are few mistakes in usage and mechanics, the writer does have some problems with sentence structure. The writing is pedestrian and the writer does not elaborate on the topic as much as he or she could have. The writer failed to provide the kind of critical analysis that the topic required.

ESSAY III (Score: 1–2)

The most pressing environmental problem today is that lots of people and companies don't care about the environment, and they do lots of things that hurt the environment.

People throw littur out car windows and don't use trash cans, even if their all over a park, soda cans and fast food wrappers are all over the place. Cigarette butts are the worst cause the filters never rot. Newspapers and junk mail get left to blow all over the neighborhood, and beer bottles too.

Companies pollute the air and the water. Sometimes the ground around a company has lots of tocsins in it. Now companies can buy credits from other companies that let them pollute the air even more. They dump all kinds of chemacals into lakes and rivers that kills off the fish and causes acid rain and kills off more fish and some trees and small animuls and insects and then noone can go swimming or fishing in the lake.

People need to respect the environment because we only have one planet, and if we keep polluting it pretty soon nothing will grow and then even the people will die.

Analysis

The writer of this essay does not define his or her thesis for this essay. Because of this lack of a clear thesis, the reader is left to infer the topic from the body of the essay. It is possible to perceive the writer's intended thesis; however, the support for this thesis is very superficial. The writer presents a list of common complaints about polluters, without any critical discussion of the problems and possible solutions. Many sentences are run-ons and the writer has made several spelling errors. While the author manages to communicate his or her position on the issue, he or she does so on such a superficial level and with so many errors in usage and mechanics that the writer fails to demonstrate an ability to effectively communicate.

Practice Test 1

Praxis I PPST
(Paper-Based Format)

PRACTICE TEST 1 (Paper-Based Format)

Section I: Reading Comprehension

TIME: *60 Minutes*
40 Questions

DIRECTIONS: A number of questions follow each of the passages in the reading section. Answer the questions by choosing the best answer from the five choices given.

Questions 1 and 2 refer to the following passage:

America's national bird, the mighty bald eagle, is being threatened by a new menace. Once decimated by hunters and loss of habitat, this newest danger is suspected to be from the intentional poisoning by livestock ranchers. Authorities have found animal carcasses injected with restricted pesticides. These carcasses are suspected to have been placed to attract and kill predators such as the bald eagle in an effort to preserve young grazing animals. It appears that the eagle is being threatened again by the consummate predator, humans.

1.   One can conclude from this passage that

(A) the pesticides used are detrimental to the environment.

(B) the killing of eagles will protect the rancher's rangeland.

(C) ranchers must obtain licenses to use the pesticides.

(D) the poisoning could result in the extinction of the bald eagle.

(E) pesticides have been obtained illegally.

2.   The author's attitude is one of

(A) detached observation.   (D) suspicion.

(B) concerned interest.   (E) unbridled anger.

(C) informed acceptance.

Questions 3 and 4 refer to the graph below.

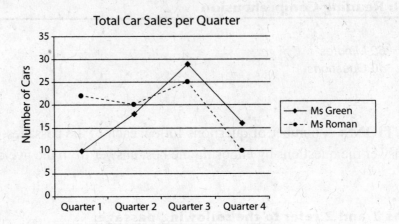

3. In which quarter did Ms. Green's sales exceed Ms. Roman's?

   (A) Quarter 1   (D) Quarter 4

   (B) Quarter 2   (E) In none of the Quarters.

   (C) Quarter 3

4. Approximately how many cars did Ms. Roman sell in Quarter 1?

   (A) 10   (D) 18

   (B) 23   (E) 25

   (C) 38

5. The disparaging remarks about her performance on the job made Alice uncomfortable.

   The word "disparaging" is closest in meaning to

   (A) complimentary.   (D) technical.

   (B) evil.   (E) insulting.

   (C) funny.

Questions 6 to 8 refer to the following passage:

INSTRUCTIONS FOR ABSENTEE VOTING

These instructions describe conditions under which voters may register for or request absentee ballots to vote in the November 5, 1991, election.

(1) If you moved on or prior to October 7, 1991, and did not register to vote at your new address, you are not eligible to vote in this election.

(2) If you move after this date, you may vote via absentee ballot or at your polling place, using your previous address as your address of registration for this election.

(3) You must register at your new address to vote in future elections.

(4) The last day to request an absentee ballot is October 29, 1991.

(5) You must be a registered voter in the county.

(6) You must sign your request in your own handwriting.

(7) You must make a separate request for each election.

(8) The absentee ballot shall be issued to the requesting voter in person or by mail.

6. A voter will be able to participate in the November 5, 1991, election as an absentee if he or she

(A) planned to register for the next election in 1992.

(B) requested an absentee ballot on November 1, 1991.

(C) voted absentee in the last election.

(D) moved as a registered voter on October 13, 1991.

(E) moved on October 7, 1991.

7. On October 15, 1991, Mr. Applebee requested an absentee ballot for his daughter, a registered voting college student, to enable her to participate in the election process. Mr. Applebee will most likely need clarification on which of the following instructions?

(A) 2   (D) 5

(B) 3   (E) 6

(C) 4

8. Which of the following best describes the most important piece of information for potential voters who want to participate in the election process, either in person or by absentee ballot?

    (A) Do not change precincts.

    (B) Do register to vote in the appropriate precinct.

    (C) You may vote at your nearest polling place.

    (D) The last day to register is always October 29.

    (E) Your absentee ballot can be used for any election when you have to be out of town.

Questions 9 and 10 refer to the following statement:

> The atrophy and incapacity which occur when a broken bone is encased in plaster and immobilized clearly demonstrate what a sedentary life-style can do to the human body.

9. In the passage above, "atrophy and incapacity" refer to

    (A) a strengthened condition brought about by rest.

    (B) a decrease in size and strength.

    (C) a type of exercise.

    (D) rest and recuperation.

    (E) the effects of body building.

10. Which of the following statements does NOT reflect the author's view of sedentary living?

    (A) If you don't use it, you lose it.

    (B) Mobility is affected by life-style.

    (C) A sedentary life-style is a healthy life-style.

    (D) A body is as a body does.

    (E) Exercise increases mobility.

Questions 11 to 15 refer to the following passage:

Frederick Douglass was born Frederick Augustus Washington Bailey in 1817 to a white father and a slave mother. Frederick was raised by his grandmother on a Maryland plantation until he was eight. It was then that he was sent to Baltimore by his owner to be a servant to the Auld family. Mrs. Auld recognized Frederick's intellectual acumen and defied the law of the state by teaching him to read and write. When Mr. Auld warned that education would make the boy unfit for slavery, Frederick sought to continue his education in the streets. When his master died, Frederick was returned to the plantation to work in the fields at age 16. Later, he was hired out to work in the shipyards in Baltimore as a ship caulker. He plotted an escape but was discovered before he could get away. It took five years before he made his way to New York City and then to New Bedford, Massachusetts, eluding slave hunters by changing his name to Douglass.

At an 1841 anti-slavery meeting in Massachusetts, Douglass was invited to give a talk about his experiences under slavery. His impromptu speech was so powerful and so eloquent that it thrust him into a career as an agent for the Massachusetts Anti-Slavery Society.

Douglass wrote his autobiography in 1845 primarily to counter those who doubted his authenticity as a former slave. This work became a classic in American literature and a primary source about slavery from the point of view of a slave. Douglass went on a two-year speaking tour abroad to avoid recapture by his former owner and to win new friends for the abolition movement. He returned with funds to purchase his freedom and to start his own anti-slavery newspaper. He became a consultant to Abraham Lincoln and throughout Reconstruction fought doggedly for full civil rights for freedmen; he also supported the women's rights movement.

11. According to the passage, Douglass's autobiography was motivated by his

(A) desire to make money for his anti-slavery movement.

(B) desire to start a newspaper.

(C) interest in authenticating his life as a slave.

(D) desire to educate people about slavery.

(E) desire to promote the Civil War.

12. The central idea of the passage is that Frederick Douglass

    (A) was influential in changing the laws regarding the education of slaves.

    (B) was one of the most eminent human rights leaders of the century.

    (C) was a personal friend and confidant to a president.

    (D) wrote a classic in American literature.

    (E) supported women's rights.

13. According to the author of this passage, Mrs. Auld taught Frederick to read because

    (A) Frederick wanted to learn like the other boys.

    (B) she recognized his natural ability.

    (C) she wanted to comply with the laws of the state.

    (D) he needed to read to work in the home.

    (E) she obeyed her husband's wishes in the matter.

14. The title that best expresses the ideas of this passage is

    (A) The History of the Anti-Slavery Movement.

    (B) The Dogged Determination of Frederick Douglass.

    (C) Reading: Window to the World.

    (D) Frederick Douglass's Contributions to Freedom.

    (E) The Oratorical and Literary Brilliance of Frederick Douglass.

15. In the context of the passage, "impromptu" is closest in meaning to

    (A) unprepared.   (D) loud and excited.

    (B) a quiet manner.   (E) elaborate.

    (C) forceful.

Question 16 refers to the following passage:

Acupuncture practitioners, those who use the placement of needles at strategic locations under the skin to block pain, have been tolerated by American physicians since the 1930s. This form of Chinese treatment has been used for about 3,000 years and until recently has been viewed suspiciously by the West. New research indicates that acupuncture might provide relief for sufferers of chronic back pain, arthritis, and recently pain experienced by alcoholics and drug users as they kick the habit.

16. According to the passage, acupuncture has been found to help people suffering from all of the following EXCEPT

(A) arthritis.

(B) recurring back pain.

(C) alcoholics in withdrawal.

(D) liver disease.

(E) drug addicts in withdrawal.

Question 17 refers to the following passage:

Each time a person opens his or her mouth to eat, he or she makes a nutritional decision. These selections make a definitive difference in how an individual looks, feels, and performs at work or play. When a good assortment of food in appropriate amounts is selected and eaten, the consequences are likely to be desirable levels of health and energy to allow one to be as active as needed. Conversely, when choices are less than desirable, the consequences can be poor health or limited energy or both. Studies of American diets, particularly the diets of the very young, reveal unsatisfactory dietary habits as evidenced by the numbers of overweight and out-of-shape young children.

17. The author's attitude toward American's dietary habits may be characterized as

(A) lacking in interest.   (D) angry.

(B) concerned.   (E) amused.

(C) informational.

Question 18 refers to the following passage:

Commercial enterprises frequently provide the backdrop for the birth of a new language. When members of different language communities need to communicate or wish to bargain with each other, they may develop a new language through a process called "pidginization." A pidgin language, or pidgin, never becomes a native language; rather, its use is limited to business transactions with members of other language communities. Pidgins consist of very simple grammatical structures and small vocabularies. They have tended to develop around coastal areas where seafarers first made contact with speakers of other languages.

18. The passage suggests which of the following about pidgins?

(A) We could expect to hear pidgins along the west coast of Africa and in the Pacific islands.

(B) Pidgins are a complicated combination of two languages.

(C) Pidgins are located in inland mountain regions.

(D) Pidgins become the main language after several generations of use.

(E) Pidgins are the languages of seafarers.

Question 19 refers to the following passage:

There are two ways of measuring mass. One method to determine the mass of a body is to use a beam-balance. By this method, an unknown mass is placed on one pan at the end of a beam. The known masses are added to the pan at the other end of the beam until the pans are balanced. Since the force of gravity is the same on each pan, the masses must also be the same on each pan. When the mass of a body is measured by comparison with known masses on a beam-balance, it is called the gravitational mass of the body.

The second method to determine the mass of a body is distinctly different; this method uses the property of inertia. To determine mass in this way, a mass is placed on a frictionless horizontal surface. When a known force is applied to it, the magnitude of the mass is measured by the amount of acceleration produced upon it by the known force. Mass measured in this way is said to be the inertial mass of the body in question. This method is seldom used because it involves both a frictionless surface and a difficult measurement of acceleration.

19. Which of the following statements can best be supported from the passage?

    (A) The gravitational and inertia mass methods measure different properties of the object.

    (B) The masses are equal when the weights are equal and cause the beam to be balanced.

    (C) Gravitational and inertial measurements do not give the same numerical value for mass.

    (D) The same result for a beam-balance method cannot be obtained at higher altitudes.

    (E) The mass of a body depends on where it is located in the universe.

Question 20 refers to the following statement:

Her introductory remarks provided a segue into the body of the speech.

20. In this context the word "segue" means

    (A) delivery.   (D) credential.

    (B) a pause.   (E) critique.

    (C) direction.

Questions 21 to 23 refer to the following passage:

One of the many tragedies of the Civil War was the housing and care of prisoners. The Andersonville prison, built by the Confederates in 1864 to accommodate 10,000 Union prisoners, was not completed when prisoners started arriving. Five months later the total number of men incarcerated there had risen to 31,678.

The sounds of death and dying were not diminished by surrender of weapons to a captor. Chances of survival for prisoners in Andersonville were not much better than in the throes of combat. Next to overcrowding, inadequate shelter caused unimaginable suffering. The Confederates were not equipped with the manpower, tools, or supplies necessary to house such a population of captives; prisoners themselves gathered lumber, logs, anything they could find to construct some sort of protection from the elements. Some prisoners dug holes in the ground, risking suffocation from cave-ins, but many hundreds were left exposed to the wind, rain, cold, and heat.

Daily food rations were exhausted by the sheer numbers they had to serve, resulting in severe dietary deficiencies. The overcrowding, meager rations, and deplorable unsanitary conditions resulted in rampant disease and a high mortality rate. The consequences of a small scratch or wound could result in death in Andersonville. During the prison's 13-month existence, more than 12,000 prisoners died and were buried in the Andersonville cemetery. Most of the deaths were caused by diarrhea, dysentery, gangrene, and scurvy that could not be treated due to inadequate staff and supplies.

21. What is the central idea of the passage?

(A) The major problem for the Confederates was finding burial spaces in the cemetery.

(B) The prison was never fully completed.

(C) Prison doctors were ill-equipped to handle emergencies.

(D) Andersonville prison was not adequate to care for three times as many prisoners as it could hold.

(E) Many prisoners died as a result of shelter cave-ins.

22. From this passage the author's attitude toward the Confederates is one of

(A) approval.   (D) indifference.

(B) impartiality.   (E) denial.

(C) contempt.

23. The first sentence of the second paragraph of this passage can best be described as

(A) a tribute.   (D) an exposé.

(B) a digression.   (E) an irony.

(C) a hypothesis.

Question 24 refers to the following statement:

Maria commented to Joe, "Ted's nose is out of joint because he wasn't invited to the reception."

24. Someone hearing the conversation would most likely conclude that Ted

    (A) had a swollen nose.

    (B) does not have a large nose.

    (C) was upset about not being asked to the reception.

    (D) was not invited to the reception because his nose was hurt.

    (E) had a bandage on his nose at the reception.

Questions 25 to 27 refer to the following passage:

To the Shakers, perfection was found in the creation of an object that was both useful and simple. Their Society was founded in 1774 by Ann Lee, an Englishwoman from the working classes who brought eight followers to New York with her. "Mother Ann" established her religious community on the belief that worldly interests were evil.

To gain entrance into the Society, believers had to remain celibate, have no private possessions, and avoid contact with outsiders. The order came to be called "Shakers" because of the feverish dance the group performed. Another characteristic of the group was the desire to seek perfection in their work.

Shaker furniture was created to exemplify specific characteristics: simplicity of design, quality of craftsmanship, harmony of proportion, and usefulness. While Shakers did not create any innovations in furniture designs, they were known for fine craftsmanship. The major emphasis was on function, and not on excessive or elaborate decorations that contributed nothing to the product's usefulness.

25. The passage indicates that members of the religious order were called "Shakers" because

    (A) they shook hands at their meetings.

    (B) they did a shaking dance at their meetings.

    (C) they took their name from the founder.

    (D) they were named after the township where they originated.

    (E) they developed a shaking disorder.

26. Which of the following is the most appropriate substitute for the use of the term "innovations" in the third paragraph?

    (A) Corrections   (D) Functions

    (B) Colors   (E) Brocades

    (C) Changes

27. The passage suggests which of the following about the Shakers?

    (A) Shaker furniture is well-proportioned and ornate in design.

    (B) Shakers believed in form over function in their designs.

    (C) Shaker furniture has seen a surge in popularity.

    (D) Shakers appeared to believe that form follows function.

    (E) Shaker furniture is noted for the use of brass hardware.

Questions 28 and 29 refer to the following passage:

James Dean began his career as a stage actor, but in motion pictures he symbolized the confused, restless, and idealistic youth of the 1950s. He excelled at film parts that called for brooding, impulsive characterizations, the personification of frustrated youthful passion. Dean made three such movies: *East of Eden, Rebel Without a Cause*, and *Giant*, and established himself as a cult hero. Tragically, his career was cut short in an automobile crash before the release of *Giant*.

28. One conclusion that could be drawn from this passage is that

    (A) James Dean was not well regarded because of the kind of characters he portrayed.

    (B) James Dean had to be replaced by another actor in *Giant* due to his death.

    (C) James Dean was adept at portraying sensitive, youthful characters.

    (D) James Dean had a long and distinguished career.

    (E) James Dean was a promising stage actor.

29. The author's attitude is one of

    (A) regret.   (D) pessimism.

    (B) anger.   (E) indifference.

    (C) humor.

Questions 30 to 32 refer to the following passage:

Benjamin Franklin began writing his autobiography in 1771, but he set it aside to assist the colonies in gaining independence from England. After a hiatus of 13 years, he returned to chronicle his life, addressing his message to the younger generation. In this significant literary work of early United States, Franklin portrays himself as benign, kindhearted, practical, and hard-working. He established a list of ethical conduct and recorded his transgressions when he was unsuccessful in overcoming temptation. Franklin wrote that he was unable to arrive at perfection, "yet I was, by the endeavor, a better and happier man than I otherwise should have been if I had not attempted it."

30. Which of the following is the LEAST appropriate substitute for the use of the term "ethical" near the end of the passage?

(A) Moral   (D) Honorable

(B) Depraved   (E) Qualifiable

(C) Virtuous

31. The passage suggests which of the following about Franklin's autobiography?

(A) It was representative of early American literature.

(B) It fell short of being a major work of literary quality.

(C) It personified Franklin as a major political figure.

(D) It was a notable work of early American literature.

(E) It was directed toward his enemies.

32. Which of the following slogans best describes Franklin's assessment of the usefulness of attempting to achieve perfection?

(A) Cleanliness is next to godliness.

(B) Nothing ventured, nothing gained.

(C) Ambition is its own reward.

(D) Time is money.

(E) Humility is everything.

Questions 33 to 35 refer to the pie chart below:

How the Average Consumer Spent Money in 2009
Total: $62,580

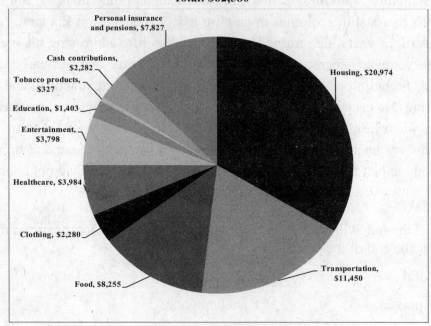

Personal insurance and pensions, $7,827

Cash contributions, $2,282

Tobacco products, $327

Education, $1,403

Entertainment, $3,798

Healthcare, $3,984

Clothing, $2,280

Food, $8,255

Housing, $20,974

Transportation, $11,450

Source: 2008 Census Bureau's Statistical Abstract of the U.S.

33. According to the graph, the average consumer spent approximately 50 percent of her/his earnings on

(A) housing and health care costs.

(B) transportation and housing.

(C) leisure pursuits and food.

(D) transportation and pensions.

(E) none of the above.

34. After transportation, the next greatest amount of money was spent on

(A) clothing.   (D) health care.

(B) other.   (E) personal insurance and pensions.

(C) food.

35. According to the graph, expenditure on health care was approximately equal to

(A) entertainment.   (D) food.

(B) insurance.   (E) other.

(C) pensions.

Questions 36 to 38 refer to the following passage:

The scarlet flamingo is practically a symbol of Florida. Once the West Indian flamingo population wintered in Florida Bay and as far north as St. John's River and Tampa Bay, but the brilliantly colored birds abandoned these grounds around 1885 due to the decimation of their numbers by feather hunters. The flock at Hialeah Race Track is descended from a handful of birds imported from Cuba in the 1930s. It took seven years before the first flamingo was born in captivity, but several thousand have since been hatched.

Flamingo raisers found that the birds require a highly specialized diet of shrimps and mollusks to maintain their attractive coloring. It is speculated that hunters as well as the birds' selective breeding habits perhaps caused the disappearance of these beautiful birds from the wild in North America.

36. The central idea of the passage is that the flamingos of Florida

(A) are a symbol of Florida.

(B) are hard to raise in captivity.

(C) are no longer found in the wild in North America.

(D) came from Cuba.

(E) eat shrimps and mollusks.

37. The word "decimation" is closest in meaning to

(A) destination.   (D) eradication.

(B) desecration.   (E) appeasement.

(C) restoration.

38. According to the passage, which of the following is responsible for the flamingo's brilliant plumage?

(A) Warm waters off the coast of Florida

(B) Selective breeding

(C) Their diet of marine organisms

(D) Shallow water plants

(E) Fish and water snakes

Questions 39 and 40 refer to the following passage:

Teachers should be cognizant of the responsibility they have for the development of children's competencies in basic concepts and principles of free speech. Freedom of speech is not merely the utterance of sounds into the air, rather, it is couched in a set of values and legislative processes that have developed over time. These values and processes are a part of our political conscience as Americans. Teachers must provide ample opportunities for children to express themselves effectively in an environment where their opinions are valued. Children should have ownership in the decision-making process in the classroom and should be engaged in activities where alternative resolutions to problems can be explored. Because teachers have such tremendous power to influence in the classroom, they must be careful to refrain from presenting their own values and biases that could "color" their students' belief systems. If we want children to develop their own voices in a free society, then teachers must support participatory democratic experiences in the daily workings of the classroom.

39. The title that best expresses the ideas in the passage is

    (A) The Nature of the Authoritarian Classroom.

    (B) Concepts and Principles of Free Speech.

    (C) Management Practices that Work.

    (D) Exploring Freedom in American Classrooms.

    (E) Developing Children's Citizenship Competencies.

40. It can be inferred from the passage that instructional strategies that assist children in the development of citizenship competencies include all of the following EXCEPT

    (A) children participation in rule making.

    (B) fostering self-esteem.

    (C) indoctrination in principles of society.

    (D) consideration of cultural and gender differences.

    (E) conflict management skills taught.

Section II: Mathematics

TIME: *60 Minutes*
         40 Questions

DIRECTIONS: Each of the questions or incomplete statements below is followed by five suggested answers or completions. Select the one that is best in each case.

1. Simplify the following expression: $6 + 2(x - 4)$.

    (A) $4x - 16$ (D) $-24x$

    (B) $2x - 14$ (E) $4x$

    (C) $2x - 2$

2. Referring to the following figure, if the measure of $\angle C$ is 20° and the measure of $\angle CBD$ is 36°, then what is the measure of $\angle A$?

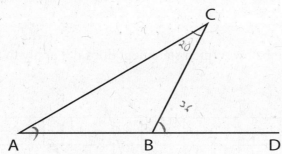

    (A) 16°   (D) 56°

    (B) 20°   (E) 144°

    (C) 36°

3. If six cans of beans cost $1.50, what is the price of eight cans of beans?

    (A) $.90   (D) $2.00

    (B) $1.00   (E) $9.60

    (C) $1.60

4. Bonnie's average score on three tests is 71. Her first two test scores are 64 and 87. What is her score on test three?

   (A) 62   (D) 151

   (B) 71   (E) 222

   (C) 74

5. In the figure below, what is the perimeter of square *ABCD* if diagonal *AC* = 8?

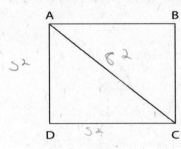

   (A) 32   (D) $16\sqrt{2}$

   (B) 64   (E) $8\sqrt{3}$

   (C) $4\sqrt{2}$

6. Examine the line below. Which statement does not apply to the graph?

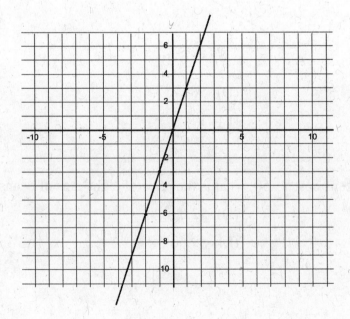

(A) Both the x-coordinates and the y-coordinates are increasing.

(B) The x-coordinate is three times the y-coordinate

(C) The y-coordinate is three times the x-coordinate

(D) The point (5, 15) will lie on the graph.

(E) The x- and y-intercepts are the same point.

7.   A jar contains 20 balls. These balls are labeled 1 through 20. What is the probability that a ball chosen from the jar has a number on it which is divisible by 4?

(A) $\dfrac{1}{20}$ (D) 4

(B) $\dfrac{1}{5}$ (E) 5

(C) $\dfrac{1}{4}$

8.   If $2x^2 + 5x - 3 = 0$ and $x > 0$, then what is the value of x?

(A) $-\dfrac{1}{2}$ (D) $\dfrac{3}{2}$

(B) $\dfrac{1}{2}$ (E) 3

(C) 1

9.   Which set of data below does not have a mean of 30?

(A) 20, 30, 30, 40   (D) 15, 45

(B) 10, 10, 10   (E) 15, 15, 15, 50, 55

(C) 22, 24, 15, 19, 40, 60

10. According to the following chart, in what year werethe total sales of Brand X television the greatest?

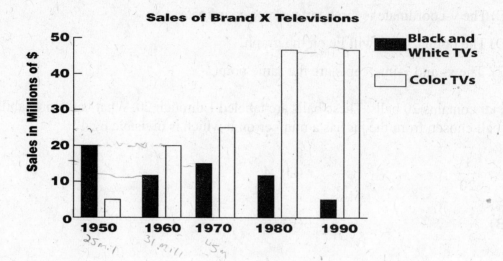

Sales of Brand X Televisions

(A) 1950

(D) 1980

(B) 1960

(E) 1990

(C) 1970

11. Ella bought two-dozen donuts. There were 6 glazed, 6 chocolate, and 12 jelly-filled donuts. What is the probability that if Ella picked a donut at random, she would select a chocolate one?

(A) $\dfrac{6}{12}$

(D) $\dfrac{1}{24}$

(B) $\dfrac{12}{18}$

(E) $\dfrac{6}{18}$

(C) $\dfrac{6}{24}$

12. Two concentric circles are shown in the figure below. The smaller circle has radius $OA = 4$ and the larger circle has radius $OB = 6$. Find the area of the shaded region.

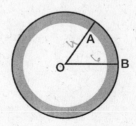

(A) 4π (D) 36π

(B) 16π (E) 100π

(C) 20π

13. Solve the following inequality for x: $8 - 2x \leq 10$.

(A) $x \leq 1$ (D) $x \geq -1$

(B) $x \geq -9$ (E) $x \leq \dfrac{5}{3}$

(C) $x \leq -1$

14. Calculate the expression shown below and write the answer in scientific notation.

0.003×1.25

(A) 3.75 (D) 3.75×10^{-3}

(B) 0.375×10^{-2} (E) 3.75×10^{3}

(C) 0.375×10^{2}

15. In the figure below $l_1 \parallel l_2$, ΔRTS is an isosceles triangle, and the measure of $\angle T = 80°$. Find the measure of $\angle OPR$.

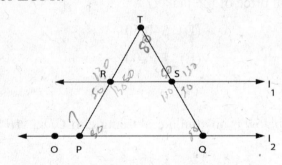

(A) $50°$ (D) $105°$

(B) $80°$ (E) $130°$

(C) $100°$

16. Danny tossed a six-sided number cube 25 times and got the results shown in the table below. What percent of the time did Danny get a 4?

Number on cube	1	2	3	4	5	6
Frequency	3	6	2	7	6	1

(A) 4%   (D) 28%

(B) 7%   (E) 33%

(C) 21%

17. The ratio of men to women at University X is 3:7. If there are 6,153 women at University X, how many men are at University X?

    (A) 879   (D) 2,637
    (B) 1,895   (E) 14,357
    (C) 2,051

18. For which set of data does the number 10 represent the mean?

    (A) 4, 5, 10, 13, 23   (D) 1, 5, 8, 11, 19
    (B) 3, 5, 5, 8, 13   (E) 7, 8, 8, 12, 15
    (C) 2, 10, 10, 10, 11

19. Linda bought a jacket on sale at a 25 percent discount. If she paid $54 for the jacket, what was the original price of the jacket?

    (A) $72.00   (D) $40.50
    (B) $67.50   (E) $36.00
    (C) $54.00

20. Assume that $\triangle ABC$ below is an equilateral triangle. If $CD \perp AB$ and $CD = 6$, what is the area of $\triangle ABC$?

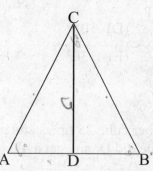

    (A) $3\sqrt{3}$ (D) 18
    (B) 12   (E) 36
    (C) $12\sqrt{3}$

21. The formula relating the Celsius (C) and the Fahrenheit (F) scales of temperature is shown below. Find the temperature in the Celsius scale when the temperature is 86° F.

$$F = \frac{9}{5}C + 32$$

(A) 25°

(B) 30°

(C) 105°

(D) 124.6°

(E) 188.6°

22. In the number 72104.58, what is the place value of the 2?

(A) Thousands

(B) Millions

(C) Ten thousands

(D) Tenths

(E) Thousandths

23. Mrs. Wall has $300,000. She wishes to give each of her six children an equal amount of her money. Which of the following methods will result in the amount that each child is to receive?

(A) 6 × 300,000

(B) 6 ÷ 300,000

(C) 300,000 ÷ 6

(D) 6 − 300,000

(E) 300,000 − 6

24. Referring to the figure below, what is the length of $\overline{PQ}$?

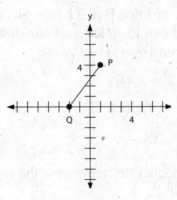

(A) $2\sqrt{5}$

(B) $5\sqrt{2}$

(C) 5

(D) 7

(E) 25

25. Bob wants to bake some cupcakes. His recipe uses $2\frac{2}{3}$ cups of flour to produce 36 cupcakes. How many cups of flour should Bob use to bake 12 cupcakes?

    (A) $\frac{1}{3}$

    (B) $\frac{8}{9}$

    (C) 1

    (D) $1\frac{1}{3}$

    (E) $1\frac{2}{3}$

26. The area of rectangle *EFGH* below is 120 and $\overline{EF}$ is twice as long as $\overline{EH}$. Which of the following is the best approximation of the length of $\overline{EH}$?

    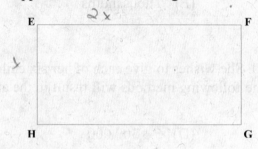

    (A) 7

    (B) 8

    (C) 10

    (D) 12

    (E) 15

27. Ricky drove from Town A to Town B in 3 hours. His return trip from Town B to Town A took 5 hours because he drove 15 miles per hour slower on the return trip. How fast did Ricky drive on the trip from Town A to Town B?

    (A) 25.5

    (B) 32

    (C) 37.5

    (D) 45

    (E) 52

28. Which of the following inequalities represents the shaded region in the figure below?

    (A) $x \geq 2$

    (B) $x \leq 2$

    (C) $y \geq 2$

    (D) $y \leq 2$

    (E) $x + y \geq 2$

Question 29 refers to the graph below.

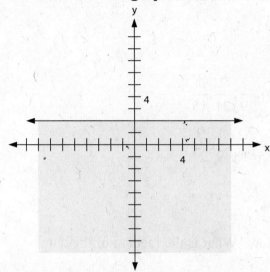

29. Given that x, y, and z are any real numbers, which of the following statements are true?

    I.   If $x > y$, then $x^2 > y^2$.

    II. If $x > y$, then $x + z > y + z$.

    III. If $x > y$, then $x - y > 0$.

    IV. If $x > y$, then $xz > yz$.

    (A) I and II only

    (B) II and III only

    (C) II and IV only

    (D) I, II, and III only

    (E) II, III, and IV only

30. Round the following number to the nearest hundredths place: 287.416.

    (A) 300

    (B) 290

    (C) 287.4

    (D) 287.41

    (E) 287.42

31. Simplify the following expression.

    $$\frac{x^2 \times x^2}{x}$$

    (A) x^6

    (B) x^7

    (C) x^8

    (D) x^{10}

    (E) x^{13}

32. List the fractions shown below from least to greatest.

$$\frac{1}{9}, \frac{2}{15}, \frac{3}{21}$$

(A) $\frac{1}{9}, \frac{2}{15}, \frac{3}{21}$ (D) $\frac{1}{9}, \frac{3}{21}, \frac{2}{15}$

(B) $\frac{2}{15}, \frac{3}{21}, \frac{1}{9}$ (E) $\frac{2}{15}, \frac{1}{9}, \frac{3}{21}$

(C) $\frac{3}{21}, \frac{1}{9}, \frac{2}{15}$

33. Examine the stem-and-leaf plot below. What is the median of the data?

Stem	Leaf
5	1
6	
7	
8	4 5 6
9	2 9
10	
11	3 4
12	1 2 4
13	8
14	4 7 8
15	1

(A) 113   (D) 121

(B) 114   (E) 125.5

(C) 117.5

34. If $x = -3$, then find the value of $-x^2 + 2x$.

(A) −15   (D) 6

(B) −3   (E) 15

(C) 3

35. If $a = b^3$ and $a = \dfrac{1}{8}$, what is the value of b?

   (A) $\dfrac{1}{512}$ (D) $\dfrac{1}{2}$

   (B) $\dfrac{1}{8}$ (E) $\dfrac{3}{2}$

   (C) $\dfrac{3}{8}$

36. In a barn there were cows and people. If we counted 30 heads and 104 legs in the barn, how many cows and how many people were in the barn?

   (A) 10 cows and 20 people   (D) 22 cows and 8 people

   (B) 16 cows and 14 people   (E) 24 cows and 4 people

   (C) 18 cows and 16 people

37. Solve for x in the following proportion.

$$\frac{12}{x-1} = \frac{5}{6}$$

   (A) 14.6   (D) 16.6

   (B) 15.4   (E) 16.8

   (C) 16

38. Ingrid earned the following scores on four history tests: 87, 76, 95, and 88. What is the lowest grade she can get on the next test to guarantee an average of at least 85?

   (A) 79

   (B) 81

   (C) 83

   (D) 87

   (E) 89

39. What is $\dfrac{1}{2} + \dfrac{1}{3}$?

    (A) $\dfrac{1}{5}$ (D) $\dfrac{2}{6}$

    (B) $\dfrac{2}{5}$ (E) $\dfrac{5}{6}$

    (C) $\dfrac{1}{6}$

40. Given that $\overline{BC} \parallel \overline{DE}$ in the following figure, write down the pair of similar ($\sim$) triangles.

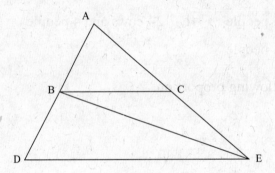

    (A) $\triangle ABC \sim \triangle ADE$ (D) $\triangle BCE \sim \triangle BAC$

    (B) $\triangle ABC \sim \triangle ABE$ (E) $\triangle ADE \sim \triangle CBE$

    (C) $\triangle ABC \sim \triangle AED$

Section III: Writing

TIME: *30 Minutes*
        38 Questions

Part A: Usage

DIRECTIONS: Each of the following sentences may contain an error in diction, usage, idiom, or grammar. Some sentences are correct. Some sentences contain one error. No sentence contains more than one error.

If there is an error, it will appear in one of the underlined portions labeled A, B, C, or D. If there is no error, choose the portion labeled E. If there is an error, select the letter of the portion that must be changed in order to correct the sentence.

EXAMPLE:

He drove <u>slowly</u> and <u>cautiously</u> in order to <u>hopefully</u> avoid having an <u>accident</u>.
     A   B   C   D

<u>No error</u>.
 E

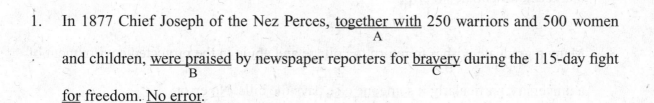

                                                (A)(B)(●)(D)(E)

1. In 1877 Chief Joseph of the Nez Perces, <u>together with</u> 250 warriors and 500 women
                                                   A

    and children, <u>were praised</u> by newspaper reporters for <u>bravery</u> during the 115-day fight
                  B   C

    <u>for</u> freedom. <u>No error</u>.
     D   E

2. The ideals <u>upon which</u> American society <u>is based</u> <u>are</u> primarily those of Europe and
                A   B   C

    not ones <u>derived from</u> the native Indian culture. <u>No error</u>.
             D   E

3. <u>An astute and powerful</u> woman, Frances Nadel <u>was</u> a beauty contest winner before she
          A   B

    <u>became</u> president of the company <u>upon the death</u> of her husband. <u>No error</u>.
     C   D   E

4. Representative Wilson <u>pointed out</u>, however, that the legislature <u>had not finalized</u> the
                A   B

   state budget and salary increases <u>had depended</u> on decisions <u>to be made</u> in a special
                                          C   D

   session. <u>No error</u>.
          E

5. Now the <u>city</u> librarian, doing more than checking out books, must help <u>to plan</u> puppet
            A   B

   shows and movies for children, garage sales for <u>used</u> books, and <u>arranging for</u> guest
                                                         C   D

   lecturers and exhibits for adults. <u>No error</u>.
                                         E

6. In order <u>to completely understand</u> the psychological <u>effects</u> of the bubonic plague,
                     A   B

   <u>one must</u> realize that one-fourth to one-third of the population in an <u>affected</u> area died.
     C   D

   <u>No error</u>.
    E

7. Rural roads, <u>known</u> in the United States as farm to market roads, have always been a
                A

   vital <u>link in</u> the econmy of <u>more advanced</u> nations because transportation of goods to
         B   C

   markets <u>is</u> essential. <u>No error</u>.
          D   E

8. <u>Many a</u> graduate <u>wishes</u> to return to college and <u>abide in</u> the protected environment of
     A   B   C

   a university, particularly if <u>someone else</u> pays the bills. <u>No error</u>.
                              D   E

9. <u>Confronted with</u> a choice of either <u>cleaning up</u> his room or <u>cleaning out</u> the garage,
       A   B   C

   the teenager became very <u>aggravated</u> with his parents. <u>No error</u>.
                           D   E

10. My brother and <u>I</u> dressed as <u>quickly</u> as we could, but we missed the school bus, <u>which</u>
                 A   B   C

    made <u>us</u> late for class today. <u>No error</u>.
       D   E

11. <u>Among</u> the activities <u>offered at</u> the local high school <u>through</u> the community education
      A   B   C

program <u>are</u> singing in the couples' chorus, ballroom dancing, and Chinese cooking.
       D

<u>No error</u>.
 E

12. If you are <u>disappointed by</u> an <u>inexpensive</u> bicycle, then an option you might consider
               A   B

is to work this summer and <u>save</u> your money for a <u>more expensive</u> model. <u>No error</u>.
                      C   D   E

13. Also being presented to the city council this morning <u>is</u> the mayor's city budget for
                                           A

next year and plans <u>to renovate</u> the <u>existing</u> music theater, so the session <u>will focus</u> on
                 B   C   D

financial matters. <u>No error</u>.
             E

14. Even a movement <u>so delicate</u> as a <u>fly's walking</u> triggers the Venus flytrap <u>to grow</u> extra
                  A   B   C

cells on the outside of <u>its</u> hinge, immediately closing the petals of the trap. <u>No error</u>.
               D   E

15. Although <u>outwardly</u> Thomas Hardy seemed quite <u>the picture</u> of <u>respectability</u> and con-
          A   B   C

tentment, his works, especially the prose, <u>deals with</u> the theme of man's inevitable suf-
                                       D

fering. <u>No error</u>.
       E

16. Though <u>unequal in</u> social standing, the everyday lives of ancient Egyptian kings and
        A

commoners <u>alike</u> are visible in the pictures of <u>them</u> found <u>inside of</u> tombs and tem-
          B   C   D

ples. <u>No error</u>.
     E

17. Sometimes considered <u>unsafe for</u> crops, land around river <u>deltas</u> <u>can be</u> excellent land
                    A   B   C

for farming because periodic flooding deposits silt rich <u>in</u> nutrients. <u>No error</u>.
                                          D   E

18. For years <u>people</u> concerned with the environment <u>have compiled</u> information which
    A B

    <u>show</u> many species are extinct and others <u>are either</u> endangered or bordering on be-
    C D

    coming endangered. <u>No error</u>.
    E

19. Little is known about Shakespeare's boyhood or his early career as an actor and

    playwright, but he <u>appears to have been</u> a financial success <u>because he bought</u> many
    A B

    properties, including <u>one of the finest</u> homes in Stratford, the town he <u>was born in</u>.
    C D

    <u>No error</u>.
    E

20. *Scared Straight*, a program designed <u>to inhibit</u> criminal <u>behavior in</u> juvenile offend-
    A B

    ers <u>who</u> seemed bound for prison as adults, had a significant <u>affect</u> on the youngsters.
    C D

    <u>No error</u>.
    E

21. The <u>average</u> American tourist feels <u>quite</u> at home in a Japanese stadium filled
    A B

    <u>at capacity</u> with sports fans watching Japan's <u>most</u> popular sport, baseball. <u>No error</u>.
    C D E

22. My brother is <u>engaged</u> to a woman <u>who</u> my parents <u>have</u> not met because she has not
    A B C

    yet <u>emigrated from</u> her native country of Ecuador. <u>No error</u>.
    D E

23. Colonel Jones <u>denies that</u> he <u>illegally</u> delivered funds to a foreign government agent or
    A B

    that <u>he</u> was involved in <u>any other</u> covert activity. <u>No error</u>.
    C D E

24. In the United States, <u>testing for</u> toxicity, determining the <u>proper</u> dose and timing
    A B

    between doses, and evaluating the vaccine for <u>effectiveness</u> <u>is</u> the method used in re-
    C D

    searching new drugs. <u>No error</u>.
    E

25. George wants <u>to know if</u> <u>it is her</u> driving that expensive red sports car
A   B

<u>at a rate of speed</u> <u>obviously exceeding</u> the posted speed limit. <u>No error.</u>
C   D   E

Part B: Sentence Correction

DIRECTIONS: In each of the following sentences, some portion of the sentence is underlined. Under each sentence are five choices. The first choice has the same wording as the original. The other four choices are reworded. Sometimes the first choice containing the original wording is the best; sometimes one of the other choices is the best. Choose the letter of the best choice. Your choice should produce a sentence which is not ambiguous or awkward and which is correct, clear, and precise.

This is a test of correct and effective English expression. Keep in mind the standards of English usage, punctuation, grammar, word choice, and construction.

EXAMPLE:

When you listen to opera, <u>a person may not appreciate it.</u>

(A) a person may not appreciate it.

(B) it may not be appreciated by a person.

(C) which may not be appreciated by one.

(D) you may not appreciate it.

(E) appreciating it may be a problem for you.

26. <u>Being that you bring home more money than I do</u>, it is only fitting you should pay proportionately more rent.

(A) Being that you bring home more money than I do

(B) Bringing home the more money of the two of us

(C) When more money is made by you than by me

(D) Because you bring home more money than I do

(E) If your bringing home more money than me

27. So tenacious is their grip on life, that sponge cells will regroup and form a new sponge even <u>when they are</u> squeezed through silk.

    (A) when they are

    (B) since they have been

    (C) as they will be

    (D) after they have been

    (E) because they should be

28. <u>Seeing as how the plane is late</u>, wouldn't you prefer to wait for a while on the observation deck?

    (A) Seeing as how the plane is late

    (B) When the plane comes in

    (C) Since the plane is late

    (D) Being as the plane is late

    (E) While the plane is landing

29. Only with careful environmental planning can we protect the <u>world we live in</u>.

    (A) world we live in

    (B) world in which we live in

    (C) living in this world

    (D) world's living

    (E) world in which we live

30. In the last three years we have added more varieties of vegetables to our garden <u>than those you suggested in the beginning</u>.

    (A) than those you suggested in the beginning

    (B) than the ones we began with

    (C) beginning with your suggestion

    (D) than what you suggested to us

    (E) which you suggested in the beginning

31. As you know, I am not easily fooled by flattery, and while <u>nice words please you,</u> they don't get the job done.

    (A) nice words please you

    (B) nice words are pleasing

    (C) nice words please a person

    (D) flattering words please people

    (E) flattering words are pleasing to some

32. Some pieces of the puzzle, in spite of Jane's search, <u>are still missing and probably will never be found</u>.

    (A) are still missing and probably will never be found

    (B) is missing still but never found probably

    (C) probably will be missing and never found

    (D) are still probably missing and to never be found

    (E) probably are missing and will not be found

33. *Gone With the Wind* <u>is the kind of a movie</u> producers would like to release because it would bring them fame.

    (A) is the kind of a movie

    (B) is the sort of movie

    (C) is the kind of movie

    (D) is the type of a movie

    (E) is the category of movie

34. Eighteenth century architecture, with its columns and balanced lines, <u>was characteristic of those of previous times in Greece and Rome</u>.

    (A) was characteristic of those of previous times in Greece and Rome

    (B) is similar to characteristics of Greece and Rome

    (C) is similar to Greek and Roman building styles

    (D) is characteristic with earlier Greek and Roman architecture

    (E) was similar to architecture of Greece and Rome

35. Plato, one of the famous Greek philosophers, won many wrestling prizes when he was a young man, thus <u>exemplifying the Greek ideal of balance between the necessity for physical activity and using one's mind</u>.

    (A) exemplifying the Greek ideal of balance between the necessity for physical activity and using one's mind

    (B) serving as an example of the Greek ideal of balance between physical and mental activities

    (C) an example of balancing Greek mental and athletic games

    (D) this as an example of the Greek's balance between mental physical pursuits

    (E) shown to be exemplifying the balancing of two aspects of Greek life, the physical and the mental

36. Allied control of the Philippine Islands during World War II proved to be <u>another obstacle as the Japanese scattered resistance</u> until the end of the war.

    (A) another obstacle as the Japanese scattered resistance

    (B) difficult because of the Japanese giving resistance

    (C) continuing scattered Japanese resistance as obstacles

    (D) as another scattered obstacle due to Japanese resistance

    (E) difficult because the Japanese gave scattered resistance

37. Flooding abated and the river waters receded as the <u>rainfall finally let up</u>.

    (A) rainfall finally let up

    (B) rain having let up

    (C) letting up of the rainfall

    (D) rainfall, when it finally let up

    (E) raining finally letting up

38. Unless China slows its population growth to zero, that country <u>would still have</u> a problem feeding its people.

    (A) would still have

    (B) will have still had

    (C) might have had still

    (D) will still have

    (E) would have still

Part C: Essay

TIME: *30 Minutes*

DIRECTIONS: You have 30 minutes to plan and write an essay on the topic below. You may write only on the assigned topic.

Make sure to give specific examples to support your thesis. Proofread your essay carefully and take care to express your ideas clearly and effectively.

Write your essay on the lined pages at the back of the book.

ESSAY TOPIC:

In the twenty-first century, the concept of heroism is dead.

ASSIGNMENT: Do you agree or disagree with the statement? Support your opinion with specific examples from history, current events, literature, or personal experience.

Answer Key

Section 1: Reading Comprehension

1. **(D)**	11. **(C)**	21. **(D)**	31. **(D)**
2. **(B)**	12. **(B)**	22. **(B)**	32. **(B)**
3. **(B)**	13. **(B)**	23. **(E)**	33. **(B)**
4. **(B)**	14. **(D)**	24. **(C)**	34. **(C)**
5. **(E)**	15. **(A)**	25. **(B)**	35. **(A)**
6. **(D)**	16. **(D)**	26. **(C)**	36. **(C)**
7. **(E)**	17. **(B)**	27. **(D)**	37. **(D)**
8. **(B)**	18. **(A)**	28. **(C)**	38. **(C)**
9. **(B)**	19. **(B)**	29. **(A)**	39. **(E)**
10. **(C)**	20. **(C)**	30. **(B)**	40. **(C)**

Section II: Mathematics

1. **(C)**	11. **(C)**	21. **(B)**	31. **(C)**
2. **(A)**	12. **(C)**	22. **(A)**	32. **(A)**
3. **(D)**	13. **(D)**	23. **(C)**	33. **(C)**
4. **(A)**	14. **(D)**	24. **(C)**	34. **(A)**
5. **(D)**	15. **(E)**	25. **(B)**	35. **(D)**
6. **(B)**	16. **(D)**	26. **(B)**	36. **(D)**
7. **(C)**	17. **(D)**	27. **(C)**	37. **(B)**
8. **(B)**	18. **(E)**	28. **(D)**	38. **(A)**
9. **(B)**	19. **(A)**	29. **(B)**	39. **(E)**
10. **(D)**	20. **(C)**	30. **(E)**	40. **(A)**

Section III: Writing

1. **(B)**	13. **(A)**	25. **(B)**	37. **(A)**
2. **(E)**	14. **(A)**	26. **(D)**	38. **(D)**
3. **(B)**	15. **(D)**	27. **(D)**	
4. **(C)**	16. **(D)**	28. **(C)**	
5. **(D)**	17. **(E)**	29. **(E)**	
6. **(A)**	18. **(C)**	30. **(A)**	
7. **(C)**	19. **(D)**	31. **(B)**	
8. **(E)**	20. **(D)**	32. **(A)**	
9. **(D)**	21. **(C)**	33. **(C)**	
10. **(C)**	22. **(B)**	34. **(E)**	
11. **(E)**	23. **(C)**	35. **(B)**	
12. **(A)**	24. **(E)**	36. **(E)**	

PRACTICE TEST 1 – Detailed Explanations of Answers

Section I: Reading Comprehension

1. **D**

    It is implied that the poisoning of animal carcasses in the habitat of bald eagles presents a new danger of extinction for America's symbol. Choices (A), (C), and (E) are not mentioned in the passage. Choice (B) suggests a reason for the poisoning; however, the overall focus of the passage does not support this.

2. **B**

    The author's use of words such as "mighty bald eagle" and "threatened by a new menace" supports concern for the topic. Therefore, choices (A) and (C) are not applicable. The author appears for the most part, to be objective. Answers (D) and (E) are too strong to be correct.

3. **B**

    Ms. Green's sales equaled, then exceeded Ms. Roman's Quarter 2.

4. **B**

    The question asks you to approximate your answer. There are no grid lines to make an exact determination, therefore you must make your best guess. Ms. Roman sold approximately 23 cars in Quarter 1.

5. **E**

    If Alice is uncomfortable with remarks about her performance on the job, it could mean either that the remarks were unkind or that compliments might lead to embarrassment. However, the prefix "dis" means to take away or not. In this instance then, we can assume that the remarks were not complimentary or funny, choices (A) and (C). Nothing in the text indicates that the remarks were technical or menacing, responses (B) and (D).

6. **D**

    Answer (D) fulfills requirements stated in rules 2 and 4 of the instructions for absentee voting. All other choices do not.

7. **E**

    Mr. Applebee's daughter must sign her own request for an absentee ballot. Since the passage indicates that she is registered, the most important instruction for her is number 6 (E).

8. **B**

    Choices (A), (D), and (E) are not stated in the passage. Choice (C) is not true unless voters have registered, answer (B).

9. **B**

    "Atrophy" and "incapacity" mean to experience a decrease in size and strength.

10. **C**

    The passage associates loss of mobility with a sedentary life-style.

11. **C**

    Douglass was interested in raising social consciousness about slavery. The passage stresses his interest in refuting those who doubted his claim to have been a slave.

12. **B**

    Choice (A) is not supported by the text. All other choices, while true, are irrelevant to the question.

13. **B**

    This choice is supported by the statement, "Mrs. Auld recognized Frederick's intellectual acumen." Choices (C) and (E) contradict information in the passage. The passage does not support choices (A) and (D).

14. **D**

    Choices (A), (B), and (C) are either too broad or too general. Choice (E) is too specific and limited to cover the information in the passage.

15. **A**

    An "impromptu" speech is one given suddenly without preparation.

16. **D**

All other choices are mentioned as providing relief from pain.

17. **B**

Use of terms "good," "consequences," and "desirable" indicate a concern for a healthy diet. Choices (A) and (C) contradict the author's attitude. Choices (D) and (E) are not supported by the text.

18. **A**

Choices (B), (C), and (D) are contradicted in the passage, and choice (E) is not relevant.

19. **B**

All other choices are not supported in the text.

20. **C**

A "segue" provides a direction or lead into the speech.

21. **D**

The passage states that housing of prisoners was "one of many tragedies of the Civil War," and that "overcrowding, meager rations… resulted in rampant disease and a high mortality rate," implying that the prison facility was inadequate for the number of prisoners. All other choices are discussed, but the main issue was overcrowded conditions.

22. **B**

The author emphasizes a lack of supplies and manpower to care for the prisoners, not a lack of interest in doing so by the Confederates. Hence, choices (C), (D), and (E) are not appropriate. Choice (A) is not suggested by the text.

23. **E**

An irony is a result that is the opposite of what might be expected or appropriate. The passage implies that being captured was not a guarantee of survival in Andersonville. This choice is supported by the second sentence of the second paragraph.

24. **C**

> The figure of speech "his or her nose is out of joint" is an expression used to indicate that someone feels slighted. It has nothing to do with the condition of someone's nose.

25. **B**

> This choice is supported by the first paragraph of the passage. All other choices are irrelevant to information in the passage.

26. **C**

> "Innovative" means to introduce something new or make changes.

27. **D**

> The passage discusses the importance of usefulness as well as simplicity to the Shakers; therefore, the function of the piece of furniture would be more important than the particular form. Choices (A), (B), and (E) are contradictory to the information given, while choice (C) is beyond information given in the text.

28. **C**

> The passage states that Dean "symbolized the confused, restless, and idealistic youth," which implies that he was adept at portraying sensitive youthful characters. Choices (A), (B), and (D) are contradictory to information in the text. Choice (E) is a conclusion not supported by the text.

29. **A**

> The author's use of the word "tragically" in reference to Dean's death indicates a feeling of regret.

30. **B**

> Depraved means corrupted or perverted. All other choices have to do with accepted standards of conduct.

31. **D**

> The author states that Franklin's work was a "significant work of early United States." Each of the other choices is not supported by the text.

32. **B**

> The final sentence of the paragraph supports this choice. Choice (C) might apply, but choice (B) is closest to the overall mood of the passage. Choices (A), (D), and (E) are not relevant to the question.

33. **B**

> Transportation and housing total about half of the $65,580.

34. **C**

> According to the graph, food is next after transportation in amount of expense paid by the consumer.

35. **A**

> According to the graph, health care was closest to entertainment in total amount spent.

36. **C**

> The author's use of the word "decimation" as well as the last sentence in the second paragraph supports this choice. All other choices are secondary to the central idea of the passage.

37. **D**

> To decimate is to eradicate or destroy a large part of something.

38. **C**

> This choice is supported by the first sentence of the second paragraph. All other choices are irrelevant to the discussion of the flamingo's plumage.

39. **E**

> The first and last sentences of the passage support this choice. Choice (A) contradicts information in the passage, and choices (B), (C), and (D) are too broad in nature and go beyond the scope of the passage.

40. **C**

> Reviewing the author's discussion of developing children's citizenship competencies, we may conclude that indoctrination is contradictory to information given in the passage.

Section II: Mathematics

1. **C**

    When simplifying algebraic expressions, always work from left to right. First perform all multiplications and divisions then once this is done, start again from the left and do all additions and subtractions.

    SUGGESTION: It can be helpful to translate the algebraic statement to English. For example, $6 + 2(x - 4)$ is "six plus two *times* the quantity x minus 4." The word *times* indicates multiplication, so we must first perform $2(x - 4)$ by using the *distributive property $a(b - c) = ab - ac$:*

    $$6 + 2(x - 4) = 6 + 2 \times x - 2 \times 4 = 6 + 2x - 8.$$

    Then we perform the subtraction to combine the terms 6 and 8:

    $$6 + 2x - 8 = 2x + (6 - 8) = 2x - 2.$$

    Note that we did not combine the $2x$ term with the other terms. This is because they are not *like terms*. Like terms are terms which have the same variables (with the same exponents). Since the terms 6 and 8 have no variable x, they are not like terms with $2x$.

2. **A**

    The sum of the measures of the interior angles of a triangle is 180°, therefore;

    $$\angle A + m\angle ABC + m\angle C = 180°.$$

    We also know that $m\angle C = 20°$, so if we substitute this into the previous equation we have

    $$m\angle A + m\angle ABC + 20° = 180°.$$

    Subtracting 20° from both sides of this equation gives us

    $$m\angle A + m\angle ABC = 160°$$

    or $m\angle A = 160° - m\angle ABC.$

    Therefore, if we know $m\angle ABC$, we are done! To find $m\angle ABC$, notice that $\angle ABD$ is a straight angle and, thus, $m\angle ABD = 180°$. But

    $$m\angle ABC + m\angle CBD = m\angle ABD.$$

    So, using the facts that

    $$m\angle CBD = 36° \text{ and } m\angle ABD = 180°,$$

    and substituting, we have

and substituting, we have

$$m\angle ABC + 36° = 180°$$

or $\quad m\angle ABC = 180° - 36° = 144°.$

Hence, $m\angle A = 160° - m\angle ABC = 160° - 144° = 16°.$

3. **D**

Let x be the cost of one can of beans. Then $6x$ is the cost of six cans of beans. So $6x = \$1.50$. Dividing both sides of the equation by 6, we get $x = \$.25$ and, hence, since $8x$ is the cost of eight cans of beans, we have

$$8x = 8 \times \$.25 = \$2.00.$$

4. **A**

Let t_1, t_2, and t_3 represent Bonnie's scores on tests one, two, and three, respectively. Then the equation representing Bonnie's average score is

$$\frac{t_1 + t_2 + t_3}{3} = 71.$$

We know that $t_1 = 64$ and $t_2 = 87$. Substitute this information into the equation above:

$$\frac{64 + 87 + t_3}{3} = 71$$

Combining 64 and 87 and then multiplying both sides of the equation by 3 gives us

$$3 \times \frac{151 + t_3}{3} = 3 \times 71$$

or $\quad 151 + t_3 = 213.$

Now subtract 151 from both sides of the equation so that

$$t_3 = 213 - 151 = 62.$$

5. **D**

Let s be the length of each side of square $ABCD$. Since triangle ADC is a right triangle, we can use the Pythagorean Theorem to solve for s. We have

$$AD^2 + DC^2 = AC^2$$

or $\quad s^2 + s^2 = 8^2.$

Simplifying the equation, we get: $2s^2 = 64$. Now divide both sides of the equation by two:

$$s^2 = 32 \text{ so } s = \sqrt{32} = \sqrt{16} \times \sqrt{2} = 4\sqrt{2}.$$

Therefore, the perimeter of square $ABCD$ is

$$P = 4s = 4 \times 4\sqrt{2} = 16\sqrt{2}.$$

6. **B**

As an example, one of the points on this graph is (1,3). This means that when $x = 1$, $y = 3$. We note that 1 is not equal to three times 3.

7. **C**

Note that the numbers 4, 8, 12, 16, and 20 are the only numbers from 1 through 20 that are divisible by 4. The probability that a ball chosen from the jar has a number on it which is divisible by 4 is given by

$$\frac{total\ number\ of\ balls\ with\ numbers\ that\ are\ divisible\ by\ 4}{total\ number\ of\ possible\ outcomes} = \frac{5}{20} = \frac{1}{4}$$

8. **B**

To solve the equation

$$2x^2 + 5x - 3 = 0,$$

we can factor the left side of the equation to get

$$(2x - 1)(x + 3) = 0.$$

Then use the following rule (this rule is sometimes called the Zero Product Property): If $a \times b = 0$, then either $a = 0$ or $b = 0$. Applying this to our problem gives us

$$2x - 1 = 0 \text{ or } x + 3 = 0.$$

Solve these two equations:

$$2x - 1 = 0 \rightarrow 2x = 1 \rightarrow x = \frac{1}{2} \text{ or } x + 3 = 0 \rightarrow x = -3.$$

But $x > 0$, so $x = \frac{1}{2}$.

9. **B**

For the set of numbers 10, 10, 10, the mean is $\dfrac{10 + 10 + 10}{3} = 10$.

10. **D**

    First find the total sales for each year by reading the graph for the sales of (i) black and white televisions and (ii) color televisions. Then combine these numbers:

    | 1950 | $20,000,000 + $5,000,000 | = | $25,000,000 |
    | 1960 | $10,000,000 + $20,000,000 | = | $30,000,000 |
    | 1970 | $15,000,000 + $25,000,000 | = | $40,000,000 |
    | 1980 | $10,000,000 + $45,000,000 | = | $55,000,000 |
    | 1990 | $5,000,000 + $45,000,000 | = | $50,000,000 |

    The greatest total sales occurred in 1980.

11. **C**

    There are a total of 24 donuts, of which 6 are chocolate. The required probability is the ratio of the number of chocolate donuts to the total number of donuts. This ratio is 6:24, which can be written as $\dfrac{6}{24}$.

12. **C**

    The area of the shaded region is equal to the area of the large circle (which has $\overline{OB}$ as a radius), minus the area of the smaller circle (which has $\overline{OA}$ as a radius). Since the area of a circle with radius r is $A = \pi r^2$, the area of the shaded region is:

    $$\pi (OB)^2 - \pi (OA)^2 = 36\pi - 16\pi = 20\pi.$$

13. **D**

    To solve this inequality, we shall use the following rules:

    (i)   If $a \leq b$ and c is any number, then $a + c \leq b + c$.

    (ii)   If $a \leq b$ and $c < 0$, then $ca \geq cb$.

    The goal in solving inequalities, as in solving equalities, is to change the inequality so that the variable is isolated (i.e., by itself on one side). So, in the equation $8 - 2x \leq 10$, we want the term $-2x$ by itself. To achieve this, use rule (i) above and add -8 to both sides obtaining

    $$8 - 2x + (-8) \leq 10 + (-8)$$

    or $-2x \leq 2$.

    Now we use rule (ii) and multiply both sides of the inequality by $-1/2$ as follows:

$$-\frac{1}{2} \times - 2x \geq -\frac{1}{2} \times 2$$

or $\quad x \geq -1.$

14. **D**

Since 0.003 has three numbers to the right of the decimal point and 1.25 has two numbers to the right of the decimal point, our answer will have (three plus two) or five numbers to the right of the decimal point. Multiplying 0.003 and 1.25, we get 0.00375, since 3 times 125 is 375. Numbers of the form $A \times 10^n$, where A is a number between 1 and 10 inclusive, and n is an integer, are in scientific notation. Thus, 0.00375 in scientific notation is 3.75×10^{-3}. Notice that when the exponent $n < 0$, the original number is smaller than A.

15. **E**

Since $\angle OPQ$ is a straight angle, $m\angle OPQ = 180°$. But

$$m\angle OPQ = m\angle OPR + m\angle RPQ,$$

so $\quad m\angle OPR + m\angle RPQ = 180°$

or $\quad m\angle OPR = 180° - m\angle RPQ.$

Thus, we need to find $m\angle RPQ$. Now, $l_1 \parallel l_2$, therefore, $m\angle RPQ = m\angle TRS$ since $\angle RPQ$ and $\angle TRS$ are corresponding angles. Recall that corresponding angles are two angles which lie on the same side of the transversal (i.e., a line intersecting other lines, in this case line TP is a transversal since it intersects both line l_1 and l_2) are not adjacent, and one is interior ($\angle RPQ$ in this problem) while the other is exterior ($\angle TRS$). Also, we know that the sum of the measures of the interior angles of a triangle is 180° and

$$m\angle T = 80°, \text{ so } m\angle TRS + m\angle RST = 180° - m\angle T = 100°.$$

But $m\angle TRS = m\angle RST$

since ΔRTS is isosceles. Thus, $m\angle TRS = 50°$. Thus,

$$m\angle RPQ = 50°$$

and $m\angle OPR = 180° - m\angle RPQ = 180° - 50° = 130°.$

16. **D**

The number of times the number cube landed on 4 is 7. Then the required percent is $\frac{7}{25} \times 100\% = 28\%.$

17. **D**

Let m = the number of men at University X. Then we have the following proportion:

$$\frac{3}{7} = \frac{m}{6,153}$$

To solve this equation, we isolate the variable (i.e., get m by itself) by multiplying both sides of the equation by 6,153 to get

$$\left(\frac{3}{7}\right) \times 6,153 = \left(\frac{m}{6,153}\right) \times 6,153 \text{ or } m = 2,637$$

18. **E**

To answer this question correctly, you need to know how to find the mean of a set of data. (Add up all of the data items and divide by the number of items.) The data in answer choice A has a median of 10, but its mean is 11. The data in answer choice B has a range of 10, but its mean is 6.8. The data in answer choice C has both a median and a mode of 10, but its mean is 8.6. For the data in answer choice D. the average of the lowest and highest numbers is 10, but the mean for all its data is 8.8. The data in answer choice E does have a mean of 10. The correct answer is E.

19. **A**

Let p be the original price of the jacket. Linda received a 25 percent discount so she paid 75 percent of the original price. Thus, 75 percent of p equals 54. Writing this in an equation, we get

$$0.75p = 54 \text{ or } \frac{3}{4}p = 54.$$

To solve this equation, multiply both sides of the equation by the reciprocal of $^3/_4$ which is $^4/_3$. This will isolate the variable p.

$$\frac{4}{3}\left(\frac{3}{4}p\right) = \left(\frac{4}{3}\right)54 \text{ or } p = \frac{216}{3} = 72$$

20. **C**

The area of

$$\Delta ABC = \frac{1}{2}\text{(base)(height)} = \frac{1}{2}(AB)(CD) = \frac{1}{2}(AB)(6) = 3(AB).$$

So we need to find AB. Let $s = AB$. Then since ΔABC is equilateral (i.e., all the sides have the same length), $BC = s$. Also, since ΔABC is equilateral, D is the midpoint of AB, so $DB = {}^s/_2$ Now $CD \perp AB$ so ΔCDB is a right triangle and we can use the Pythagorean Theorem:

$$(CD)^2 + (DB)^2 = (BC)^2.$$

As $CD = 6$, this equation becomes

$$6^2 + \frac{s}{2}^2 = s^2,$$

or $\quad 36 + \frac{s^2}{4} = s^2.$

To solve for s, subtract $\frac{s^2}{4}$ from both sides:

$$36 = s^2 - \frac{s^2}{4} = \frac{3}{4}s^2.$$

Now multiply both sides of the equation by the reciprocal of $\frac{3}{4}$ which is $\frac{4}{3}$:

$$\frac{4}{3}(36) = s^2$$

or $\quad s^2 = 48.$

Hence, $s = \sqrt{48} = \sqrt{16} \times \sqrt{3} = 4\sqrt{3}$

The area of $\Delta ABC =$

$$3s = 3(4\sqrt{3}) = 12\sqrt{3}$$

21. **B**

Substituting $F = 86$ into the formula

$$F = \frac{9}{5}C + 32$$

we get

$$86 = \frac{9}{5}C + 32.$$

To solve for C, first subtract 32 from both sides:

$$86 - 32 = \frac{9}{5}C + 32 - 32$$

or $$54 = \frac{9}{5}C.$$

Now multiply both sides of this equation by the reciprocal of $\frac{9}{5}$ which is $\frac{5}{9}$:

$$\left(\frac{5}{9}\right)54 = \left(\frac{5}{9}\right)\frac{9}{5}C \text{ or } \frac{270}{9} = C \text{ or } C = 30$$

22. **A**

72104.58 is read "seventy-two **thousand**, one hundred four and fifty-eight hundredths."

23. **C**

Another way to phrase the second sentence is: She wants to divide her money equally among her six children. Therefore, each child is to receive $300,000 \div 6$.

24. **C**

To find the distance between two points (x_1, y_1) and (x_2, y_2), we may use the following formula:

$$d = \sqrt{(x_2 - x_1)^2 + (y_2 - y_1)^2}$$

For our two points, $P = (1, 4)$ and $Q = (-2, 0)$, the above formula gives us the length of segment PQ:

$$d = \sqrt{(-2-1)^2 + (0-4)^2} = \sqrt{(-3)^2 + (-4)^2} \sqrt{9 + 16} = \sqrt{25} = 5$$

25. **B**

Bob wants to bake 12 cupcakes. The recipe is for 36 cupcakes. Therefore, Bob wants to make $\frac{12}{36}$ or $\frac{1}{3}$ of the usual amount of cupcakes. Thus, Bob should use $\frac{1}{3}$ of the recipe's flour or $\left(\frac{1}{3}\right)\left(\frac{8}{3}\right) = \frac{8}{9}$

Note we used $\frac{8}{3}$ since $2\frac{2}{3} = \frac{8}{3}$.

26. **B**

Let x be the length of EH, then the length of EF is $2x$. The area of a rectangle is length (EF) times width (EH). So we have

$$(2x)(x) = 120 \text{ or } 2x^2 = 120.$$

To solve for x divide both sides of the equation by 2 to get $x^2 = 60$. Note that $49 < x^2 < 64$, so

$$\sqrt{49} < \sqrt{x^2} < \sqrt{64} \text{ or } 7 < x < 8.$$

But 60 is closer to 64 than it is to 49, so 8 is the best approximation of x which represents the length of EH.

27. **C**

Let s_1 and s_2 be Ricky's speed (rate) on the trip from A to B and the return trip from B to A, respectively. Then, since he drove 15 miles per hour slower on the return trip, $s_2 = s_1 - 15$. Recall that rate times time equals distance. So the distance from A to B is $(s_1)3 = 3s_1$ and the distance from B to A is

$$(s_2)5 = 5s_2 = 5(s_1 - 15) = 5s_1 - 75.$$

But the distance from Town A to Town B is the same as the distance from Town B to Town A, so we have the following equation:

$$3s_1 = 5s_1 - 75.$$

To solve this equation, first add 75 to both sides of the equation:

$$3s_1 + 75 = 5s_1 - 75 + 75 \text{ or } 3s_1 + 75 = 5s_1.$$

Now to isolate the variable, subtract $3s_1$ from both sides:

$$3s_1 + 75 - 3s_1 = 5s_1 - 3s_1 \text{ or } 75 = 2s_1.$$

To finish the problem, divide both sides of the equation by 2:

$$s_1 = \frac{75}{2} = 37.5.$$

Thus, Ricky drove 37.5 miles per hour on his trip from Town A to Town B.

28. **D**

The shaded region consists of all the points on the horizontal line passing through the point (0, 2) and those below the line. All of these points have y coordinate less than or equal to 2. Thus, our answer is $y \leq 2$.

29. **B**

Statement I is not always true. For example, let $x = 2$ and $y = -3$. Then $x > y$, but $x^2 = 4$ and $y^2 = 9$ so $x^2 < y^2$. Statement IV is not always true. For example, let $x = 5$, $y = 1$, and $z = -2$. Then $xz = -10$ and $yz = -2$ so that $xz < yz$. Statements II and III are true.

30. **E**

The 1 is in the hundredths place. If the number to the immediate right of the 1 (i.e., the number in the thousandths place) is greater than or equal to 5, we increase 1 to 2, otherwise do not change the 1. Then we leave off all numbers to the right of the 1. In our problem a 6 is in the thousandths place so we change the 1 to a 2 to get 287.42 as our answer.

31. **C**

Recall the following Laws of Exponents:

$$x^p \times x^q = x^{p+q} \text{ and } \frac{x^p}{x^q} = x^{p-q}.$$

So, $x^2 \times x^7 = x^{2+7} = x^9$. Hence,

$$\frac{x^2 \times x^7}{x} = \frac{x^9}{x^1} = x^{9-1} = x^8.$$

32. **A**

We need to write the three fractions with the same denominator. So, find the least common multiple (LCM) of 9, 15, and 21.

$$9 = 3^2, 15 = 3 \times 5, \text{ and } 21 = 3 \times 7$$

Therefore, the LCM is

$$3^2 \times 5 \times 7 = 315.$$

Then $\dfrac{1}{9} = \dfrac{5 \times 7}{5 \times 7} \times \dfrac{1}{9} = \dfrac{35}{315}$,

$$\frac{2}{15} = \frac{3 \times 7}{3 \times 7} \times \frac{2}{15} = \frac{42}{315},$$

and $\frac{3}{21} = \frac{3 \times 5}{3 \times 5} \times \frac{3}{21} = \frac{45}{315}.$

Clearly,

$$\frac{35}{315} < \frac{42}{315} < \frac{45}{315}$$

and hence, in order, from least to greatest, we have:

$$\frac{1}{9}, \frac{2}{15}, \frac{3}{21}.$$

33. **C**

There are 16 data, so that the median is the mean of the 8th and 9th values. The eighth value is 114 and the ninth value is 121. Thus, the median equals

$$\frac{114 + 121}{2} = \frac{235}{2} = 117.5.$$

34. **A**

If $x = -3$ then

$$-x^2 + 2x = -(-3)^2 + 2(-3) = -(9) + (-6) = -15.$$

35. **D**

If $a = b^3$ and $a = \frac{1}{8}$, then substituting into the first equation we have

$$\frac{1}{8} = b^3 \text{ or } \left(\frac{1}{2}\right)^3 = b^3 \text{ so } b = \frac{1}{2}$$

36. **D**

Let x be the number of people in the barn. Then, since each person and cow has only one head, the number of cows must be $30 - x$. Since people have two legs, the number of human legs totals $2x$. Similarly, since the number of legs each cow has is 4, the total number of cow legs in the barn is $4(30 - x)$. Thus, we have this equation:

$$2x + 4(30 - x) = 104.$$

To solve this equation, use the distributive property:

$$a(b - c) = ab - ac.$$

We get

$$4(30 - x) = (4 \times 30) - (4 \times x) = 120 - 4x.$$

Our equation reduces to:

$$2x + 120 - 4x = 104 \text{ or } 120 - 2x = 104.$$

Now subtract 120 from both sides or the equation to get

$$-2x = 104 - 120 = -16.$$

Dividing both sides of the equation by –2: $x = 8$. Therefore, there were 8 people and $30 - 8 = 22$ cows in the barn.

37. **B**

To solve the proportion

$$\frac{12}{x - 1} = \frac{5}{6}$$

multiply both sides of the equation by 6 and by $(x - 1)$ so that we have

$$6(x - 1) \times \frac{12}{x - 1} = 6(x - 1) \times \frac{5}{6} \text{ or } 72 = 5(x - 1).$$

Now, use the distributive property:

$$a(b - c) = ab - ac$$

to get $72 = 5x - 5$. Add 5 to both sides of the equation:

$$77 = 5x$$

and then divide both sides by 5:

$$x = \frac{77}{5} = 15.4.$$

38. **A**

In order for Ingrid to achieve an average of at least 85, her test scores must total at least $(85)(5) = 425$. Her total for the four tests she has already taken is $87 + 76 + 95 + 88 = 346$. Thus, the minimum grade that she needs on her fifth test is $425 - 346 = 79$.

39. **E**

First of all the least common multiple (LCM) of 2 and 3 is $2 \times 3 = 6$, so let's rewrite the expression so that both fractions have 6 as a common denominator:

$$\frac{1}{2} + \frac{1}{3} = \frac{3}{3} \times \frac{1}{2} + \frac{2}{2} \times \frac{1}{3} = \frac{3}{6} + \frac{2}{6} = \frac{5}{6}.$$

40. **A**

Two triangles are similar if we can find two pairs of angles, one in each triangle, that are congruent. Given that $BC \parallel DE$ we know that $(\angle ABC, \angle BDE)$ and $(\angle ACB, \angle CED)$ are two pairs of corresponding and hence congruent angles. Thus, taking care in the order that we write the angles so that we match the correct angles, $\triangle ABC \sim \triangle ADE$.

Section III: Writing

1. **B**

    "Were praised" is a plural verb; since the subject is Chief Joseph, a singular proper noun, the verb should be "was praised." The intervening phrase of choice (A), "*together with* 250 warriors and 500 women and children," does not change the singular subject. Choice (C), "bravery," is the correct noun form, and choice (D), "for," is idiomatically correct in that phrase.

2. **E**

    Choice (A), "upon which," is a correct prepositional phrase. Choice (B), "is based," agrees with its subject, "society." In choice (C), "are" agrees with its subject, "ideals." "Derived from" in choice (D) is correct idiomatic usage.

3. **B**

    Two past actions are mentioned. The earlier of two past actions should be indicated by past perfect tense, so the answer is "had been." Choice (C) is correct. Choice (A) contains two adjectives as part of an appositive phrase modifying the subject, and choice (D), "upon the death," is idiomatically correct.

4. **C**

    Choice (C) should be "depend," not "had depended" because that use of past perfect would indicate prior past action. There is a series of events in this sentence: first, the legislature "had not finalized" the budget (B); then, Representative Wilson "pointed out" this failure (A). Choice (C) needs to be present tense as this situation still exists, and (D) is future action.

5. **D**

    In order to complete the parallelism, choice (D) should be "arrangements." Choice (A) is a noun used as an adjective. "To plan" (B) is an infinitive phrase followed by noun objects: "puppet shows and movies" and "garage sales." Choice (C), "used," is a participate modifying books.

6. **A**

    An infinitive, "to understand," should never be split by any adverbial modifier, "completely." Choice (B), "effects," is the noun form, and choice (D), "affected," is the adjective form. "One must," choice (C), is used in standard English.

7. **C**

    "More" is used to compare two things. Since the number of nations is not specified, "more" cannot be used in this sentence. Choice (A), "known," modifies "roads"; choice (B) is idiomatically correct; choice (D), "is," agrees in number with its subject, "transportation."

8. **E**

    Choice (A), "many a," should always be followed by the singular verb, "wishes," of choice (B). Choice (C) is idiomatically correct. In "someone else," (D), "else" is needed to indicate a person other than the student would pay the bills.

9. **D**

    Choice (D) should read, "became very irritated." "To aggravate" means "to make worse"; "to irritate" means "to excite to impatience or anger." A situation is "aggravated" and becomes worse, but one does not become "aggravated" with people. Choices (A), (B), and (C) are correctly used idioms.

10. **C**

    The reference in choice (C) is vague because it sounds as if the bus made the two students late. Choice (A) is a correct subject pronoun; choice (B) is the correct adverb form to modify "dressed"; choice (D) is a correct object pronoun.

11. **E**

    Choice (A), "among," indicates choice involving more than two things. The prepositions in (B) and (C) are correct. "Are," (D), is a plural verb, agreeing in number with the compound subject "singing… dancing…cooking."

12. **A**

    One is "disappointed by" a person or action but "disappointed in" what is not satisfactory. "Inexpensive," (B), is the adjective form. Parallel with "to work," choice (C), "save," had the word "to" omitted. Choice (D) compares the two models, one "inexpensive" and one "more expensive."

13. **A**

    The verb should be plural, "are," in order to agree with the compound subject, "budget…plans." Choice (B) begins an infinitive phrase which includes a participle, "existing," (C). Choice (D) is idiomatically correct.

14. **A**

The expression should be phrased "as delicate as." Choice (B) uses a possessive before a gerund; choice (C) is correctly used; and choice (D) is a possessive pronoun of neuter gender which is appropriate to use in referring to a plant.

15. **D**

The verb "deal" must agree with the subject, "works," and not a word in the intervening phrase. "Outwardly," choice (A), is an adverb modifying "seemed." Choices (B) and (C), "the picture of respectability," describe the subject; (D) is idiomatically correct.

16. **D**

The word "of" in "inside of" is redundant and should not be used. Choice (A) is idiomatically correct and signals two classes of people once considered unequal in merit, and choice (B), "alike," is appropriate when comparing the two. Choice (C), "them," is correct pronoun usage.

17. **E**

Choice (A), "unsafe for," is idiomatically correct; choice (B), "deltas," is a plural noun. Choice (C), "can be," is grammatically correct. The preposition "in," choice (D), is correct.

18. **C**

The verb in this subordinate clause is incorrect; the clause begins with, "which," and this word refers to "information." Therefore, the clause, in order to agree with the antecedent, must read, "which shows." The verb "shows" should not be made to agree with "species" and "others." Choices (A), "people," and (B), "have compiled," agree in number. "Either" in choice (D) is correctly placed after the verb to show a choice of "endangered" or "becoming endangered."

19. **D**

Do not end a sentence with a preposition; the phrase should read, "in which he was born." The verbs show proper time sequence in (A) and (B); choice (C) is correct pronoun usage and correct superlative degree of adjective.

20. **D**

   The noun form "effect" is the correct one to use. Choice (A), "to inhibit," is an infinitive; choice (B) is correctly worded; in choice (C), the nominative case "who" is the correct subject of "seemed."

21. **C**

   The idiom should be "filled to capacity." The adjective in choice (A), "average," is correct, as is the adverb in choice (B). Choice (D), "most," is appropriate for the superlative degree.

22. **B**

   The subordinate clause, "who my parents have not met," has as its subject "parents," which agrees with choice (C), "have…met." Therefore, the pronoun is a direct object of the verb and should be in the objective case, "whom." Both choice (A) and choice (D) are idiomatically correct.

23. **C**

   The pronoun reference is unclear. The meaning of the sentence indicated that Colonel Jones denies involvement in any other covert activity. The agent from a foreign country may or may not have been involved in other covert activities, but that is not the issue here. The verb tense of choice (A) is correct. Choice (B) is the correct adverb form, and "other" in choice (D) is necessary to the meaning of the sentence.

24. **E**

   Choice (A), "testing," is parallel to "determining" and "evaluating." "Proper" in choice (B) and "effectiveness" in choice (C) are correct. In choice (D) "is" must be singular because all three steps mentioned comprise the one process.

25. **B**

   Choice (A) is correct. Choice (B) should read, "it is she"; nominative case pronoun is required following a linking verb. Choice (C) is proper English, and the correct form of the modifiers appears in choice (D).

26. **D**

   "Because" is the correct word to use in the cause-and-effect relationship in this sentence. Choice (A), "being that"; choice (E), "than me"; and choice (B), "the more," are not grammatically correct. Choice (C), "is made by you," is in the passive voice and not as direct as (D).

27. **D**

"After they have been" completes the proper time sequence. Choice (A), "when"; choice (B), "have been"; and choice (C), "will be," are the wrong time sequences. Choice (E), "should be," is an idea not contained in the original sentence.

28. **C**

"Since the plane is late" shows correct time sequence and good reasoning. Choice (A), "seeing as how," and choice (D), "being as," are poor wording. Choices (B), "when," and (E), "while," are the wrong time, logically, to be on the observation deck.

29. **E**

Since a sentence should not end with a preposition, choices (A) and (B) are eliminated. Choices (C), "living in this world," and (D), "world's living," introduce new concepts.

30. **A**

The construction, "than those," clarifies the fact that more vegetables have been added. Choice (C), "your suggestion"; choice (D), "than what"; and choice (E), "which," do not contain the idea of adding more varieties of vegetables. Choice (B) ends with a preposition.

31. **B**

The voice must be consistent with "I," so (B) is the only possible correct answer. All other choices have a noun or pronoun that is not consistent with "I"; choice (A), "you"; choice (C), "a person"; choice (D), "people"; and choice (E), "some."

32. **A**

The correct answer has two concepts—pieces are missing and pieces will probably never be found. Choice (B) has a singular verb, "is." Choice (C) indicates the pieces "probably will be" missing, which is not the problem. Choice (D) and choice (E) both indicate the pieces are "probably" missing, which is illogical because the pieces either are or are not missing.

33. **C**

   Choice (A), "the kind of a," and choice (D), "the type of a," are incorrect grammatical structures. Choice (E) introduces the new concept of "category." Choice (B), "sort of," is poor wording.

34. **E**

   Choice (E) is clear and concise and shows the correct comparison of architecture. The antecedent of "those" in choice (A) is not clear. Choice (B) is comparing "characteristics," not just architecture. Choice (C) is awkward, and choice (D) incorrectly uses an idiom, "characteristic with."

35. **B**

   Choice (B) is clear and direct. Choices (A) and (E) are too wordy. Choice (C) has the wrong concept, "balancing games." Choice (D) "this as an example" is poorly worded.

36. **E**

   An opposing force "gives" scattered resistance; therefore, choice (A) is incorrect. Choices (B), (C), and (D) are poorly worded and do not have the correct meaning.

37. **A**

   Choice (A) produces a complete sentence: "rainfall" is the subject and "let up" is the verb. None of the other choices produces a complete sentence.

38. **D**

   This choice uses the correct tense, "will have," showing action in the future. All the other verbs listed do not show correct future verb construction.

PPST Essay Scoring Guide

The PPST essay sections are scored by two writing experts on the basis of the criteria outlined below. In addition to comparing your essay to those included in our practice tests, you may use these guidelines to estimate your score on this section. Remember that your score is the sum of the scores of two writing experts, so provided you respond to the assigned topic, your score will fall somewhere between two and twelve. Scores will be assigned based on the following guidelines:

6   An essay receiving a score of 6 may contain one or two spelling or punctuation errors, but overall it exhibits a high degree of proficiency and thought on the assigned topic.

An essay scoring a 6

- is both well organized and well developed

- engages important concepts and explains them clearly

- varies expression and language

- demonstrates deft use of language

- is virtually free from errors involving syntax and structure

5   An essay receiving a score of 5 exhibits a high degree of proficiency and thought on the assigned topic, however it contains a number of minor mistakes.

An essay scoring a 5

- is both well organized and well developed

- engages important concepts and explains them

- varies expression and language somewhat

- demonstrates deft use of language

- is virtually free from errors involving syntax and structure

4   An essay receiving a score of 4 responds to the assignment and exhibits some degree of deeper understanding.

An essay scoring a 4

- demonstrates adequate organization and development

- engages and explains some important concepts, but not all that are necessary to demonstrate full understanding

- exhibits adequate use of language

- contains some syntactical and structural errors, without excessive repetition of those errors

3 An essay receiving a score of 3 exhibits some degree of understanding, but its response to the topic is obviously deficient.

An essay scoring a 3 is deficient in one or more of the following areas:

- insufficient organization or development

- insufficient engagement or explanation of important concepts

- consistent repetition of syntactical or structural errors

- redundant or unsuitable word choice

2 An essay receiving a score of 2 exhibits limited understanding and its response to the topic is seriously deficient.

An essay scoring a 2 is deficient in one or more of the following areas:

- weak organization or development

- very few pertinent details

- consistent and serious errors in syntax, structure

- consistent and serious errors in word choice

1 An essay receiving a score of 1 exhibits a lack of basic writing skills.

An essay scoring a 1 is disorganized, undeveloped, contains consistent repetition of errors, or is incomprehensible.

SAMPLE SCORED ESSAYS WITH EXPLANATIONS

Essay #1—(Score = 5–6)

A poll was recently conducted to determine American heroes. Sadly, most of the heroes listed in the top ten are cartoon characters or actors who portray heroic roles. What does this say about American ideals? Perhaps we do not know enough, or perhaps we know too much in order to have heroes. Having access to instant information about a variety of military, political and religious figures, citizens of modern society have outgrown the innocence of previous centuries.

The ancient hero possessed many idealized virtues, such as physical strength, honesty, courage, and intelligence. Oedipus saved his people from pestilence by solving the riddle of the Sphinx. As leader, he was sworn to find the murderer of the previous king; Oedipus' brave pursuit of justice was conducted with honesty and integrity. Beowulf, another famous ancient hero, existed at a time when life was wild, dangerous, unpredictable.

Modern society is missing several of the ingredients necessary to produce a hero of this calibre. For one thing, there are no mythical monsters such as the Sphinx or Grendel. War is left as the stuff of heroic confrontation, but modern wars only add to our confusion. Men have been decorated for killing their brothers and friends in the Civil War; America fought the Germans in World War I and the Germans and Japanese in World War II, but our former enemies are our current allies. As for honesty, modern role models too often let us down. The media exposes politicians who are involved in scandal, sports figures who do drugs, and religious leaders who make multi-million dollar incomes.

No wonder Americans name Superman and actors John Wayne and Clint Eastwood to the list of modern heroes. These heroes are larger than life on the theatre screen, and their vices are at least predictable and reasonably innocuous. Wisely, we have chosen those who will not surprise us with ugly or mundane reality.

ANALYSIS

Essay I has a score range of 5–6. It is the strongest of the four essays. Although it is not perfect, it shows a good command of the English language and depth of thought. The writer employs a traditional essay structure: the first paragraph is the introduction and ends with the thesis statement; the second and third paragraphs discuss traditional and contemporary heroes, as stated in the last sentence of the thesis paragraph; the fourth paragraph concludes. Each of the two body paragraphs has a clear topic sentence. The writer gives several distinct examples to support his ideas. Vocabulary is effective, and sentence structure is varied.

Essay #2—(Score = 4–5)

Heroes are people who perform the extraordinary and who are highly regarded by society. These outstanding people have characteristics that are desirable to everyone, but the ways in which heroes use their talents glorify them even more. A true hero will do anything in his power to help others.

Two heroes from modern literature exhibit the quality of self-sacrifice. In Remarque's novel *All Quiet on the Western Front*, Paul Baumer is a German ground soldier who endures many disappointments and difficulties while fighting for his country. Paul does not shirk his duties as a soldier of the German people. Moreover, Paul goes out of his way to train the raw recruits and to care for a soldier suffering from shell shock. Another hero, Willy Loman in *Death of a Salesman* makes all the everyday sacrifices a father makes for children and a husband makes for his wife. Willy drives long distances in order to make a living. When Willy feels he is hindering his family, he makes the ultimate sacrifice of suicide to get out of the way.

The true heroes of today are the common people, not unlike Willy and Paul. Stories regularly appear in the newspapers of everyday heroes. The woman with knowledge of CPR saves a drowning child from certain death. A neighbor saves two children from an apartment fire. Teachers take the extra time to listen to a student's personal problem. Parents stand tough against their child's unreasonable demands. Adults who stop to help a stranded motorist are all heroic in their own way.

Every day they stand behind their ideals, living up to their moral standards, in order to help others. It is the day-to-day dedication that makes these twentieth-century heroes extraordinary.

ANALYSIS

Essay II has a score range of 4–5. It still has the traditional essay organization, but the thesis paragraph and conclusion are a bit less focused and less interesting than in Essay I. The paper is supported by examples, but the sentence structure is not varied enough. The last sentence of the third paragraph is weak.

Essay #3—(Score = 3–4)

I would say that there are some heroes still left in modern society. Although we don't have heroes like we used to, our heroes are different now.

When I was a child, I thought that Superman was a real person. He was my hero. He was strong and always won the fights he got into. Villains didn't stand a chance with him. My parents thought I should watch *Sesame Street*, but I wanted to go to the moves to see Luke Skywalker. Even though I later knew it was not real, I still enjoy going to the movies. I want to see a good conflict between the forces of good and the forces of evil, especially when justice rules.

Now I am more realistic. My heroes are good people or successful people. My uncle, for example. He owns his own business and lets me work there part time to earn money. That's what I want to be, someone who is successful and independent but will still help out a young person. When a person is brave, that's heroism too. My friend's brother has a medal for being a hero in Vietnam. You have different ways to be brave now. The innocent days of childhood are gone, but there are still people to be admired.

ANALYSIS

Essay III has a score range of 3–4. There is a thesis in the opening paragraph, and the remaining two paragraphs are organized so as to support that thesis. However, this paper is not as strong as the previous two. The conclusion is not well defined. Also, the writer uses mixed voice, slang, and contractions. His use of the first person pronoun becomes intrusive, and all examples are drawn from his personal experience. The sentence structure could be better, and there is even a fragment.

Essay #4—(Score = 1–2)

It is not true that there are no heroes nowadays. Everywhere you look, a person see heroes to believe in.

When you go to the movie theatre, many movies are about good guys versus bad buys. Not just Westerns. Sometimes the good cop gets killed. But he usually kills a few criminals for himself before he dies. In many movies, justice wins when the villain is defeated. No matter who wins, people in the audience know what is right and what is wrong because the heroes kill because he needs to defend themselves or because the guy needed to be killed. Rambo would not kill anyone except the enemy. This teaches good values about heroes and their motives since people like to go to the movies, they see a lot of heroes.

ANALYSIS

Essay IV has a score range of 1–2. It is the weakest of the four essays. The ideas are inexact, and the sentences are ill-formed. This essay uses mixed voice and slang. There is an agreement error and a fragment. The most serious faults of this essay are the lack of specific examples and the use of sweeping generalizations. The concluding two sentences are exceptionally poor in clarity of thought and wording.

Practice Test 2

Praxis I PPST
Paper-Based Format

PRACTICE TEST 2 (Paper-Based Format)

Section I: Reading Comprehension

TIME: *60 Minutes*
40 Questions

DIRECTIONS: A number of questions follow each of the passages in the reading section. Answer the questions by choosing the best answer from the five choices given.

Questions 1 to 5 refer to the following passage:

Spa water quality is maintained through a filter to ensure cleanliness and clarity. Wastes such as perspiration, hairspray, and lotions which cannot be removed by the spa filter can be controlled by shock treatment or super chlorination every other week. Although the filter traps most of the solid material to control bacteria and algae and to oxidize any organic material, the addition of disinfectants such as bromine or chlorine is necessary.

As all water solutions have a pH which controls corrosion, proper pH balance is also necessary. A pH measurement determines if the water is acid or alkaline. Based on a 14-point scale, a pH reading of 7.0 is considered neutral while a lower reading is considered acidic, and a higher reading indicates alkalinity or basic. High pH (above 7.6) reduces sanitizer efficiency, clouds water, promotes scale formation on surfaces and equipment, and interferes with filter operation. When pH is high, add a pH decrease such as sodium bisulphate (e.g., Spa Down). Because the spa water is hot, scale is deposited more rapidly. A weekly dose of a stain and scale fighter also will help to control this problem. Low pH (below 7.2) is equally damaging, causing equipment corrosion, water which is irritating, and rapid sanitizer dissipation. To increase pH add sodium bicarbonate (e.g., Spa Up).

The recommended operating temperature of a spa (98° – 104°) is a fertile environment for the growth of bacteria and viruses. This growth is prevented when appropriate sanitizer levels are continuously monitored.

Bacteria can also be controlled by maintaining a proper bromine level of 3.0 to 5.0 parts per million (ppm) or a chlorine level of 1.0 – 2.0 ppm. As bromine tablets should not be added directly to the water, a bromine floater will properly dispense the tablets. Should chlorine be the chosen sanitizer, a granular form is recommended, as liquid chlorine or tablets are too harsh for the spa.

1. Although proper chemical and temperature maintenance of spa water is necessary, the most important condition to monitor is preventing

    (A) growth of bacteria and virus.

    (B) equipment corrosion.

    (C) soap build up.

    (D) scale formation.

    (E) cloudy water.

2. Of the chemical and temperature conditions in a spa, the condition most dangerous to one's health is

    (A) spa water temperature above 104°.

    (B) bromine level between 3.0 and 5.0.

    (C) pH level below 7.2.

    (D) spa water temperature between 90° and 104°.

    (E) cloudy and dirty water.

3. The primary purpose of the passage is to

    (A) relate that maintenance of a spa can negate the full enjoyment of the spa experience.

    (B) provide evidence that spas are not a viable alternative to swimming pools.

    (C) convey that the maintenance of a spa is expensive and time consuming.

    (D) explain the importance of proper spa maintenance.

    (E) give specific details for proper spa maintenance.

4. The spa filter can be relied upon to

(A) control algae and bacteria.

(B) trap most solid material.

(C) oxidize organic material.

(D) assure an adequate level of sanitation.

(E) maintain clear spa water.

5. Which chemical should one avoid when maintaining a spa?

(A) Liquid chlorine   (D) Baking soda

(B) Bromine   (E) All forms of chlorine

(C) Sodium bisulfate

Questions 6 to 10 refer to the following passage:

The relationship of story elements found in children's generated stories to reading achievement was analyzed. Correlations ranged from .61101 (p = .64) at the beginning of first grade to .83546 (p = .24) at the end of first grade, to .85126 (p = .21) at the end of second grade, and to .82588 (p=.26) for fifth/sixth grades. Overall, the correlation of the story elements to reading achievement appeared to indicate a high positive correlation trend even though it was not statistically significant.

Multiple regression equation analyses dealt with the relative contribution of the story elements to reading achievement. The contribution of certain story elements was substantial. At the beginning of first grade, story conventions added 40 percent to the total variance while the other increments were not significant. At the end of first grade, story plot contributed 44 percent to the total variance, story conventions contributed 20 percent, and story sources contributed 17 percent. At the end of second grade, the story elements contributed more equal percentages to the total partial correlation of .8513. Although none of the percentages were substantial, story plot (.2200), clausal connectors (.1858), and T-units (.1590) contributed the most to the total partial correlation. By the fifth and sixth grades three other story elements—T-units (.2241), story characters (.3214), and clausal connectors (.1212)—contributed most to the total partial correlation. None of these percentages were substantial.

6. Which of the following is the most complete and accurate definition of the term "statistically significant" as used in the passage?

   (A) Consists of important numerical data

   (B) Is educationally significant

   (C) Departs greatly from chance expectations

   (D) Permits prediction of reading achievement by knowing the story elements

   (E) Indicates that two measures (reading achievement and story elements) give the same information

7. The passage suggests which of the following conclusions about the correlation of story elements to reading achievement?

   (A) That there are other more important story elements that should also be included in the analyses

   (B) That children's inclusion of story elements in their stories causes them to achieve higher levels in reading

   (C) That these story elements are important variables to consider in reading achievement

   (D) That correlations of more than 1.0 are needed for this study to be statistically significant

   (E) That this correlation was not statistically significant because there was little variance between story elements and reading achievement

8. The relative contribution of story conventions and story plot in first grade suggests that

   (A) children may have spontaneously picked up these story elements as a result of their exposure to stories.

   (B) children have been explicitly taught these story elements.

   (C) these story elements were not important because in fifth/sixth grades other story elements contributed more to the total correlation.

   (D) other story elements were more substantial.

   (E) children's use of story conventions and plots were not taken from story models.

9. The content of the passage suggests that the passage would most likely appear in which of the following?

(A) *Psychology Today*   (D) *Language Arts*

(B) *The Creative Writer*   (E) *Reading Research Quarterly*

(C) *Educational Leadership*

10. "None of these percentages were substantial" is the last statement in the passage. It refers to the story elements

(A) for fifth/sixth grades.

(B) for second grade.

(C) at the end of first grade.

(D) at the beginning of first grade.

(E) for all of the grades, i.e., first grade, second grade, and fifth/sixth grade.

Questions 11 to 13 refer to the following passage:

There is an importance of learning communication and meaning in language. Yet the use of notions such as communication and meaning as the basic criteria for instruction, experiences, and materials in classrooms may misguide a child in several respects. Communication in the classroom is vital. The teacher should use communication to help students develop the capacity to make their private responses become public responses. Otherwise, one's use of language would be in danger of being what the younger generation refers to as mere words, mere thoughts, and mere feelings.

Learning theorists emphasize specific components of learning: behaviorists stress behavior in learning; humanists stress the affective in learning; and cognitivists stress cognition in learning. All three of these components occur simultaneously and cannot be separated from each other in the learning process. In 1957, Festinger referred to dissonance as the lack of harmony between what one does (behavior) and what one believes (attitude). Attempts to separate the components of learning either knowingly or unknowingly create dissonances wherein language, thought, feeling, and behavior become diminished of authenticity. As a result, ideas and concepts lose their content and vitality, and the manipulation and politics of communication assume prominence.

11. Which of the following best describes the author's attitude toward the subject discussed?

   (A) A flippant disregard   (D) A passive resignation

   (B) A mild frustration   (E) An informed concern

   (C) A moral indignation

12. The primary purpose of the passage is to

   (A) explain the criteria for providing authentic communication in classroom learning.

   (B) discuss the relationships between learning and communication.

   (C) assure teachers that communication and meaning are the basic criteria for learning in classrooms.

   (D) stress the importance of providing authentic communication in classroom learning.

   (E) address the role of communication and meaning in classrooms.

13. Which of the following is the most complete and accurate definition of the term "mere" as used in paragraph 2?

   (A) Small   (D) Poor

   (B) Minor   (E) Insignificant

   (C) Little

Questions 14 to 16 refer to the following passage:

In 1975, Sinclair observed that it had often been supposed that the main factor in learning to talk is being able to imitate. Schlesinger (1975) noted that at certain stages of learning to speak, a child tends to imitate everything an adult says to him or her, and it therefore seems reasonable to accord to such imitation an important role in the acquisition of language.

Moreover, various investigators have attempted to explain the role of imitation in language. In his discussion of the development of imitation and cognition of adult speech sounds, Nakazema (1975) stated that although the parent's talking stimulates and accelerates the infant's articulatory activity, the parent's phoneme system does not influence the child's articulatory mechanisms. Slobin and Welsh (1973) suggested that imitation is the reconstruction of the adult's utterance and that the child does so by employing the grammatical rules that he has developed at a specific time. Schlesinger proposed that by imitating the adult the child practices new grammatical constructions. Brown and Bellugi (1964) noted that a child's imitations resemble spontaneous speech in that they drop inflections, most function words, and sometimes other words. However, the word order of imitated sentences usually was preserved. Brown and Bellugi assumed that imitation is a function of what the child attended to or remembered. Shipley et al. (1969) suggested that repeating an adult's utterance assists the child's comprehension. Ervin (1964) and Braine (1971) found that a child's imitations do not contain more advanced structures than his or her spontaneous utterances; thus, imitation can no longer be regarded as the simple behavioristic act that earlier scholars assumed it to be.

14. The author of the passage would tend to agree with which of the following statements?

   (A) Apparently, children are physiologically unable to imitate a parent's phoneme system.

   (B) Apparently, children require practice with more advanced structures before they are able to imitate.

   (C) Apparently, children only imitate what they already do, using whatever is in their repertoire.

   (D) Apparently, the main factor in learning to talk remains being able to imitate.

   (E) Apparently, children cannot respond meaningfully to a speech situation until they have reached a stage where they can make symbol-orientation responses.

15. The primary purpose of the passage is to

   (A) explain language acquisition.

   (B) explain the role of imitation in language acquisition.

   (C) assure parents of their role in assisting imitation in language acquisition.

   (D) relate the history of imitation in language acquisition.

   (E) discuss relationships between psychological and physiological processes in language acquisition.

16. An inference that parents may make from the passage is that they should

   (A) be concerned when a child imitates their language.

   (B) focus on developing imitation in their child's language.

(C) realize that their child's imitations may reflect several aspects of language acquisition.

(D) realize that their talking may over-stimulate their child's articulatory activity.

(E) not be concerned as imitation is too complex for anyone to understand.

Questions 17 and 18 refer to the following passage:

A major problem with reading/language arts instruction is that practice assignments from workbooks often provide short, segmented activities that do not really resemble the true act of reading. Perhaps more than any computer application, word processing is capable of addressing these issues.

17. The author would tend to agree that a major benefit of computers in reading/language arts instruction is

(A) that the reading act may be more closely resembled.

(B) that short segmented assignments will be eliminated.

(C) that the issues in reading/language arts instruction will be addressed.

(D) that computer application will be limited to word processing.

(E) that reading practice will be eliminated.

18. The appropriate use of a word processor to assist in making practice resemble a reading act is

(A) detailed.   (D) alluded to.

(B) desirable.   (E) costly.

(C) unstated.

Questions 19 to 21 refer to the following passage:

In view of the current emphasis on literature-based reading instruction, a greater understanding by teachers of variance in cultural, language, and story components should assist in narrowing the gap between reader and text and improve reading comprehension. Classroom teachers should begin with students' meaning and intentions about stories before moving students to the commonalities of story meaning based on common background and culture. With teacher guidance, students should develop a fuller understanding of how complex narratives are when they are generating stories as well as when they are reading stories.

19. Which of the following is the intended audience for the passage?

    (A) Students in a reading class

    (B) Teachers using literature-based curriculum

    (C) Professors teaching a literature course

    (D) Parents concerned about their child's comprehension of books

    (E) Teacher educators teaching reading methods courses

20. Which of the following is the most complete and accurate definition of the term "variance" as used in the passage?

    (A) Change   (D) Deviation

    (B) Fluctuations   (E) Incongruity

    (C) Diversity

21. The passage supports a concept of meaning primarily residing in

    (A) culture, language, and story components.

    (B) comprehension.

    (C) student's stories only.

    (D) students only.

    (E) students and narratives.

Questions 22 to 25 refer to the following passage:

As noted by Favat in 1977, the study of children's stories has been an ongoing concern of linguists, anthropologists, and psychologists. The past decade has witnessed a surge of interest in children's stories from researchers in these and other disciplines. The use of narratives for reading and reading instruction has been commonly accepted by the educational community. The notion that narrative is highly structured and that children's sense of narrative structure is more highly developed than expository structure has been proposed by some researchers.

Early studies of children's stories followed two approaches for story analysis: the analysis of story content or the analysis of story structure. Story content analysis has centered primarily on examining motivational and psychodynamic aspects of story characters as noted in the works of Erikson and Pitcher and Prelinger in 1963 and Ames in 1966. These studies have noted that themes or topics predominate and that themes change with age.

Early research on story structure focused on formal models of structure, such as story grammar and story schemata. These models specified basic story elements and formed sets of rules similar to sentence grammar for ordering the elements.

The importance or centrality of narrative in a child's development of communicative ability has been proposed by Halliday (1976) and Hymes (1975). Thus, the importance of narrative for language communicative ability and for reading and reading instruction has been well documented. However, the question still remains about how these literacy abilities interact and lead to conventional reading.

22. This passage is most probably directed at which of the following audience?

(A) Reading educators   (D) Reading researchers

(B) Linguists   (E) Anthropologists

(C) Psychologists

23. According to the passage, future research should address

(A) how story structure and story schema interact with comprehension.

(B) how children's use and understanding of narrative interacts and leads to conventional reading.

(C) how basal texts and literature texts differ from children's story structure.

(D) how story content interacts with story comprehension.

(E) how narrative text structure differs from expository text structure.

24. The major distinction between story content and story structure is that

(A) story content focuses on motivational aspects whereas story structure focuses on rules similar to sentence grammar.

(B) story content focuses on psychodynamic aspects whereas story structure focuses on formal structural models.

(C) story content and story structure essentially refer to the same concepts.

(D) story content focuses on themes and topics whereas story structure focuses on specific basic story elements.

(E) story content focuses primarily on characters whereas story structure focuses on story grammar and schemata.

25. Which of the following is the most complete and accurate definition of the term "surge" as used in the following sentence?

    The past decade has witnessed a surge of interest in children's stories from researchers in these and other disciplines.

    (A) A heavy swell   (D) A sudden increase

    (B) A slight flood   (E) A sudden rush

    (C) A sudden rise

Questions 26 to 29 refer to the following passage:

Seldom has the American school system not been the target of demands for change to meet the social priorities of the times. This theme has been traced through the following significant occurrences in education: Benjamin Franklin's advocacy in 1749 for a more useful type of education; Horace Mann's zealous proposals in the 1830s espousing the tax-supported public school; John Dewey's early twentieth-century attack on traditional schools for not developing the child effectively for his or her role in society; the post-Sputnik pressure for academic rigor; the prolific criticism and accountability pressures of the 1970s, and the ensuing disillusionment and continued criticism of schools even in the new millenium. Indeed, the waves of criticism about American education have reflected currents of social dissatisfaction for any given period of this country's history.

As dynamics for change in the social order result in demands for change in the American educational system, so in turn insistence has developed for revision of teacher education (witness the more recent Holmes report (1986)). Historically, the education of American teachers has reflected evolving attitudes about public education. With slight modifications, the teacher education pattern established following the demise of the normal school during the early 1900s has persisted in most teacher preparation programs. The pattern has been one requiring certain academic and professional (educational) courses often resulting in teachers prone to teach as they had been taught.

26. The author of this passage would probably agree with which of the following statements?

    (A) Teacher education courses tend to be of no value.

    (B) Social dissatisfaction should drive change in the American school systems.

(C) Teacher education programs have changed greatly since normal schools were eliminated.

(D) Critics of American education reflect vested interests.

(E) Teachers' teaching methods tend to reflect what they have learned in their academic and professional courses.

27. The evolving attitudes about public education are

(A) stated.   (D) unchanged.

(B) unstated.   (E) unwarranted.

(C) alluded.

28. One possible sequence of significant occurrences in education noted in the passage is

(A) Mann's tax-supported public schools, post-Sputnik pressures for academic rigor, and the Holmes' report.

(B) Franklin's more useful type of education, Dewey's educating children for their role in society, and Mann's tax-supported public schools.

(C) Mann's tax-supported public schools, the Holmes report, and post-Sputnik pressures for academic rigor.

(D) Franklin's more useful type of education, the Holmes report, and accountability pressures of the 1970s.

(E) Mann's tax-supported public schools, accountability pressures of the 1970s, and the post-Sputnik pressures for academic rigor.

29. Which of the following statements most obviously implies dissatisfaction with preparation of teachers in the United States?

(A) Demands for change in the American education system lead to insistence for revision of teacher education programs.

(B) The pattern of teacher education requires certain academic and professional education courses.

(C) The education of U.S. teachers has reflected evolving attitudes about public education.

(D) Teachers tend to teach as they were taught.

(E) Teacher education has changed very little since the decline of the normal school.

Questions 30 to 33 refer to the following poem:

HAWK ON A FRESHLY PLOWED FIELD

My Lord of the Field, proudly perched on the sod,
You eye with disdain
And mutter with wings
As steadily each furrow I tractor-plod.
"Intruder!" you glare, firmly standing your ground,
Proclaim this fief yours
By Nature so willed—
Yet bound to the air on my very next round.
You hover and soar, skimming close by the earth,
Distract me from work
To brood there with you
Of changes that Man wrought your land—for his worth.
In medieval days, lords were god over all:
Their word was the law.
Yet here is this hawk
A ruler displaced—Man and Season forestall.
My Lord of the Field, from sight you have flown
For purpose untold,
When brave, you return
And perch once again, still liege-lord—but Alone.

Jacqueline K. Hultquist (1952)

30. Which of the following is the most complete and accurate definition of the term "liege-lord" as used in the poem?

    (A) Monarch

    (B) King

    (C) Owner

    (D) Sovereign

    (E) Master

31. Which of the following best describes the author's attitude toward the hawk?

    (A) Whimsical

    (B) Romantic

    (C) Pensive

    (D) Intimidating

    (E) Fearful

32. Which of the following groups of words about the hawk carry human qualities?

    (A) Mutter, brood, and ruler

    (B) Brave, disdain, and perch

    (C) Mutter, disdain, and perch

    (D) Brave, brood, and distract

    (E) Mutter, disdain, and skimming

33. Which of the following is the most complete and accurate definition of the term "medieval" as used in the poem?

    (A) Antiquated   (D) Antebellum

    (B) Feudal   (E) Antediluvian

    (C) Old

Questions 34 to 37 refer to the following passage:

Reduced to its simplest form, a political system is really no more than a device enabling groups of people to live together in a more or less orderly society. As they have developed, political systems generally have fallen into the broad categories of those which do not offer direct subject participation in the decision-making process, and those which allow citizen participation—in form, if not in actual effectiveness.

Let us consider, however, the type of political system that is classified as the modern democracy in a complex society. Such a democracy is defined by Lipset (1963) as "a political system which supplies regular constitutional opportunities for changing the governing officials, and a social mechanism which permits the largest possible part of the population to influence major decisions by choosing among alternative contenders for political office."

Proceeding from another concept (that of Easton and Dennis), a political system is one of inputs, conversion, and outputs by which the wants of a society are transformed into binding decisions. Easton and Dennis (1967) observed: "To sustain a conversion process of this sort, a society must provide a relatively stable context for political interaction, set of general rules for participating in all parts of the political process." As a rule, this interaction evolves around the settling of differences (satisfying wants or demands) involving the elements of a "political regime," which consists of minimal general goal constraints, norms governing behavior, and structures of authority for the input-output function.

In order to persist, a political system would seem to need a minimal support for the political regime. To insure the maintenance of such a support is the function of political socialization, a process varying according to political systems but toward the end of indoctrinating the members to the respective political system. "To the extent that the maturing members absorb and become attached to the overarching goals of the system and its basic norms and come to approve its structure of authority as legitimate, we can say that they are learning to contribute support to the regime." The desired political norm (an expectation about the way people will behave) is that referred to as political efficacy—a feeling that one's action can have an impact on government.

Adapted from Easton, B. and J. Dennis, "The Child's Acquisition of Regime Norms: Political Efficacy" American Political Science Review, March 1967.

34. Political efficacy according to the passage is

   (A) most likely to be found where citizen participation is encouraged.

   (B) most likely to be found where little direct citizen participation is offered.

   (C) in an expanding concept of political efficiency.

   (D) in a diminishing concept of political efficiency.

   (E) in a figurehead political system.

35. Political socialization is a process that

   (A) occurs only in democracies.

   (B) occurs only in totalitarian regimes.

   (C) occurs in any type of political system.

   (D) occurs less frequently in recent years.

   (E) occurs when members reject the goals of the system.

36. As used in the passage, which of the following is the most complete and accurate defini-

tion of the term "conversion"?

(A) Transformation   (D) Resolution

(B) Changeover   (E) Passing

(C) Growth

37. The major distinction between the concepts of Easton and Dennis as opposed to the concepts of Lipset is that

(A) the concepts of Easton and Dennis are based on the wants of a society, whereas Lipset's concepts are based on change of governing officials.

(B) Easton and Dennis's concepts are based on arbitrary decisions, whereas Lipset's concepts are based on influencing major decisions.

(C) Easton and Dennis's concepts must have a set of general rules, whereas Lipset's concepts provide for irregular constitutional opportunities.

(D) Easton and Dennis's concepts have no inputs, conversion, and outputs, whereas Lipset's concepts allow for no regular constitutional opportunities.

(E) Easton and Dennis's concepts evolve around the settling of differences, whereas Lipset's concepts permit the largest conflict possible.

Questions 38 to 40 refer to the following passage:

Assignment: Research for a White Paper Proposing U.S. Foreign Policy

Imagine you are in charge (or assigned to) a foreign policy desk in the U.S. Department of State. Select one of the following regions (descriptors are merely suggestions):

Western Europe—A Changing Alliance

Eastern Europe—Out from Behind the Iron Curtain

The U.S.S.R.—Still an Enigma

The Middle East—History and Emotions

Africa—Rising Expectations in the Postwar Continent

South and Southeast Asia—Unrest in Far Away Places

The Far East—Alienation and Alliance

The Western Hemisphere—Neighbors; Pro and Con

Through research, prepare a White Paper for that area which will indicate:

1.   a General Policy Statement toward the nations of that region;

2.   a statement as to how World War II set the stage for that policy;

3.   a summary of the major events since 1945 in that region which have affected U.S. foreign policy;

4.   a list of suggested problems and/or possibilities for near-future interactions of that region and the U.S.

38.   In order to complete this assignment, research into which of the following disciplines (areas of study) would be most appropriate?

(A)   History, Economics, Political Science, and Language

(B)   History, Political Science, Education, Economics

(C)   Political Science, Economics, Geography, and Religion

(D)   Geography, Education, History, and Political Science

(E)   History, Political Science, Economics, and Culture

39.   Which of the following is the most complete and accurate definition of the term "enigma" as used in the passage?

(A)   Problem   (D)   Secret

(B)   Riddle   (E)   Mystery

(C)   Puzzle

40.   Which of the following is the most appropriate secondary school audience for the assignment?

(A)   Students in a World Geography class

(B)   Students in a World History class

(C)   Students in a Content Area Reading class

(D)   Students in an Economics class

(E)   Students in an American Government class

Section II: Mathematics

TIME: 60 Minutes
40 Questions

DIRECTIONS: Each of the questions or incomplete statements below is followed by five suggested answers or completions. Select the one that is best in each case.

1. If 406.725 is rounded off to the nearest tenth, the number is

   (A) 406.3.
   (B) 406.5.
   (C) 406.7.
   (D) 406.8.
   (E) 407.0.

2. The mean IQ score for 1,500 students is 100, with a standard deviation of 15. Assuming normal curve distribution, how many students have an IQ between 85 and 115? Refer to the figure shown below.

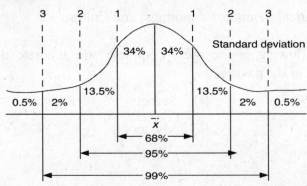

   (A) 510
   (B) 750
   (C) 1,020
   (D) 1,275
   (E) 1,425

3. The sum of 12 and twice a number is 24. Find the number.

   (A) 6
   (B) 8
   (C) 10
   (D) 11
   (E) 12

4. Twice the sum of 10 and a number is 28. Find the number.

    (A) 4   (D) 14

    (B) 8   (E) 24

    (C) 12

5. Two college roommates spent $2,000 for their total monthly expenses. A pie graph below indicates a record of their expenses.

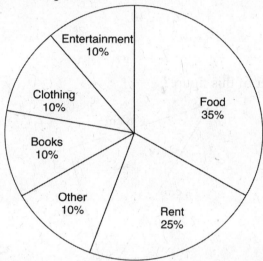

    Based on the above information, which of the following statements is accurate?

    (A) The roommates spent $700 on food alone.

    (B) The roommates spent $550 on rent alone.

    (C) The roommates spent $300 on entertainment alone.

    (D) The roommates spent $300 on clothing alone.

    (E) The roommates spent $300 on books alone.

6. You can buy a telephone for $24. If you are charged $3 per month for renting a cell phone from the telephone company, how long will it take you to recover the cost of the cell phone if you buy one?

    (A) 6 months   (D) 9 months

    (B) 7 months   (E) 10 months

    (C) 8 months

7.   What would be the measure of the third angle in the following triangle?

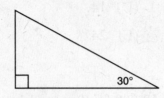

(A) 45°   (D) 70°

(B) 50°   (E) 240°

(C) 60°

8.   What is the perimeter of this figure?

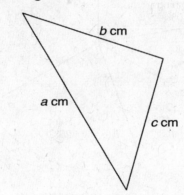

(A) *abc* cm   (D) $(a + b + c)$ cm²

(B) *abc* cm²   (E) *abc* cm³

(C) $(a + b + c)$ cm

9.   What is the perimeter of the given triangle?

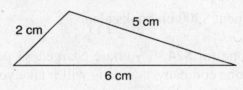

(A) 6 cm   (D) 13 cm

(B) 11 cm   (E) 15 cm

(C) 12 cm

10. Assuming that the quadrilateral in the following figure is a parallelogram, what would be its area?

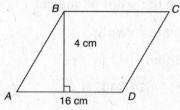

(A) 32 cm

(B) 40 cm

(C) 40 cm²

(D) 64 cm

(E) 64 cm²

11. Refer to the figure below to determine which of the following statements is correct.

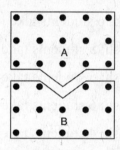

I.   Figures A and B have the same area.

II. Figures A and B have the same perimeter.

(A) I only

(B) II only

(C) Both I and II

(D) Neither I nor II

(E) Can't be determined.

12. Which of the following is NOT a proper subset of $\{1, 2, 3, 4\}$?

(A) $\{1, 2\}$

(B) $\{1, 2, 3\}$

(C) $\{1, 2, 4\}$

(D) $\{1, 3, 4\}$

(E) $\{1, 2, 5\}$

13. Which of the following is an example of a rational number?

(A) $\sqrt{2}$

(B) $6\sqrt{3}$

(C) $4\frac{1}{2}$

(D) $7 + \frac{3}{2}$

(E) $2 - \frac{1}{20}$

14. Which of the following statements includes a cardinal number?

    (A) There are 15 volumes in the set of periodicals.

    (B) I received my 14th volume recently.

    (C) The students meet at Room 304.

    (D) My phone number is 213-617-8442.

    (E) James lives on 3448 Lucky Avenue.

15. In a group of 30 students, 12 are studying mathematics, 18 are studying English, 8 are studying science, 7 are studying both mathematics and English, 6 are studying English and science, 5 are studying mathematics and science, and 4 are studying all three subjects. How many of these students are taking only English? How many of these students are not taking any of these subjects?

    (A) 9 students take only English; 6 students take none of these subjects.

    (B) 10 students take only English; 5 students take none of these subjects.

    (C) 11 students take only English; 5 students take none of these subjects.

    (D) 12 students take only English; 6 students take none of these subjects.

    (E) 13 students take only English; 4 students take none of these subjects.

16. For the given Venn diagram, find $n(A \cap B \cap C)$:

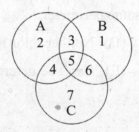

    (A) 3   (D) 6

    (B) 4   (E) 7

    (C) 5

17. Find the next three terms in this sequence: 1, 4, 9, 16, …

    (A) 19, 24, 31   (D) 25, 36, 49

    (B) 20, 25, 31   (E) 25, 34, 43

    (C) 21, 28, 36

18. Assume that one pig eats 4 pounds of food each week. There are 52 weeks in a year. How much food do 10 pigs eat in a week?

    (A) 40 lb.   (D) 20 lb.

    (B) 520 lb.   (E) 60 lb.

    (C) 208 lb.

19. Suppose that a pair of pants and a shirt cost $65 and the pants cost $25 more than the shirt. What did they each cost?

    (A) The pants cost $35 and the shirt costs $30.

    (B) The pants cost $40 and the shirt costs $25.

    (C) The pants cost $43 and the shirt costs $22.

    (D) The pants cost $45 and the shirt costs $20.

    (E) The pants cost $50 and the shirt costs $15.

20. There are five members in a basketball team. Supposing each member shakes hands with every other member of the team before the game starts, how many handshakes will there be in all?

    (A) 6   (D) 10

    (B) 8   (E) 12

    (C) 9

21. Which figure can be obtained from figure Y by translation?

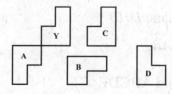

    (A) A   (D) D

    (B) B   (E) None of the above

    (C) C

22. Which of the polygons below is a triangular pyramid?

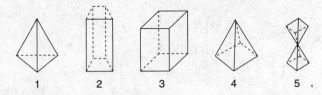

1   2   3   4   5

(A) 1   (D) 4

(B) 2   (E) 5

(C) 3

23. The figure below represents a portion of a square pyramid viewed from above. Which of the following statements is true?

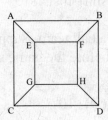

(A) Edges $\overline{AE}$ and $\overline{BF}$ intersect.

(B) Lines $\overleftrightarrow{AE}$ and $\overleftrightarrow{BF}$ intersect.

(C) Line segment $\overline{CG}$ intersects plane DHB.

(D) Face $CGEA$ intersects plane DHB.

(E) Line $\overleftrightarrow{CG}$ intersects line $\overleftrightarrow{AB}$.

24. Below is a rectangular pyramid ABCDE.

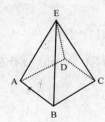

How many vertices does it have?

(A) 3   (D) 6

(B) 4   (E) 7

(C) 5

25. Tom bought a piece of land selling for $20,000. If he had to pay 20 percent of the price as a down payment, how much was the down payment?

(A) $2,500   (D) $4,500

(B) $3,000   (E) $5,000

(C) $4,000

26. A desktop computer sells for $3,200 to the general public. If you purchase one in the university, the price is reduced by 20 percent. What is the sale price of the computer?

(A) $640   (D) $2,560

(B) $2,000   (E) $3,180

(C) $2,410

27. In order for Sue to receive a final grade of C, she must have an average greater than or equal to 70% but less than 80% on five tests. Suppose her grades on the first four tests were 65%, 85%, 60%, and 90%. What range of grades on the fifth test would give her a C in the course?

(A) 40 up to but excluding 95

(B) 45 up to but excluding 95

(C) 47 up to but excluding 90

(D) 49 up to but excluding 98

(E) 50 up to but excluding 100

28. A certain company produces two types of lawnmowers. Type A is self-propelled while type B is not. The company can produce a maximum of 18 mowers per week. It can make a profit of $15 on mower A and a profit of $20 on mower B. The company wants to make at least 2 mowers of type A but not more than 5. They also plan to make at least 2 mowers of type B. Let x be the number of type A produced, and let y be the number of type B produced.

From the above, which of the following is NOT one of the listed constraints?

(A) $x \geq 2$ (D) $y < 5$

(B) $x \leq 5$ (E) $y \geq 2$

(C) $x + y \leq 18$

29. Mr. Smith died and left an estate to be divided among his wife, two children, and a foundation of his choosing in the ratio of 8:6:6:1. How much did his wife receive if the estate was valued at $300,000?

(A) $114,285.71   (D) $120,421.91

(B) $85,714.29   (E) $14,285.71

(C) $125,461.71

30. There were 19 hamburgers for nine people on a picnic. How many whole hamburgers were there for each person if they were divided equally?

(A) 1   (D) 4

(B) 2   (E) 5

(C) 3

31. George has four ways to get from his house to the park. He has seven ways to get from the park to the school. How many ways can George get from his house to school by way of the park?

(A) 4   (D) 3

(B) 7   (E) 11

(C) 28

32. If it takes one minute per cut, how long will it take to cut a 15-foot long timber into 15 equal pieces?

(A) 5   (D) 20

(B) 10   (E) 15

(C) 14

33. Ed has six new shirts and four new pairs of pants. How many combinations of new shirts and pants does he have?

   (A) 10   (D) 20

   (B) 14   (E) 24

   (C) 18

34. The property tax rate of the town of Grandview is $32 per $1,000 of assessed value. What is the tax if the property is assessed at $50,000?

   (A) $32   (D) $1,600

   (B) $1,000   (E) $2,000

   (C) $1,562

35. Ralph kept track of his work time in gardening. Refer to the broken-line graph below:

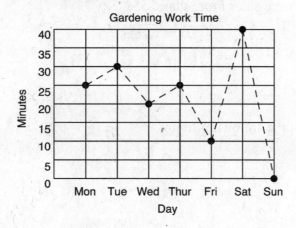

How many minutes did he average per day?

   (A) 10 min.   (D) 23.05 min.

   (B) 20 min.   (E) 25 min.

   (C) 21.43 min.

36. Mary had been selling printed shirts in her neighborhood. She made this pictograph to show how much money she made each week.

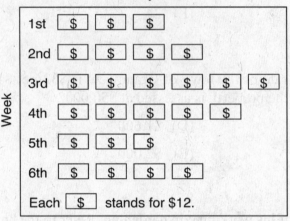

Weekly Sales

How many weeks were sales more than $55?

(A) 1 week

(D) 4 weeks

(B) 2 weeks

(E) 5 weeks

(C) 3 weeks

37. Find the volume of the following figure.

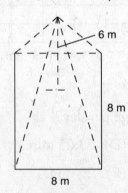

(A) 48 m²

(D) 192 m³

(B) 64 m²

(E) 384 m³

(C) 128 m³

38. The result of Mary's spring semester grades follow. Find her grade point average for the term (A = 4, B = 3, C = 2, D = 1, F = 0).

Course	Credits	Grades
Biology	5	A
English	3	C
Math	3	A
French	3	D
P.E.	2	B

(A) 3.80

(B) 3.50

(C) 2.94

(D) 2.00

(E) 1.86

39. In a biology class at International University, the grades on the final examination were as follows:

91	81	65	81
50	70	81	93
36	90	43	87
96	81	75	81

Find the mode.

(A) 36

(B) 70

(C) 81

(D) 87

(E) 96

40. One commonly used standard score is a z-score. A z-score gives the number of standard deviations by which the score differs from the mean, as shown in the following example.

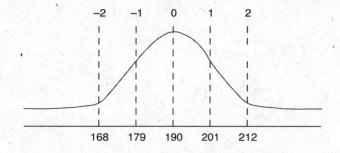

The mean (x) is 190 and the standard deviation(s) is 11. The score of 201 has a z-score of 1 and the score of 168 has a z-score of -2. Consider the mean height of a certain group of people as 190 cm with a standard deviation of 11 cm. Suppose Glenn's height has a z-score of 1.6, what is his height? (Note $z = \frac{x - \bar{x}}{s}$.)

(A) 207.60 cm

(B) 190 cm

(C) 201 cm

(D) 179 cm

(E) 212 cm

Section III: Writing

TIME: *30 Minutes*
38 Questions

Part A: Usage

DIRECTIONS: Each of the following sentences may contain an error in diction, usage, idiom, or grammar. Some sentences are correct. Some sentences contain one error. No sentence contains more than one error.

If there is an error, it will appear in one of the underlined portions labeled A, B, C, or D. If there is no error, choose the portion labeled E. If there is an error, select the letter of the portion that must be changed in order to correct the sentence.

EXAMPLE:

He drove <u>slowly</u> and <u>cautiously</u> in order to <u>hopefully</u> avoid having an <u>accident</u>.
      A   B   C   D
<u>No error</u>.
  E

1. *Huckleberry Finn*, by <u>general consensus agreement</u> Mark Twain's <u>greatest</u> work, is
                            A   B

    <u>supremely</u> the American <u>Classic</u>; it is also one of the great books of the world.
      C   D

    <u>No error</u>.
      E

2. The U.S. <u>Constitution</u> <u>supposes</u> what the history of all governments <u>demonstrate</u>, that
               A   B   C

    the executive is the branch <u>most</u> interested in war and most prone to it. <u>No error</u>.
                            D   E

3. Mama, the <u>narrator</u> of Alice Walker's short story "Everyday Use," <u>speaks</u> fondly of
           A   B

    her daughter upon her return home after a long absence <u>like</u> Mama is <u>proud</u> of her.
                                            C   D

    <u>No error</u>.
      E

4. <u>Nearly</u> one <u>hundred</u> years after the impoverished Vincent van Gogh died, his paintings
    A   B

  <u>had sold</u> for more than a <u>million dollars</u>. <u>No error</u>.
   C   D   E

5. Many athletes <u>recruited</u> for football by college coaches <u>expect</u> that they will, <u>in fact</u>,
            A   B   C

  receive an education when they <u>accept</u> a scholarship. <u>No error</u>.
                      D   E

6. <u>Hopefully</u>, by the end of the <u>Twentieth Century</u>, computer scientists will invent ma-
   A   B

  chines with <u>enough</u> intelligence to work without breaking down <u>continually</u>. <u>No error</u>.
          C   D   E

7. Studies <u>showing</u> that the earth includes a <u>vast series</u> of sedimentary rocks, some with
         A   B

  <u>embedded</u> fossils <u>that</u> prove the existence of ancient organisms. <u>No error</u>.
    C   D   E

8. When Martin Luther King, <u>Jr.</u>, wrote his famous letter from the Birmingham jail, he
                   A

  advocated neither evading <u>or</u> defying the law; <u>but</u> he accepted the idea that a penalty
                       B   C

  <u>results from</u> breaking a law, even an unjust one. <u>No error</u>.
     D   E

9. <u>The eighteenth century</u> philosopher Adam Smith <u>asserted</u> that a nation <u>achieves</u>
         A   B   C

  the best economic results when individuals work both for their own interests and

  <u>to gain more goods</u>. <u>No error</u>.
        D   E

10. According to Niccolo Machiavelli, wise rulers <u>cannot</u> and <u>should not</u> keep their word
                                         A   B

  when such integrity would be to <u>their</u> disadvantage and when the reasons for the
                                  C

  promise no longer <u>exist</u>. <u>No error</u>.
             D   E

11. The Milky Way galaxy, which <u>comprises</u> millions of stars, has both <u>thin and congest-</u>
                          A   B

  ed spots, but shines <u>their</u> <u>brightest</u> in the constellation Sagittarius. <u>No error</u>.
                    C   D   E

12. <u>To learn</u> an ancient language <u>like</u> Latin or Greek is one way to discover the roots of
       A   B

    Western Culture; studying Judaeo-Christian religious <u>beliefs</u> <u>is</u> another. <u>No error</u>.
                                               C   D   E

13. Many political conservatives <u>contribute</u> the problems of modern American society to
                                 A

    the twin evils of the New Deal and <u>secular humanism</u>, both <u>of which</u> <u>are</u> presumed to
                                       B   C   D

    stem from Marxism. <u>No error</u>.
                    E

14. <u>Having minimal exposure</u> to poetry when they <u>attended</u> school, most Americans <u>chose</u>
              A   B   C

    to watch television or <u>to read</u> popular magazines for entertainment. <u>No error</u>.
                         D   E

15. What makes <u>we</u> humans <u>different from</u> other animals <u>can be defined</u> at least <u>partly</u> by
                 A   B   C   D

    our powerful and efficient intelligence. <u>No error</u>.
                                        E

16. When one contrasts the ideas of the Romantic William Wordsworth <u>with</u> <u>those</u> of Neo-
                                                                    A   B

    classicist John Dryden, <u>one finds</u> that neither of the poets <u>differ</u> as much as one would
                                   C   D

    expect. <u>No error</u>.
               E

17. Carl Jung's hypothesis of the collective unconscious <u>suggests</u> that we inherit
                                                    A

    <u>cultural-experimental</u> memory in the form of mythological archetype, <u>which arise</u>
           B   C

    from repeated <u>patterns</u> of human behavior. <u>No error</u>.
                    D   E

18. Bertrand Russell believed that a free <u>person's</u> liberation is <u>effected</u> by a contempla-
                                              A   B

    tion of <u>Fate</u>; one achieves emancipation through passionate pursuit of eternal things,
              C

    <u>not through</u> the pursuit of private happiness. <u>No error</u>.
       D   E

19. <u>Latin American</u> literature <u>includes</u> the works of Gabriel Garcia Marquez, Pablo
    A   B

    Neruda, and Jorge Luis Borges; each of these <u>acclaimed</u> artists has won <u>their</u> share of
                                                  C   D

    prizes. <u>No error</u>.
            E

20. The reason <u>a large percentage</u> of American college students <u>located</u> Moscow in Cali-
               A   B

    fornia is <u>because</u> they <u>were not required</u> to learn the facts of geography. <u>No error</u>.
              C   D   E

21. Astronomers and physicists <u>tell</u> us that the universe is <u>constant</u> expanding <u>and that</u> it
                               A   B   C

    <u>comprises</u> numerous galaxies like ours. <u>No error</u>.
    D   E

22. <u>Less</u> students chose liberal arts and <u>sciences</u> majors in the 1980s than in the 1960s
    A   B

    <u>because of</u> the contemporary view that a college education <u>is</u> a ticket to enter the job
    C   D

    market. <u>No error</u>.
            E

23. Span of control is the term <u>that</u> refers to the <u>limits</u> of a leader's <u>ability for managing</u>
                                A   B   C

    those employees <u>under</u> his/her supervision. <u>No error</u>.
                    D   E

24. <u>Because some</u> people believe <u>strongly</u> that channelling, the <u>process by which</u> an in-
    A   B   C

    dividual goes into a trance-like state and communicates the thoughts of an ancient

    warrior or guru to an audience, helps them cope with modern problems, but others

    condemn the whole idea <u>as</u> mere superstition. <u>No error</u>.
                           D   E

25. The reed on a woodwind instrument is <u>essential</u> <u>being that</u> it <u>controls the quality</u> of
                                         A   B   C

    tone and sound. <u>No error</u>.
    D   E

Part B: Sentence Correction

DIRECTIONS: In each of the following sentences, some portion of the sentence is underlined. Under each sentence are five choices. The first choice has the same wording as the original. The other four choices are reworded. Sometimes the first choice containing the original wording is the best; sometimes one of the other choices is the best. Choose the letter of the best choice. Your choice should produce a sentence which is not ambiguous or awkward and which is correct, clear, and precise.

This is a test of correct and effective English expression. Keep in mind the standards of English usage, punctuation, grammar, word choice, and construction.

EXAMPLE:

When you listen to opera, a person may not appreciate it.

(A) a person may not appreciate it.

(B) it may not be appreciated by a person.

(C) which may not be appreciated by one.

(D) you may not appreciate it.

(E) appreciating it may be a problem for you.

26. Two-thirds of American 17-year-olds do not know that the Civil War takes place between 1850–1900.

(A) takes place   (D) have taken place

(B) took place   (E) is taking place

(C) had taken place

27. Both professional and amateur ornithologists, people that study birds, recognize the Latin or scientific names of bird species.

(A) people that study birds

(B) people which study birds

(C) the study of birds

(D) people who study birds

(E) in which people study birds

28. Many of the oil-producing states spent their huge surplus tax revenues during the oil boom of the 1970s and early 1980s <u>in spite of the fact that</u> oil production from new wells began to flood the world market as early as 1985.

    (A) in spite of the fact that

    (B) even in view of the fact that

    (C) however clearly it was known that

    (D) even though

    (E) when it was clear that

29. The president of the community college reported <u>as to the expectability of the tuition increase as well as the actual amount</u>.

    (A) as to the expectability of the tuition increase as well as the actual amount

    (B) that the tuition will likely increase by a specific amount

    (C) as to the expectability that tuition will increase by a specific amount

    (D) about the expected tuition increase of five percent

    (E) regarding the expectation of a tuition increase expected to be five percent

30. Although Carmen developed an interest in classical music, <u>she did not read notes and had never played an instrument</u>.

    (A) she did not read notes and had never played an instrument

    (B) she does not read notes and has never played an instrument

    (C) it is without being able to read notes or having played an instrument

    (D) she did not read notes nor had she ever played them

    (E) it is without reading notes nor having played an instrument

31. Political candidates must campaign on issues and ideas that strike a chord within their constituency but <u>with their goal to sway</u> undecided voters to support their candidacy.

    (A) with their goal to sway

    (B) need also to sway

    (C) aiming at the same time to sway

    (D) also trying to sway

    (E) its goal should also be in swaying

32. The major reasons students give for failing courses in college <u>is that they have demand-ing professors and work at</u> full- or part-time jobs.

    (A) is that they have demanding professors and work at

    (B) are demanding professors and they work at

    (C) is having demanding professors and having

    (D) are demanding professors, in addition to working at

    (E) are that they have demanding professors and that they have

33. <u>Having command of color, symbolism, as well as technique,</u> Georgia O'Keeffe is con-sidered to be a great American painter.

    (A) Having command of color, symbolism, as well as technique

    (B) Having command of color, symbolism, and her technical ability

    (C) Because of her command of color, symbolism, and technique

    (D) With her command of color and symbolism and being technical

    (E) By being in command of both color and symbolism and also technique

34. <u>Whether the ancient ancestors of American Indians actually migrated or did not</u> across a land bridge now covered by the Bering Strait remains uncertain, but that they could have has not been refuted by other theories.

    (A) Whether the ancient ancestors of American Indians actually migrated or did not

    (B) That the ancient ancestors of American Indians actually did migrate

    (C) The actuality of whether the ancient ancestors of American Indians migrated

    (D) Whether in actuality the ancient ancestors of American Indians migrated or not

    (E) That the ancient ancestors of American Indians may actually have migrated

35. Caution in scientific experimentation can <u>sometimes be related more to integrity than to lack of knowledge</u>.

    (A) sometimes be related more to integrity than to lack of knowledge

    (B) sometimes be related more to integrity as well as lack of knowledge

    (C) often be related to integrity as to lack of knowledge

    (D) be related more to integrity rather than lack of knowledge

    (E) be related often to integrity, not only to lack of knowledge

36. Separated by their successful rebellion against England from any existing form of government, the citizens of the United States <u>have developed a unique constitutional political system</u>.

    (A) have developed a unique constitutional political system

    (B) had developed a very unique constitutional political system

    (C) had developed their constitutional political system uniquely

    (D) have developed their political system into a very unique constitutional one

    (E) have a unique political system, based on a constitution

37. <u>Returning to the ancestral home after 12 years, the house itself seemed much smaller to Joe</u> than it had been when he visited it as a child.

    (A) Returning to the ancestral home after 12 years, the house itself seemed much smaller to Joe

    (B) When Joe returned to the ancestral home after 12 years, he thought the house itself much smaller

    (C) Joe returned to the ancestral home after 12 years, and then he thought the house itself much smaller

    (D) After Joe returned to the ancestral home in 12 years, the house itself seemed much smaller

    (E) Having returned to the ancestral home after 12 years, it seemed a much smaller house to Joe

38. Historians say that the New River of North Carolina, Virginia, and West Virginia, <u>which is 2,700 feet above sea level and 2,000 feet above</u> the surrounding foothills, is the oldest river in the United States.

    (A) which is 2,700 feet above sea level and 2,000 feet above

    (B) with a height of 2,700 feet above sea level as well as 2,000 feet above that of

    (C) 2,700 feet higher than sea level and ascending 2,000 feet above

    (D) being 2,700 feet above sea level and 2,000 feet high measure from that of

    (E) located 2,700 feet high above sea level while measuring 2,000 feet above

Part C: Essay

TIME: *30 Minutes*

DIRECTIONS: You have 30 minutes to plan and write an essay on the topic below. You may write only on the assigned topic.

Make sure to give specific examples to support your thesis. Proofread your essay carefully and take care to express your ideas clearly and effectively.

ESSAY TOPIC:

Many leaders have suggested that instead of a military draft we should require all young people to perform public service in some way for a set period of time. The service could be military or any other reasonable form of service.

ASSIGNMENT: Do you agree or disagree with the statement? Support your opinion with specific examples from history, current events, literature, or personal experience.

Answer Key

Section 1: Reading Comprehension

1. **(A)**	11. **(E)**	21. **(E)**	31. **(C)**
2. **(A)**	12. **(D)**	22. **(D)**	32. **(A)**
3. **(D)**	13. **(E)**	23. **(B)**	33. **(B)**
4. **(B)**	14. **(C)**	24. **(B)**	34. **(A)**
5. **(A)**	15. **(B)**	25. **(D)**	35. **(C)**
6. **(D)**	16. **(C)**	26. **(E)**	36. **(A)**
7. **(C)**	17. **(A)**	27. **(B)**	37. **(A)**
8. **(A)**	18. **(C)**	28. **(A)**	38. **(E)**
9. **(E)**	19. **(B)**	29. **(E)**	39. **(C)**
10. **(A)**	20. **(C)**	30. **(E)**	40. **(E)**

Section II: Mathematics

1. **(C)**	11. **(B)**	21. **(C)**	31. **(C)**
2. **(C)**	12. **(E)**	22. **(A)**	32. **(C)**
3. **(A)**	13. **(D)**	23. **(B)**	33. **(E)**
4. **(A)**	14. **(A)**	24. **(C)**	34. **(D)**
5. **(A)**	15. **(A)**	25. **(C)**	35. **(C)**
6. **(C)**	16. **(C)**	26. **(D)**	36. **(B)**
7. **(C)**	17. **(D)**	27. **(E)**	37. **(C)**
8. **(C)**	18. **(A)**	28. **(D)**	38. **(C)**
9. **(D)**	19. **(D)**	29. **(A)**	39. **(C)**
10. **(E)**	20. **(D)**	30. **(B)**	40. **(A)**

Section III: Writing

1. (A)	13. (A)	25. (B)	37. (B)
2. (C)	14. (C)	26. (B)	38. (A)
3. (C)	15. (A)	27. (D)	
4. (C)	16. (D)	28. (D)	
5. (B)	17. (E)	29. (B)	
6. (A)	18. (E)	30. (A)	
7. (A)	19. (D)	31. (B)	
8. (B)	20. (C)	32. (E)	
9. (D)	21. (B)	33. (C)	
10. (E)	22. (A)	34. (B)	
11. (C)	23. (C)	35. (A)	
12. (A)	24. (A)	36. (A)	

PRACTICE TEST 2 – Detailed Explanations of Answers

Section I: Reading Comprehension

1. **A**

    Choices (B), (D), and (E) present minor problems in spa maintenance, whereas choice (C) cannot be prevented. As bacteria and virus are controlled by both temperature and chemicals, it becomes a possible source of health problems if ignored.

2. **A**

    Choices (B), (C), and (D) are correct levels or degrees. Although choice (E) is important, it is not as dangerous as choice (A) where temperatures in excess of 104° can cause dizziness, nausea, fainting, drowsiness, and reduced awareness.

3. **D**

    Choices (A), (B), and (C) represent an inference that goes beyond the scope of the passage and would indicate biases of the reader. Although the passage explains spa maintenance, choice (E), the information is not adequate to serve as a detailed guide.

4. **B**

    The other choices (A), (C), and (D) refer to chemical or temperature maintenance. Although choice (E) helps to ensure clarity, choice (B) is explicitly stated in the passage.

5. **A**

    Choices (B), (C), and (D) are appropriate chemicals. Although chlorine is an alternative to bromine, this passage indicates it should be granular as indicated in choice (A); liquid and tablet chlorines are too harsh for spas, thus all forms are not acceptable as indicated by choice (E).

6. **D**

    Choices (A) and (B) appear to be acceptable, whereas choice (E) indicates a perfect correlation. Although choice (C) is a definition of statistical significance, choice (D) is correct as the passage is about correlational statistical significance which permits prediction.

7. **C**

Choice (A) goes beyond the information provided in the passage. Choice (B) is incorrect as correlation cannot indicate causality, and choice (E) states incorrectly there was no variance. Choice (D) is not statistically possible. The high positive correlation trend indicates that these variables are important to consider for future research, thus choice (C).

8. **A**

Choices (B), (C), (D), and (E) represent inferences that are based on inadequate information which go beyond the scope of the passage. As these story elements are not taught explicitly in the first grade or prior to entering school, children apparently have picked up these elements from their exposures to stories as indicated by choice (A).

9. **E**

Although the content might be appropriate for each of the journals, choices (A), (B), (C), and (D), the style of writing suggests that it would be most appropriate for choice (E), *Reading Research Quarterly,* as this passage reports research results.

10. **A**

The passage provides information for the grade level and mentions if it was significant or substantial. As this statement follows information provided for fifth/sixth grades, it refers to that level, thus choice (A).

11. **E**

Choices (A), (B), (C), and (D) all connote extreme or inappropriate attitudes not expressed in the passage. The author presents an informed concern—choice (E).

12. **D**

For the other choices, (A), (B), (C), and (E), the criteria, the role, the discussion, and the assurance for communication or learning are not provided in the passage. The passage stresses the importance of authenticity in communication—choice (D)

13. **E**

Each of the choices is a possible definition, but the passage overall suggests that communication needs to be developed so that students' responses may become more significant and authentic—choice (E).

14. **C**

Choices (A), (B), and (E) are not supported by the passage. Choice (D) represents an incorrect conclusion. Choice (C) is supported by the various investigators' explanations.

15. **B**

As stated explicitly in the passage, the various investigators have attempted to explain the role of imitation in language—choice (B). The other choices go beyond the scope of the passage.

16. **C**

As the investigators studied different aspects of language while attempting to explain the role of imitation in language, choice (C) is correct. The other choices go beyond the scope of the passage.

17. **A**

The passage explicitly states that computers are capable of addressing the issues of practice and the true act of reading, choice (A). The other choices represent inferences that are not supported by the passage.

18. **C**

Although the reader might make inferences to select choices (A), (B), (D), and (E), ways to use a word processor to make practice resemble the true reading act are not stated in the passage, thus choice (C).

19. **B**

Although audiences in choices (A), (C), (D), and (E) may benefit from the information provided in the passage, the passage explicitly states that a greater understanding of the information in the passage should assist teachers—choice (B).

20. **C**

Each of the choices is a definition of variance. However, for this passage, choice (C) is the most appropriate.

21. **E**

Although meaning is found in the components of each choice, the passage states that we should begin with students' meaning before moving to the commonalities of story meaning—choice (E).

22. **D**

As the passage presents information by various researchers on children's stories, the passage ends with an unanswered question that still needs to be addressed by reading researchers as provided in choice (D).

23. **B**

Although more information may be needed about story content and story structure as indicated in choices (A), (C), (D), and (E), the main question that remains to be answered is choice (B).

24. **B**

Each choice provides partially correct information about story content and story structure; choice (B) provides the most complete response.

25. **D**

Each choice is a possible definition. However, choice (D) is most appropriate as there was an increased interest by researchers in these and other areas even though it has been an ongoing concern of some researchers.

26. **E**

Choices (A) and (C) are not supported by the passage. Choices (B) and (D) go beyond the passage. The last sentence states "The pattern . . . resulting in teachers prone to teach as they had been taught"—thus choice (E).

27. **B**

The other choices (A), (C), (D), and (E) are not supported by the passage. Although the passage mentions that teacher education has reflected evolving attitudes about education, the attitudes are not spelled out—choice (B).

28. **A**

Only choice (A) has the correct sequence; the other sequences are incorrect.

29. **E**

Choices (A), (B), (C), and (D) are statements about education, teacher education, and teachers. Choice (E)'s statement that teacher education has changed very little implies that this lack of change could be a source of dissatisfaction.

30. **E**

Choices (A), (B), and (D) suggest rights either by heredity or supreme authority, whereas choice (C) indicates rights just by possession. The hyphenated term "liege-lord" connotes both entitled rights and power to command respect. Thus choice (E), "master" (one who assumes authority and property rights through ability and power to control), best represents the hawk.

31. **C**

Choices (A), (D), and (E) are not supported by the passage. Choice (B) represents a possible conclusion, but choice (C) suggests real thought about the hawk.

32. **A**

Each of the other choices contains a term which does not refer to human qualities. The other qualities may refer to the hawk, e.g., "perch" or to the author of the passage, e.g., "disdain."

33. **B**

Choices (D) and (E) are incorrect because of definitions. Choices (A) and (C) are possible definitions, but feudal most clearly denotes an association to the Middle Ages.

34. **A**

The passage explicitly states that political efficacy is a feeling that one's actions can have an impact on government—choice (A). Choices (C), (D), and (E) are not supported by the passage. Choice (B) is incorrect.

35. **C**

Choices (A), (B), (D), and (E) are not supported by the passage. The passage states "...political socialization, a process varying according to political systems but toward the end of indoctrinating the members to the respective political system"— choice (C).

36. **A**

Although the other choices (B), (C), (D), and (E) are possible definitions, the passage explicitly states that "a political system is one of inputs, conversions, and outputs by which the wants of a society are transformed into binding decisions"—thus choice (A).

37. **A**

Choices (B), (C), (D), and (E) contain an incorrect concept of either Easton and Dennis or Lipset. Only choice (A) has the correct concepts for both Easton and Dennis and Lipset.

38. **E**

Choices (A), (B), (C), and (D) each contain an area which is considered a component of culture, such as religion, education, and language. Thus, choice (E) is the most appropriate response.

39. **C**

Although each definition appears appropriate, choices (B), (D), and (E) assume that a solution is known, or has been known at one time, and could be solved. Although choice (A) suggests difficulty in solving, choice (C) suggests a situation that is intricate enough to perplex the mind. Choice (C) is most appropriate for this passage as a definition of enigma is an inexplicable situation.

40. **E**

Although choices (A), (B), (C), and (D) may touch on such a topic, the roles and functions of governmental offices and departments are generally addressed in an American Government class, thus choice (E).

Section II: Mathematics

1. **C**

    7 is in the tenths place. Since the next digit (2) is below 5, drop this digit and retain the 7. The answer, therefore, is 406.7.

2. **C**

    The mean IQ score of 100 is given. One standard deviation above the mean is 34% of the cases, with an IQ score from 100 to 115. One standard deviation below the mean is another 34% of the cases, with an IQ score from 85 to 100. So, a total of 68% of the students have an IQ between 85 and 115. Therefore, $1,500 \times .68 = 1,020$.

3. **A**

    $$12 + 2x = 24$$
    $$2x = 24 - 12$$
    $$2x = 12$$
    $$x = 6$$

4. **A**

    $$(10 + x)2 = 28$$
    $$20 + 2x = 28$$
    $$2x = 28 - 20$$
    $$2x = 8$$
    $$x = 4$$

5. **A**

    $$\$2,000 \times .35 = \$700.$$

    The rest have wrong computations.

6. **C**

    Let x = length of time (# of mos) to recover cost.

    $$3x = 24$$
    $$x = \frac{24}{3}$$
    $$x = 8 \text{ mos.}$$

7. **C**

    With one right angle (90°) and a given 30° angle, the missing angle, therefore, is a 60° angle.

    $$90° + 30° = 120°; \ 180° - 120° = 60°$$

8. **C**

    The perimeter is the distance around the triangle which is, therefore,

    $(a + b + c)$ cm.

9. **D**

    The perimeter is the distance around the triangle. Therefore,

    2 cm + 6 cm + 5 cm = 13 cm.

10. **E**

    The area of a parallelogram is base × height. Therefore,

    $A = bh = (16 \text{ cm}) \times (4 \text{ cm}) = 64 \text{ cm}^2$.

11. **B**

    Figure A has an area of about 9 square units while Figure B has an area of about 7 square units. Both Figures A and B have the same perimeter of about 12 units.

12. **E**

    Only (E) has an element (which is 5) not present in the given set of {1, 2, 3, 4}.

13. **D**

    Nine is the square of an integer. 17, 11, and 15 are not squares of an integer, therefore, they are irrational numbers. 7 is not the cube of an integer, hence, it is an irrational number as well.

14. **A**

    15 is used as a cardinal number. The rest are either ordinal (B) or nominal, (C), (D), (E), numbers.

15. **A**

Use the Venn diagram (as shown below) with three circles to represent the set of students in each of the listed subject matter areas. Start with four students taking all three subjects. We write the number 4 in the region that is the intersection of all these circles. Then we work backward: Since seven are taking math and English, and four of these have already been identified as also taking English, math, and science, there must be exactly three taking only math and English. That is, there must be three in the region representing math and English, but not science. Continuing in this manner, we enter the given data in the diagram.

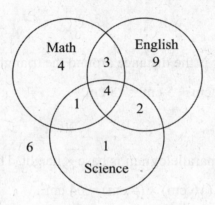

16. **C**

There is one region in the intersection of all three sets. Thus,

$$n(A \cap B \cap C) = 5.$$

17. **D**

The sequence 1, 4, 9, 16 is the sum of the odd numbers.

1.   1
2. $1 + 3 = 4$
3. $1 + 3 + 5 = 9$
4. $1 + 3 + 5 + 7 = 16$

Thus, the fifth number is $1 + 3 + 5 + 7 + 9 = 25$.

The sixth number is $1 + 3 + 5 + 7 + 9 + 11 = 36$.

The seventh number is $1 + 3 + 5 + 7 + 9 + 11 + 13 = 49$.

18. **A**

Here one must use only the needed information. Do not be distracted by superfluous data. Simple multiplication will do. If one pig eats four pounds of food per week, how much will 10 pigs eat in one week? $10 \times 4 = 40$ pounds. The problem intentionally contains superfluous data (52 weeks), which should not distract the reader from its easy solution. Ratio and proportion will also work here

$$\frac{1}{10} = \frac{4}{x}, \ x = 40 \text{ pounds/week.}$$

19. **D**

Let the variable S stand for the cost of the shirt. Then the cost of the pair of pants is $S + 25$ and

$$S + (S + 25) = 65$$
$$2S = 65 - 25$$
$$2S = 40$$
$$S = 20$$

$20 (cost of shirt)

$20 + $25 = $45 (cost of pants)

20. **D**

The possible handshakes are illustrated by listing all the possible pairs of letters, thus

AB	AC	AD	AE
BC	BD	BE	
CD	CE		
DE			

(a total of 10 handshakes)

21. **C**

Only (C) involves a change by only translation.

22. **A**

(B) is a rectangular prism. (C) is a square prism. (D) is a square pyramid. (E) is neither a prism nor a pyramid.

23. **B**

If one continues lines $\overleftrightarrow{AE}$ and $\overleftrightarrow{BF}$, they intersect at a common vertex. The rest do not.

24. **C**

Points ABCDE are the vertices, thus 5.

25. **C**

Let

D = down payment
D = $20,000 × .20
D = $4,000

26. **D**

20% of $3,200 = $640 (amount price reduced)
$3,200 − $640 = $2,560 (sale price)

27. **E**

Let x = 5th grade

$$\text{Average} = \frac{65+85+60+90+x}{5}$$

For Sue to obtain a C, her average must be greater than or equal to 70 but less than 80.

$$70 \leq \frac{65+85+60+90+x}{5} < 80$$
$$70 \leq \frac{300+x}{5} < 80$$
$$5(70) \leq 5(300+x \div 5) < 5(80)$$
$$350 \leq 300+x < 400$$
$$350-300 \leq x < 400-300$$
$$50 \leq x < 100$$

Thus, a grade of 50 up to but not including a grade of 100 will result in a C.

28. **D**

   All but (E) are constraints. The constraint for y is to make at least two mowers.

29. **A**

   The ratio 8:6:6:1 implies that for each $8 the wife received, each child received $6 and the foundation $1. The estate is divided into $8 + 6 + 6 + 1$, or 21 equal shares. The wife received $\frac{8}{21}$ of $300,000 or $114,285.71, each child received $\frac{6}{21}$ of $300,000, or $85,714.29, and the foundation received $\frac{1}{21}$ of $300,000 or $14,285.71. As a check,

   $114,285.71 + \$85,714.29 + \$85,714.29 + \$14,285.71 = \$300,000$.

30. **B**

   Simple division: $\frac{19}{9} = 2$ whole hamburgers with one left over.

31. **C**

   Simple multiplication: $7 \times 4 = 28$.

32. **C**

   For a 15 ft. log, it will take 14 cuts to make 15 equal pieces. Therefore, 14 minutes for 14 cuts.

33. **E**

   Simple multiplication.

   $6 \times 4 = 24$.

34. **D**

   First find out how many shares of $1,000 there are in $50,000

   $\$50,000 \div 1,000 = 50$

   Then multiply the shares by the cost ($50 \times \$32$) and the answer is $1,600.

35. **C**

   Find the sum of the seven days. Thus:

   $M = 25$;

   $T = 30$;

   $W = 20$;

$$Th = 25;$$
$$F = 10;$$
$$Sat = 40;$$
$$Sun = 0,$$

or a total of 150 minutes. Find the average by dividing 150 by 7 = 21.43 minutes.

36. **B**

If each ☐$☐ stands for $12, weeks 3 and 4 had a sale of $72 and $60, respectively. The rest are below $55.

37. **C**

The volume of a pyramid is

$$V = \frac{1}{3}Bh,$$

where B is the area of the base and h is the height of the pyramid. Thus,

$$V = \frac{1}{3}(64)(6)$$

$$= \frac{1}{3}(384) = 128 \text{ m}^3.$$

38. **C**

Total the number of credits earned (in this case = 16 credits). Multiply the credit and the weight for the earned grade per subject (e.g., biology = 5 × 4 = 20). Then add the total of the products of the credits and corresponding weights (in this case = 47). Then divide 47 by 16 to get the grade point average of 2.94. See table below.

$$\text{Biology} = 5 \times 4 = 20$$
$$\text{English} = 3 \times 2 = 6$$
$$\text{Math} = 3 \times 4 = 12$$
$$\text{French} = 3 \times 1 = 3$$
$$\text{P.E.} = 2 \times 3 = 6$$

$$GPA = \frac{20 + 6 + 12 + 3 + 6}{16} = \frac{47}{16} = 2.94$$

39. **C**

Mode is the most frequent score. 81 appeared five times and is therefore the mode.

40. **A**

Following the formula

$$z = \frac{x - \bar{x}}{s.d.}$$

thus, $1.6 = x - \dfrac{190}{11}$

$17.60 = x - 190$

$x = 190 + 17.60$

$x = 207.60$ cm (Glenn's height)

Section III: Writing

1. **A**

   Choice (A) is obviously wordy, "consensus" meaning the same thing as "general agreement," so it is the best choice. None of the others has a usage error. Choice (B) is acceptable in that it implies a well-known fact that Twain wrote many other works. Choice (C) underscores the claim made in the whole sentence by establishing the book as the "best" American work. Finally, choice (D) is acceptable because of commas in other parts of the sentence. Choice (E) clearly does not apply.

2. **C**

   This question has several potential errors. Choice (A) requires that you know to capitalize historical documents, so it is correct. Choice (B) calls into question the attribution of human rationality to an inanimate object, but since the Constitution actually does have logical premises, we can correctly say that the document can posit the premise stated. Choice (D) is acceptable because the superlative is referenced within the sentence; one should know that the U.S. government has three branches. That leaves choices (C) and (E). Choice (C) is the verb in the clause beginning with the word "what"; it is plural, and therefore, incorrect because it does not agree with its subject "history," a singular noun. Do not be fooled by the intervening plural word "governments." Since choice (C) is the error, choice (E) would no longer be considered.

3. **C**

   Even though people use "like" as a conjunction in conversation and public speaking, it is a preposition, and formal written English requires "as," "as if," or "as though," when what follows is a clause. No other choice is even suspect.

4. **C**

   One could question the use of "nearly" (A), but it is correct. One might argue also that "million dollars" (D) should be written "$1 million," but choice (C) is so clearly an incorrect use of the past perfect tense that the other possibilities, remote at best, pale by comparison. The simple past tense ("sold"), the present progressive tense ("are selling"), or the present perfect progressive tense ("have been selling") could each be used correctly depending on the meaning intended.

5. **B**

   This choice is not as obvious, but authorities agree that the use of "expect" to mean "suppose" or "believe" (the usage here) is either informal or colloquial, but again not formal written English. The next most likely choice, (E), would suggest that informal or colloquial usage is appropriate. The third most likely choice, (D), brings to mind the distinction between "accept" and "except," a word pair often confused. However, "accept" is correct here.

6. **A**

   Regardless of its popular usage "hopefully" is an adverb trying to be a clause ("it is hoped" or "I hope"). However, instances still exist that require a distinction between the two uses. To be clear, use "hopefully" when you mean "in a hopeful manner." ["He wished hopefully that she would accept his proposal of marriage."] Choice (D) appears suspicious. "Continually" means recurrence at intervals over a period of time, so it is correctly used to imply that machines do break down often. (B) Capitalizing "Twentieth Century" is also appropriate as it is here used as the specific historical period (like the "Middle Ages"). We would not capitalize the phrase if it were used simply to count, as in "The twentieth century from now will surely find enormous changes in the world." It is incorrect to hyphenate a number-noun phrase like this one when it stands alone as a noun phrase. Choice (C), "enough," is correct as used.

7. **A**

   The two most suspicious choices are (A) and (D) because the item is a sentence fragment. No reasonable substitute for (D) would solve both the logic problem (incomplete thought) and the punctuation problem (comma splice if you omit "that"). Changing "showing" to "show" would, however, make the clause into a complete sentence with correct punctuation. Neither choice (B) nor choice (C) provoke suspicion.

8. **B**

   Again, the two most questionable choices, (B) and (C), compete for our attention. The use of "but" makes sense because it shows contrast to the previous idea. ("Don't evade or defy the law, *but* if caught breaking a law, accept the penalty.") The use of "or," however, is clearly not parallel to the immediately preceding use of "neither." The proper phrase is "neither . . . nor" for negative alternate choices. Neither choice (A) nor choice (D) demands a second look.

9. **D**

This choice involves parallel construction, or the lack of it. The word "both" introduces a pair of phrases, one a prepositional phrase ("for their own interests"), the other an infinitive phrase ("to gain more goods"). Aside from being inelegant, "to gain more goods" is also not the same structure and should be changed to "their own gain" to make the two phrases perfectly parallel. Choices (B) and (C) are not problematic. Choice (A) properly modifies "philosopher".

10. **E**

The other choices all fail to exhibit inappropriate usage. Choice (A), "cannot," is spelled as one word; choice (B), "should not," is parallel to "cannot" and adds meaning necessary to the thought. Choice (C) is a correct plural possessive pronoun, the antecedent of which is "rulers." Finally, choice (D) is a third-person plural verb agreeing with its subject, "reasons."

11. **C**

"Milky Way galaxy" is the singular antecedent, for which the pronoun referent should be "its" (inanimate object). Do not be confused by the intervening words ("stars" and "spots"); it is the galaxy which shines in this sentence, not the stars or the spots. Choice (A) is the correct usage of "comprises." Choice (B) is an appropriate pair of adjectives with no apparent problem. Choice (D) is appropriate because the sentence has an internally supplied superlative sense; it does not need a "brightest of" phrase.

12. **A**

Again, non-parallel structure is the key of this and many other test items. Because of the overwhelming importance of understanding balance in sentence structure, tests like this one emphasize parallel sentence structures. "To learn" clashes with "studying" in the parallel clause. You cannot choose "studying." "Learning" substituted for "To learn" would make the clauses parallel. Choice (B) is a correct use of "like" as a preposition (objects: "Latin," "Greek"). Choice (D) is correctly singular as the verb of the noun phrase "studying . . . beliefs." Nothing is incorrect about choice (C).

13. **A**

This is a colloquial, nonstandard substitution for the correct word, "attribute." Choice (B) is correctly lowercase, not capitalized. Choice (C) is a correct, if a bit stiff, phrase. Choice (D) is a correct plural verb the subject of which is "both," also plural.

14. **C**

This is an incorrect simple past verb tense. You have to spot the context clue "most Americans" "attended" school (B) in the past, which suggests they no longer do so now. They must then "choose" their entertainment. Choice (A) is questionable, but the present participial phrase suggests coincidence with the time "most Americans" "attended school." It is, therefore, correct. Choice (D) is correctly an infinitive that is parallel to "to watch."

15. **A**

The two most questionable choices are (A) and (B). Choice (A) is incorrectly a subjective case pronoun when it should be objective (object of verb "makes," subject "What"). If you know the difference between "different from" (correctly used in this sentence) and "difference than" (correctly used only to introduce a clause), then choice (B) is no longer viable. Besides being a passive construction, choice (C) has no objectionable qualities; it is grammatically correct. So is choice (D) correctly an adverb that has meaning in context.

16. **D**

This is a case of subject-verb disagreement related to the definition of the word "neither" (subject) as singular. Its verb must also be singular, and "differ" is plural. Choice (A) correctly uses English idiom ("compare to"—"contrast with"). Choice (B) refers clearly to "ideas," its antecedent, and agrees with it (both plural). Choice (C) is a singular verb agreeing with its subject, "one."

17. **E**

Everything in the sentence is acceptable or correct usage, even though some of it may be a bit stuffy and pedantic, i.e., choice (B). You might question choice (A) in that instead of suggesting, perhaps asserting or stating would be more appropriate. Even though these terms clearly differ, there is nothing wrong with using "suggests" (correct subject-verb agreement with "hypothesis") because a hypothesis can suggest as well as theorize, assert, etc. Choice (C) correctly agrees with its subject "which" (plural, antecedent "archetypes"). Choice (D) might be considered redundant ("repeated" and "patterns"), but that is not apparent from the context.

18. **E**

You are likely to have chosen either (B) or (C) here. The affect/effect word pair often confuses students, and this instance is one in which "effected" is correctly used as a verb meaning "brought about" or "caused to happen." The question in choice (C) is whether or not to capitalize the word "Fate." When it refers to the collective term for the Greek concept of destiny (actually gods, the Fates), as it does here, it is appropriately capitalized. Choices (A) and (D) do not seem questionable.

19. **D**

Again, the problem here is pronoun-antecedent agreement. "Their" does not refer to the three writers collectively; its antecedent is "each," which is always singular, not plural ("each one"). There is nothing wrong with choices (A), (B), (C) and (D).

20. **C**

The error here is known as faulty predication ("reason . . . is because"). The usage rule is that "because" is redundant for "reason." Choice (A) is appropriate, if a bit general (not 30 or 70 percent, for example). The verb in choice (B) is correct and in the past tense, as is the verb phrase in choice (D).

21. **B**

Choice (A) is a verb correctly in agreement with its compound subject. Choice (C) is an appropriate parallel structure requiring no punctuation. Choice (D) correctly uses the word "comprises" and makes it agree with its subject. Only choice (B) seems incorrect. The structure requires the adverb form "constantly," since it describes an adjective, "expanding."

22. **A**

This is the classic confusion of "less" for the correct "fewer." "Few(er)" refers to countable things or persons; "little (less)" refers to things that can be measured or estimated but not itemized. The only other choice to examine is choice (D), but it is the appropriate tense referring to the "contemporary" (now) view.

23. **C**

Choice (A) is a correct use of the relative pronoun. Nothing is unusual about (B). (C) is the culprit here: it should be the infinitive form to adhere to the idiom, "ability to (verb)." (D) is an appropriate reference to hierarchy and responsibility.

24. **A**

The sentence as it stands is illogical. Removing "Because" will make it sensible. Choice (B) is an appropriate adverb modifying "believe"; choice (C) is a clear and effective subordination of an explanation of a term. Choice (D) uses "as" properly as a preposition.

25. **B**

   "Being that" is colloquial for "because," which is better for at least the reason that it is shorter, but also that it is more formal. No other choices seem out of bounds.

26. **B**

   This question of appropriate verb tense requires the simple past tense verb "took" because the Civil War happened in a finite time period in the past. The other choices all fail that test. The original and choice (E) are present tense, and do not logically fit the facts. Choice (D) is the present perfect tense, which suggests a continuous action from the past to the present. Choice (C) is the past perfect tense, which suggests a continuing action from one time in the past to another in the more recent past.

27. **D**

   We can eliminate fairly quickly choices (C) and (E) as either inappropriate or awkward appositives to "ornithology," instead of "ornithologists." Neither is (A) the best choice even though some may consider it acceptable. Likewise, choice (B) tends to be limited to nonrestrictive clauses, unlike this one. Choice (D) then correctly uses a "personal" relative pronoun.

28. **D**

   Choices (A), (D), and (E) are the best candidates because they are more concise than the other two choices. Each does express the same idea, but choice (E) does not as strongly indicate the contrast between the two clauses in the sentence as do choices (A) and (D). Choice (D) clearly makes its point in fewer words and is the better choice.

29. **B**

   The phrase "as to" often is overblown and unclear, so it is best to eliminate it when there are other choices. Likewise, "expectability" does not exactly roll off your tongue. That leaves choices (B) and (D). Choice (D) adds a definite figure, unwarranted by the original sentence. It also is duller than choice (B), which does change the wording for the better and also indicates that the "actual amount" is to be announced, rather than that it is already known.

30. **A**

   Choices (C) and (E) introduce unnecessary absolute phrases beginning with "it," which makes the sentences wordy. They can be eliminated immediately. Choice (D) has an illogical comparison suggesting notes = instrument, so it, too, is not the best choice. Between choices (A) and (B) the difference boils down to the present tense vs. the past tense. Choice (A) uses past tenses, which seem better in sequence to follow the past tense verb "developed."

31. **B**

     Choices (A), (C), and (D) can be disqualified quickly because they are not parallel to the structure of the main clause. Choice (E) is ungainly and introduces a vague pronoun "its" (unclear antecedent). Choice (B) reads well and has the virtue of brevity.

32. **E**

     The choices are easy to discern in this sentence. The original verb does not agree with its subject, nor is the structure parallel. The former reason also eliminates choice (C). Choice (B) does not have parallel structure (phrase and clause). Choice (D) does not logically agree with the subject ("reasons") since it names one ("demanding professors") but relegates the other reason to an afterthought. Choice (D) has both parallel structure and subject-verb agreement; it also names two reasons.

33. **C**

     The original suffers from inadequate causal relationship and non-parallel structure. Choices (D) and (E) are both unnecessarily wordy; (D) is still not parallel, and (E) is internally illogical ("both" with three things). Choice (B) switches its structure at the end. Although it is technically parallel, it is still awkward because of the addition of the possessive pronoun "her." Choice (C) solves both problems by clearly showing cause and by being parallel (three nouns in series).

34. **B**

     This sentence presents an incomplete comparison and a redundancy ("Whether"/"or did not"/"remains uncertain"). Choice (B) eliminates both problems clearly. Choice (C) tries to undo the damage, but it remains inelegant in syntax and leaves partial redundancy ("whether"/"remains uncertain"). Choice (D) is worse in both respects. Choice (E) clears up the syntax but leaves some redundancy ("may actually have"/"remains uncertain"). Choice (B) eliminates both problems clearly.

35. **A**

     The sentence as is reads well; it is perfectly balanced. Choice (B) introduces an incomplete comparison ("more" but no "than"). Choice (C) awkwardly uses "as to." Choices (D) and (E) make a scrambled mess by introducing illogical structures.

36. **A**

     "Unique" means just that; it should not have qualifiers like "very" or "nearly." That eliminates choices (B) and (D). Choice (C) changes the meaning by making the development unique, instead of the system. Choice (E) uses an inappropriate verb tense because the first part of the sentence suggests the Revolutionary War period, definitely in the past.

37. **B**

The original sentence (A) has a dangling modifier (participial phrase); it remains that way in choice (E). The house cannot return to itself, nor can "it" (pronoun for house). Choice (D) seems to leave something out: "returned to . . . home in 12 years." Choice (C) solves the original problem but is unnecessarily wordy. Choice (B) properly solves the dangling modifier problem by subordinating the return in an adverbial clause.

38. **A**

Choice (A) is the only response that makes sense. Each of the others introduces illogical comparisons or structures (non-parallel); choices (B), (D), and (E) are also verbose. Choice (C) is concise but not parallel.

PPST Essay Scoring Guide

The PPST essay sections are scored by two writing experts on the basis of the criteria outlined below. In addition to comparing your essay to those included in our practice tests, you may use these guidelines to estimate your score on this section. Remember that your score is the sum of the scores of two writing experts, so provided you respond to the assigned topic, your score will fall somewhere between two and twelve. Scores will be assigned based on the following guidelines:

6   An essay receiving a score of 6 may contain one or two spelling or punctuation errors, but overall it exhibits a high degree of proficiency and thought on the assigned topic.

An essay scoring a 6

- is both well organized and well developed.

- engages important concepts and explains them clearly.

- varies expression and language.

- demonstrates deft use of language.

- is virtually free from errors involving syntax and structure.

5   An essay receiving a score of 5 exhibits a high degree of proficiency and thought on the assigned topic, however it contains a number of minor mistakes.

An essay scoring a 5

- is both well organized and well developed.

- engages important concepts and explains them.

- varies expression and language somewhat.

- demonstrates deft use of language.

- is virtually free from errors involving syntax and structure.

4   An essay receiving a score of 4 responds to the assignment and exhibits some degree of deeper understanding.

An essay scoring a 4

- demonstrates adequate organization and development.

- engages and explains some important concepts, but not all that are necessary to demonstrate full understanding.

- exhibits adequate use of language.

- contains some syntactical and structural errors, without excessive repetition of those errors.

3   An essay receiving a score of 3 exhibits some degree of understanding, but its response to the topic is obviously deficient.

An essay scoring a 3 is deficient in one or more of the following areas:

- insufficient organization or development.

- insufficient engagement or explanation of important concepts.

- consistent repetition of syntactical or structural errors.

- redundant or unsuitable word choice.

2   An essay receiving a score of 2 exhibits limited understanding and its response to the topic is seriously deficient.

An essay scoring a 2 is deficient in one or more of the following areas:

- weak organization or development.

- very few pertinent details.

- consistent and serious errors in syntax, structure.

- consistent and serious errors in word choice.

1   An essay receiving a score of 1 exhibits a lack of basic writing skills.

An essay scoring a 1 is disorganized, undeveloped, contains consistent repetition of errors, or is incomprehensible.

SAMPLE SCORED ESSAYS WITH EXPLANATIONS

Essay #1—(Score = 5–6)

The cynic in me wants to react to the idea of universal public service for the young with a reminder about previous complaints aimed at the military draft. These complaints suggest that wars might never be fought if the first people drafted were the adult leaders and lawmakers. Still, the idea of universal public service sounds good to this concerned citizen who sees everywhere—not just in youth—the effects of a selfish and self-indulgent culture.

One reads and hears constantly about young people who do not care about the problems of our society. These youngsters seem interested in money and the luxuries money can buy. They do not want to work from the minimum wage up, but want instead to land a high paying job without "paying their dues." An informal television news survey of high school students a few years ago suggested that students had the well entrenched fantasy that with no skills or higher education they would not accept a job paying less than $20 an hour. Perhaps universal service helping out in an urban soup kitchen for six months would instill a sense of selflessness rather than selfishness.

The shiny gleam of a new expensive sports sedan bought on credit by a recent accounting student reflects self indulgence that might be toned down by universal service. That self indulgence may reflect merely a lack of discipline, but it also may reflect a lack of purpose in life. Philosophers, theologians and leaders of all types suggest throughout the ages that money and objects do not ultimately satisfy. Helping others—service to our fellow human beings—often does. Universal public service for that accounting student might require a year helping low income or senior citizens prepare income tax forms. This type of service would dim that self indulgence, give the person some experience in the real world, and also give satisfaction that one's life is not lived only to acquire things.

Universal service might also help young people restore faith in their nation and what it means to them. Yes, this is the land of opportunity, but it is also a land of forgotten people, and it is a land that faces outside threats. Part of the requisite public service should remind young people of their past and of their responsibility to the future.

ANALYSIS

Essay I has a score range of 5-6. It uses a traditional structure: the first paragraph states the topic, the second and third present development with specific examples from personal observation. The fourth ends the essay, but it is not as strong a conclusion as it could be. The writer probably ran out of time. The essay as a whole is unified and uses pertinent examples to support the opinion stated. The sentence structure varies, and the vocabulary is effective. Generally, it is well done within the 30-minute time limit.

Essay #2—(Score = 4–5)

If we were to have the draft today he would be obligated, by law, to register for the military draft. This is done so that in case of a war or something catastrophic these boys and men can be called on for active duty in the military. It is good to know that we will have the manpower in case of a war but my opinion on the military draft is negative. I don't like the idea of forcing someone to sign up at a certain age for something that they don't want to happen. Of course, I know that we need some sort of military manpower on hand just in case, but it would be so much better if it was left to the individual to decide what area to serve in and what time.

When a boy turns 18, he's a rebel of sorts. He doesn't want someone telling him what to do and when to do it; he's just beginning to live. In Switzerland, when a boy turns 18, he goes into some branch of the military for a time of training. He is given his gun, uniform and badge number. Then, once a year for about two weeks he suits up for retraining. He does this until he is about 65 years old. Now in a way this is like a draft but the men love it and feel that it is honorable. I think that they like it because it does not discriminate and their jobs pay them for the time away. Switzerland seems to give the 18 year old somewhat of a choice what division to go in and whether or not to join. They're not as strict on joining as we are so it's more of an honorable thing to do.

Of course, I'd love to see it as strictly up to the individual but it can't be that way. We have too many enemies that we might go to war with and we would need a strong military. Switzerland has nothing to worry about as long as they have their banks.

ANALYSIS

Essay II has a score range of 4-5. It displays competence in overall thought. It does not state its topic quite as well as Essay I. The extended example of Swiss military conscription is the main strength of the essay. The writer hedges a bit but manages to convey an opinion.

Sentences have some variety, and the vocabulary is competent. Some spelling and grammatical errors interfere with the communication.

Essay #3—(Score = 3–4)

I agree with the many leaders who suggest we require young people to serve the public in some way, rather than the military draft.

There are several reasons this could benefit our country. The first being giving the young people, perhaps just out of high school, with no job experience, an opportunity to give something to his community. In return for this, he gains self-respect and pride.

Whether it be taking flowers to shut-ins or just stopping for a chat in a rest home, a young person would have gained something and certainly given, perhaps hope, to that elder person. I can tell from my own experience, not quite old enough for the military draft, how enriched I feel when visiting the elderly. They find joy in the simplest things, which in turn, teaches me I should do the same.

Another thing gained by doing voluntary type work, is a sense of caring about doing the job right—quality! If you can't do it for your country, what else matters?

ANALYSIS

Essay III has a score range of 3-4. It has major faults, not the least of them the lack of a clear sense of overall organization. The thoughts do have some coherence, but they don't seem to have a plan, except to express agreement with the statement. Examples from personal observation do help, but the paragraphs are not well developed. Several severe grammatical problems interfere with the communication.

Essay #4—(Score = 1–2)

Feeling strongly against the draft, as I do. I could not agree with the idea of requiring young people to serve in the military. I feel this would say something about the world situation. I believe the leaders and people would have to give up the idea of peace totally. Which would eventually lead to our own destruction.

Although I do believe young people should serve their country in a peaceful more useful way. They should be more politically aware of what the government is trying to do.

They should work in a peaceful way to try and make changes that work for the good of all people of the world.

There has never in the history of the world been a military state that survived.

ANALYSIS

Essay IV has a score range of 1-2. It has many problems. Not only does it fail to present a coherent argument, it also shows a fundamental lack of understanding of sentence structure. The concluding statement seems to come out of nowhere. The writer also confuses the topic with that of required military service, which would be only part of universal service.

Practice Test 3

Praxis I PPST
(Computer-Based Format)

Section I: Reading Comprehension

TIME: *75 Minutes*
          46 Questions

DIRECTIONS: A number of questions follow each of the passages in the reading section. Answer the questions by choosing the best answer from the five choices given.

Questions 1 to 3 refer to the following passage:

Representatives of the world's seven richest and most industrialized nations held a three-day economic summit in London on July 14-16, 1991. On the second day of the summit, the Soviet Union's Mikhail Gorbachev, who appealed for help, was offered support by the seven leaders for his economic reforms and his "new thinking" regarding political reforms. However, because the allies were split on giving a big aid package to Gorbachev, the seven leaders decided to provide help in the form of technical assistance in fields such as banking and energy, rather than in hard cash.

1.   Which of the following statements best synthesizes what the passage is about?

   (A) A seven-nation economic summit was held in London in July 1991.

   (B) An economic summit of the world's richest nations was held in London in July.

   (C) Mikhail Gorbachev appealed for help and the seven leaders agreed to support his economic reforms.

   (D) At a three-day economic summit held in London in July 1991, leaders of the world's seven richest and most industrialized nations agreed to provide technical assistance to Gorbachev.

   (E) Representatives of the world's seven most industrialized nations, at a summit conference in London, were split on giving Gorbachev assistance in the form of hard cash.

2.   The passage implies

   (A) that, under the leadership of Gorbachev, the Soviet Union is faced with a financial crisis.

   (B) that Gorbachev's "new thinking" on democratic reforms needs support from the seven nations meeting in London.

(C) that the seven leaders meeting in London were split on giving Gorbachev economic and political support.

(D) that with only technical assistance from the seven nations that met in London, the Soviet Union under the leadership of Gorbachev is heading for economic disaster.

(E) that with the support of political and economic reforms along with provisions for technical assistance from the seven nations that met in London, the Soviet Union under the leadership of Gorbachev can achieve political and economic stability.

3. The passage suggests that technical assistance will be provided to the Soviet Union

(A) only in the fields of banking and energy.

(B) in the fields of banking and energy and possibly other fields also.

(C) by the U.S. in the fields of banking and energy.

(D) by any of the seven nations that met at a summit in London.

(E) by all seven nations—U.S., Great Britain, France, Germany, Italy, Canada, and Japan.

Questions 4 to 6 refer to the following passage:

A follow-up survey of the 1990 census showed an estimated undercount of 5.2 million people nationwide. This "undercount" was greatest in California where approximately 1.1 million people were not recorded. This estimated undercount was based on a post-census survey of 171,390 households nationwide. Failure to achieve an accurate count would affect federal funding and political representation. If the higher numbers were used, California would gain eight congressional seats instead of seven and about $1 billion in federal funds. Last July 14, 1991, however, Commerce Secretary Robert Mosbacher decided to stick to the original figures of the 1990 census.

4. Which of the following statements gives the main idea of the passage you just read?

(A) California would gain an additional congressional seat and more federal money if the 1.1 million people undercounted in the census were included.

(B) The population in a state is the basis for determining the political representation for that state.

(C) An undercount in the census, if not considered, will be a disadvantage to any state.

    (D) A post-census survey is necessary in getting to a more accurate population figure for the states.

    (E) California will suffer the most because of the 1.1 million undercount in the 1990 census.

5. If the 1.1 million undercount was considered for California

    (A) it would settle any political dispute arising from the undercount.

    (B) it would give California eight congressional seats and $1 billion in federal funds.

    (C) it would discourage the practice of a post-census survey.

    (D) it would create political unrest for other states.

    (E) it would reverse the decision made by Commerce Secretary Mosbacher.

6. What will it mean for California if the original figures of the 1990 census remain the same?

    (A) No additional federal funding will be given.

    (B) There will be no additional political representation.

    (C) The amount of federal funding and number of congressional seats will remain the same.

    (D) The census undercount will not make a difference.

    (E) The results of the follow-up survey of the 1990 census will be meaningless.

Questions 7 to 10 refer to the following passage:

    A big toxic spill took place on the upper Sacramento River in California on July 13, 1991 about 10 P.M. when a slow moving Southern Pacific train derailed north of the town of Dansmuir. A tank car containing 19,500 gallons of pesticide broke open and spilled into the river. This pesticide is used to kill soil pests. Since the spill, thousands of trout and other fish were poisoned along a 45-mile stretch of river. In addition, 190 people were treated at a local hospital for respiratory and related illnesses. Residents along the river have been warned to stay away from the tainted water. Once this water reaches Lake Shasta, a source of water for millions of Californians, samples will be taken to assess the quality of the water.

7. Which of the following statements conveys the message in the passage?

    (A) Pesticides intended to kill soil pests can be dangerous to all living things.

    (B) Water uncontaminated by pesticides is safe to drink.

    (C) Take every precaution not to come in contact with the pesticide infected water.

    (D) Pesticides that killed thousands of trout and other fish will not necessarily kill human beings.

    (E) Only residents along the tainted river need worry.

8. The Southern Pacific train that derailed was a

    (A) passenger train.

    (B) cargo train.

    (C) commuter train.

    (D) cargo and passenger train.

    (E) special train.

9. The most serious problem that can come about as a result of the toxic spill is

    (A) possible movement of residents in Dansmuir to another place of residence.

    (B) reduction in tourism attraction for Dansmuir and other nearby areas.

    (C) the negative effects on those whose livelihood depends on the fishing industry.

    (D) when the tainted water reaches Lake Shasta, which is a source of water supply for millions of Californians.

    (E) the uncertain length of time it will take to make the tainted water safe and healthy again.

10. This unfortunate incident of toxic spill resulting from train derailment implies

    (A) the need for more environmental protection.

    (B) other means for transporting pesticides need to be considered.

    (C) that there should be more precaution for trains running by nighttime.

    (D) that there should be an investigation as to the cause of the train derailment and effective measures to prevent its occurrence again should be applied.

    (E) that there should be research on how to expedite making infected water safe and healthy again.

Questions 11 to 13 refer to the following passage:

Labor Day, a national holiday observed in the United States, is really a day we should remember to give thanks to the labor unions. In the days before the unions became effective, a holiday meant a day off, but the loss of a day's pay to working people. It was not until World War II that unions succeeded, through negotiations with the federal government, in making paid holidays a common practice.

11. The main idea in the passage above is

    (A) the role labor unions played in employer-employee relations.

    (B) Labor Day as a national holiday in the U.S.

    (C) the role labor unions played in effecting paid holidays.

    (D) the dispute between paid and unpaid holidays.

    (E) Labor Day before World War II.

12. The passage implies that before World War II

    (A) a holiday gave working people a chance to rest from work.

    (B) Labor Day meant losing a day's pay.

    (C) a holiday was a day to make up for upon returning to work.

    (D) labor unions were ineffective.

    (E) taking off from work set a worker one day behind in his or her work.

13. As a national holiday, Labor Day should really be a day to remember and be thankful for

    (A) working people.

    (B) help from the federal government.

    (C) paid holidays.

    (D) labor unions.

    (E) a free day.

Question 14 refers to the following passage:

President Bush's proposed educational "program of choice" will give parents more say in choosing schools for their children. This will encourage states and local districts to change their laws so that parents can apply their tax dollars toward the public or private school to which they choose to send their children, rather than be forced to send their child to the public school in their district or pay for private school tuition.

14. President Bush's proposed educational program implies

(A) the freedom to choose.

(B) competition among schools.

(C) school standards need to be raised.

(D) more money is needed.

(E) curricula should be improved.

Questions 15 to 17 refer to the following passage:

Ash from Mt. Pinatubo in the Philippines has been found to contain gold and other precious metals. However, officials warned against any hopes of a new "gold rush." They found gold content of only 20 parts per billion, which is far below commercial levels. Other metals found were chromium, copper, and lithium.

15. The passage indicates

(A) the possibility of existing gold mines beneath Mt. Pinatubo.

(B) the need for further exploration of what else lies beneath the volcano.

(C) that there is a new resource for boosting the economy of the Philippines.

(D) other active volcanoes might be worth exploring as possible gold resources.

(E) that the gold content of the ash from Mt. Pinatubo does not warrant a commercial level.

16. Which of the following is the best title for the passage above?

(A) A New Gold Rush

(B) Mt. Pinatubo's Gold Mine

(C) Ash Content from Mt. Pinatubo

(D) A Philippine Discovery

(E) Precious Metals

17. What is the first research that should be done on the ash content?

   (A) Research on the ash content from the eruption of Mt. Fujiyama in Japan

   (B) Potential market value of the gold and other metals contained in the volcanic ash from Mt. Pinatubo

   (C) Further excavation into possible gold underneath Mt. Pinatubo

   (D) Research on what lies underneath active volcanoes

   (E) A comparison of volcanic ash content with what lies underneath the same volcano when it is inactive

Questions 18 to 20 refer to the following passage:

   Gary Harris, a farmer from Conrad, Montana, has invented and patented a motorcycle helmet. It provides a brake light which can signal traffic intentions to other drivers behind. In the U.S., all cars sold are now required to carry a third, high-mounted brake light. Harris's helmet will meet this requirement for motorcyclists.

18. The passage is primarily about

   (A) a new invention for motorcyclists.

   (B) a requirement for all cars in the U.S.

   (C) a brake light for motorcyclists.

   (D) Harris's helmet.

   (E) Gary Harris, inventor.

19. An implication regarding the new invention is

   (A) any farmer can come up with a similar traffic invention.

   (B) the new brake light requirement for cars should likewise apply to motorcycles.

   (C) the new brake light requirement for cars cannot apply to motorcycles.

   (D) if you buy a car from outside of the U.S., you are exempted from the brake light requirement.

   (E) as an inventor, Gary Harris can make more money if he leaves farming.

20. Because of the new brake light requirement for cars

    (A) drivers can readily see the traffic signals of car drivers ahead of them.

    (B) less accidents can happen on the road.

    (C) car prices will go up and will be less affordable to buy.

    (D) more lights on the road can be hazardous.

    (E) more traffic policemen will be needed.

Questions 21 to 24 refer to the following passage:

> Lead poisoning is considered by health authorities to be the most common and devastating environmental disease of young children. According to studies made, it affects 15% to 20% of urban children and from 50% to 75% of inner-city, poor children. As a result of a legal settlement in July 1991, all of California's Medi-Cal eligible children, ages one through five, will now be routinely screened annually for lead poisoning. Experts estimate that more than 50,000 cases will be detected in California because of the newly mandated tests. This will halt at an early stage a disease that leads to learning disabilities and life-threatening disorders.

21. Lead poisoning among young children, if not detected early, can lead to

    (A) physical disabilities.   (D) heart disease.

    (B) mental disabilities.   (E) death.

    (C) learning disabilities.

22. The new mandate to screen all young children for lead poisoning is required of all

    (A) young children in California.

    (B) children with learning disabilities.

    (C) Medi-Cal-eligible children, ages one through five, in California.

    (D) minority children in California.

    (E) all school-age children in California.

23. According to findings, more cases of lead poisoning are found among

    (A) urban children.   (D) children in rural areas.

    (B) inner-city poor children.   (E) middle-class children.

    (C) immigrant children.

24. The implication of this new mandate in California regarding lead poisoning is that

(A) non-eligible children will not be screened.

(B) children older than five years will not be screened.

(C) middle-class children will not be screened.

(D) new immigrant children will not be screened.

(E) thousands of young children in California will remain at risk for lead poisoning.

Question 25 refers to the following passage:

As millions of children returned to school in the year 2008 – 2009, teachers in California faced the reality of what many consider was the worst fiscal crisis to hit the schools in more than a decade. This crisis caused reductions in teaching positions, increases in class sizes, cuts in teacher paychecks in some school districts, reductions in special programs, and reductions in school supplies.

25. Those who were most affected by the effects of the financial crisis in California schools were the

(A) teachers.   (D) paraprofessionals.

(B) parents.   (E) students.

(C) school administrators.

Questions 26 to 28 refer to the following passage:

The U.S. Postal Service issued a 50-cent stamp in Anchorage, Alaska, on October 12, 1991, to commemorate the 500th anniversary of the arrival of the Italian explorer Christopher Columbus in the New World. The stamp depicted how America may have appeared to Asians crossing the Bering Strait. The stamp series showed the pre-Columbian voyages of discovery.

26. Which of the following makes an appropriate title for the passage?

(A) The Discovery of the Americas

(B) 500th Anniversary of the Discovery of America

(C) The Significance of the Bering Strait

(D) A Commemorative New U.S. Postal Stamp

(E) A Tribute to Asians

27. The passage implies that

    (A) historical facts need to be verified.

    (B) Christopher Columbus was not the first to arrive in the New World.

    (C) Asians discovered America.

    (D) Native Americans came from Asia.

    (E) history books need to be rewritten.

28. Which of the following would you consider as the most historically significant?

    (A) Asians crossed over the Bering Strait to the New World before Columbus came.

    (B) It has been 500 years since Christopher Columbus arrived in the New World.

    (C) A tribute to Christopher Columbus was held on October 12, 1991.

    (D) Native Americans are of Asian origin.

    (E) There were other voyages undertaken before Christopher Columbus'.

Questions 29 and 30 refer to the following passage:

A 150 million-year-old allosaurus skeleton which appears to be intact was found on September 9, 1991, by a Swiss team in north-central Wyoming. This Zurich-based company sells fossils to museums. They were digging on private property, but the fossil actually showed up on federal land.

Immediately, the federal government sealed off the site along the foot of Big Horn Mountains in Wyoming and deployed rangers from the Bureau of Land Management to prevent vandalism. Paleontologists believe that this discovery could lead them to a vast dinosaur graveyard.

29. The passage above can best be utilized by a classroom teacher in

    (A) reading.   (D) zoology.

    (B) mathematics.   (E) history.

    (C) biology.

30. A teaching strategy that the classroom teacher can use appropriately with the students regarding the allosaurus fossil discovery is

    (A) the problem-solving approach.

    (B) the survey approach.

    (C) the deductive approach.

(D) the comparative study approach.

(E) the historical approach.

Questions 31 to 33 refer to the following passage:

Popular U.S. attractions such as Disneyland, the Golden Gate Bridge, Las Vegas, and the Statue of Liberty have attracted millions of foreign tourists whose spending helped the U.S. post a $31.7 billion service trade surplus in 1990 compared with a $101 billion merchandise trade deficit in the same year. The heavy-spending Japanese tourists accounted for the biggest portion of the tourism trade surplus, spending $5.5 billion more touring the U.S than U.S. tourists spent visiting Japan. Canadians also outspent American tourists to Canada by $2.2 billion.

31. The main idea of the passage is

(A) foreign tourists in the U.S. spend more than American tourists spend abroad.

(B) there are more tourist attractions in the U.S. than any foreign country.

(C) Japanese tourists are the biggest spenders among tourists to the U.S.

(D) Canadians rank second to Japan in tourism spending in the U.S.

(E) tourism is very important to the economy of the U.S.

32. A significant implication of the passage is that

(A) Japan will have to reduce its tourist spending in the U.S.

(B) the U.S. should increase its tourist spending in Japan.

(C) tourist spending in the U.S. reduces its trade deficit.

(D) Canada needs to improve its tourism attractions.

(E) Japan has more money on which to spend on tourism than any other country.

33. Based on the passage, which of the following would be an appropriate topic of discussion with students?

(A) International relations

(B) Global relations

(C) Balance in global tourism industry

(D) Interdependency of nations

(E) Global competition

Questions 34 and 35 refer to the following passage.

San Francisco was named the world's favorite travel destination in the prestigious 1991 Condé Nast Traveler magazine poll. It was considered the best city in the world that year, beating out Florence, Italy (No. 2), and London and Vienna which tied for No. 3. A red-carpet gala in the City Hall rotunda is planned in which Mayor Agnos will laud the city's 60,000 tourism industry workers including hotel maids, taxi drivers, bellhops, and others in the local hospitality industry.

34. An appropriate title for the passage is

    (A) San Francisco: World's Favorite Travel Destination.

    (B) A Gala for San Francisco's Tourism Workers.

    (C) San Francisco: Top in Ranking.

    (D) Best City in the World.

    (E) Top City in 1991.

35. The prestigious citation for the city of San Francisco could mean in practical terms

    (A) increasing tourism attractions for city runner-ups in the poll.

    (B) more openings for tourism industry workers.

    (C) higher pay demands from hotel maids, bellhops, and other workers.

    (D) more tourists will come to the city.

    (E) more money coming to the city from its tourism industry.

Questions 36 to 38 refer to the following passage.

Results of a study released by the College Board and the Western Interstate Commission for Higher Education showed that by 1994, the majority of California's high school graduates would be non-white and that by 1995, one-third of all the nation's students would be from minority groups. It was also predicted that, nationally, the total non-white and Hispanic student population for all grade levels would increase from 10.4 million in 1985–1986 to 13.7 million in 1994–1995. The figures suggest that now, more than ever, equal educational opportunity for all students must be our nation's number one priority.

36. The foregoing passage suggests that

    (A) this nation is, educationally, at risk.

    (B) something needs to be done to reduce the growing numbers of minority students in the school system.

    (C) urgent educational reforms are needed to provide equal opportunity for all students.

    (D) a Spanish bilingual system be endorsed.

    (E) immigration laws be strictly enforced to balance the numbers of white and non-white student populations.

37. Because of changes in demographics, what preparation is needed in California in the area of teacher preparation?

    (A) Recruit of more minority teachers

    (B) Increase budget appropriation for schools

    (C) Enforce school desegregation

    (D) Encourage non-Hispanic, white students to enroll in private schools

    (E) Revise teacher preparation programs to reflect appropriate preparation for multi-cultural classrooms

38. What problem could result from the increasing minority population in the nation?

    (A) Strong resentment from whites towards the school administration

    (B) Increase in enrollment in private and parochial schools

    (C) "White flight" to the suburbs where minorities are not yet the majority

    (D) School budget crisis

    (E) Inappropriate and inadequate school curriculum and teacher preparation to meet the needs in multicultural classrooms

Questions 39 and 40 refer to the following passage.

The United States' final offer on a lease agreement for the Subic Bay Naval Base in the Philippines was rejected by the Philippine Senate. Hence, for the first time in nearly a century, U.S. military strategy for the Asia-Pacific region will no longer be centered on the Philippines, and the nation's economic survival and development will no longer rely on U.S. dependency. Somehow, this dependency on the U.S. has served as an impediment to the Philippines' ability to join East Asia's economic boom.

39. Which of the following best summarizes what the passage is about?

    (A) Philippine-U.S. military relations have come to an end.

    (B) The Philippines' economic dependency on the U.S. ended with its Senate's rejection of the U.S. lease offer.

    (C) The U.S. lease offer for the Subic Bay Naval Base was rejected by the Philippine Senate, hence the U.S. will no longer have its military base in the Asia-Pacific region.

    (D) The Philippines is now on its own in its economic survival and development.

    (E) The U.S. military strategy for the Asia-Pacific region will no longer be on the Philippines following the Philippine Senate's rejection of the U.S. lease offer.

40. The U.S. military's pullout from Subic Bay would mean

    (A) fewer jobs for Filipinos.

    (B) fewer Americans in the Philippines.

    (C) a chance for the Philippines to survive on its own.

    (D) weakening of U.S.-Philippine relations.

    (E) less protection for the Philippines.

Questions 41–45 are based on the following excerpt. Read the poem carefully before choosing your answers.

The Rape of the Lock

1   One speaks the glory of the British Queen,
         And one describes a charming Indian screen;
         A third interprets motions, looks, and eyes;
         At every word a reputation dies.
5   Snuff, or the fan, supply each pause of chat,
         With singing, laughing, ogling, and all that.
         Meanwhile, declining from the noon of day,
         The sun obliquely shoots his burning ray;
         The hungry judges soon the sentence sign,
10   And wretches hang that jurymen may dine;

                              by Alexander Pope

41. The last two lines suggest that this society

   (A) takes pride in its justice system.

   (B) speedily administers justice for humanitarian reasons.

   (C) sentences the wrong people to death.

   (D) sentences people for the wrong reasons.

   (E) has no problem with the death penalty.

42. Lines 1–6 suggest that this society

   I.   indulges in gossip that slanders the Queen.

   II.   engages in serious discussions about affairs of state.

   III. engages in gossip that ruins reputations.

   (A) I and III.   (D) I, II, and III.

   (B) III only.   (E) I only

   (C) II only.

43. The juxtaposition of lines 1 and 2 suggests that the people

   (A) talk of trivia.

(B) revere the monarchy and Indian screens equally.

(C) are Imperialists.

(D) are Royalists.

(E) show how different people are.

44. The word "obliquely" (line 8) in this context could mean or functions as all of the following EXCEPT:

(A) perpendicularly.

(B) at a steep angle.

(C) a pun on hidden meanings.

(D) a pun on stealth.

(E) a nautical reference.

45. The change in voice from the first half of the excerpt into the second is best described as one from

(A) light to dark.

(B) critical to amused.

(C) sarcastic to light-hearted.

(D) amused to sadness.

(E) sarcastic to bleak

46. The intention of an "utterance" is

(A) private, available only to the speaker of the utterance.

(B) public, measurable by various outward criteria.

(C) unknowable to either the speaker or the listener of the utterance.

(D) translatable into the "deep structure" of the utterance.

(E) usually derogatory.

Section II: Mathematics

TIME: *75 Minutes*
          46 Questions

DIRECTIONS: Each of the questions or incomplete statements below is followed by five suggested answers or completions. Select the one that is best in each case.

1.   What is the least common denominator of $\frac{2}{15}$, $\frac{1}{21}$, and $\frac{4}{35}$?

  (A) 105   (D) 735

  (B) 35   (E) 175

  (C) 415

2.   On July 19, a Friday, Dick received a letter to have a class reunion exactly four years from that day. On what day of the week is his reunion?

  (A) Monday   (D) Thursday

  (B) Tuesday   (E) Friday

  (C) Wednesday

3.   John and Mary are working on a job together. If John does it alone, it will take him seven days, while Mary can do it alone in five days. How long will it take them to do it together?

  (A) 12 days   (D) 3 and $\frac{1}{2}$ days

  (B) 2 days   (E) 6 days

  (C) 2 and $\frac{11}{12}$ days

4.   How much water is needed to add to a half-pint of syrup with 60 percent sugar to obtain a drink with 5 percent sugar?

  (A) 3 pints   (D) 5.5 pints

  (B) 2.5 pints   (E) 7 pints

  (C) 4 pints

5. Which of the following is true about triangle *ABC*? (The triangle is not drawn to scale.)

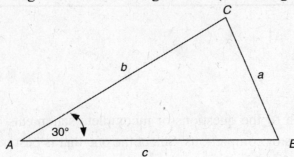

(A) Sides *b* and *c* are equal in measurement.

(B) Angle *A* is the smallest angle.

(C) Side *a* is not the longest side.

(D) Angle *B* or *C* must be a right angle.

(E) Side *b* must be greater than side *a* in measurement.

6. If the diameter of circle *A* is twice that of circle *B*, what is the ratio of the area of circle *A* to the area of circle *B*?

(A) 2 to 1   (D) π to 1

(B) 3 to 1   (E) 8 to 1

(C) 4 to 1

7. A solid cube has a volume of 8. What is the volume of the cube whose sides are twice that of this cube?

(A) 16   (D) 36

(B) 28   (E) 64

(C) 32

8. Jack flies from New York to Los Angeles. His plane leaves New York at 2:15 p.m. The flying time is 5 hours and 45 minutes. Since New York is three hours ahead of Los Angeles, what time does he arrive in Los Angeles?

(A) 11:00 p.m.   (D) 5:00 p.m.

(B) 8:00 p.m.   (E) 4:45 p.m.

(C) 7:45 p.m.

9. Bob has 50 coins, all nickels and dimes, worth a total of $4.85. How many nickels does he possess?

   (A) 30   (D) 37

   (B) 15   (E) 3

   (C) 7

10. A steamboat goes 24 miles upstream and then returns to its original position. The round trip takes six hours. The water flows at three miles per hour. What is the speed of the boat in still water?

   (A) 10 miles/hour   (D) 7 miles/hour

   (B) 9 miles/hour   (E) 6 miles/hour

   (C) 8 miles/hour

11. If ten babies drink a total of ten gallons of milk in ten days, how many gallons of milk will 20 babies drink in 20 days?

   (A) 20   (D) 35

   (B) 25   (E) 40

   (C) 30

12. Jane has three kinds of coins, quarters, dimes, and nickels, totalling 24 in number and worth $3.00. How many coins of each kind does she have?

   (A) Jane has 12 nickels, 4 dimes, and 8 quarters.

   (B) Jane has 9 nickels, 8 dimes, and 7 quarters.

   (C) Jane has 6 nickels, 12 dimes, and 6 quarters.

   (D) Jane has 3 nickels, 16 dimes, and 5 quarters.

   (E) There is no unique answer; further information is needed.

13. A parallelogram *ABCD* has all its sides measure 4, one of the diagonals ▬ also measures 4. What is its area?

   (A) Its area is 16.

   (B) Its area is 32.

   (C) Its area is $4\sqrt{3}$.

   (D) Its area is $8\sqrt{3}$.

   (E) Its area cannot be found; further information is needed.

14. Jack gave one-third of his money to his daughter and one-quarter of his money to his son. He then had $150,000 left. How much money did he have before he gave away some?

(A) $225,000

(B) $250,000

(C) $300,000

(D) $360,000

(E) $400,000

15. The fraction $\dfrac{1}{\left(\sqrt{3}-\sqrt{2}\right)}$ is equivalent to

(A) $\sqrt{3}+\sqrt{2}$.

(B) $\sqrt{3}-\sqrt{2}$.

(C) $\dfrac{1}{\left(\sqrt{3}+\sqrt{2}\right)}$.

(D) 1.

(E) 0.

16. If Don and Ron can paint a house in five days, and Ron can paint it alone in seven days, how long will it take Don to paint it alone?

(A) 2 days

(B) 7 days

(C) 17.5 days

(D) 9.75 days

(E) 11.25 days

17. If the volume of a cube is 8, how long is its main diagonal (the line segment joining the two farthest corners)?

(A) $2\sqrt{2}$

(B) $3\sqrt{2}$

(C) $2\sqrt{3}$

(D) $3\sqrt{3}$

(E) The length of the main diagonal cannot be found for lack of information.

18. Norman lives six blocks north and six blocks east of Bob. The town is made up of all square blocks. How many ways can Bob walk to Norman's house covering only 12 blocks?

(A) 2 ways

(B) 924 ways

(C) 36 ways

(D) 4,096 ways

(E) Infinitely many ways

19. If the area of a right isosceles triangle is 4, how long are its sides?

    (A) $2\sqrt{2}$, $2\sqrt{2}$, 4

    (B) 2, 2, $2\sqrt{2}$

    (C) 3, 3, $3\sqrt{2}$

    (D) $3\sqrt{2}$, $3\sqrt{2}$, 6

    (E) There is not enough information given to determine the lengths.

20. Donald gave Louie a number of marbles to share with Dewey and Huey. Making sure that he got his share, Louie took one-third of the marbles and hid them. Dewey, after hearing from Donald that he is entitled to one-third of the marbles as well, went and hid one-third of the remaining marbles. Not knowing what was going on, Daisy took two marbles from the pile. When Huey came, there were only 10 marbles left. How many marbles did Donald give to Louie in the beginning?

    (A) 18

    (B) 21

    (C) 24

    (D) 27

    (E) There is not enough information given to determine the number of marbles.

21. A steamboat left Hong Kong on May 25, at 6 a.m., New York time. It sailed 400 hours and arrived in New York. When did it arrive?

    (A) 10 p.m., June 9   (D) 4 p.m., June 10

    (B) 10 p.m., June 10   (E) 4 p.m., June 11

    (C) 10 p.m., June 11

22. Joan is eight years older than Georgette. Joan was twice as old as Georgette eight years ago. How old are they now?

    (A) Joan is 30 and Georgette is 22.

    (B) Joan is 28 and Georgette is 20.

    (C) Joan is 26 and Georgette is 18.

    (D) Joan is 24 and Georgette is 16.

    (E) There is not enough information given to determine.

23. A river flows at a speed of five miles per hour. A steamboat went upstream for five hours and stopped at a point 20 miles from where it started. What is the speed of the steamboat in still waters?

    (A) 9 miles per hour

    (B) 12 miles per hour

    (C) 14 miles per hour

    (D) 18 miles per hour

    (E) The speed of the boat cannot be found for lack of information.

24. Sarah bought 10 pounds of apples and nuts. Apples are 89 cents a pound, and nuts are $1.29 a pound. She spent a total of $10.10. How many pounds of nuts did she buy?

    (A) 1   (D) 4

    (B) 2   (E) 5

    (C) 3

25. Jim and Joe were running together. Jim's average speed was 400 meters per minute. Jim started running four minutes before Joe. Ten minutes after Joe started, he caught up with Jim. What was Joe's average speed?

    (A) 440 meters per minute   (D) 500 meters per minute

    (B) 450 meters per minute   (E) 560 meters per minute

    (C) 480 meters per minute

26. If 96 chickens and rabbits are put together, they have a total of 312 legs. How many chickens are there?

    (A) 36   (D) 24

    (B) 60   (E) 42

    (C) 72

27. Harold decided to cut down his sugar consumption in coffee, tea, and other drinks. He had been consuming 120 grams of sugar a day. He was determined to cut down two grams per week until he no longer used sugar in his drinks. Starting from the first day that he began cutting down his sugar, how much sugar would he have consumed before he arrived at his goal?

    (A) 92,160 grams   (D) 8,200 grams

    (B) 10,900 grams   (E) 24,780 grams

    (C) 72,000 grams

28. John and Kevin have a total of $97. John has $9 more than Kevin. How much money does Kevin have?

    (A) $40   (D) $46

    (B) $42   (E) $48

    (C) $44

29. Three circles of equal radii with centers A, B, and C are lying on a straight line and tangent to each other as in the figure shown below. A tangent line to circle C is drawn from A, meeting circle B at S and T, and tangent to circle C at D. What is the ratio of the line segment $\overline{ST}$ to the radii?

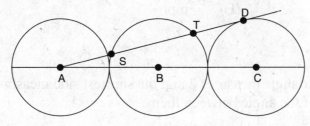

    (A) $\dfrac{\sqrt{3}}{2}$ (D) 1

    (B) $\dfrac{3}{2}$ (E) $\sqrt{2}$

    (C) $\sqrt{3}$

30. If a number times itself is added to five times itself, the result is 24. What could this number possibly be?

    (A) 3 or 8   (D) −3 or −8

    (B) −3 or 8   (E) −4 or 6

    (C) 3 or −8

31. $(630 \times .4) + (2{,}370 \times .4) =$

    (A) 120   (D) 1,500

    (B) 1,200   (E) 15,000

    (C) 12,000

32. What is the measurement of an angle of a regular pentagon?

   (A) 72°

   (B) 108°

   (C) 100°

   (D) 84°

   (E) 104°

33. A boat travels 15 mph going downstream and 8 mph going upstream. How fast is the waterflow?

   (A) $\frac{7}{2}$ mph

   (B) 3 mph

   (C) $\frac{9}{2}$ mph

   (D) 4 mph

   (E) $\frac{5}{2}$ mph

34. The longest side of a triangle measures 2 and the shortest side measures 1. What cannot be the measurement of the angle between them?

   (A) 30°

   (B) 60°

   (C) 70°

   (D) 20°

   (E) 90°

35. Which of the following is closest to the graph of the equation $y = x^2$?

   (A)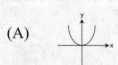

   (B)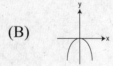

   (C)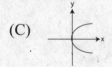

   (D)

   (E)

36. Roger took off at 8:00 a.m. driving 45 mph. Bill went after him two hours later and caught up with him at 4:00 p.m. How fast did Bill drive?

    (A) 70 mph   (D) 55 mph

    (B) 65 mph   (E) 50 mph

    (C) 60 mph

37. The expression $\dfrac{x+1}{x-1} - \dfrac{x-1}{x+1}$ simplifies to

    (A) -1.   (D) $\dfrac{4x}{x^2-1}$.

    (B) 1.   (E) $\dfrac{x}{x^2-1}$.

    (C) $\dfrac{2x}{x^2-1}$.

38. If an equilateral triangle has an area of $\sqrt{3}$, what are the lengths of its sides?

    (A) 1   (D) $\dfrac{5}{2}$

    (B) $\dfrac{3}{2}$ (E) 3

    (C) 2

39. Jane went shopping. On her first trip, she bought six pairs of shoes, all at the same price, and three pairs of socks, also at the same price (shoes and socks are not necessarily of the same price), and she spent $96. On her second trip, she went to the same shop and bought four more pairs of the same socks and returned a pair of shoes; she spent $2. How much does a pair of her shoes cost?

    (A) $10   (D) $16

    (B) $12   (E) $18

    (C) $14

40. Triangle ABC is inscribed in a circle with center O at the midpoint of the side BC. If angle B measures $47°$, what is the measurement of angle C?

    (A) $43°$ (D) $37°$

    (B) $47°$ (E) There is insufficient information

    (C) $53°$

41. Which of the following numbers is greatest?

    (A) .0054

    (B) .054

    (C) .0544

    (D) .0545

    (E) .0499

42. How many of the six numbers in the table have a 4 in the hundreds or the hundredths place?

543.403	345.349	98.084
824.547	431.008	84.43

    (A) One

    (B) Two

    (C) Three

    (D) Four

    (E) Five

43. Henry ate 1500 calories yesterday, and 15% of the calories came from fat. How many calories of fat did Henry eat?

    (A) 100

    (B) 225

    (C) 150

    (D) 15

    (E) 300

44. Consider the following numbers: $.89, \frac{7}{9}, \frac{6}{7}, .75, .\overline{6}$

    Which answer below shows the numbers arranged in ascending order?

    (A) $.\overline{6}, .75, \frac{7}{9}, \frac{6}{7}, .89$

    (B) $.89, \frac{7}{9}, \frac{6}{7}, .75, .\overline{6}$

    (C) $\frac{6}{7}, .75, .\overline{6}, .89, \frac{7}{9}$

    (D) $.89, \frac{6}{7}, \frac{7}{9}, .75, .\overline{6}$

    (E) $.75, .\overline{6}, .89, \frac{7}{9}, \frac{6}{7}$

45. Which inequality or equation below is correct?

   (A) $.857 > \dfrac{7}{8}$

   (B) $.3 > .34$

   (C) $\dfrac{6}{11} = \dfrac{18}{23}$

   (D) $3\dfrac{1}{5} < 3.09$

   (E) $\dfrac{1}{9} = .\overline{1}$

46. Which statement correctly describes the relationship shown in the table below?

x	y
11	17
19	33
27	49
35	65

   (A) There is no relationship between the x-values and the y-values.

   (B) As the y-value increases by 8, the x-value increases by 16.

   (C) As the x-value increases by 8, the y-value increases by 16.

   (D) The y-value is found by multiplying the x-value by 3 and then adding 1.

   (E) The x-values increase as the y-values decrease.

Section III: Writing

TIME: *30 Minutes*
44 Questions

Part A: Usage

DIRECTIONS: Each of the following sentences may contain an error in diction, usage, idiom, or grammar. Some sentences are correct. Some sentences contain one error. No sentence contains more than one error.

If there is an error, it will appear in one of the underlined portions labeled A, B, C, or D. If there is no error, choose the portion labeled E. If there is an error, select the letter of the portion that must be changed in order to correct the sentence.

EXAMPLE:

He drove <u>slowly</u> and <u>cautiously</u> in order to <u>hopefully</u> avoid having an <u>accident</u>.
       A   B   C   D
<u>No error</u>.
  E

1. <u>Which</u> suspension bridge <u>is</u> the <u>longest</u>, the Verrazano-Narrows Bridge in New York
    A   B   C

    City <u>or</u> the Golden Gate Bridge in San Francisco? <u>No error</u>.
     D   E

2. A main function <u>of proteins</u>, whether <u>they come</u> from <u>plant or animal sources</u>, <u>is</u> the
               A   B   C   D

    building of body tissue. <u>No error</u>.
                     E

3. <u>Recognizing</u> that we <u>had worked</u> very hard to complete our project, the teacher told
    A   B

    Janice and <u>I</u> that we could give it to her <u>tomorrow</u>. <u>No error</u>.
         C   D   E

4. <u>According to</u> the United States Constitution, the legislative branch of the government
      A

    <u>has</u> powers <u>different than</u> <u>those</u> of the executive branch. <u>No error</u>.
    B   C   D   E

5. After <u>being studied</u> for the <u>preceding ten years</u> by the National Heart, Lung, and Blood
           A   B

Institute, the relationship of high levels of cholesterol in the blood to the possibility of

<u>having</u> heart attacks <u>was reported</u> in 1984. <u>No error.</u>
  C   D   E

6. The book *Cheaper By the Dozen* <u>demonstrates</u> that each of the children of Frank and
                           A

Lillian Gilbreth <u>was expected</u> <u>to use</u> <u>his or her</u> time efficiently. <u>No error.</u>
           B   C   D   E

7. His aversion <u>with</u> snakes made camping an unpleasant activity <u>for him</u> and <u>one</u> <u>that</u> he
           A   B   C D

tried diligently to avoid. <u>No error.</u>
                  E

8. The story of the American pioneers, <u>those</u> who willingly left the safety of <u>their</u> homes
                              A   B

to move into unsettled territory, <u>show</u> <u>us</u> great courage in the face of danger. <u>No error.</u>
                            C D   E

9. <u>Because of</u> the long, cold winters <u>and</u> short summers, farming in high latitudes is
    A   B

<u>more difficult</u> <u>than</u> low latitudes. <u>No error.</u>
    C   D   E

10. When my sister and <u>I</u> <u>were</u> in Los Angeles, <u>we</u> hoped that both of us could be <u>a contes-</u>
                     A B   C   D

tant on a quiz show. <u>No error.</u>
                  E

11. After he <u>had broke</u> the vase <u>that</u> his mother <u>had purchased</u> in Europe, he tried to buy a
             A   B   C

new one for his father and <u>her.</u> <u>No error.</u>
                      D   E

12. Some of the people <u>with whom</u> the witness <u>worked</u> <u>were engaged</u> in covert activities
                   A   B   C

<u>on behalf of</u> the United States government. <u>No error.</u>
    D   E

13. <u>Because of</u> their cold personalities and hot tempers, <u>neither</u> John Adams <u>nor</u> his son
    A   B   C

John Quincy Adams <u>were</u> especially successful in politics. <u>No error</u>.

              D   E

14. <u>Among</u> the reasons <u>for United States participation</u> in World War II <u>were</u> the Japanese
    A   B   C

attack on the <u>naval base</u> at Pearl Harbor on December 7, 1941. <u>No error</u>.
             D   E

15. Some parents make a <u>greater</u> attempt to frighten <u>their</u> children about the dangers of
                     A   B

driving <u>than</u> <u>teaching</u> them safe driving habits. <u>No error</u>.
       C   D   E

16. The high standard <u>of living</u> in Sweden <u>is shown</u> by <u>their</u> statistics <u>of life expectancy</u>
                  A   B   C   D

and per capita income. <u>No error</u>.
                      E

17. The snow leopard <u>is</u> a wild mammal in Central Asia <u>that has</u> large eyes, a four-foot
                 A   B

body, <u>and</u> <u>white and bluish gray in color</u>. <u>No error</u>.
       C   D   E

18. Selecting a lifetime vocation, <u>a young person</u> may have to choose either a vocation
                                  A

that he enjoys <u>and</u> a vocation that will make <u>him</u> rich; that choice is perhaps the <u>most</u>
                B   C   D

<u>important</u> one he will ever make. <u>No error</u>.
                               E

19. Failing a test because the student <u>is</u> nervous <u>is</u> understandable; <u>to fail</u> because <u>he or</u>
                              A   B   C   D

she did not study is quite another matter. <u>No error</u>.
                                      E

20. Although she <u>had grown up</u> in the North and <u>had been</u> neither a slave <u>or</u> a slave owner,
                  A   B   C

Harriet Beecher Stowe <u>vividly</u> portrayed life on a slave-holding plantation in her fa-
                            D

mous book. <u>No error</u>.
           E

21. The reason Jason failed <u>his</u> speech was <u>because</u> he suffered <u>such stage fright</u> <u>that he</u>
                       A   B   C

    <u>refused</u> to give his final speech. <u>No error</u>.
     D   E

22. <u>After completing the typing course</u>, he made <u>less</u> errors and typed <u>more rapidly</u> than
             A   B   C

    <u>anyone else</u> in his office. <u>No error</u>.
      D   E

23. Learning the basic <u>components of good nutrition</u> is <u>important for</u> the young adult <u>who</u>
                      A   B

    <u>want</u> <u>to gain independence</u> by living in his or her own apartment. <u>No error</u>.
     C   D   E

24. Because condominiums offer the advantages of property ownership <u>along with</u> <u>those</u>
                                                        A   B

    of apartment rental, <u>this</u> <u>has made</u> condominiums popular since the 1970s. <u>No error</u>.
                      C   D   E

25. Students <u>who</u> eat every day in the college cafeteria <u>generally</u> tire of the <u>frequent</u> rep-
            A   B   C

    etitious menu <u>that is provided</u>. <u>No error</u>.
                 D   E

Part B: Sentence Correction

DIRECTIONS: In each of the following sentences, some portion of the sentence is underlined. Under each sentence are five choices. The first choice has the same wording as the original. The other four choices are reworded. Sometimes the first choice containing the original wording is the best; sometimes one of the other choices is the best. Choose the letter of the best choice. Your choice should produce a sentence which is not ambiguous or awkward and which is correct, clear, and precise.

This is a test of correct and effective English expression. Keep in mind the standards of English usage, punctuation, grammar, word choice, and construction.

EXAMPLE:

When you listen to opera, <u>a person may not appreciate it.</u>

(A) a person may not appreciate it.

(B) it may not be appreciated by a person.

(C) which may not be appreciated by one.

(D) you may not appreciate it.

(E) appreciating it may be a problem for you.

26. Wealthy citizens often protest <u>about the building of</u> low-cost housing in the affluent communities where they reside.

    (A) about the building of

    (B) whether they should build

    (C) if builders should build

    (D) the building of

    (E) whether or not they should build

27. Siblings growing up in a family do not necessarily have equal opportunities to achieve, <u>the difference being their placement in the family, their innate abilities, and their personalities.</u>

    (A) the difference being their placement in the family, their innate abilities, and their personalities.

(B) because of their placement in the family, their innate abilities, and their personalities.

(C) and the difference is their placement in the family, their innate abilities, and their personalities.

(D) they have different placements in the family, different innate abilities, and different personalities.

(E) their placement in the family, their innate abilities, and their personalities being different.

28. Two major provisions of the United States Bill of Rights <u>is freedom of speech and that citizens are guaranteed a trial by jury</u>.

(A) is freedom of speech and that citizens are guaranteed a trial by jury.

(B) is that citizens have freedom of speech and a guaranteed trial by jury.

(C) is freedom of speech and the guarantee of a trial by jury.

(D) are freedom of speech and that citizens are guaranteed a trial by jury.

(E) are freedom of speech and the guarantee of a trial by jury.

29. Poets of the nineteenth century tried <u>to entertain their readers but also with the attempt of teaching them</u> lessons about life.

(A) to entertain their readers but also with the attempt of teaching them

(B) to entertain their readers but also to attempt to teach them

(C) to both entertain their readers and to teach them

(D) entertainment of their readers and the attempt to teach them

(E) both to entertain and to teach their readers

30. The city council decided to remove parking meters <u>so as to encourage</u> people to shop in Centerville.

(A) so as to encourage

(B) to encourage

(C) thus encouraging

(D) with the desire

(E) thereby encouraging

31. Visiting New York City for the first time, <u>the sites most interesting to Megan were</u> the Statue of Liberty, the Empire State Building, and the Brooklyn Bridge.

    (A) the sites most interesting to Megan were

    (B) the sites that Megan found most interesting were

    (C) Megan found that the sites most interesting to her were

    (D) Megan was most interested in

    (E) Megan was most interested in the sites of

32. Although most college professors have expertise in their areas of specialty, <u>some are more interested in continuing their research than in teaching undergraduate students</u>.

    (A) some are more interested in continuing their research than in teaching undergraduate students.

    (B) some are most interested in continuing their research rather than in teaching undergraduate students.

    (C) some prefer continuing their research rather than to teach undergraduate students.

    (D) continuing their research, not teaching undergraduate students, is more interesting to some.

    (E) some are more interested in continuing their research than to teach undergraduate students.

33. <u>Whether adult adoptees should be allowed to see their original birth certificates or not</u> is controversial, but many adoptive parents feel strongly that records should remain closed.

    (A) Whether adult adoptees should be allowed to see their original birth certificates or not

    (B) Whether or not adult adoptees should be allowed to see their original birth certificates or not

    (C) The fact of whether adult adoptees should be allowed to see their original birth certificates

    (D) Allowing the seeing of their original birth certificates by adult adoptees

    (E) That adult adoptees should be allowed to see their original birth certificates

34. <u>Having studied theology, music, along with medicine</u>, Albert Schweitzer became a medical missionary in Africa.

    (A) Having studied theology, music, along with medicine

    (B) Having studied theology, music, as well as medicine

    (C) Having studied theology and music, and, also, medicine

    (D) With a study of theology, music, and medicine

    (E) After he had studied theology, music, and medicine

35. When the Mississippi River threatens to flood, sandbags are piled along its banks, <u>and they do this to keep its waters from overflowing</u>.

    (A) and they do this to keep its waters from overflowing.

    (B) to keep its waters from overflowing.

    (C) and then its waters won't overflow.

    (D) and, therefore, keeping its waters from overflowing.

    (E) and they keep its waters from overflowing.

36. <u>Because of the popularity of his light verse</u>, Edward Lear is seldom recognized today for his travel books and detailed illustrations of birds.

    (A) Because of the popularity of his light verse

    (B) Owing to the fact that his light verse was popular

    (C) Because of his light verse, that was very popular

    (D) Having written light verse that was popular

    (E) Being the author of popular light verse

37. Lincoln's Gettysburg Address, <u>despite its having been very short and delivered after a two-hour oration by Edward Everett</u>, is one of the greatest speeches ever delivered.

    (A) despite its having been very short and delivered after a two-hour oration by Edward Everett

    (B) which was very short and delivered after a two-hour oration by Edward Everett

    (C) although it was very short and delivered after a two-hour oration by Edward Everett

    (D) despite the fact that it was very short and delivered after a two-hour oration by Edward Everett

    (E) was very short and delivered after a two-hour oration by Edward Everett

38. China, <u>which ranks third in area and first in population among the world's countries</u>, also has one of the longest histories.

    (A) which ranks third in area and first in population among the world's countries

(B) which ranks third in area and has the largest population among the world's countries

(C) which is the third largest in area and ranks first in population among the world's countries

(D) in area ranking third and in population ranking first among the world's countries

(E) third in area and first in the number of people among the world's countries

39. <u>Leonardo da Vinci was a man who</u> was a scientist, an architect, an engineer, and a sculptor.

(A) Leonardo da Vinci was a man who

(B) The man Leonardo da Vinci

(C) Being a man, Leonardo da Vinci

(D) Leonardo da Vinci

(E) Leonardo da Vinci, a man who

40. <u>The age of 35 having been reached</u>, a natural-born United States citizen is eligible to be elected President of the United States.

(A) The age of 35 having been reached

(B) The age of 35 being reached

(C) At 35, when that age is reached

(D) When having reached the age of 35

(E) When he or she is 35 years old

41. <u>It was my roommate who caught the thief stealing my wallet, which is the reason</u> I gave him a reward.

(A) It was my roommate who caught the thief stealing my wallet, which is the reason

(B) My roommate caught the thief stealing my wallet, which is the reason

(C) Because my roommate caught the thief stealing my wallet,

(D) That my roommate caught the thief stealing my wallet is the reason why

(E) My roommate having caught the thief stealing my wallet,

42. <u>The fewer mistakes one makes in life</u>, the fewer opportunities you have to learn from your mistakes.

(A) The fewer mistakes one makes in life

(B) The fewer mistakes you make in life

(C) The fewer mistakes he or she makes in life

(D) The fewer mistakes there are in one's life

(E) The fewer mistakes in life

43. Although the word "millipede" means one thousand feet, millipedes have no more than 115 pairs of legs that are attached to the segments of their bodies.

(A) that are attached to the segments of their bodies.

(B) each of which are attached to a segment of their bodies.

(C) attaching themselves to segments of their bodies.

(D) whose attachment is to the segments of their bodies.

(E) the attachment of which is to the segments of their bodies.

44. Father Junipero Sera, who was a Franciscan missionary sent from Spain to Mexico, where he taught and worked among the Indians and then founded many missions in California that later became cities.

(A) where he taught and worked among the Indians

(B) there he taught and worked among the Indians

(C) he taught and worked among the Indians

(D) taught and worked among the Indians

(E) teaching and working among the Indians

Part C: Essay

TIME: *30 Minutes*

DIRECTIONS: You have 30 minutes to plan and write an essay on the topic below. You may write only on the assigned topic.

Make sure to give specific examples to support your thesis. Proofread your essay carefully and take care to express your ideas clearly and effectively.

ESSAY TOPIC:

"There is a wonderful, mystical law of nature that the three things we crave most in life—happiness, freedom, and peace of mind—are always attained by giving them to someone else."

ASSIGNMENT: Do you agree or disagree with the statement? Support your opinion with specific examples from history, current events, literature, or personal experience.

Answer Key

Section 1: Reading Comprehension

1. **(D)**	13. **(D)**	25. **(E)**	37. **(E)**
2. **(E)**	14. **(B)**	26. **(D)**	38. **(E)**
3. **(B)**	15. **(E)**	27. **(B)**	39. **(E)**
4. **(A)**	16. **(C)**	28. **(A)**	40. **(C)**
5. **(B)**	17. **(B)**	29. **(D)**	41. **(D)**
6. **(C)**	18. **(A)**	30. **(E)**	42. **(B)**
7. **(C)**	19. **(B)**	31. **(A)**	43. **(B)**
8. **(B)**	20. **(A)**	32. **(C)**	44. **(A)**
9. **(D)**	21. **(E)**	33. **(C)**	45. **(D)**
10. **(D)**	22. **(C)**	34. **(A)**	46. **(B)**
11. **(C)**	23. **(B)**	35. **(E)**	
12. **(B)**	24. **(E)**	36. **(C)**	

Section II: Mathematics

1. **(A)**	13. **(D)**	25. **(E)**	37. **(D)**
2. **(C)**	14. **(D)**	26. **(A)**	38. **(C)**
3. **(C)**	15. **(A)**	27. **(E)**	39. **(C)**
4. **(D)**	16. **(C)**	28. **(C)**	40. **(A)**
5. **(C)**	17. **(C)**	29. **(C)**	41. **(D)**
6. **(C)**	18. **(B)**	30. **(C)**	42. **(C)**
7. **(E)**	19. **(A)**	31 **(B)**	43. **(B)**
8. **(D)**	20. **(D)**	32 **(B)**	44. **(A)**
9. **(E)**	21. **(B)**	33. **(A)**	45. **(E)**
10. **(B)**	22. **(D)**	34. **(E)**	46. **(C)**
11. **(E)**	23. **(A)**	35. **(A)**	
12. **(E)**	24. **(C)**	36. **(C)**	

Section III: Writing

1. **(C)**	12. **(E)**	23. **(C)**	34. **(E)**
2. **(E)**	13. **(D)**	24. **(C)**	35. **(B)**
3. **(C)**	14. **(C)**	25. **(C)**	36. **(A)**
4. **(C)**	15. **(D)**	26. **(D)**	37. **(C)**
5. **(A)**	16. **(C)**	27. **(B)**	38. **(A)**
6. **(E)**	17. **(D)**	28. **(E)**	39. **(D)**
7. **(A)**	18. **(B)**	29. **(E)**	40. **(E)**
8. **(C)**	19. **(C)**	30. **(B)**	41. **(C)**
9. **(D)**	20. **(C)**	31. **(D)**	42. **(B)**
10. **(D)**	21. **(B)**	32. **(A)**	43. **(A)**
11. **(A)**	22. **(B)**	33. **(E)**	44. **(D)**

Section I: Reading Comprehension

1. **D**

   The question asks for the best synthesis of the passage and choice (D) is the best and most complete answer. Choices (A), (B), (C), and (E) are not as complete. For example, choice (A) left out the duration of the conference, choice (B) left out the number of the nations represented at the summit, choice (C) left out both the duration of the conference and the number of the nations represented at the summit, and choice (E) left out the number of nations represented and support for Gorbachev's "new thinking."

2. **E**

   Of the choices provided, choice (E) gives the most logical and sound implication of the passage. Choice (A) falls short of the capabilities of Gorbachev's leadership; in choice (B) the "new thinking" referred to already has the support of the seven leaders at the summit; choice (C) is a rather sweeping, unfair statement; and choice (D) left out support for economic and political reforms.

3. **B**

   The mention of banking and energy did not rule out technical assistance in other fields, hence, choice (B) is the correct answer. Choice (A) limited the assistance to only the fields of banking and energy; in choice (C) the statement is only partly true—the U.S. is not alone in providing support; in choice (D) the statement implies that there is no consensus among the seven nations; and in choice (E) technical assistance can likewise come from other nations outside of the seven.

4. **A**

   The question asks for the main idea in the passage and choice (A) provides the best and complete main idea. Choices (B), (C), and (D) are generalizations derived from the passage and choice (E), while it is true and specific to the passage, is stated in the negative.

5. **B**

   Choice (B) gives the most specific consequence for California. The other choices, while all plausible or possible answers, do not get to the "root" of the issue specific to California.

6. **C**

Based on the passage the answer to this question is choice (C)—two things are mentioned that would affect California: federal funding and the number of congressional seats. While choices (A) and (B) are correct, they are incomplete. Choices (D) and (E) are consequential generalizations which, while correct deductions, are not mentioned in the passage.

7. **C**

The question asks for the "message" conveyed in the passage. Choice (C) is the correct answer, as it gives a warning. In choice (A), pesticides cannot necessarily be dangerous to all living things—some are good for the protection of plants, for example; in choice (B), water can be contaminated by something other than pesticides; the statement in choice (D) may be true, but it is certainly not the best answer.

8. **B**

The train is definitely a cargo train, hence, choice (B) is the correct answer. In choice (A), if it were a passenger train, hundreds would have been killed; in choices (C) and (D), according to the clues, the choices here don't apply; and in choice (E) the answer used "special train" but could have appropriately used "cargo train" instead.

9. **D**

The question here asks for the most "serious problem" that can come about; so, of all the choices, (D) provides the most serious problem resulting from the pesticide spill for Californians. Choices (A), (B), (C), and (E) are not life-threatening as is choice (D).

10. **D**

Answer choice (D) is the most logical and straightforward answer. Choice (D) prioritizes which action should be first taken, and is therefore the correct answer. While the choices in (A), (B), (C), and (E) are sound answers, they don't list the most urgent thing to do.

11. **C**

The correct answer here is choice (C) because this choice synthesizes the key or main idea in the passage. The other choices, while partly true, don't describe the main idea.

12. **B**

> Before World War II, which were the depression years, one can easily presume that people were more practical or money minded, hence, Labor Day as celebrated then could mean the loss of a day's pay for working people. Hence, choice (B) is the correct answer. While choices (A), (C), (D), and (E) are also possible answers they don't get to the "root" of the issue.

13. **D**

> Explicitly provided in the passage is choice (D), the correct answer. Choices (A), (B), (C), and (E), while they may all be true and correct, are not what is precisely given in the passage.

14. **B**

> The question asks for implication. The most straight forward implication of the choices provided is (B). Choice (A) is too general and is actually given in the passage. Choice (C) is an eventual consequence of the proposed program and the same can be said of choices (D) and (E).

15. **E**

> The gold content found in the volcanic ash from Mt. Pinatubo could easily stir or trigger a "gold rush." However, people are warned that the gold content found is not at a "commercial level." Hence, choice (E) is the correct answer. The other choices provided are all mere speculations.

16. **C**

> Choice (C) is the most appropriate answer—it also synthesizes the content of the reading passage; hence, it is the correct answer. Choices (A) and (B) are both incorrect. Choices (D) and (E) are somewhat applicable as titles but do not really synthesize the main idea of the passage as choice (C).

17. **B**

> If priorities will have to be established, to determine the most immediate research needed on the ash content from Mt. Pinatubo, choice (B) will have to be the most logical choice because there is already some data with which to work. Other research possibilities such as those in choices (A), (C), (D), and (E) will have to come later.

18. **A**

The best and correct answer here is choice (A)—it's the main idea of the passage. Choice (B) is incorrect. Choice (C) is partially correct—if it has to be specific, it should refer to the brake lights on the helmet. Choice (D) is incomplete as a key or main idea of the passage and the same could be said of choice (E).

19. **B**

It would follow that the rationale behind the new brake light requirement for cars in California is the same for all other vehicles on the road. Hence, choice (B) is the correct answer. The implication provided in choice (A) is not necessarily true; choice (C) is illogical; in choice (D) any car driven in California, wherever its been bought, cannot be exempted from the requirement; and in choice (E) Harris can go on inventing while remaining a farmer—he'll make more money doing both.

20. **A**

Choice (A) is the most logical and appropriate answer, hence, it is the correct answer. Choice (B) can be, but is not necessarily true; choice (C) is a logical possibility but will not drastically raise car prices beyond affordability; choice (D) may be true, but not as road hazards; and choice (E), the contrary may also be true.

21. **E**

All the choices in this question are possible answer; however, since the question asks for what lead poisoning, if not detected early "can lead to," it calls for the ultimate consequence. Hence, choice (E) is the correct answer inasmuch as the passage states "life-threatening disorders" as among the possible consequences.

22. **C**

The correct answer to this question is choice (C)—it gives the complete and precise category. Other choices are incomplete—(A) left out the age group and the medical eligibility; (B) is narrowed down and all inclusive of "children with learning disabilities" and choices (D) and (E) are incorrect.

23. **B**

As indicated by figures in the passage, the correct answer is (B). Other choices (A), (C), (D), and (E) are obviously incorrect. This is an example of a question in which the incorrect choices are not possible answers. The correct answer is derived from the figures provided in the passage.

24. **E**

    The implications provided in choices (A) through (E) are correct. However, each of the implications for choices (A) through (D) are narrowed down to only one specific category of children—not any one is inclusive of all that needs to be addressed. Hence, choice (E) is the best and appropriate answer because it addresses the thousands who will not be screened which include those in choices (A) through (D).

25. **E**

    If schools exist to serve the best interest of students, then the correct answer for this question is (E). Choices (A) through (D) are also correct; however, the group that will be most affected by the financial crisis in California would have to be the "students." The fact remains that schools exist to serve the best interest of students.

26. **D**

    A title is supposed to synthesize the main idea and (D) does. Choice (A) left out the main idea of a commemorative stamp; choice (B) is incorrect because it implies Columbus discovered the Americas; choice (C) is not the main idea of the passage; and choice (E), while it may be implied in the passage, does not synthesize its focus.

27. **B**

    The underlying fact behind the passage is explicitly implied; therefore, (B) is the correct answer. Choice (A), while true, is a generalized implication, not addressing the specific issue; choice (C) is debatable and so is choice (D); choice (E) like (A) is also a generalized implication.

28. **A**

    Of the choices given (A) is the most historically significant, and, therefore, the correct answer. Choice (B) is significant but left out the fact that Columbus was not the first to arrive in the New World, the main point in the passage; choice (C) is a mere commemoration day; choice (D) remains a debatable assumption; and choice (E) is not specific enough as an historically significant fact.

29. **D**

    Since *zoology* is the study of animals choice (D) is the correct and appropriate answer. The other choices which are other subject areas, as in choices (A), (B), (C), and (E), while they may be used by the classroom teacher, they are not quite the most appropriate subject areas.

30. **E**

A study of a 150 million-year-old fossil will require digging up into history; hence, choice (E) is the correct answer. Choice (A) could be used if there is a problem focus in the passage; choices (B), (C), and (D) are poor and incorrect choices. *Survey* applies to a descriptive study; *deductive* is an approach that proceeds from a generalization or theory, and *comparative* requires two things to compare which is not addressed in the passage.

31. **A**

Answer choice (A) clearly synthesizes the main idea in the passage; hence, it is the correct answer. Choice (B) is more of an implication, hence, the wrong answer; choice (C) is merely stating a fact which does not speak of the main idea; the same can be said of choice (D); and choice (E), while it may be true, is not really the passage's main idea.

32. **C**

The most sound and significant implication of the passage is stated in (C); hence, this is the correct answer. Choices (A) and (B) are not sound, they reflect a rather immature reasoning; choice (D) merely states some degree of competitiveness which is not the issue's focus; and choice (E) is a "so what" kind of statement and not a sound implication.

33. **C**

The passage is really on global tourism providing comparisons and implying some inter-nation balance in tourism trade; hence, choice (C) is the appropriate and correct answer. Choices (A), (B), (D), and (E) are stated in general terms, missing out on the specific focus or topic of the passage, hence, not the logical and immediate topics to discuss.

34. **A**

The most appropriate and complete title is expressed in (A); hence this is the correct answer. Choice (B) merely states a planned activity and does not address the main idea; choice (C) is incomplete—it does not specify the basis for ranking; the same can be said for choices (D) and (E), likewise, incomplete titles.

35. **E**

The best answer in considering "practical terms" will have to be (E) which is the correct answer. Choice (A) is an implication that does not apply to San Francisco; choice

(C) is a possible consequence but an undesirable one; and choice (D) is a true implication but the "practicality" is merely implied. Choice (E) says this explicitly.

36. **C**

The suggestion in choice (C) is the most sound and logical if equal opportunity for all students is to be our nation's priority; hence, this is the correct answer. Choice (A) is a mere statement of concern and does not provide a plan for action; choice (B) is illogical—you cannot cut down the number of minority students who are already in the system; choice (D) disregards other languages existing in the school system and in the community at large; and choice (E) is only secondary to the major issue.

37. **E**

Since the passage points out the fact that there will soon be more minority students in the classroom, priority should be in providing the appropriate teacher preparation; hence, the correct answer is (E). Choice (A) is a need but secondary to those who are already in the system; choice (B) has always been an issue even before the rapid changes in the demographics; choice (C) is something that has triggered legislations since the 1950s—the natural composition of the classroom today is already desegregated. While the other choices are a need, the one that needs immediate action is choice (E).

38. **E**

The answer to this question has to tie in with the foregoing answer; hence, the correct choice is (E). Choices (A), (B), (C), and (D), while also problems arising from the changes in demographics, are secondary to choice (E).

39. **E**

The most complete summary of the passage is stated in (E); hence, this is the correct answer. Choice (A) is not true, therefore, is incorrect; choice (B) is rather put in general terms—the U.S. pullout is not the only issue related to the Philippine economy. The interdependence of nations will remain no matter what, i.e., trade relations will continue; choice (C) is incorrect. The U.S. military strategy will have to be relocated elsewhere in the Asia-Pacific region, the same can be said for choice (D)—the Philippines will not be completely on its own—it continues to maintain its trade relations with the U.S. and other trading partners.

40. **C**

The passage is quite explicit in stating that the U.S. presence on the Philippines has been an impediment to the nation's capability in joining East Asia's "economic boom"; hence, the correct answer is choice (C). Choices (A), (B), (D), and (E) are all possible consequences but are all quite debatable.

41. **D.**

The prisoners are speedily sentenced because the judges and the jurymen are hungry and want to go home for supper as the day ends—the prisoners may be guilty, but the wrong reasons determine their sentences choice (D). No doubt the people do believe in the system, but the sarcasm of the piece suggests that this society uses the system for personal selfish benefits—certainly not a humanitarian society. And, while choice (E), the society has no problem with the death penalty, may be true, it does not adequately capture the sarcasm of the last two lines.

42. **B**

The society depicted is shallow and trivial, engaging in chatty conversations that everyone takes seriously. Serious as the discussions may be, they possibly involve extramarital affairs rather than affairs of state choices (C, D)—such gossip ruins reputations choice (B). The gossiping involves the Queen, but it is not revealed that she is slandered (which would involve maliciousness), which, if you hadn't already done so, eliminates (D and E) along with (A).

43. **B**

The question wants you to analyze the clash or conflict of two very different concepts in conversation: the glory of the Queen in one breath and a fire screen (or room divider) in another. The juxtaposition is not so much to suggest trivia or seriousness (the Queen's glory is serious but the furniture is not), but that this society holds both in equal reverence choice (B). No real evidence is given that the people are Royalists or Imperialists. The poem may imply, in the first two lines, that people are interested in different things, but again, there is no real evidence, at issue is the clash of the two.

44. **A**

There is a clever use of the language in this one adverb. It stands for the angle of the sun as it declines at a steep angle but also for the hidden meanings behind the word as it refers to this society: the deceit, the amorality. It certainly does not mean that the sun is at a perpendicular angle choice (A), nor does it imply anything about the sea.

45. **D**

The move is light to dark in the physical movement of the day but not specifically in the voice. On analysis you will find the "coming down" of mood from amusement at the chat of the day—the trivia—to a sadness of the effect of the hunger of the court officials, a hunger that sends men to the gallows. The answer is choice (D).

46. **B**

Like meaning, the intention of an utterance is "on the surface," manifested within the particular situation and measurable by outward criteria pertinent to the situation. Choice (B) is thus correct. Intention is not a private act occurring in the mind of a speaker; if one couldn't express one's intentions verbally to another person, one wouldn't be able to articulate them to oneself. Therefore, choice (B) is correct. For the same reason, choice (A) cannot be correct. If intentions were unknowable, it would make no sense to speak of intentions at all; hence, choice (C) is incorrect. Finally, the notion that intention is public and "on the surface" contradicts previous linguistic theories of "deep structure," which maintained that one must translate a given sentence into another set of words in order for its intention to be clear. The problem with such a notion is that there is nothing to guarantee the adequacy of the translation and thus we are involved in an infinite regress. If the intention of an utterance cannot be made clear by the utterance itself, it is unlikely another set of words would possess such clarity. Choice (D) is therefore incorrect. And, while (E) may be true in some circumstances, it is not *de facto* with regard to utterances.

Section II: Mathematics

1. **A**

   The least common denominator of the fractions is the least common multiple of their denominators: 15, 21, and 35. Since

   $$15 = 3 \times 5,$$
   $$21 = 3 \times 7,$$
   and $35 = 5 \times 7,$

   we see that their least common multiple is $3 \times 5 \times 7 = 105$.

2. **C**

   Since his reunion will be $365 \times 4 + 1 = 1,461$ days from a Friday, dividing 1,461 by 7 yields a remainder of 5. Therefore, his reunion is 5 days from a Friday, which makes it on a Wednesday.

3. **C**

   In one day, John can do $^1/_7$ of the work, and Mary can do $^1/_5$; together, they can do

   $$\frac{1}{5} + \frac{1}{7} = \frac{12}{35}$$

   of the job. To finish the whole job, it takes

   $$\frac{35}{12} = 2 \text{ and } \frac{11}{12} \text{ days.}$$

4. **D**

   Since the sugar content is 60 percent of $\frac{1}{2}$ pint and will not be changed after the water is added, we obtain an equation by equating the sugar content before and after adding in x pints of water. The equation is then

   $$\frac{1}{2} \times 60\% = \frac{1}{2} + x \times 5\%$$

   $$\text{or } 30 = 2\frac{1}{2} + 5x$$
   $$60 = 5 + 10x$$
   $$55 = 10x$$
   $$5.5 = x$$

5. **C**

Since the only information we have concerning the triangle is that angle *A* measures 30°, we know that in a triangle, the largest angle faces the longest side, the sum of the three angles of a triangle is 180°, and a 30° angle is not the largest angle. Therefore, *a* is not the longest side.

6. **C**

The diameter of circle *A* is twice that of circle *B*, so if the radius of *B* is *r*, then the radius of *A* is 2*r*. Since the area of a circle with radius *r* is πr^2, the area of *B* is πr^2, while the area of *A* is

$$\pi(2r)^2 = 4\pi r^2,$$

therefore the ratio is 4:1.

7. **E**

Since the cube has a volume of 8, its sides have length 2. The cube whose sides are twice that would be of length 4, so the volume of the other cube is

$$4 \times 4 \times 4 = 64.$$

8. **D**

2:15 + 5:45 = 8:00 means he arrives in Los Angeles at 8 p.m. New York time. But New York is 3 hours ahead of Los Angeles, so the Los Angeles time of arrival is 5 p.m.

9. **E**

We set up two equations. Let *n* be the number of nickels, and let *d* be the number of dimes. We have

$$n + d = 50.$$

Since each nickel is worth 5 cents and each dime is worth 10 cents, we have

$$5n + 10d = 485.$$

Multiplying the first equation by 10, we obtain

$$10n + 10d = 500.$$

Subtracting the second equation from it, we obtain $5n = 15$, or $n = 3$.

10. **B**

Let *s* be the speed of the boat in still water. Then the speed of the boat upstream is (*s* – 3) miles per hour, and the speed of the boat downstream is (*s* + 3) miles per hour. Therefore, the time going upstream,

$$\frac{24}{s - 3}$$

hours plus the time going downstream,

$$\frac{24}{s+3}$$

hours, equals 6 hours.

$$\frac{24}{s-3}+\frac{24}{s+3}=6, \quad \frac{(s+3)}{(s+3)(s-3)}+\frac{(s-3)}{(s+3)(s-3)}=\frac{6}{24}=\frac{1}{4}$$

$$\frac{2s}{(s+3)(s-3)}=\frac{1}{4}, \quad 8s=(s+3)(s-3)=s^2-9$$

$$s^2-8s-9=0;$$
$$(s-9)(s+1)=0;$$
$$s=9 \text{ or } -1,$$

but we require $s > 0$. Thus $s = 9$ miles per hour.

11. **E**

Since 10 babies drink 10 gallons of milk in 10 days, each baby drinks; $^1/_{10}$ gallon of milk per day. Each baby drinks 2 gallons of milk in 20 days, so 20 babies will drink $2 \times 20 = 40$ gallons of milk in 20 days.

12. **E**

Let x be the number of nickels, y be the number of dimes, and z be the number of quarters. We have two equations:

$$x + y + z = 24$$

and $5x + 10y + 25z = 300$

and three unknowns. Therefore, no unique answer can be found without one more equation.

13. **D**

Draw both diagonals to divide the parallelogram into four equal parts. Each part is a right triangle with hypotenuse measuring 4 and one side measuring 2. Therefore, the other side must measure $2\sqrt{3}$ by the Pythagorean Theorem. The area of this triangle is

$$\left(\frac{1}{2}\right) \times (2 \times 2\sqrt{3}) = 2\sqrt{3},$$

and the area of the parallelogram is four times that, which is $8\sqrt{3}$.

14. **D**

Let the amount of money he had before be x. We have
$$x - \left(\frac{1}{3}\right)x - \left(\frac{1}{4}\right)x = 150,000 .$$

Or, $\left(\frac{5}{12}\right)x = 150,000$.

Therefore, $x = 360,000$.

15. **A**

If we multiply both the numerator and denominator by the conjugate of the expression $\sqrt{3} - \sqrt{2}$, namely, $\sqrt{3} + \sqrt{2}$, the numerator becomes $\sqrt{3} + \sqrt{2}$, and the denominator becomes $3 - 2 = 1$.

16. **C**

Since Don and Ron can paint the house in 5 days, they finish $\frac{1}{5}$ of the job in a day. Now Ron's contribution in a day is $\frac{1}{7}$ of the job, so
$$\frac{1}{5} - \frac{1}{7}$$
is Don's contribution in a day, which amounts to $\frac{2}{35}$ Therefore, if Don is to do it alone, it will take him
$$\frac{35}{2} = 17.5 \text{ days.}$$

17. **C**

Since the volume of the cube is 8, each side has a measure of 2, and the main diagonal is found with the extended Pythagorean Theorem. Thus, the main diagonal is
$$\sqrt{2^2 + 2^2 + 2^2} = \sqrt{12} = 2\sqrt{3}$$

18. **B**

Each way for Bob to walk to Norman's consists of six blocks northward and six blocks eastward in different orders. The total number of ways of walking is then the same as the number of ways to choose 6 out of 12 things, and the number is
$$12 \times 11 \times 10 \times 9 \times 8 \times 7 \text{ divided by } 6 \times 5 \times 4 \times 3 \times 2, \text{ or } 924.$$

19. **A**

For a right isosceles triangle, the area is half of the product of the two equal sides. Let x represent each leg. Then $\frac{1}{2}(x)(x) = \frac{1}{2}x^2 = 4$, $x^2 = 8$.

Therefore, each of the equal sides measure $\sqrt{8}$, or $2\sqrt{2}$, and the hypotenuse must be 4.

20. **D**

Let the number of marbles in the beginning be x. We have

$$x - \left(\frac{1}{3}\right)x - \left(\frac{1}{3}\right)\left(\frac{2}{3}\right)x - 2 = 10.$$

Solving the equation, $x = 27$.

21. **B**

We divide 400 by 24 (number of hours in a day); we obtain a partial quotient of 16 and a remainder of 16. This means that it takes 16 days and 16 hours for the trip. With 31 days in May, the boat must arrive on June 10. And 16 hours from 6 a.m. is 10 p.m.

22. **D**

If we let Joan's age be x, then Georgette's age is $(x - 8)$. Solving the equation
$$(x - 8) = 2[(x - 8) - 8] = 2x - 32,$$
we obtain $x = 24$.

23. **A**

Since the boat took five hours to go 20 miles, its speed upstream was four miles per hour. But the water effect was five miles per hour. If that effect had been taken away, the boat would have been five miles faster; therefore, the boat in still waters goes $4 + 5 = 9$ miles per hour.

24. **C**

Suppose Sarah bought x pounds of apples and y pounds of nuts. We have the following equations to solve:
$$x + y = 10$$
$$89x + 129y = 1{,}010$$
Solving these equations give $x = 7$, $y = 3$.

25. **E**

When Joe caught Jim, Jim had been running for $(10 + 4) = 14$ minutes, at the rate of 400 meters per minute. So the total distance covered was $(14 \times 400) = 5,600$ meters. But Joe covered this distance in 10 minutes. Thus, his average speed was

$$\frac{5,600}{10} = 560 \text{ meters per minute.}$$

26. **A**

Since a chicken has two legs and a rabbit has four legs, letting x be the number of chickens and y be the number of rabbits, we have the following equations to solve:

$$
\begin{aligned}
x + y &= 96 \\
2x + 4y &= 312 \\
x &= 96 - y \\
\frac{2x + 4y}{2} &= 312 \\
x + 2y &= 156 \\
96 - y + 2y &= 156 \\
96 + y &= 156 \\
y &= 60 \\
x + 60 &= 96 \\
x &= 36
\end{aligned}
$$

27. **E**

In the first week, he consumed 118 grams of sugar daily; in the second week, he consumed 116 grams of sugar daily, etc. We are then to add $118 + 116 + 114 + \ldots + 2$ and since there are seven days in a week, the result must be multiplied by 7. Observing that

$$118 + 116 + 114 + \ldots + 2 \quad = \quad 2 \times (1 + 2 + 3 + \ldots + 59)$$

$$= \quad 2 \times (1 + 59) \left(\frac{59}{2}\right) = 3,540$$

And $\quad 3,540 \times 7 = 24,780.$

28. **C**

Let x be the amount of money Kevin has, and let y be the amount of money John has. Then $y + x = 97$, and $y - x = 9$. Subtracting the two equations, we have

$$2x = 88, \text{ or } x = 44.$$

29. **C**

If we draw a perpendicular line from *B* to the tangent line, say *BE*, then the right-angled triangles *ABE* and *ACD* are similar, so *BE* equals half of *CD*, the radius. *BET* is also a right-angled triangle, and *BT* is a radius. Using the Pythagorean Theorem, *ET* measures

$$\frac{\sqrt{3}}{2}$$

of the radius. Thus, *ST* measures $\sqrt{3}$ of the radius.

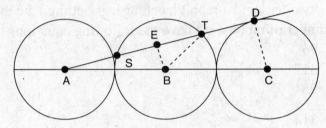

30. **C**

Letting this number be *x,* we have
$$x^2 + 5x = 24, \text{ or } x^2 + 5x - 24 = 0,$$
or $(x + 8)(x - 3) = 0$,
so $x = 3$ or $x = -8$.

31. **B**

By the Distributive Law, $(630 \times .4) + (2,370 \times .4) = (630 + 2,370) \times (.4) = (3,000) \times (.4) = 1,200$.

32. **B**

We do not need to memorize any formula. If we inscribe the regular pentagon in a circle, the angle with the vertex at the center facing each side is
$$\frac{360°}{5} = 72°,$$
and each of the other angles of that triangle must be
$$\frac{(180° - 72°)}{2} = 54°.$$
Thus, each of the angles is 108°.

33. **A**

Let x be the speed of the boat in still waters, and let y be the speed of the waterflow. Then $x + y = 15$ mph, and $x - y = 8$ mph. Subtracting the equations, we get $2y = 7$, or
$$y = \frac{7}{2}.$$

34. **E**

Since a 90° angle must be the largest in a triangle, it must face the longest side, and the angle between the longest side and the shortest side is not facing the longest side.

35. **A**

$y = x^2$ has a graph like (A). (B) is the graph of $y = -x^2$; (C) is the graph of $x = y^2$; (D) is the graph of $x = -y^2$; and (E) is not even the graph of a second degree equation.

36. **C**

Since Bill took six hours to catch up, and Roger has gone 90 miles, Bill was
$$\frac{90}{6} = 15$$
miles closer each hour. Thus, he was driving 60 miles per hour.

37. **D**

The common denominator is $x^2 - 1$, and the numerator is
$$(x + 1)^2 - (x - 1)^2 = 4x.$$

38. **C**

Using the Pythagorean Theorem and the formula for the area of a triangle,

$$b = a \text{ and } h = \frac{s^2}{4}\sqrt{3} = \sqrt{3}. \text{ Then, } \frac{s^2}{4} = 1, \text{ so s=2.}$$

where a is the length of the sides.

39. **C**

Let the price for a pair of shoes be x, and let the price for a pair of socks be y. Then,
$$6x + 3y = 96,$$

and $4y - x = 2$.

Solving these equations, we have $x = 14$.

40. **A**

Since $\overline{BC}$ is the diameter of the circle, angle A is a right angle. Therefore, angle C is complementary to angle B, i.e., $90° - 47° = 43°$.

41. **D**

Answer choices (B), (C), and (D) are tied with the largest digits in the hundredths and thousandths places. However, answer choice (D) has a larger digit in the ten-thousandths place than either of answer choices (B) and (C). Here is the order of the five numbers, from least to greatest: .0054, .0499, .054, .0544, .0545.

42. **C**

Each of 345.349 and 824.547 has the digit 4 in the hundredths place. The number 431.008 has the digit 4 in the hundreds place.

43. **B**

The number of calories of fat is equal to the product of 15% and 1500, which is $(.15)(1500) = 225$.

44. **A**

Change each of the five numbers to its approximate decimal equivalent to the nearest hundredth. Then .89 remains the same, $\frac{7}{9} \approx .78$, $\frac{1}{9}$, .75 remains the same, and $.\overline{6} \approx .67$ We note that $.67 < .75 < .78 < .86 < .89$. Therefore, the correct ascending order for the original five numbers is $.\overline{6}$ .75, $\frac{7}{9}$, $\frac{6}{7} \approx .86$, .89.

45. **E**

The decimal equivalent of $\frac{1}{9}$ is .111111…. Answer choice (A) is wrong because $\frac{7}{8} = .875$, which is greater than .857. Answer choice (B) is wrong because $.\overline{3} = .33333…$, which is less than .34. Answer choice (C) is wrong because $(6)(23) \uparrow (11)(18)$. Answer choice (D) is wrong because $3\frac{1}{5} = 3.2$, which is greater than 3.09.

46. **C**

Beginning with the lowest value of x, each successive value is found by adding 8. For example $11 + 8 = 19$ and $19 + 8 = 27$. Beginning with the lowest value of y, each successive value is found by adding 16. For example, $17 + 16 = 33$ and $33 + 16 = 49$.

Section III: Writing

1. **C**

    As you read the sentence, you should recognize that choice (C) presents an error in comparison. The comparison of two bridges requires the comparative form "longer." All of the other choices are acceptable in standard written English. Choice (A), the interrogative adjective "Which," introduces the question; choice (B), "is," agrees with its singular subject "bridge"; and choice (D), "or," is a coordinating conjunction joining the names of the two bridges.

2. **E**

    The correct response to this question is choice (E). All labeled elements are choices acceptable in standard written English. Choice (A), "of proteins," is a prepositional phrase that modifies the word "function"; in choice (B), the pronoun "they "is plural to agree with its antecedent, "proteins," and the verb "come" is also plural to agree with its subject, "they"; choice (C), "plant or animal sources," is idiomatic; and choice (D), "is," is singular to agree with its singular subject, "function."

3. **C**

    The error is choice (C), "I," which is in the nominative case. Because the words "Janice" and "I" serve as indirect objects in the sentence, the correct pronoun is the first person objective form, "me." Choice (A), "Recognizing," is a participle introducing an introductory participial phrase modifying "teacher;" choice (B), "had worked," is a verb in the past perfect tense because the action in the phrase was completed before the action in the main clause occurred; and choice (D), "tomorrow," is an adverb modifying the verb "could give."

4. **C**

    The error occurs at choice (C), where the preposition "from" is idiomatic after the word "different." Although some experts insist upon the use of "from" after the adjective "different," others accept the use of "different than" in order to save words. An example would be "different than you thought"; the use of "from" would require the addition of the word "what." Choice (A), "According to," is a preposition correctly introducing a prepositional phrase; choice (B), "has," is third person singular to agree with its subject "branch"; and choice (D), "those," is a plural pronoun to agree with its antecedent "powers."

5. **A**

    Choice (A) should be a gerund in the present perfect form (having "been studied") to indicate that the action expressed by the gerund occurred before the relationship was reported. Choice (B), "preceding ten years," is idiomatic. Choice (C), "having," is a gerund introducing the phrase "having heart attacks" which is the object of the preposition "of"; and choice (D), the past tense passive verb "was reported," is singular to agree with its subject, "relationship."

6. **E**

    Your answer should be choice (E), indicating that this sentence contains no error in standard written English. Choice (A), "demonstrates," is present tense third person singular to agree with its subject, "book"; choice (B), "was expected," uses the third person singular form of "to be" to agree with its subject "each;" choice (C), the infinitive "to use," is idiomatic after the passive verb "was expected"; and choice (D), "his or her," is singular to agree with its antecedent, the indefinite pronoun "each," and provides gender neutrality.

7. **A**

    You should recognize in choice (A) that the idiomatically acceptable preposition to follow "aversion" is "to." The other choices in the sentence are acceptable in standard written English. Choice (B), "for him," is a prepositional phrase modifying "activity"; choice (C), "one," is a pronoun appropriate to refer to its antecedent "activity"; and choice (D), "that," is a relative pronoun introducing a restrictive adjective subordinate clause modifying "one."

8. **C**

    Choice (C) contains the error because the subject of the verb "show" is "story," a singular noun that calls for the third person singular verb, "shows." The rest of the sentence represents correct usage. Choices (A) and (B), "those" and "their," are plural pronouns that agree with the antecedent "pioneers"; and choice (D), "us," is in the objective case because it is the indirect object in the sentence.

9. **D**

    Choice (D) presents an error in comparison, appearing to compare "farming" with "low latitudes" when what is intended is a comparison of "farming in high latitudes" with "farming in low latitudes." The corrected sentence reads: "Because of the long, cold winters and short summer growing season, farming in high latitudes is more difficult than farming in low latitudes." The other choices all represent appropriate usage in standard written English. Choice (A), "Because of," is idiomatically correct as a preposition; choice (B), "and," is a coordinating conjunction joining the nouns "winters" and "summers." Choice (C), "more difficult," is the comparative form appropriate to compare two items.

10. **D**

The error is in choice (D). The word "contestant" is a predicate nominative in the subordinate noun clause, and it must agree in number with the plural subject of the clause, the pronoun "both," to which it refers. The noun clause should, therefore, read: "that both of us could be contestants on a quiz show." Choice (A), "I," is part of the compound subject of the introductory adverb clause and is, correctly, in the nominative case. Choice (B), "were," is plural to agree with its compound subject. Choice (C), "we," is plural to agree with its compound antecedent, "sister and I," and is in the nominative case because it is the subject of the verb "hoped."

11. **A**

The error is in choice (A). The auxiliary verb "had" calls for the past participle form of the verb "break," which is "broken." All of the other choices are acceptable in standard written English. Choice (B), "that," is the correct relative pronoun to follow "vase" and introduce the subordinate adjective clause; choice (C), "had purchased," is the past perfect form of the verb to indicate action completed in the past before the action of the verb in the main clause; and choice (D), "her," is the object of the preposition "for."

12. **E**

This sentence contains no error in standard written English. Choice (A), the prepositional phrase "with whom," introduces an adjective clause modifying the word "people." The relative pronoun "whom" is in the objective case because it serves as the object of the preposition "with." The simple past tense "worked" is appropriate for choice (B); choice (C), "were engaged," is plural to agree with its subject "some"; and choice (D) is an idiomatic expression replacing the preposition "for."

13. **D**

Your reading of the sentence should indicate that choice (D), "were," presents an error in subject-verb agreement. A compound subject joined by "or" or "neither...nor" calls for a verb that agrees in number with the second part of the compound subject, which is, in this case, singular. The correct choice is the verb "was." The other choices represent correct usage. Choice (A), "Because of," is idiomatic; and choices (B) and (C) are correlative conjunctions.

14. **C**

Again the error is one of agreement of the subject and verb. Choice (C), "were," is plural; because its subject is "attack," not "reasons," which is the object of the preposition "among" and therefore cannot be the subject of the sentence, the verb should be the singular "was." Choice (A), "Among," introduces a prepositional phrase; choice (B) is an idiomatically acceptable prepositional phrase to modify the noun "reasons;" choice (D), "naval base," poses no error in usage.

15. **D**

Your analysis of this sentence should disclose an error in parallelism in choice (D). "Teaching" should be replaced by "to teach," an infinitive parallel with "to frighten." Both infinitives modify the noun "attempt." The other choices all represent standard usage in written English. Choice (A), "greater," is the comparative form of the adjective, correctly used to compare two items; choice (B), "their," is a plural possessive pronoun agreeing in number with its plural antecedent, "parents"; and choice (C), "than," is idiomatic to introduce the second part of the comparison.

16. **C**

You should recognize that the possessive pronoun in choice (C), "their," is not the appropriate pronoun to use in referring to a country. Choice (A), "of living," and choice (D), "of life expectancy," are both idiomatically acceptable prepositional phrases; choice (B), "is shown," is passive and agrees in number with its singular subject, "standard."

17. **D**

Choice (D), "white and bluish gray in color," is the third in a series of objects of the verb "has." The error lies in its lack of parallelism with the other two objects, "eyes" and "body." Corrected, the sentence reads: "The snow leopard is a wild mammal in Central Asia that has large eyes, a four-foot body, and a white and bluish gray color." The other choices are all acceptable in standard written English. Choice (A), "is," is singular to agree with its subject "leopard." Choice (B), "that has," is composed of the relative pronoun "that" referring to the noun "mammal," and the verb "has," that agrees with its subject in number. Choice (C), "and," is a coordinating conjunction correctly used to join the three objects of the verb.

18. **B**

You should recognize that choice (B), "and," is not the correct correlative conjunction to follow "either." The correct word is "or." The other choices all represent acceptable choices in standard written English. Choice (A), "a young person," is correctly placed immediately after the introductory participial phrase that modifies it; choice (C), "him," is singular to agree with its antecedent "person" and objective because it is the object of the verb "make." Choice (D), "most important," is in the superlative form because the comparison involves more than two choices.

19. **C**

Choice (C), "to fail," is incorrect in standard written English. The sentence contains two parallel ideas that should be expressed with the same grammatical form. Because "Failing" is a gerund, the "infinitive" to "fail" should be replaced with "failing" to make the construction parallel. Choice (A), "is," agrees in number with its subject, "student"; choice (B), "is," agrees in number with its subject, "Failing"; and choice (D) is singular to agree with its antecedent, "student," and indicates no sexual preference.

20. **C**

You should recognize that choice (C), "or," is in error because the correlative conjunction that should follow "neither" is "nor." All other choices are correct. Choice (A), "had grown up," is idiomatically acceptable and it and choice (B), "had been," are in the past perfect tense to indicate that the actions occurred before the action mentioned in the main clause; choice (D), "vividly," is an adverb correctly modifying the verb "portrayed."

21. **B**

As you read the sentence, you should recognize that choice (B) is incorrect because "that" is the relative pronoun that should introduce a noun clause following "reason"; another option would be to revise the sentence by omitting the words "The reason," but that is not an option provided on this test. Choice (A), "his," is the correct possessive pronoun to refer to "Jason." Choice (C), "such stage fright," is idiomatic, and choice (D) is the relative pronoun, subject, and verb of an adjective clause modifying "fright."

22. **B**

Your recognition that the word "less" is used with a singular noun and the word "fewer" is appropriate before a plural noun will lead you to locate the error in choice (B). Choice (A) is an introductory participial phrase, correctly followed by the pronoun it modifies. Choice (C) is the comparative adverb, the correct choice to compare two people ("anyone else" is singular), and choice (D) is idiomatic as a singular indefinite pronoun.

23. **C**

You should recognize that the verb "want" in choice (C) does not agree with its subject "who," a pronoun that is singular to agree with its antecedent, "adult." The word ordering used in choices (A), (B), and (D) are all idiomatic in standard written English.

24. **C**

As you read the sentence, you should recognize that the pronoun "this" in choice (C) does not have a clear antecedent in the sentence. The other choices are all correct in standard written English. Choice (A), "along with," is idiomatic and serves as one preposition. Choice (B), "those," has as its antecedent "advantages," and choice (D), "has made," is in the present perfect tense because the action began in the past and continues into the present.

25. **C**

You should find the error at choice (C), where the adverb "frequently" is needed to modify the adjective "repetitious"; "frequent" is an adjective and does not correctly modify another adjective. Choice (A), the pronoun "who," correctly refers to its antecedent "Students"; choice (B), the adverb "generally," modifies the verb; and choice (D) is a relative pronoun "that" and its verb, "is provided," that comprise the adjective clause modifying "menu."

26. **D**

Because the verb "protest" can be transitive and have a direct object, choice (D) avoids awkward wordiness and use of the unnecessary preposition "about." Choices (B) and (E) include unnecessary words and uses the pronoun "they" that has no clear antecedent; choice (C) is also unnecessarily wordy and contains the repetitious words, "builders should build."

27. **B**

Choice (B) best shows the causal relationship between sibling opportunities and their placement in the family, their abilities, and their personalities, and retains the subordination of the original sentence. Choices (A) and (E) provide dangling phrases. Choice (C) with its use of the coordinating conjunction "and" treats the lack of opportunity and its cause as if they are equal ideas and does not show the causal relationship between them, and choice (D) results in a run-on sentence.

28. **E**

> Only choice (E) corrects the two major problems in the sentence, the lack of subject-verb agreement and the lack of parallelism. In choices (A), (B), and (C), the verb "is" does not agree with its plural subject, "provisions." Choices (A) and (D) have unlike constructions serving as predicate nominatives, the noun "freedom" and the clause "that citizens are guaranteed a trial by jury." Choice (E) correctly uses the plural verb "are" to agree with the plural subject, and the predicate nominative is composed of two parallel nouns, "freedom" and "guarantee."

29. **E**

> The errors found in the original sentence, choice (A), involve parallelism and redundancy. Choice (E) uses the parallel infinitives "to entertain" and "to teach" as direct objects and eliminates the repetition created in the use of both "tried" and "attempt" in the original sentence. Choices (B) and (C) provide parallel construction, but choice (B) retains the redundancy and choice (C) incorrectly splits the infinitive "to entertain"; although choice (D) provides parallelism of the nouns "entertainment" and "attempt," the redundancy still remains, and the word order is not idiomatic.

30. **B**

> Choice (B) adequately conveys the reason for removal of the parking meters with the least wordiness. Choices (A) and (D) contain unnecessary words; choices (C) and (E) have dangling participial phrases.

31. **D**

> Choice (D), in which "Megan" correctly follows the phrase, conveys the meaning with the least wordiness. The problem with choice (A) is the introductory participial phrase; it must be eliminated or followed immediately by the word modified. Choice (B) does not solve the problem of the dangling phrase; choices (C) and (E) add words unnecessary to the meaning of the sentence.

32. **A**

> The given sentence is acceptable in standard written English. Each of the alternate choices introduces a problem. Choice (B) uses the superlative form of the adjective, "most interested," when the comparative form "more interested" is correct for the comparison of two options; choices (C) and (E) introduce a lack of parallelism; and choice (D) is not idiomatic.

33. E

The noun clause in choice (E) is idiomatically acceptable. The use of "Whether" in choices (A) and (B) leads the writer to add "or not," words that contribute nothing to the meaning and result in awkwardness of construction. In choice (C), "the fact of whether," is not idiomatic, and choice (D) with its awkward gerund phrase is also not idiomatic.

34. E

This sentence presents two problems, namely use of a preposition instead of a coordinating conjunction to join the objects of the participle "having studied" and failure to show a time relationship. Choice (E) corrects both problems. Choice (B) simply replaces the preposition "along with" by "as well as"; choice (C) unnecessarily repeats the conjunction "and" rather than using the quite appropriate series construction. None of the choices (A), (B), (C), or (D) correctly shows the time relationship.

35. B

This sentence contains the ambiguous pronoun "they," for which there is no antecedent and fails to show the relationship of the ideas expressed. Choice (B) eliminates the clause with the ambiguous pronoun and correctly expresses the reason for the sandbag placement. Choice (C) suggests that the two clauses joined by "and" are equal and does not show the subordinate relationship of the second to the first. Choice (D) introduces a dangling phrase with a coordinating conjunction, "and," that suggests the joining of equals; and choice (E) retains both errors from the original sentence.

36. A

This sentence is correct in standard written English. Choices (B) and (C) introduce unnecessary words that add nothing to the meaning and make the sentence awkward and wordy; choices (D) and (E) do not correctly show relationship.

37. C

Choice (C) shows the relationship accurately and eliminates the awkward gerund construction as the object of the preposition "despite." The adjective clause in choice (B) fails to show the relationship of the original sentence; choice (D) introduces the superfluous words "the fact that." Choice (E) inappropriately places the qualifying information in equal and parallel construction to the main idea of the sentence.

38. A

This sentence is correct in standard written English. Choices (B) and (C) lose the strength of the parallelism in choice (A). Choice (D), although containing parallel construction, is idiomatically awkward with its participial phrases. Choices (B), (C), and (E) all exhibit wordiness.

39. **D**

The original sentence, choice (A), contains the obvious and redundant words "was a man who." Choices (B), (C), and (E) are also unnecessarily verbose. Choice (D) makes the statement in the most direct way possible and represents correct standard usage.

40. **E**

Choice (E) eliminates the awkward participial phrase with its passive verb, and, in direct fashion, clearly shows the desired relationship. Choices (A), (B), and (D) retain the awkward construction; choice (C) is repetitious, wordy, and not idiomatic.

41. **C**

The error in this sentence involves the use of the pronoun "which," that refers not to a single antecedent but to the entire main clause in the sentence. A pronoun should have a single noun or pronoun as its antecedent. Choice (C) most economically shows the causal relationship of the original sentence and effectively eliminates the pronoun altogether. Although choice (B) eliminates unnecessary words, the basic problem remains; choice (D) is also wordy and repetitive; and choice (E) is not idiomatic.

42. **B**

The problem in this sentence involves the need for consistent pronoun use and for parallel construction. Because the portion of the sentence not underlined uses the pronouns "you" and "your," the first part of the sentence must also use the second person pronoun. Choice (B) alone accomplishes that consistency and yet retains parallel construction.

43. **A**

This sentence contains no error in standard written English. Each of the possible revisions makes no real improvement, and choice (B) adds an error in subject-verb agreement. Choice (C) creates confusion in pronoun reference with the addition of "themselves," and choices (D) and (E) are not idiomatic.

44. **D**

This exercise is a sentence fragment, not a complete sentence. The subject has no verb but is followed by two subordinate clauses. To correct this sentence, eliminate the subordinating conjunction, "where," and the subject of the subordinate clause, "he," to provide a predicate for the subject, "Father Junipero Serra." Choice (D) accomplishes what is necessary. Choices (B) and (C) result in run-on sentences; and choice (E) substitutes a verbal phrase for the necessary predicate and does not solve the problem of the fragment.

PPST Essay Scoring Guide

The PPST essay sections are scored by two writing experts on the basis of the criteria outlined below. In addition to comparing your essay to those included in our practice tests, you may use these guidelines to estimate your score on this section. Remember that your score is the sum of the scores of two writing experts, so provided you respond to the assigned topic, your score will fall somewhere between two and twelve. Scores will be assigned based on the following guidelines:

6 An essay receiving a score of 6 may contain one or two spelling or punctuation errors, but overall it exhibits a high degree of proficiency and thought on the assigned topic.

An essay scoring a 6

- is both well organized and well developed

- engages important concepts and explains them clearly

- varies expression and language

- demonstrates deft use of language

- is virtually free from errors involving syntax and structure

5 An essay receiving a score of 5 exhibits a high degree of proficiency and thought on the assigned topic, however it contains a number of minor mistakes.

An essay scoring a 5

- is both well organized and well developed

- engages important concepts and explains them

- varies expression and language somewhat

- demonstrates deft use of language

- is virtually free from errors involving syntax and structure

4 An essay receiving a score of 4 responds to the assignment and exhibits some degree of deeper understanding.

An essay scoring a 4

- demonstrates adequate organization and development

- engages and explains some important concepts, but not all that are necessary to demonstrate full understanding

- exhibits adequate use of language

- contains some syntactical and structural errors, without excessive repetition of those errors

3 An essay receiving a score of 3 exhibits some degree of understanding, but its response to the topic is obviously deficient.

An essay scoring a 3 is deficient in one or more of the following areas:

- insufficient organization or development

- insufficient engagement or explanation of important concepts

- consistent repetition of syntactical or structural errors

- redundant or unsuitable word choice

2 An essay receiving a score of 2 exhibits limited understanding and its response to the topic is seriously deficient.

An essay scoring a 2 is deficient in one or more of the following areas:

- weak organization or development

- very few pertinent details

- consistent and serious errors in syntax, structure

- consistent and serious errors in word choice

1 An essay receiving a score of 1 exhibits a lack of basic writing skills.

An essay scoring a 1 is disorganized, undeveloped, contains consistent repetition of errors, or is incomprehensible.

SAMPLE SCORED ESSAYS WITH EXPLANATIONS

Essay #1—(Score = 5-6)

Happiness, freedom, and peace of mind are goals that everyone wants in life. Yet they are very abstract and difficult to measure. Happiness is a frame of mind that means we enjoy what we do. Freedom is the ability to do what we want, although it is limited to not doing anything that takes away freedom from other people. Peace of mind is a feeling that we are all right and that the world is a good place. How does one achieve these important goals? They can best be acquired when we try to give them to other people rather than when we try to get them ourselves.

The people who feel happiest, experience freedom, and enjoy peace of mind are most often people who are concentrating on helping others. In 1997, Mother Theresa of Calcutta died, but she remains an example for me today. Because she took care of homeless people and was so busy, she probably didn't have time to worry about whether she was happy, free, and peaceful. She always looked cheerful in her pictures.

There are other people in history who seem to have attained the goals we all want by helping others. Jane Addams established Hull House in the slums of Chicago to help other people, and her life must have brought her great joy and peace of mind. She gave to the mothers in the neighborhood freedom to work and know that their children were being taken care of; and Jane Addams apparently had the freedom to do what she wanted to help them.

On the other hand, there are people in literature who directly tried to find happiness, freedom, and peace of mind; and they were often miserable. The two people who come to mind are Scrooge and Silas Marner. Scrooge had been selfish in the past, and he wouldn't give anything for the poor. He wasn't a bit happy even at Christmas. Later, when he began helping others, he became happy. Silas Marner was very selfish, hoarding his money and thinking it would make him happy. Only when he tried to make little Eppie happy was he able to be happy, too, even without his stolen money.

If we want to achieve happiness, freedom, and peace of mind, we should get involved in helping others so much that we forget ourselves and find joy from the people we are helping. When we try to give away the qualities we want, we find them ourselves.

ANALYSIS

Essay I has a score range of 5-6. It is well organized, with the opening paragraph serving as the introduction and stating the thesis of the paper in its last sentence. Defining the terms serves as an effective way to introduce the paper. The last paragraph concludes the essay, restating the thesis. The three middle paragraphs support the thesis with specific examples that are adequately explained and have a single focus. Transitions effectively relate the ideas. The sentence structure varies, and the vocabulary is effective. There are no major errors in sentence construction, usage, or mechanics. Although the essay would benefit from some minor revisions, it is well done considering the 30 minute time limit imposed upon the writer.

Essay #2—(Score = 4–5)

I think there is a basic problem in this quotation. I do not think that anyone can give happiness, freedom, or peace of mind to anybody. Those things have to come from inside the person, not from someone else, no matter how hard they try to give them to him. That means that the person trying to make someone else happy, free, and peacefull will be frusterated because he really can't do what he wants to do. And if he is frustrated, he won't be happy, free, and peacefull himself.

I think an example of this in history is when the missionaries went to Oregon in early United States history and tried to help the Indians, and the Indians got smallpox and then killed the missionaries. So no one was happy, free, or had a peacefull mind. That's happened with other missionaries in China and other places, too. It just wasn't possible to give happiness, freedom, and peace of mind to anyone else, and the people giving it often lost it themselves.

I know an example from my own life. My parents have tried very hard to make my little sister happy. They have done everything for her and, I'll tell you, she's so spoiled that nothing makes her happy. When they gave her a new bicycle, she was unhappy because she didn't like the color. I'd think she'd be glad just to have a nice bike. I know they never gave me one as nice as they gave her.

So I really think that whoever said the quotation was not right at all. You can't give happiness, freedom, and peace of mind to someone else at all, so you can't get those qualities by giving them.

ANALYSIS

Essay II has a score range of 4-5. It is organized clearly, with an introduction in the first paragraph, a clear statement of thesis, and a conclusion in the last paragraph. Although a few sentences are not relevant to the topic being discussed, the writer attempts to maintain one focus and to support his position with specific details. Paragraphing is good. The use of "I think" and "I know" weakens the essay, and pronouns without clear antecedents occur throughout the essay. Sentence patterns and vocabulary lack variety, and there are some errors in spelling, usage, and sentence construction. Transitions are also lacking.

Essay #3—(Score = 3–4)

I agree with the idea that you don't get happiness without trying to make other people happy. But I'm not sure that you *always* get happiness when you give it to someone else, you may try to make someone else happy and you're miserable even though you do it.

For instance, I've tried many times to make my grandmother happy. No matter what I do, she complains about me and tells my mother I should do everything different. She didn't even act like she liked my Christmas present last year, and she sure didn't make me happy either. Its just the opposite when you let someone else be free he takes away from your freedom and you don't feel free at all.

So, all in all, I think maybe sometimes you get happiness and freedom when you give it to others but most of the time things just get worse.

ANALYSIS

Essay III has a score range of 3-4. The writer attempts to introduce his topic in the first paragraph, but the thesis is not stated precisely. Although the last paragraph serves as a conclusion, it, too, lacks clarity and singleness of purpose. Paragraph 2 gives a specific illustration to develop the theme, but paragraph 3 lacks specific detail. Although there are some transitional words, the essay rambles with words and ideas repeated. In addition, the essay contains errors in usage, sentence construction, and mechanics.

Essay #4—(Score = 1–2)

I don't think you can give happiness or piece of mind to anyone maybe you can give freedom. My folks are giving me more freedom now that I useta have, so you can give that to someone else. But nobody knows what makes me happy so I can be happy only if I decide what it is I want and go out and get it for myself. And then I'll have piece of mind, too.

Happiness don't come much but I'm happyest when I'm with a bunch of friends and we are having fun together. That's what friends like being together with other people. but nobody gives me that kind of happiness I have to find a bunch of friends I like and than be with them. And thats real freedom, too, but nobody gave it to any of us. My folks think they can make me happy by giving me gifts but usually I don't like what they give me, and there idea of going for a ride or eating together isn't my idea of being happy.

ANALYSIS

Essay IV has a score range of 1-2. The writer states the thesis in the first sentence and maintains a consistent position, but fails to have an introductory paragraph; and there is no conclusion at all. The writer does give some specific details but rambles, failing to use the details effectively to support his thesis. In addition, there are serious errors in sentence construction like the run-on sentence in the beginning of the paper. There are also major problems with spelling, usage, and mechanics.

Practice Test 4

Praxis I PPST
Computer-Based Format

Section I: Reading Comprehension

TIME: *75 Minutes*
46 Questions

DIRECTIONS: A number of questions follow each of the passages in the reading section. Answer the questions by choosing the best answer from the five choices given.

Question 1 refers to the following statement:

The funnel cloud appeared capricious with its destruction, darting from one street to another, obliterating any object in its path.

1. In this context the word "capricious" means

    (A) unpredictable.   (D) adaptable.

    (B) intense.   (E) belligerent.

    (C) threatening.

Questions 2 and 3 refer to the following passage:

Many times different animal species can inhabit the same environment and share a common food supply without conflict, because each species occupies a separate niche defined by its specific physical adaptations and habits. For example, the little green heron, equipped with legs too short to do much wading, fishes from shore for its food. The Louisiana heron wades out a little further into the shallows during the daytime hours, while the yellow-crowned night heron stalks the same shallows after dark. Diet also varies in size and amount, according to the size of the bird.

2. According to the passage, which one of the following basic assumptions can be made about how a bird's diet varies according to size?

    (A) Small birds can eat twice their weight.

    (B) The larger birds can swallow larger fish and water snakes.

(C) Birds have to adapt their diets according to what is available within their environment.

(D) Fishing from shore is difficult for smaller birds.

(E) The type of bill is an adaptation for the type of food the animal eats.

3. The title that best expresses the ideas of this passage is

(A) The Heron Family.

(B) Diet Variations of Birds.

(C) A Separate Niche at the Same Pond.

(D) Long-Legged Fishing.

(E) Fishing Habits of the Heron.

Questions 4 and 5 refer to the following passage:

Most Americans assume that English is the language of the United States, but they are naive to imagine that every American speaks it fluently. According to the 1980 U.S. census, 11 percent of Americans come from non-English-speaking homes. Over one percent of the U.S. population speaks English not well or not at all.

Non-English speakers reside in all 50 states. In some 23 states, the non-English speaking minority makes up 10 percent or more of the total population. All of American history is characterized by this language phenomenon. For those misguided Americans who believe that their country is and always has been a monolingual country, the facts just do not support their claim.

4. This selection implies that the author's attitude toward a belief that America is a monolingual country is one of

(A) impartiality.   (D) anger.

(B) indifference.   (E) optimism.

(C) criticism.

5. Which of the following statements can best be inferred from the information given?

(A) Non-English languages are found primarily along the East and West Coast areas.

(B) No indicators suggest that the percentages of non-English speaking populations will decrease.

(C) This language situation is relatively new to the United States.

(D) In the next decade the United States should become primarily monolingual.

(E) The United States is comparable to Great Britain in percentage of non-English speakers.

Questions 6 to 8 refer to the following passage:

The Indians of California had five varieties of acorn which they used as their principle source of food. This was a noteworthy accomplishment in technology since they first had to make the acorn edible. A process had to be developed for leaching out the poisonous tannic acid. They ground the acorns into a meal and then filtered it many times with water. This had to be done through sand or through tightly woven baskets. Early Indian campsites reveal the evidence of the acorn-processing labor necessary to provide enough food for their subsistence. The women patiently ground acorns into meal with stone pestles. The result, a pinkish flour that was cooked into a mush or thin soup, formed the bulk of their diet.

6. The central idea of the passage is the early Indians of California

(A) had ample food sources.

(B) left evidence of their meal processing at ancient campsites.

(C) differed from other Indians in their use of natural resources.

(D) contributed distinctive talents and technological expertise in providing food sources.

(E) produced finely crafted woven baskets.

7. According to the passage, which of the following was a technological innovation developed by the early California Indians in the production of food?

(A) Irrigation of crops

(B) Grinding meal

(C) Filtration system

(D) Dams

(E) Removal of tannic acid

8. It can be inferred from the passage that the early Indians faced a major problem in their production of food. What was it?

(A) They needed many pounds of acorns to produce enough meal.

(B) Acorns had to be carried a great distance to their campsites for grinding.

(C) The acorn grinding took many hours of hard labor.

(D) Acorns were scarce.

(E) It was difficult to filter the meal without losing it.

Question 9 refers to the following statement:

There was a vestige of the original manuscript for us to review.

9. In the context of the passage, "vestige" means

(A) reproduction.   (D) engraving.

(B) cartoon.   (E) trace.

(C) counterfeit.

Questions 10 to 12 refer to the following passage:

Beginning readers, and those who are experiencing difficulty with reading, benefit from assisted reading. During assisted reading the teacher orally reads a passage with a student or students. The teacher fades in and out of the reading act. For example, the teacher lets his or her voice drop to a whisper when students are reading on their own at an acceptable rate and lets his/her voice rise to say the words clearly when the students are having difficulty.

Students who are threatened by print, read word-by-word, or rely on grapho-phonemic cues will be helped by assisted reading. These students are stuck on individual language units which can be as small as a single letter or as large as phrases or sentences. As Frank Smith (1977) and other reading educators have noted, speeding up reading, not slowing it down, helps the reader make sense of a passage: This strategy allows students to concentrate on meaning as the short-term memory is not overload by focusing on small language units. As the name implies, assisted reading lets the reader move along without being responsible for every language unit; the pressure is taken off the student. Consequently, when the reading act is sped up, it sounds more like language, and students can begin to integrate the cueing systems of semantics and syntax along with grapho-phonemics.

10. As a strategy, assisted reading is best for

    (A) beginning readers who are relying on grapho-phonemic cues.

    (B) learning disabled readers who are experiencing neurological deficits.

    (C) beginning readers who are relying on phonographic cues.

    (D) remedial readers who are experiencing difficulty with silent reading.

    (E) beginning readers who are experiencing difficulty with silent reading.

11. Language units as presented in the passage refer to

    (A) individual letters, syllables, or phrases.

    (B) individual letters, syllables, or sentences.

    (C) individual letters, phrases, or paragraphs.

    (D) individual letters, phrases, or sentences.

    (E) individual letters, sentences, or paragraphs.

12. According to the passage, to make sense of a passage a reader must

    (A) focus on small language units.

    (B) overload short-term memory.

    (C) slow down when reading.

    (D) read word-by-word.

    (E) speed up the reading act.

Questions 13 to 16 refer to the following passage:

The information about the comparison of the technology (duplex versus one-way video and two-way audio) and the comparison of site classes versus regular classes tends to indicate that although there was not much of an apparent difference between classes and technology, student participation and student involvement were viewed as important components in any teaching/learning setting. For the future, perhaps revisiting what learning is might be helpful so that this component of distance learning can be more adequately addressed. The question remains whether or not student participation can be equated with learning. Participation per se does not demonstrate learning. A more rigorous instrument which assesses and determines learning may need to be addressed with future distance learning studies.

13. "Duplex", as used in the passage, suggests which of the following when comparing distance learning technology?

   (A) One-way video and two-way audio

   (B) One-way video and one-way audio

   (C) Two-way video and two-way audio

   (D) Two-way video and one-way audio

   (E) Two-way video

14. Which of the following is the most complete and accurate definition of the term "rigorous" as used in the passage?

   (A) Harsh   (D) Dogmatic

   (B) Austere   (E) Precise

   (C) Uncompromising

15. The author of the passage would tend to agree with which of the following statements?

   (A) Learning consists of more than student participation.

   (B) Duplex technology is better than one-way video and two-way audio.

   (C) Student participation and student involvement are not important in learning.

   (D) An instrument which assesses and demonstrates learning is not currently available.

   (E) A review of learning is not important as the topic has been thoroughly researched.

16. The primary purpose of the passage is to

   (A) delineate the issues in distance learning.

   (B) note student participation in distance learning and question this role in learning.

   (C) detail the comparison of site classes versus regular classes.

   (D) share information about duplex technology versus one-way video and two-way audio.

   (E) request an assessment instrument which includes a learning component.

Questions 17 and 18 refer to the following passage:

Eyes are. There is no doubt about it—they are certainly in existence. Eyes have many purposes in this world. Eyes are to see with, to be seen, to be heard, and even to be felt. I suppose they could be tasted, and in some cases could be smelled. Now anything that can satisfy all five of the body's senses must have a great deal of value.

To begin with, I shall start with the thing that enables us to see the other kinds of eyes, and that is the eye—e-y-e. It is a very delicate and effeminate mechanism, as any optician or optometrist will tell you. However, if one of these is not close at hand, just consult a hygiene, psychology, or physics text-book. It (the eye) is also very intricate; the cornea, iris, retina, and crystal-line lens are a few of its main members. Each is arranged very neatly in its proper place, where it helps form a part of a very necessary whole.

17. Which of the following is the most complete and accurate definition of the term "ef-feminate" as used in the passage?

   (A) Womanish

   (B) Unmanly

   (C) Emasculate

   (D) Soft, delicate

   (E) Female

18. The author's attitude about the subject discussed is best described as

   (A) flippant disregard.

   (B) moral indignation.

   (C) critical.

   (D) imaginative.

   (E) humorous.

Questions 19 to 21 refer to the following passage:

The Matsushita Electric Industrial Co. in Japan has developed a computer program that can use photographs of faces to predict the aging process and, also, how an unborn child will look. The system can show how a couple will look after 40 years of marriage and how newlyweds' future children will look. The computer analyzes facial characteristics from a photograph based on shading and color differences, and then creates a three-dimensional model in its memory. The system consists of a personal computer with a program and circuit board and will be marketed by the Matsushita Company soon.

19. The main idea in the passage you just read is about a computer that

   (A) shows the aging process.

   (B) chooses the right mate.

   (C) predicts the number of children for newlyweds.

   (D) predicts the looks of future children as well as their parents.

   (E) analyzes photographs.

20. The new computer program developed in Japan uses

   (A) a three-dimensional face model.

   (B) photographs of faces to predict the aging process and looks of an unborn child.

   (C) shading and color differences in photographs.

   (D) a personal computer and circuit board.

   (E) facial characteristics from a photograph.

21. What might result from their new computer system developed in Japan?

   (A) The U.S. will develop an even more sophisticated computer system.

   (B) Competition among trading partners of Japan will be keener.

   (C) Japan's economy will skyrocket.

   (D) The trade imbalance between Japan and the U.S. will increase.

   (E) The next computer system Japan will develop will be even more refined and sophisticated.

Questions 22 and 23 refers to the following passage:

On September 17, 1991, a communications power failure brought New York's three big airports to a virtual stop for several hours. Air traffic control centers communicate with planes through a network of radio towers linked to them by phone. Due to this power failure, local air traffic centers could not communicate properly amongst themselves or with other U.S. airports.

22. What could have happened to airplanes en route to New York when the power failure took place?

   (A) They could have turned back from where they came.

   (B) They could have encircled New York until the control towers were able to communicate with the pilots.

(C) They could have been diverted to other airports by other air control centers.

(D) They could have slowed down their speed while waiting for the power failure to be corrected.

(E) They could have landed, as usual, at the New York airports.

23. What can air travelers learn from this power failure incident?

(A) Expect delays or being diverted to other airports for landing.

(B) Take the train instead.

(C) Prepare for the unexpected each time you fly.

(D) A power failure in New York can happen again.

(E) Flight delays are due to failure in communications systems.

Questions 24 to 27 refer to the following passage:

New health research shows that regular vigorous exercise during the middle and late years of life not only keeps the heart healthy, but also may protect against colon cancer, one of the major killers in the U.S. The researchers in the study compared the rate of colon cancer among those who were physically inactive with those who were either active or highly active. Seventeen thousand one hundred forty eight men, ages 30 to 79, were covered in the study. Among men judged to be inactive there were 55 cases of colon cancer; among those moderately active, there were 11; and only 10 cases of colon cancer were found among the very active ones.

24. Which of the following makes an appropriate title for the passage?

(A) New Health Research on Colon Cancer

(B) Colon Cancer: A Major Killer in the U.S.

(C) Regular Vigorous Exercise May Prevent Colon Cancer

(D) Results of Research on Colon Cancer

(E) A Prescription for Preventing Colon Cancer

25. Based on the result of the research, what generalization regarding colon cancer for men and women can be made?

(A) Women are more susceptible to disease than are men.

(B) Women are more likely to participate in surveys.

(C) Young men are more susceptible to colon cancer than are all women.

(D) Men are more inactive than women.

(E) Regular exercise is highly beneficial for older men and women.

26. What important message did you get from the passage?

(A) Regular exercise is good for the health.

(B) Only middle-aged men get colon cancer.

(C) Women need not worry about colon cancer.

(D) Regular exercise is needed only by older people.

(E) Children are too young to exercise.

27. What is the major limitation of the study?

(A) It did not explain "vigorous exercise."

(B) It did not include children.

(C) It did not include men below 30.

(D) It did not include women of the same age group.

(E) It did not include a large enough sample.

Questions 28 to 33 are based on the following passage.

Cacti and other succulent plants originate in areas where water is only occasionally available and are, therefore, conditioned to deal with long periods of drought. They possess structural modifications enabling them to store moisture for use in times of scarcity.

Such adaptations may be similar in both groups. (All cacti are succulents but not all succulents are cacti.) Storage areas include thickened leaves, stems, and corms. Leaves, which transpire precious moisture, may be eliminated altogether (with the stem taking over the process of photosynthesis), or the moisture in the leaves may be protected from evaporation by a leathery surface or covered with wiry or velvety hairs, thick spines, or even with a powdery coating.

The very shape of many succulents provides the same protection; globular and columnar forms offer the least exposed area to the drying effects of sun and wind.

Many times there are "look-alikes" in the two groups. Certain cacti coming from the New World closely resemble counterparts in the Euphorbias of Africa.

How then do we differentiate between cacti and other succulents? It is not always easy. Presence or absence of leaves can be helpful; size and brilliance of flowers are also helpful, but the real test comes by learning to recognize the areole.

The areole is possessed by cacti alone and consists of cushion-like modifications on the body of the cactus from which arise spines, hairs (and the barbed hairs or spines of Opuntia), flowers, fruit, and often new growth.

The flowers of cacti are usually more conspicuous and most often appear from areoles near the top of the plant. In other succulents they are inclined to be less showy and more likely to emerge from between the leaves or from the base.

In addition, with a very minor possible exception (a form of Rhipsalis), all cacti are native to the Western Hemisphere. It is sometimes hard to believe this because of the vast areas of escaped cacti in many parts of the world today.

The majority of other succulents (excluding Agave, Echeveria, Sedum, Sempervivum and a few others) are indigenous to Africa and a few scattered areas in the Eastern Hemisphere.

Both cacti and other succulents are excellent subjects for the outdoor garden, greenhouse, or windowsill. They require a minimum of care, provided that they have a requisite amount of sunlight and that their condition of hardiness is respected.

28. Which of the following is the best title for the passage?

(A) Succulents and Non-Succulents

(B) Regions of the World and their Vegetation

(C) Distinguishing Between Succulents and Cacti

(D) Characteristics of Cacti and Other Succulents

(E) Subjects for the Outdoor Garden

29. Which features from the list below best distinguish cacti from other succulents?

(A) Absence of leaves; presence of areoles; large, brilliant flowers; nativity to the Western Hemisphere.

(B) The flowers of cacti are usually more conspicuous and most often appear near the top of the plant; the areole is possessed by cacti alone.

(C) The areole; presence of leaves; flowers which are likely to emerge from between the leaves or from the base.

(D) Presence or absence of leaves; showy flowers which always appear at the top of the plant; indigenous to Africa and a few scattered areas in the Eastern Hemisphere.

(E) The majority of other succulents are indigenous to Africa and a few scattered areas in the Eastern Hemisphere.

30. Which of the following statements best describes the attitude of the author toward cacti and succulents?

(A) Cacti are to be chosen over succulents for the home.

(B) Either are excellent subjects to study in the wild, but to preserve their beauty they should not be removed to the home.

(C) Both are excellent subjects for the outdoor garden, greenhouse, or windowsill.

(D) Both feature interesting adaptations; the cacti is the preferred.

(E) Both are excellent subjects for botanists to study.

31. The most compelling reason for choosing cacti over other succulents for a windowsill would be which of the following?

(A) Cacti require less care than do other succulents.

(B) The shape of the cacti is more appealing than that of the other succulents.

(C) Succulents from the Eastern Hemisphere do not adapt well to the Western Hemisphere.

(D) The flowers of cacti are usually more conspicuous and most often appear from areoles near the top of the plant.

(E) The flowers of cacti are usually more conspicuous and most often appear between the leaves or at the base.

32. Which of the following would probably best describe the author's reaction to the many laws being enacted to protect the cacti and to prevent their being removed from desert areas or vandalized?

    (A) Apathy

    (B) Confusion

    (C) Despair

    (D) Understanding

    (E) Distaste

33. According to the passage, which of the following statements are true?

    I.   The areole distinguishes cacti from other succulents.

    II. Cactus flowers are more conspicuous and tend to emerge from between the leaves or near the base.

    III. The adaptations to conserve moisture are not very similar in cacti and other succulents.

    (A) I and III only

    (B) II only

    (C) I and II only

    (D) III only

    (E) I only

Questions 34 to 40 are based on the following passage written by Martin Luther King, Jr.

1   We cannot walk alone, and as we walk, we must make the pledge that we shall always march ahead. We cannot turn back. There are those who are asking the devotees of civil rights: "When will you be satisfied?" We can never be satisfied as long as the Negro is the victim of unspeakable horrors

5   of police brutality. We can never be satisfied as long as our bodies, heavy with the fatigue of travel, cannot gain lodging in the motels of the highways and the hotels of the cities. We can never be satisfied as long as the Negro's basic mobility is from a smaller ghetto to a larger one. We can never be satisfied as long as our children are stripped of their selfhood and robbed of

10 their dignity by signs stating "For Whites Only."

    We cannot be satisfied so long as the Negro in Mississippi cannot vote and the Negro in New York believes he has nothing for which to vote. No, no, we will not be satisfied until justice rolls down like water and righteousness like a mighty stream.

15   I am not unmindful that some of you have come here out of great trials and tribulations. Some of you have come from narrow jail cells. Some of you have come from areas where your quest for freedom left you battered by the storms of persecution and staggered by the winds of police brutality. You have been the veterans of creative suffering. Continue to work with the faith

20   that unearned suffering is redemptive.

Go back to Mississippi. Go back to Alabama; go back to South Carolina; go back to Georgia; go back to Louisiana; go back to the slums and ghettoes of our northern cities knowing that somehow this situation can and will be changed. Let us not wallow in the valley of despair.

25   I say to you today, my friends, even though we face the difficulties of today and tomorrow, I still have a dream. It is a dream deeply rooted in the American dream. I have a dream that one day this Nation will rise up and live out the true meaning of its creeds—"we hold these truths to be self-evident that all men are created equal."

30   I have a dream that one day on the red hills of Georgia the sons of slaves and the sons of former slaveowners will be able to sit down together at the table of brotherhood. I have a dream that one day even the state of Mississippi, sweltering with the heat of injustice, sweltering with the heat of oppression, will be transformed into an oasis of freedom and justice.

35   I have a dream that my four little children will one day live in a Nation where they will not be judged by the color of their skins, but by the conduct of their character.

I have a dream that one day in Alabama, with this vicious racist, its Governor, having his lips dripping the words of interposition and nullifica-

40   tion—one day right there in Alabama, little black boys and black girls will be able to join hands with little white boys and little white girls as brothers and sisters.

I have a dream that one day every valley shall be exalted: every hill and mountain shall be made low, the rough places will be made plane, the

45   crooked places will be made straight and the glory of the Lord shall be revealed and all flesh shall see it together.

50 This is our hope. This is the faith that I go back to the South with. With this faith, we will be able to hew out of the mountains of despair a stone of hope. With this faith, we will be able to transform the jangling discord of our Nation into a beautiful symphony of brotherhood. With this faith, we will be able to work together; to play together; to struggle together; to go to jail together; to stand up for freedom together knowing that we will be free one day....

34. In line 39 the word "interposition" most nearly means

    (A) a mixing, a conglomeration.

    (B) a lofty height or position.

    (C) a coming together, a union.

    (D) a uniting.

    (E) an intervention.

35. In lines 13–14 the words "justice rolls down like water and righteousness like a mighty stream" can best be described as

    (A) onomatopoeic words.

    (B) an alliterative expression.

    (C) an understatement.

    (D) an analogy.

    (E) a fantasy.

36. The Southern states, the slums, and the ghettos in the fourth paragraph were listed

    (A) in order to show that though the United States is large, racial inequality is limited to two main areas.

    (B) in order to name the areas from which most of the audience came.

    (C) in order to single out areas where political leaders were most biased.

    (D) to warn those areas of the violence planned.

    (E) to remind people in those areas that even though times may be rough, not to give up.

37. King reminded the audience that "unearned suffering is redemptive" in line 20. The best explanation for this statement is that

    (A) some suffering is earned; it is deserved.

(B) some suffering is justified; it is purifying, as such.

(C) unearned suffering is cruel and unforgivable.

(D) unearned suffering is desirable.

(E) some undeserved suffering is freeing and releasing.

38. The "old saying" which best fits lines 36–38 is

(A) "A soft answer turneth away wrath."

(B) "You can't judge a book by its cover."

(C) "Birds of a feather flock together."

(D) "Let sleeping dogs lie."

(E) "A good name is rather to be chosen than great riches."

39. King compares his audience to those who had fought in great battles by calling them

(A) veterans.   (D) flesh.

(B) battered.   (E) devotees.

(C) staggered.

40. King used the analogy of winds for police brutality because winds

(A) rise up and then die.

(B) turn first one way and then another.

(C) are easy to protect oneself against.

(D) can be harnessed and used as a windmill.

(E) when strong can be damaging and a fearful obstacle

Read the passage below; then answer the four questions that follow.

The price of cleaning up the environment after oil spills is on the increase, especially after the recent spill off the U.S. Gulf Coast that created miles of sludge-covered beach. While numerous smaller spills have occurred along the coast of California, none have been as disastrous as the spills in Alaska and the Gulf Coast. Tides and prevailing winds carried much of this oil to shore in a matter of days. Workers tried to contain the oil with weighted, barrel-shaped plastic tubes stretched along the sand near the water.

They hoped to minimize the damage. Generally, the barriers were success-ful, but there remained many miles of oil-covered sand. Cleanup crews shov-eled the oil-covered sand into plastic bags for removal.

Coastal states are responding to the problem in several ways. California is considering the formation of a department of oceans to oversee protec-tion programs and future cleanups. Several states called for a commission of independent experts to recommend solutions, while other states have suggested training the National Guard in cleanup procedures. Other states are calling for the creation of an oil spill trust fund large enough to cover the costs of a major spill. Still other states are demanding federal action and funding. Regardless of the specific programs that may be enacted by the various states or the federal government, continued offshore drilling and the shipping of oil in huge tankers creates a constant threat to the nation's shoreline.

41. Which oil spill affected area is not mentioned in the passage?

(A) Pacific Coast

(B) Alaskan coast

(C) California coast

(D) Florida Coast

(E) Gulf Coast

42. What was the purpose of the barrel-shaped plastic tubes?

(A) To keep sightseers away from the oil

(B) To keep oil-soaked animals off the beach

(C) To force the oil to soak into the sand

(D) To keep the oil from spreading on the beach

(E) To clean the oil saturated water.

43. Which of the following solutions is NOT discussed in the passage?

(A) Create an oil cleanup trust fund

(B) Increase federal funding for cleanups

(C) Reduce oil production

    (D) Use the National Guard for cleanups

    (E) A special commission of independent experts

44. What is the author's opinion of the hazards created by oil spills?

    (A) Oil spills must be expected if the present methods of production and shipment continue.

    (B) Oil spills are the result of untrained crews.

    (C) Oil spills would not be a problem if the government was better prepared to clean up.

    (D) Oil spills are the responsibility of foreign oil producers.

    (E) Oil spills are just part of the cost of doing business.

Read the index below; then answer the two questions that follow.

> Gloves, 59
> Goggles, 59
> Grinders, portable, 66
> Grinding operations, 126–140
>   grinding wheels, 126–129
>   selecting and using the wheel, 129–140
> Grinding wheel selection and use, 129–140
>   center punch sharpening, 133
>   chisel head grinding, 135
>   grinding metal stock, 131–133
>   hand sharpening twist drills, 138
>   installing the wheel, 130
>   screwdriver tip dressing, 133
>   sharpening a twist drill by machine, 139
>   sharpening a twist drill for drilling brass, 139
>   sharpening metal-cutting chisels, 136–138
>   thinning the web of a twist drill, 139
>   tin snips sharpening, 134
>   truing and dressing the wheel, 131
> Grinding wheels, 126–129
>   markings and composition, 127
>   sizes and shapes, 127

45. To which page(s) would one turn for information on how to install a grinding wheel?

    (A) 126–140   (D) 126–129

    (B) 136–138   (E) 66

(C) 130

46. Which of the following best describes the organizational scheme used to index the section dealing with grinding wheel selection and use?

(A) by type of wheel

(B) by physical characteristics

(C) by task

(D) by type of drill

(E) by page sequence

Section II: Mathematics

TIME: *75 Minutes*
46 Questions

DIRECTIONS: Each of the questions or incomplete statements below is followed by five suggested answers or completions. Select the one that is best in each case.

1. The cost of gas for heating a house in Riverview, Florida is $1.83 per cubic foot. What is the monthly gas bill if the customer uses 145 cubic feet?

    (A) $265.35   (D) $79.23

    (B) $145.00   (E) $200.00

    (C) $183.00

2. Which of the following figures below represent simple closed curves?

    (A) a and b   (D) d and e

    (B) a, b, and c   (E) c, d, and e

    (C) c and d

3. The wear-out mileage of a certain tire is normally distributed with a mean of 30,000 miles and a standard deviation of 2,500 miles, as shown below. What will be the percentage of tires that will last at least 30,000 miles?

    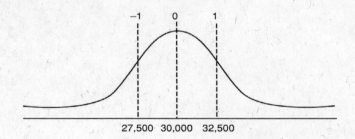

(A) 40% (D) 55%

(B) 45% (E) 60%

(C) 50%

4. How many lines of symmetry, if any, does the following figure have?

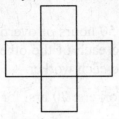

(A) 1 (D) 4

(B) 2 (E) 5

(C) 3

5. Suppose a person 2 m tall casts a shadow 1 m long when a tree has an 8 m shadow. How high is the tree?

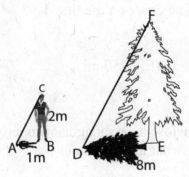

(A) 8 m (D) 16 m

(B) 10 m (E) 18 m

(C) 14 m

6. How many 12 oz. cans of orange juice would it take to give 75 people an 8 oz. cup of orange juice?

(A) 112 cans (D) 900 cans

(B) 75 cans (E) 50 cans

(C) 600 cans

7. A car rental agency charges $139 per week plus $0.08 per mile for an average size car. How far can you travel to the nearest mile on a maximum budget of $350?

   (A) 2,637 mi.   (D) 1,737 mi.

   (B) 2,640 mi.   (E) 4,375 mi.

   (C) 2,110 mi.

8. Suppose 4 people have to split 50 hours of overtime. Twice the number of hours must be assigned to one worker as to each of the other three. Find the number of hours of overtime that will be assigned to each worker.

   (A) 10 hrs. for the first three workers; 20 hrs. for the 4th worker

   (B) 8 hrs. for the first three workers; 16 hrs. for the 4th worker

   (C) 9 hrs. for the first three workers; 18 hrs. for the 4th worker

   (D) 11 hrs. for the first three workers; 22 hrs. for the 4th worker

   (E) 12 hrs. for the first three workers; 24 hrs. for the 4th worker

9. Peter took a 1,500 mile trip in 5 days. Each day, he drove 30 miles more than the day before. How many miles did he cover on the first day?

   (A) 375 mi.   (D) 240 mi.

   (B) 294 mi.   (E) 250 mi.

   (C) 230 mi.

10. Mr. Reagan needs 75 m to enclose his rectangular property. If the length of the property is 5 m more than the width, what are the dimensions of his property? Note the figure below.

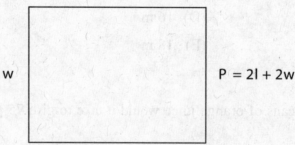

$$w \qquad\qquad P = 2l + 2w$$

$$l = w + 5$$

   (A) $w = 16.25$ m; $l = 21.25$ m

   (B) $w = 18.25$ m; $l = 19.25$ m

   (C) $w = 13.00$ m; $l = 24.50$ m

(D) $w = 17.50$ m; $l = 20.00$ m

(E) $w = 35.00$ m; $l = 40.00$ m

11. Which of the following sets is graphed below?

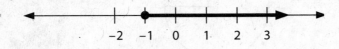

(A) $\{x \mid x \geq -1\}$ (D) $\{x \mid x < -1\}$

(B) $\{x \mid x > -1\}$ (E) $\{x \mid x \neq -1\}$

(C) $\{x \mid x \leq -1\}$

12. Sal has a set of blocks. If 8 percent of this collection is shown in the box below, how many blocks did Sal have?

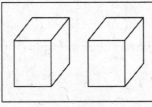

(A) 8   (D) 64

(B) 16   (E) 100

(C) 25

13. Solve the following problem: $|x - 3| < 2$

(A) $-5 < x < 5$ (D) $1 < x < 5$

(B) $x = -5$ or 5 (E) $x = 5$

(C) $x < 5$

14. Which answer choice below shows a true equation?

(A) $(37 \times 23) = (23 \times 73)$

(B) $12(20 + 5) = 240 + 60$

(C) $3 + (54 + 98) = (3 - 54) + 98$

(D) $125 = (10 \times 100) + (1 \times 25)$

(E) $75 + 87 = 87 \times 75$

15. The area of the circle below is 144π square feet. If $\overline{OB}$ is increased by 2 feet, what is the area of the new circle (in square feet)?

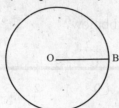

(A) 4π

(B) 121π

(C) 146π

(D) 169π

(E) 196π

16. On what interval is the following function positive?

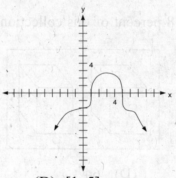

(A) $[0, 2]$

(B) $(0, 2)$

(C) $(0, 2]$

(D) $[1, 5]$

(E) $(1, 5)$

17. In the following figure, $\overline{AB} \perp \overline{BC}$, $\overline{AC} = 10$, and $\overline{AB} = 6$. What is the area of $\triangle ABC$?

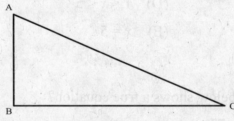

(A) 24

(B) 48

(C) 121

(D) 240

(E) 480

18. According to the graph below, during how many months was supply greater than demand?

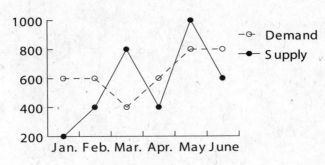

Supply vs. Demand

- -○ Demand
- ● Supply

(A) 0   (D) 3

(B) 1   (E) 4

(C) 2

19. What is the greatest common divisor of 120 and 252?

(A) 2   (D) 12

(B) 3   (E) 2,520

(C) 6

20. How many negative integers are between −9 and 5?

(A) 13   (D) 8

(B) 10   (E) 6

(C) 9

21. Dan flies north at a speed of 200 miles per hour, and Tom flies east at a speed of 150 miles per hour. Head wind and air resistance all having been taken into consideration, how far are they apart two hours later?

(A) 300 miles   (D) 450 miles

(B) 350 miles   (E) 500 miles

(C) 400 miles

22. The sum of the base and altitude of a triangle is 12 and the area is 16. What are the base and altitude of the triangle?

(A) 2 and 10   (D) 3 and 9

(B) 6   (E) 5 and 7

(C) 4 and 8

23. The repeating decimal 0.36363636...., when written as a fraction is

    (A) $\dfrac{9}{25}$

    (B) $\dfrac{4}{11}$

    (C) $\dfrac{63}{175}$

    (D) $\dfrac{8}{13}$

    (E) Not expressible as a fraction.

24. An isosceles triangle ABC is inscribed in a circle with center O in such a way that OBC forms an equilateral triangle. The measurement of angle ABC is

    (A) 80°.   (D) 65°.

    (B) 75°.   (E) 60°.

    (C) 70°.

25. If subtracting 13 from a number is the same as taking $\dfrac{3}{4}$ of the number, what is the number?

    (A) 52   (D) 76

    (B) 39   (E) 97

    (C) 48

26. Mr. Jones is nine times as old as his grandson. If they are 56 years apart, how old is his grandson?

    (A) 9   (D) 6

    (B) 8   (E) 5

    (C) 7

27. Bob is lending money at 6 percent simple interest. How much does he need to lend at the beginning of the year to yield $1,000 by the end of the year? (Figure to the nearest dollar.)

    (A) $850   (D) $943

    (B) $950   (E) $927

    (C) $894

28. The expression $x^n - y^n$

 (A) can be factored only when n is odd.

 (B) can never be factored.

 (C) can always be factored.

 (D) can be factored only when n is a power of 4.

 (E) can be factored only when n is twice an odd integer.

29. If one root of the equation $ax^2 + bx + c = 0$ is 2, the other root must be

 (A) $\dfrac{c}{2}$. (D) $\dfrac{b}{2c}$.

 (B) $\dfrac{c}{2a}$. (E) $\dfrac{a}{2c}$.

 (C) $\dfrac{c}{2b}$.

30. If five gallons of 50% alcohol solution is mixed with three gallons of 20% alcohol solution, what is the resulting solution?

 (A) 38.75% (D) 42.25%

 (B) 37.5% (E) 32.25%

 (C) 35%

31. Divide $3\dfrac{1}{5}$ by $1\dfrac{1}{3}$.

 (A) $2\dfrac{2}{5}$ (D) $4\dfrac{4}{15}$

 (B) $3\dfrac{1}{15}$ (E) 8

 (C) $3\dfrac{3}{5}$

32. Change 125.937% to a decimal.

 (A) 1.25937 (D) 1,259.37

 (B) 12.5937 (E) 12,593.7

 (C) 125.937

33. Evaluate $4(a + b) + 2[5 - (a^2 + b^2)]$, if $a = 2, b = 1$.

   (A) 6
   (D) 20
   (B) 7
   (E) 62
   (C) 12

34. Find the mean of the following scores:

   5, 7, 9, 8, 5, 8, 9, 8, 7, 8, 7, 5, 9, 5, 8, 5, 9, 6, 5

   (A) 5
   (D) 8
   (B) 6
   (E) 9
   (C) 7

35. What percent is 260 of 13?

   (A) .05%
   (D) .5%
   (B) 5%
   (E) 20%
   (C) 50%

36. How many corners does a cube have?

   (A) 4
   (D) 12
   (B) 6
   (E) 24
   (C) 8

37. Subtract $4\frac{1}{3} - 1\frac{5}{6}$.

   (A) $3\frac{2}{3}$
   (D) $2\frac{1}{6}$
   (B) $2\frac{1}{2}$
   (E) None of these.
   (C) $3\frac{1}{2}$

38. In rhombus *ABCD,* which of the following are true?

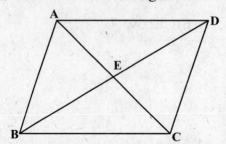

I. $\angle BAE$ and $\angle ECD$ are congruent.

II. $\angle ADE$ and $\angle CDE$ are congruent.

III. $\angle ABE$ and $\angle ADE$ are congruent.

(A) I only.

(B) II only.

(C) I and II only.

(D) I and III only.

(E) I, II, and III.

39. The rates of a laundry are $6.25 for the first 15 pieces and $0.35 for each additional piece. If the laundry charge is $8.35, how many pieces were laundered?

(A) 5

(B) 6

(C) 15

(D) 21

(E) 25

40. The enrollment in Eastern High School is 1,050. If the attendance for a month was 94 percent, how many students were absent during the month?

(A) 50

(B) 63

(C) 420

(D) 987

(E) 1,044

41. Which answer choice below shows how you can find 20% of 75?

(A) 20×75

(B) 20×7.5

(C) $.20 \times 75$

(D) $.20 \times .75$

(E) $2 \times .75$

42. What would be a reasonable estimate for the answer to the following problem: $63 \times .12$

(A) .63

(B) 6.3

(C) 630

(D) 6,300

(E) 63,000

43. Which expression below could be used to show how many more laps Carrie swam than Antoine?

    Carrie's laps: $9x - 2$

    Antoine's laps: $3x + 5$

    (A) $9x - 2 - 3x + 5$

    (B) $(9x - 2) \cdot (3x + 5)$

    (C) $(9x - 2) + (3x + 5)$

    (D) $(9x - 2) - (3x + 5)$

    (E) $(3x + 5) - (9x - 2)$

44. Which equation below could be used to solve the following problem?

    Nancy and her sister Karen wanted to buy their father a Father's Day present. Nancy had 4 more than double the number of dollars that Karen had. Together they had $19. How much money did each have?

    (A) $2x + 4 = 19$

    (B) $4x + 2 + x = 19$

    (C) $2(x + 4) + x = 19$

    (D) $4x + 2 = 19$

    (E) $2x + 4 + x = 19$

45. Which equation below could be used to generate the table of values shown?

x	y
5	24
10	12
20	6
60	2

    (A) $\dfrac{120}{x}$

    (B) $y = 120x$

    (C) $y = \dfrac{x}{120}$

    (D) $y = 120 - x$

    (E) $x = 120 - y$

46. Which ordered pair could also be included in the table below?

x	y
3	15
4	20
5	25
6	30

(A) (7, 42)

(B) (8, 64)

(C) (2, 10)

(D) (1, 6)

(E) (0, 5)

Section III: Writing

TIME: *30 minutes (38 minutes multiple-choice; 30 minutes essay)*
44 multiple-choice Questions and one essay question

Part A: Usage

DIRECTIONS: Each of the following sentences may contain an error in diction, usage, idiom, or grammar. Some sentences are correct. Some sentences contain one error. No sentence contains more than one error.

If there is an error, it will appear in one of the underlined portions labeled A, B, C, or D. If there is no error, choose the portion labeled E. If there is an error, select the letter of the portion that must be changed in order to correct the sentence.

EXAMPLE:

He drove <u>slowly</u> and <u>cautiously</u> in order to <u>hopefully</u> avoid having an <u>accident</u>.
      A   B   C   D

<u>No error</u>.
  E

                                        Ⓐ Ⓑ ● Ⓓ Ⓔ

1. Each campus appointed <u>their</u> own committee to apply the <u>findings of</u> the city-wide
                         A   B

  survey concerning ways <u>in which</u> the school district <u>can</u> save money. <u>No error</u>.
                                C   D   E

2. When <u>I</u> asked Gary and John what would be <u>good</u> for dinner, the boys said they <u>could</u>
                                        A   B

  <u>care less</u> <u>about eating</u> liver for the main dish with spinach for a vegetable. <u>No error</u>.
     C   D   E

3. John will be <u>liable for</u> damages to Mrs. Simon's car because he was <u>fascinated by</u> his
                A   B

  new red truck and driving so <u>fast</u> that he failed to <u>conform to</u> a law limiting the speed
                                   C   D

  of any vehicle within the city limits. <u>No error</u>.
                                     E

4. I <u>have seen</u>, <u>more than</u> anything <u>else</u>, that self-esteem is a <u>problem in</u> many people of
      A   B   C   D

  all ages and nationalities. <u>No error</u>.
                           E

5. Mr. Burgess made sure the ten-year-olds were <u>accommodated with</u> quarters for a
                                                          A
    video games party; afterwards, he declined <u>to say how</u> much the event cost him but <u>al-</u>
                                                    B
    <u>lowed as how</u> it was more than he <u>had expected</u>. <u>No error</u>.
          C   D   E

6. This afternoon's boating accident <u>having</u> turned out <u>differently</u> through the efforts of
                                           A   B
    Jack Williams, a fellow vacationer <u>who</u> knows CPR, <u>so</u> the little girl has survived.
                                          C   D
    <u>No error</u>.
       E

7. Three hundred <u>years ago</u> John Milton <u>protested against</u> laws which required a govern-
                       A   B
    ment official to <u>approve of</u> <u>any</u> manuscript before it was published. <u>No error</u>.
                          C   D   E

8. Frequently <u>called</u> the "Fourth Estate," journalists have <u>rapidly</u> <u>developed into</u> power-
                    A   B   C
    ful people, influencing public opinion and government policy that <u>has</u> a bearing on the
                                                                          D
    course of history. <u>No error</u>.
                           E

9. Totaling <u>more than expected</u>, the groom's wedding expenses <u>included</u> hiring a limou-
                     A   B
    sine for the trip to the airport after the wedding, <u>buying gifts</u> for his groomsmen, and <u>a</u>
                                                             C
    <u>tuxedo</u> for the ceremony. <u>No error</u>.
       D   E

10. <u>Our viewing</u> these photographs of Dad standing in front of the throne at Macchu Pichu
         A
    <u>brings</u> back pleasant memories for <u>we</u> children, reminding us <u>of the need for</u> more
        B   C   D
    family get-togethers. <u>No error</u>.
                              E

11. Finally confessing to the <u>theft of</u> money collected for a class movie, Jules said <u>he only</u>
                                  A   B
    stole money once in his life and <u>his</u> conscience would not allow <u>him</u> to enjoy spending
                                         C   D
    it. <u>No error</u>.
           E

12. If <u>a person</u> is a criminal, <u>he</u> should be punished for <u>it</u>; unfortunately, many criminals
    A   B   C

are <u>never</u> caught. <u>No error</u>.
   D   E

13. An intriguing habit many hawks have <u>is bringing</u> a fresh green branch <u>daily</u> to line the
                                    A   B

nest <u>during the season</u> in which <u>they</u> are mating and rearing their young. <u>No error</u>.
      C   D   E

14. Hawks and owls can be seen <u>more frequent</u> in populated areas than <u>most people</u>
                              A   B

<u>suppose</u>, and it is <u>possible</u> to hear screech owls at night when the adult birds feed their
 C   D

chicks. <u>No error</u>.
        E

15. The grass was <u>growing over</u> the curb and the oak tree had a branch hanging almost <u>to</u>
             A   B

the ground, so we decided to trim <u>it</u> before the neighbors became <u>annoyed with us</u>.
                                 C   D

<u>No error</u>.
 E

16. Charles Draper developed the <u>theory of</u> and invented the <u>technology for</u> inertial navi-
                                 A   B

gation, a guidance system <u>which</u> does not <u>rely on</u> external sources. <u>No error</u>.
                            C   D   E

17. Inertial navigation is a system of navigation <u>employed</u> in submarines when <u>they are</u>
                                           A   B

underwater, missiles used <u>for</u> defense purposes, aircraft, and <u>to get</u> man to the moon in
                           C   D

the Apollo exploration series. <u>No error</u>.
                          E

18. Much <u>to</u> <u>everyone's</u> surprise, the company president, <u>known for</u> his intelligence and
        A   B   C

good business judgment, <u>and enjoying</u> a hobby of sky diving. <u>No error</u>.
                     D   E

19. <u>They</u> are very <u>grateful the city</u> has <u>set up</u> a special fund which <u>helps pay</u> for electric
    A   B   C   D

 bills of the elderly and the handicapped. <u>No error</u>.
                                   E

20. <u>In order to</u> stay cool during the summer months, Americans <u>not only</u> are using ceiling
    A   B

 fans, but they are also using devices <u>to add humidity</u> to the air in <u>particularly</u> arid cli-
                                 C   D

 mates such as Arizona. <u>No error</u>.
                      E

21. <u>After seeing</u> the technique demonstrated on television, Janie baked homemade bread
    A

 for the first time yesterday, <u>and her</u> brother thought it tasted <u>good</u>, an opinion everyone
                              B   C

 <u>agreed with</u>. <u>No error</u>.
   D   E

22. Although not <u>so</u> prevalent as they once were, <u>hood</u> ornaments still exist, <u>some of which</u>
           A   B   C

 are quite distinctive, <u>such as</u> the symbol for Mercedes-Benz and Jaguar. <u>No error</u>.
                   D   E

23. If I <u>were</u> that tourist, I would not <u>argue with</u> those two members of the Guardia Civil
      A   B

 because, although they are <u>speaking politely</u>, it is obvious they are <u>becoming angry</u>.
                            C   D

 <u>No error</u>.
   E

24. Mr. Burns is fully <u>aware of</u> statistics proving the <u>harmful</u> consequences of smoking;
                    A   B

 <u>irregardless</u>, he <u>persists</u> in his habit. <u>No error</u>.
   C   D   E

25. David was not capable <u>to win</u> the singles tennis match because he
                      A

 <u>had been</u> injured <u>in</u> a game last week and the doctor prohibited him <u>from</u> playing for
   B   C   D

 two weeks. <u>No error</u>.
           E

Part B: Sentence Correction

DIRECTIONS: In each of the following sentences, some portion of the sentence is underlined. Under each sentence are five choices. The first choice has the same wording as the original. The other four choices are reworded. Sometimes the first choice containing the original wording is the best; sometimes one of the other choices is the best. Choose the letter of the best choice. Your choice should produce a sentence which is not ambiguous or awkward and which is correct, clear, and precise.

This is a test of correct and effective English expression. Keep in mind the standards of English usage, punctuation, grammar, word choice, and construction.

EXAMPLE:

When you listen to opera, <u>a person may not appreciate it.</u>

(A) a person may not appreciate it.

(B) it may not be appreciated by a person.

(C) which may not be appreciated by one.

(D) you may not appreciate it.

(E) appreciating it may be a problem for you.

26. The new secretary proved herself <u>to be not only capable and efficient but also a woman who was adept</u> at working under pressure and handling irate customers.

   (A) to be not only capable and efficient but also a woman who was adept

   (B) not only to be capable or efficient but also a woman who was adept

   (C) not only to be capable and efficient but also a woman who was adept

   (D) to be not only capable and efficient but also adept

   (E) to be not only capable and efficient but also an adept woman

27. <u>Hunting, if properly managed and carefully controlled,</u> can cull excess animals, thereby producing a healthier population of wild game.

   (A) Hunting, if properly managed and carefully controlled,

   (B) Managing it wisely, carefully controlled hunting

    (C) Managed properly hunting that is carefully controlled

    (D) Properly and wisely controlled, careful hunting

    (E) If properly managed, hunting, carefully controlled,

28. In spite of my reservations, <u>I agreed on the next day to help her put up new wallpaper</u>.

    (A) I agreed on the next day to help her put up new wallpaper.

    (B) I agreed on the next day to help put up her new wallpaper.

    (C) I agreed to help her put up new wallpaper on the next day.

    (D) I, on the next day, agreed to help her put up new wallpaper.

    (E) I agreed to, on the next day, help her put up new wallpaper.

29. <u>We saw many of, though not nearly all, the existing Roman ruins</u> along the Mediterranean coastline of Africa.

    (A) We saw many of, though not nearly all, the existing Roman ruins

    (B) We saw many, though not nearly all, of the existing Roman ruins

    (C) Seeing many, though not nearly all, of the existing Roman ruins

    (D) Having seen many of, though not nearly all, the existing Roman ruins

    (E) Many of, though not nearly all, the existing Roman ruins we saw

30. <u>The horned owl is a carnivore who hunts a diversity of creatures, like</u> hares, grouse, and ground squirrels.

    (A) The horned owl is a carnivore who hunts a diversity of creatures, like

    (B) The horned owl, a carnivore who hunts a diversity of creatures like

    (C) A hunting carnivore, the horned owl likes a diversity of creatures

    (D) The horned owl likes a diversity of carnivorous creatures, such as

    (E) The horned owl is a carnivore who hunts a diversity of creatures, such as

31. In many of his works Tennessee Williams, <u>of whom much has been written</u>, has as main characters drifters, dreamers, and those who are crushed by having to deal with reality.

    (A) of whom much has been written

    (B) of who much has been written

    (C) of whom much has been written about

    (D) about him much having been written

    (E) much having been written about him

32. The world history students wanted to know <u>where the Dead Sea was at and what it was famous for</u>.

    (A) where the Dead Sea was at and what it was famous for.

    (B) where the Dead Sea is at and for what it is famous.

    (C) where the Dead Sea is located and why it is famous.

    (D) at where the Dead Sea was located and what it was famous for.

    (E) the location of the Dead Sea and what it is famous for.

33. Literary historians <u>cannot help but admit that they do not know</u> whether poetry or drama is the oldest form of literature.

    (A) cannot help but admit that they do not know

    (B) cannot admit that they do not admit to knowing

    (C) cannot help admitting that they do not know

    (D) cannot help but to admit that they do not know

    (E) cannot know but admit that they do not

34. Getting to know a person's parents <u>will often provide an insight to</u> his personality and behavior.

    (A) will often provide an insight to

    (B) will often provide an insight into

    (C) will often provide an insight for

    (D) will provide often an insight for

    (E) often will provide an insight with

35. Upon leaving the nursery, Mr. Greene, together with his wife, <u>put the plants in the trunk of the car they had just bought</u>.

    (A) put the plants in the trunk of the car they had just bought.

    (B) put in the plants to the trunk of the car they had just bought.

    (C) put into the trunk of the car they had just bought the plants.

    (D) put the plants they had just bought in the trunk of the car.

    (E) put the plants into the trunk of the car.

36. The way tensions are increasing in the Middle East, some experts <u>are afraid we may end up with a nuclear war</u>.

    (A) are afraid we may end up with a nuclear war.

    (B) being afraid we may end up with a nuclear war.

    (C) afraid that a nuclear war may end up over there.

    (D) are afraid a nuclear war may end there.

    (E) are afraid a nuclear war may occur.

37. <u>Whether Leif Erickson was the first to discover America or not</u> is still a debatable issue, but there is general agreement that there probably were a number of "discoveries" through the years.

    (A) Whether Leif Erickson was the first to discover America or not

    (B) That Leif Erickson was the first to discover America

    (C) That Leif Erickson may have been the first to have discovered America

    (D) Whether Leif Erickson is the first to discover America or he is not

    (E) Whether or not Leif Erickson was or was not the first discoverer of America

38. <u>People who charge too much are likely to develop</u> a bad credit rating.

    (A) People who charge too much are likely to develop

    (B) People's charging too much are likely to develop

    (C) When people charge too much, likely to develop

    (D) That people charge too much is likely to develop

    (E) Charging too much is likely to develop for people

39. The museum of natural science has a special exhibit of gems and minerals, <u>and the fifth graders went to see it on a field trip</u>.

    (A) and the fifth graders went to see it on a field trip.

    (B) and seeing it were the fifth graders on a field trip.

    (C) when the fifth graders took a field trip to see it.

    (D) which the fifth graders took a field trip to see.

    (E) where the fifth graders took their field trip to see it.

40. <u>When the case is decided, he plans appealing</u> if the verdict is unfavorable.

    (A) When the case is decided, he plans appealing

    (B) When deciding the case, he plans appealing

    (C) After the case is decided, he is appealing

    (D) After deciding the case, he is planning to appeal

    (E) When the case is decided, he plans to appeal

41. <u>We decided there was hardly any reason for his allowing us</u> to stay up later on week-nights.

    (A) We decided there was hardly any reason for his allowing us

    (B) We, deciding there was hardly any reason for his allowing us,

    (C) Deciding there was hardly any reason, we allowed

    (D) We decided there were none of the reasons for him to allow us

    (E) For him to allow us there was hardly any reason we decided

42. At this time <u>it is difficult for me agreeing with your plan of having everyone</u> in the club working on the same project.

    (A) it is difficult for me agreeing with your plan of having everyone

    (B) I find it difficult to agree to your plan of having everyone

    (C) for my agreement with your plan is difficult for everyone

    (D) an agreement to your plan seems difficult for everyone

    (E) finding it difficult for me to agree to your plan of having everyone

43. When the Whites hired a contractor to do remodeling on their home, he <u>promised to completely finish the work inside of three months</u>.

    (A) promised to completely finish the work inside of three months.

    (B) promised to complete the work within three months.

    (C) completely promised to finish the work inside of three months' span.

    (D) promising to completely finish the work in three months.

    (E) completely finished the work within three months.

44. <u>The more we use machines</u>, the more human beings live at odds with their environment.

    (A) The more we use machines

    (B) The more they use machines

    (C) The more machines are used by us

    (D) As our use of machines is increased

    (E) As we add to our use of machines

Part C: Essay

TIME: *30 Minutes*

DIRECTIONS: You have 30 minutes to plan and write an essay on the topic below. You may write only on the assigned topic.

Make sure to give specific examples to support your thesis. Proofread your essay carefully and take care to express your ideas clearly and effectively.

Write your essay on the lined pages at the back of the book.

ESSAY TOPIC:

Television often causes the viewer to lose touch with reality and become completely passive and unaware. Like other addictions, television provides a pleasurable escape route from the daily grind.

ASSIGNMENT: Do you agree or disagree with the statement? Support your opinion with specific examples from history, current events, literature, or personal experience.

Answer Key

Section 1: Reading Comprehension

1. (A)	13. (C)	25. (E)	37. (E)
2. (B)	14. (E)	26. (A)	38. (B)
3. (C)	15. (A)	27. (D)	39. (A)
4. (C)	16. (B)	28. (D)	40. (E)
5. (B)	17. (D)	29. (B)	41. (D)
6. (D)	18. (D)	30. (C)	42. (D)
7. (C)	19. (D)	31. (D)	43. (C)
8. (E)	20. (B)	32. (D)	44. (A)
9. (E)	21. (E)	33. (E)	45. (C)
10. (A)	22. (C)	34. (E)	46. (C)
11. (D)	23. (A)	35. (D)	
12. (E)	24. (C)	36. (E)	

Section II: Mathematics

1. (A)	13. (D)	25. (A)	37. (B)
2. (A)	14. (B)	26. (C)	38. (E)
3. (C)	15. (E)	27. (D)	39. (D)
4. (D)	16. (E)	28. (C)	40. (B)
5. (D)	17. (A)	29. (B)	41. (C)
6. (E)	18. (C)	30. (A)	42. (B)
7. (A)	19. (D)	31. (A)	43. (D)
8. (A)	20. (D)	32. (A)	44. (E)
9. (D)	21. (E)	33. (C)	45. (A)
10. (A)	22. (C)	34. (C)	46. (C)
11. (A)	23. (B)	35. (B)	
12. (C)	24. (B)	36. (C)	

Section III: Writing

1. (A)	12. (C)	23. (E)	34. (B)
2. (C)	13. (B)	24. (C)	35. (D)
3. (D)	14. (A)	25. (A)	36. (E)
4. (E)	15. (C)	26. (D)	37. (B)
5. (C)	16. (E)	27. (A)	38. (A)
6. (A)	17. (D)	28. (C)	39. (D)
7. (B)	18. (D)	29. (B)	40. (E)
8. (D)	19. (A)	30. (E)	41. (A)
9. (D)	20. (B)	31. (A)	42. (B)
10. (C)	21. (D)	32. (C)	43. (B)
11. (B)	22. (A)	33. (C)	44. (B)

Section I: Reading Comprehension

1. **A**

   "Capricious" means unpredictable.

2. **B**

   This choice is supported by the last sentence in the passage.

3. **C**

   The author discusses how the birds share the same food supply but occupy different areas of the pond. Each of the other choices is too broad and general.

4. **C**

   The author's terms "misguided" and "facts just do not support their claim" indicate more than impartiality, choice (A), or indifference, choice (B), for those who believe that America is or ever was a monolingual country. Nothing in the passage characterizes anger, choice (D), or an optimistic nature, choice (E).

5. **B**

   Choices (A), (D), and (E) generalize beyond information in the passage. Choice (C) contradicts information given in the passage.

6. **D**

   This choice is supported in the second sentence. All other choices are secondary to the central idea.

7. **C**

   The passage states that this was a "noteworthy accomplishment in technology."

8. **E**

   The passage emphasizes the complicated process of filtering the meal through sand or tightly woven baskets. Choices (A), (B), and (C), while true, are not the most difficult problem. Choice (D) is contradictory to information given in the text.

9. **E**

In the context of the passage, vestige means a small remaining amount.

10. **A**

Choices (D) and (E) are incorrect as the strategy is for oral reading, not silent reading. Choices (B) and (C) are not supported by the passage—thus choice (A) is correct.

11. **D**

Choices (A), (B), (C), and (E) include syllable and paragraph elements which are not supported by the passage. The passage states " . . . individual language units which can be as small as a single letter or as large as phrases or sentences."

12. **E**

Choices (A), (B), (C), and (D) are not supported by the passage. The passages states that "speeding up reading, not slowing it down, helps the reader make sense of a passage."

13. **C**

The passage compares duplex versus one-way video and two-way audio. The reader must infer that duplex indicates two-way video and two-way audio since duplex refers to two. The other choices (A), (B), (D), and (E) are incorrect.

14. **E**

Choices (A), (B), (C), and (D) are inappropriate for defining an instrument which assesses learning and demonstrates learning.

15. **A**

Choices (B), (C), (D), and (E) are not supported by the passage.

16. **B**

While choices (A), (C), (D), and (E) are mentioned briefly in the passage, the passage focuses on student participation and learning.

17. **D**

Choices (A), (B), (C), and (E) appear to be definitions of effeminate. However, for this passage choice (D) is most appropriate since it relates to the eyes.

18. **D**

     Choices (A), (B), and (C) are not supported by the passage. The passage hints at choice (E), but the passage remains primarily imaginative, thus choice (D) is correct.

19. **D**

     Choice (D) states the most complete main idea in the passage, hence, it is the correct answer. Choice (A) addresses only one part of the correct answer; choices (B) and (C) are incorrect; and choice (E) is an in-complete answer.

20. **B**

     Of the choices provided, (B) provides the most complete answer—namely, the two things that the computer program does: predicts the aging process and predicts how an unborn child will look. The other choices, (A), (C), (D), and (E) while all true, are incomplete in providing the main capability of the new computer program developed in Japan.

21. **E**

     A logical answer to this question has got to be (E). With this new computer system it certainly will follow that Japan will do a more refined and sophisticated system next. Choices (A) and (B) are related—the answers are natural outgrowths of the competitive market among nations; and choices (C) and (D) have been an on-going trend anyway.

22. **C**

     In an emergency situation, the most sound and logical thing to do would have to be (C). Choice (A) is not the best thing to do in the situation; choice (B) is running a risk of consuming the fuel; the same could be said of choice (D); and choice (E) is too risky, hence, incorrect.

23. **A**

     For air travelers who are aware of possible communications breakdown due to a power failure, choice (A) is the best and correct answer. Choice (B) could be true only to certain people; choice (C) is a good answer but does not relate to the specific incident; choice (D) is besides the point; and choice (E) is an incorrect generalization—delays are caused by other reasons besides a power failure.

24. **C**

A title is supposed to synthesize the main idea of a passage. In this passage the best synthesis is (C), hence, the correct answer. Choices (A), (B), (D), and (E) are possible titles but are all incomplete as titles.

25. **E**

Regular exercise, according to research, is highly beneficial. Choices (A), (B), (C), and (D), are illogical and incorrect.

26. **A**

The answer in (A) is sound and is the best and correct answer. Choice (B) is an incorrect answer; choice (C) is an incorrect implication; the same can be said of choices (D) and (E).

27. **D**

The study covered only men, hence, a major limitation is the fact that it did not include women of the same age group. The correct answer, therefore, is (D). Choice (A) may not be an essential in the study, hence, definitely not a major limitation; choice (B), while a limitation, cannot be considered "major." Besides, "children" could include babies through young adolescents—a rather wide age range. Choice (C) is also a limitation, but it does not state the precise age range. Choice (E) is incorrect since more than 17,000 men were included in the study.

28. **D**

The title in (A) is too broad; only cacti and succulents are studied here. (B) is not accurate. Regions of the world are not the primary topic of the passage. (C) The passage deals with more than just distinguishing between cacti and succulents. (E) is too limiting.

29. **B**

Not all cacti are without leaves so (A) is not the correct answer. Cacti are usually without leaves; cacti are indigenous to the Western Hemisphere. (C) is incorrect. (D) is incorrect. Flowers on a cacti usually emerge from the top, not the base. (E) is a true statement, but it is not a statement that BEST distinguishes cacti from other succulents.

30. **C**

The writer never implies that cacti are to be chosen over other succulents. The wording of the choice ("Cacti are to be chosen over succulents...") implies that cacti are not themselves succulents. Choice (A) is not the best answer. The author does not suggest that they are to be left in the wild, but states that they are excellent subjects for a garden, greenhouse, or windowsill. Choice (B) is incorrect. The author implies that they are excellent subjects for botanists or the home gardener. Choice (C) is the correct answer. Choices (D) and (E) are incorrect. Both feature interesting adaptations, but the author does not state that one is preferred over the other.

31. **D**

Statement (A) is not implied by the passage; nothing suggests that cacti require less care. The author does not indicate that the shape of cacti is more appealing than that of other succulents. Choice (B) is incorrect. The author does not indicate that succulents from one hemisphere do not adapt well to the other, or vice versa. Choice (C) is not the best answer. The flowers of cacti do not appear between the leaves or at the base. Choice (E) is incorrect.

32. **D**

Considering the author's fondness for cacti and other succulents, he would probably view laws to protect them with understanding choice (D), not disinterest or apathy, choice (A), confusion choice (B), despair choice (C), or distaste (E).

33. **E**

Paragraph 6 states that only cacti have areoles. I is a true statement. Paragraph 7 states that cactus flowers are more conspicuous, but they most often appear from areoles near the top of the plant. II is a false statement. The second paragraph states that the adaptations made by both cacti and other succulents "may be similar"; III is a false statement. Since only (I) is true, the correct answer is choice (E).

34. **E**

The word "interposition" means most nearly an intervention or a mediation. Answer choice (E) most nearly satisfies that definition. A conglomeration is not an intervention or a coming between but a mixing; choice (A) would not be the best choice. One who intervenes does not necessarily have to be in a lofty position; choice (B) is not, therefore, the best answer; perhaps the person who chose this answer selected it merely because both the word being considered and the answer contained the letters "position." After an intervention there may be a coming together choice (C) or a uniting choice (D), but interposition does not necessarily ensure this result; choices (C) and (D) are not, therefore, the best answers.

35. **D**

In lines 13–14 the words "justice rolls down like water and righteousness like a mighty stream" can best be described as a comparison, or an analogy choice (D). Since an onomatopoeic word is formed by making an imitation of the sound associated with the object or action, onomatopoeic, choice (A) is not the best answer. An alliterative expression repeats the same sound; this has not been done in the phrase "justice rolls down like water and righteousness like a mighty stream"; choice (B) is incorrect. Using terms like "mighty stream" and "righteousness" are not understatements; choice (C) should not be selected. The words in question were not fanciful words but words which were capable of being fulfilled. Choice (E) should not be selected since it expresses this quotation as being a fantasy.

36. **E**

The Southern states, the slums, and the ghettos in the fourth paragraph were listed to inspire hope; even if those areas were desolate at this time, King had faith that in the future things would change. Choice (E) is the best answer. Unfortunately, racial bias and inequality were not just evident in one area. Choice (A), then, was an inadequate answer. The audience did not necessarily come from the areas listed above; choice (B) is not the best answer. Biased political leaders are not restricted to slums, ghettos, and Southern states; choice (C) is not the best choice. King did not plan violence, so choice (D) is not appropriate.

37. **E**

King reminded the audience that "unearned suffering is redemptive" in line 20. The best explanation for this statement is that King was suggesting that some undeserved suffering may actually be freeing and releasing. Choice (E) is the best choice. King makes no reference to the fact that some of the suffering endured was earned or deserved. Choice (A) is not the best choice. King does not see suffering as being justified or purifying so choice (B) is incorrect. King does not view unearned suffering as unforgivable; choice (C) is incorrect. King does not advocate followers seeking to suffer for no reason; he does not see unearned suffering as something to be sought or desired. Choice (D) is incorrect.

38. **B**

The "old saying" which best fits lines 36–38 is choice (B), "You can't judge a book by its cover." King is looking forward to the day when people are judged by their character and not by their skin color. Choice (B) is the answer to be chosen. Although choice (A) is an oft-repeated statement and even though it does not fit at this point, it does fit some of King's speeches. Choice (A) should not be chosen. Judging little children by their skin color does not relate to birds of a feather flocking together; choice (C) should not be chosen. Not disturbing the situation, or letting sleeping dogs lie, does not relate to the color of the children's skin; choice (D) does not fit. "A good name is rather to be chosen than great riches," but this has nothing to do with judging children by their skin color. Choice (E) is not the best answer.

39. **A**

King best compared his audience to those who had fought in great battles by calling them choice (A) veterans. It is true that the audience may have been choice (B) battered, but that does not necessarily go along with war alone; victims of other situations may be battered. Choice (B) should not be chosen. The audience may be opposed and may stagger, but this does not necessarily relate to war; staggered choice (C) is not a good choice. Flesh choice (D) does not necessarily relate to war; choice (D) should not be selected. A devotee choice (E) may or may not relate to war; choice (E) should not be chosen.

40. **E**

King used the analogy of winds for police brutality because winds when strong can be damaging and a fearful obstacle; choice (E) is the best choice. Winds do rise up and then die, but that analogy is not the best here; it does not seem to relate to the police. Choice (A) is not the best answer. A reference to the police as turning first one way and then another, choice (B) is not the best answer. Since winds are not always easy to protect one's self against, choice (C) is not the best choice. A wind which can be harnessed and used by a windmill does not seem to be a good analogy here; one does not usually think of harnessing police. Choice (D) is not the best answer.

41. **D**

Choice (D) is correct because the passage specifically mentions the California coast, the Alaskan coast, and the U. S. Gulf Coast as sites of oil spills.

42. **D**

Choice (D) is correct because workers were trying to keep the oil in the water and away from the beach. Choices (A) and (B) are incorrect because neither sightseers nor animals are discussed in the passage. Choice (C) is incorrect because the cleanup crews wanted to remove the oil, not let it soak into the sand.

43. **C**

Choice (C) is correct. This question must be answered using the process of elimination. Cleanup trust funds, increased federal spending, using the National Guard, and creating a department of oceans are all discussed in the passage. Therefore, choices A, B, and D are incorrect. Only choice C names a solution not mentioned in the passage.

44. **A**

Choice (A) is correct. The last sentence of the passage specifically states that spills are a constant threat if offshore drilling and the shipment of oil in tankers continues. Choice (B) is incorrect because the passage does not discuss crews or training programs. While the passage does imply that the government should be better prepared to clean up, the author does not state that oil spills would cease to be a problem if the government was better prepared. Therefore, choice (C) is incorrect. Choice (D) is incorrect because foreign oil producers are not mentioned.

45. **C**

Choice (A), "Grinding operations, 126–140," would be expected to discuss how the grinders are operated, but "grinding wheels" is too general in the context of the question posed. Pages 136–138, choice (B) describe an unrelated function. Choice (D), "Grinding wheels, 126–129," is overly broad, particularly when considered alongside choice (C), which proves to be the best choice because it specifically uses the phrase "installing the wheel."

46. **C**

While the extract is surely arranged alphabetically choice (E), there is another pattern that emerges—one governed by task. This is clear by the preponderance of task-oriented descriptors (e.g., "grinding," "sharpening," "truing and dressing," etc.). Choice

(B), "Physical characteristics," addresses a level of detail that does not figure to any appreciable extent in the passage. Thus, choice (C) is the best answer.

Section II: Mathematics

1. **A**

   Multiply $1.83 by 145 and the answer is $265.35.

2. **A**

   By definition, a simple curve is a curve that can be traced in such a way that no point is traced more than once with the exception that the tracing may stop where it started. A closed curve is a curve that can be traced so that the starting and stopping points are the same. Therefore, a and b are simple closed curves. The rest are not.

3. **C**

   In a normal distribution, half the data are always above the mean. Since 30,000 miles is the mean, half or 50 percent of the tires will last at least 30,000 miles.

4. **D**

   A line of symmetry for a figure is a line on which you can stand a mirror, so that the image you see in the mirror is just like the original figure. The given figure has two diagonal lines of symmetry one horizontal line of symmetry and one vertical line of symmetry.

5. **D**

   This can be solved using ratio and proportion, thus, 2 is to 1 as x is to 8.
   $$\frac{2}{1} = \frac{x}{8}$$
   so $x = 16$ m.

6. **E**

   First find how many ounces of orange juice is needed, so multiply 75×8 oz. $= 600$ oz. needed. Then divide 600 by 12 oz. which equals 50. Thus it would take 50 - 12 oz. cans of juice to serve 75 people 8 oz. each.

7. **A**

   m = number of miles you can travel

   $0.08m$ = amount spent for m miles travelled at 8 cents per mile,

   (rental fee + mileage charge = total amount spent)

$$\$139 + \$0.08m = \$350$$

$$139 - 139 + 0.08m = 350 - 139$$

$$\frac{0.08m}{0.08} = \frac{211}{0.08}$$

$$m = 2,637.5$$

$$m = 2,637$$

8. **A**

Let x = number of hours of overtime for the 1st worker,

x = number of hours of overtime for the 2nd worker,

x = number of hours of overtime for the 3rd worker,

$2x$ = number of hours of overtime for the 4th worker.

$$x + x + x + 2x = 50$$

$$5x = 50$$

$$x = \frac{50}{5}$$

$$x = 10 \text{ hrs of overtime for the 1st three workers}$$

$$2x = 20 \text{ hrs of overtime for the 4th worker}$$

9. **D**

Let m = number of miles covered the 1st day.

$m + 30$ = number of miles covered the 2nd day,

$m + 30 + 30$ = number of miles covered the 3rd day,

$m + 30 + 30 + 30$ = number of miles covered the 4th day,

$m + 30 + 30 + 30 + 30$ = number of miles covered the 5th day.

$$m + m + 30 \text{ and so on}\ldots = 1,500$$

$$5m + 30 (10) = 1,500$$

$$5m + 300 = 1,500$$

$$5m = 1,500 - 300$$

$$5m = 1,200$$

$$m = \frac{1,200}{5}$$

$$m = 240 \text{ mi}$$

10. **A**

Using the formula
$$P = 2w + 2l$$
$$75 = 2w + 2(w + 5)$$
$$75 = 2w + 2w + 10$$
$$75 = 4w + 10$$
$$65 = 4w$$
$$16.25 = w$$
The width is therefore 16.25 m and the length is w + 5 or 16.25 + 5 = 21.25 m.

11. **A**

Note that there is a solid dot on –1 which means to include –1 in the set. The numbers to the right of –1 are shaded; this means to include these numbers also. Hence, this is the graph of all numbers greater than or equal to –1 ($\{x \mid x \geq -1\}$).

12. **C**

Let 2 be the number of blocks that Sal has. Then, 8% of x is 2 according to the given figure. Thus, we have the equation: .
.08x = 2 or, dividing both sides by .08,

$$x = \frac{2}{.08} = \frac{2}{.08} \times \frac{100}{100} = \frac{200}{8} = 25$$

13. **D**

$|x - 3| < 2$ is equivalent to $-2 < x - 3 < 2$. To solve this double inequality, we must add 3 to all three sides:
$$3 + -2 < x - 3 + 3 < 2 + 3 \text{ or } 1 < x < 5.$$

14. **B**

By the Distributive Law, 12(20 + 5) = (12)(20) + (12)(5). The right side of this identity can be simplified to 240 + 60.

15. **E**

The area of a circle is r² where r is the radius. In the given circle, $\overline{OB}$ is the radius and $A = 144\pi$. So, $144\pi = \pi r^2$ so that r = 12. If we increased the radius by 2 feet so that now r = 14, the area of the new circle is
$$A = \pi (14)^2 = 196\pi.$$

16. **E**

   A function is positive when the points on its graph lie above the x-axis. In our graph this occurs when x is between 1 and 5 or (1, 5).

17. **A**

   Since $\overline{AB} \perp \overline{BC}$, we know that $\triangle ABC$ is a right triangle and thus we may use the Pythagorean Theorem to find the length of $\overline{BC}$ (let x be the length of $\overline{BC}$):

$$(AC)^2 = (AB)^2 + (BC)^2$$

   or $\qquad (10)^2 = 6^2 + x^2$

   or $\qquad 100 = 36 + x^2$.

   To solve this, subtract 36 from both sides of the equation to get: $64 = x^2$ so that $x = 8$. The area of $\triangle ABC =$

$$\frac{1}{2}(AB)(BC) = \frac{1}{2}(6)(8) = 24.$$

18. **C**

   According to the graph, the supply was greater than the demand in March and May only.

19. **D**

   The greatest common divisor (GCD) is the greatest integer which divides both 120 and 252. To find the GCD, factor both numbers and look for common factors.

$$120 = 2^3 \times 3 \times 5$$

   and $\qquad 252 = 2^2 \times 3^2 \times 7$,

   so the GCD $= 2^2 \times 3 = 12$.

20. **D**

   The list of all the negative integers between –9 and 5 is:

   $-8, -7, -6, -5, -4, -3, -2, -1$.

21. **E**

   Since they travel on the two sides of a right-angled triangle, the Pythagorean Theorem yields

$$400^2 + 300^2 = 500^2.$$

22. **C**

Let b be the base and a be the altitude of the triangle. We have the equations:
$$a + b = 12,$$
and $$\frac{ab}{2} = 16$$
To solve these equations, substitute $b = 12 - a$ into the second equation, we have
$$a(12 - a) = 32,$$
or $$12a - a^2 = 32,$$
or $$a^2 - 12a + 32 = (a - 8)(a - 4) = 0;$$
thus, $a = 4$ or 8, and $b = 8$ or 4 respectively.

23. **B**

Since a two-digit repeating decimal is the two digits over 99, we have
$$\frac{36}{99} = \frac{4}{11}$$

24. **B**

Since the angle BOC measures $60°$, angle BAC measures $30°$, each of angles ABC and ACB will be half of
$$\frac{(180° - 30°)}{2} = 75°$$

25. **A**

Since
$$x - 13 = \frac{3x}{4}$$
or $4x - 52 = 3x$,
we have $x = 52$.

26. **C**

Letting Mr. Jones' age be x, and his grandson's be y, we have $x = 9y$ and $x - y = 56$. Substitute the first into the second equation,
$$9y - y = 56, y = 7.$$

27. **D**

His principal and interest need to be 1,000, which is 1.06 times his principal. Thus, we divide 1,000 by 1.06 and it is close to 943.

28. **C**

In fact,
$$x^n - y^n = (x - y)(x^{n-1} + x^{n-2}y + x^{n-3}y^2 + \ldots + y^{n-1}).$$

29. **B**

The original equation is equivalent to
$$x^2 + \frac{bx}{a} + \frac{c}{a} = 0.$$
The product of the two roots must equal $\frac{c}{a}$.

Since 2 is one root $\frac{c}{a} \div 2 = \frac{c}{2a}$

30. **A**

The alcohol content is
$$5 \times 0.5 + 3 \times 0.2 = 3.1 \text{ gallons},$$
and the total amount of solution is 8 gallons.
$$3.1 \div 8 = .3875 = 38.75\%.$$

31. **A**

In order to divide $3\frac{1}{5}$ by $1\frac{1}{3}$, we must first change both mixed numbers into improper fractions.

$$\frac{16}{5} \div \frac{4}{3} = \frac{16}{5} \times \frac{3}{4}$$

$$= \frac{4}{5} \times \frac{3}{1}$$

$$= \frac{12}{5}$$

Since the result is an improper fraction, we must convert it back into a mixed number.

$$\frac{12}{5} = \frac{10}{5} + \frac{2}{5}$$

$$= 2 + \frac{2}{5}$$

Therefore, the correct answer is $2\frac{2}{5}$.

32. **A**

To change a percent to a decimal, drop the percent sign and move the decimal point two place values to the left. The correct answer is 1.25937.

33. **C**

Substitute 2 for each a, 1 for each b, and simplify the expres-sion.

$$4(2 + 1) + 2[5 - (2^2 + 1^2)] = 4(2 + 1) + 2[5 - (4 + 1)]$$
$$= 4(3) + 2[5 - (5)]$$
$$= 4(3) + 2[0]$$
$$= 12 + 0$$
$$= 12$$

34. **C**

To find the mean, first add the individual scores together. The sum is 133. Next, count the number of scores which is 19 and divide 19 into 133, for a mean of 7.

35. **B**

In order to find what percent of 260 is 13, one needs only to form the following equation:

$$x\%(260) = 13$$
$$\frac{x(260)}{100} = 13$$
$$260x = 13(100)$$
$$x = \frac{1300}{260} = 5 \text{ percent} = 5\%$$

The other answer choices are incorrect. Choice (A) is obtained by dividing 13 by 260 and attaching the percent symbol. Choice (D) is obtained by again dividing 13 by 260, moving the decimal point one place to the right and attaching the percent symbol. Choice (E) is obtained by dividing 260 by 13 and attaching the percent sign. Finally, choice (C) is absurd because 50% of 260 is half of 260 which is 130 or 10 times 13.

36. **C**

> Referring to the figure shown below, it is easy to see that a cube has 8 corners. There are four in the front (points 1, 2, 3, and 4) and four in the back (points 5, 6, 7, and 8).

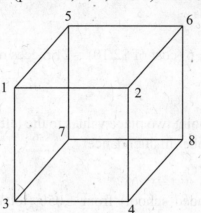

37. **B**

$$4\frac{1}{3} - 1\frac{5}{6} = 4\frac{2}{6} - 1\frac{5}{6}$$

$$= 3\frac{2+6}{6} - 1\frac{5}{6}$$

$$= 3\frac{8}{6} - 1\frac{5}{6}$$

$$= 2\frac{3}{6} = 2\frac{1}{2}$$

38. **E**

All three statements are true. Since a rhombus is a parallelogram, sides $\overline{BA}$ and $\overline{CD}$ are parallel. Using $\overline{AC}$ as a transversal, $\angle BAE$ and $\angle ECD$ are alternate interior angles and are therefore congruent making I true. The diagonals of a rhombus bisect the angles and so $\angle ADE$ and $\angle CDE$ are congruent making II true. In a rhombus, all four sides are congruent so triangle ABD is isosceles with congruent sides AB and $\overline{AD}$. The angles opposite those congruent sides are congruent, so $\angle ABE$ and $\angle ADE$ are congruent making III true. Therefore, the answer is choice (E).

39. **D**

The total cost is $8.35; subtract $6.25 for the cost of the first 15 pieces of laundry.

$$8.35 - 6.25 = \$2.10$$

Divide $2.10 by $0.35 to determine the number of pieces of laundry over 15.

$$.35\overline{)2.10}$$

$$35\overline{)210}$$

15 (cost of $6.25) + 6 (cost of $2.10) = 21 pieces of laundry.

40. **B**

Move the decimal point two place values to the left and drop the percent sign, then multiply to fi nd the number in attendance.

$(1,050)(.94) = 987.00$

Subtract 987 (attended school) from 1,050 (total enrolled) to find the number absent.

$1,050 - 987 = 63$

The correct answer is 63.

41. **C**

The phrase "20% of 75" means the same as "20% multiplied by 75." Changing 20% to .20, we can also multiply .20 by 75.

42. **B**

The number .12 can be rounded off to .1, so that the multiplication becomes $63 \times .1 = 6.3$

43 **D**

The required expression is represented by the number of laps that Carrie swam minus the number of laps that Antoine swam. This expression is $(9x - 2) - (3x + 5)$.

44. **E**

Let x represent the number of dollars that Karen had. Then the expression "4 more than double x" becomes $2x + 4$, which is the number of dollars that Nancy had.

The sum of these two amounts is $19, so the equation becomes $2x + 4 + x = 19$.

45. **A**

   By substituting each ordered pair into answer choice (A), we have a correct equality. For example, by substituting the first and last ordered pairs, we have $24 = \dfrac{120}{5}$ and $2 = \dfrac{120}{60}$. These ordered pairs do not satisfy the other answer choices.

46. **C**

   For each ordered pair, we notice that the y value is five time as large as the x value. In answer choice (C), the y value of 10 is five times as large as the x value of 2. This relationship does not exist in the other answer choices.

Section III: Writing

1. **A**

   "Campus" is a singular noun; therefore, the pronoun referring to "campus" should be "its" so that the pronoun will agree with its antecedent. Choices (B), "findings of," and (C), "in which," both have prepositions appropriately used. Choice (D), "can," is a helping verb in the correct tense.

2. **C**

   Choice (C) should read, "could not care less." A person using this expression is indicating his total lack of interest in something; to say, "I could care less" indicates some interest, so the correct expression is "I could not care less." Choice (A) is the correct subject pronoun; choice (B), "good," is the adjective form used to follow the linking verb "be" and choice (D) is a gerund used as the object of a preposition.

3. **D**

   The idiom is "conform with" a law; something or someone will "conform to" an environment. Choices (A) and (B) are correctly used idioms. Choice (C) is the proper form of the adjective.

4. **E**

   Choice (A), "have seen," is the present perfect tense, which is used to make a statement about something occurring in the past but continuing into the present. The speaker has observed the problem of lack of self-esteem, but this problem has not stopped in the present time. Choice (B) is a comparative form, and "else" of choice (C) is necessary when comparing one thing with the group of which it is a member or part. (The observation about self-esteem is but one of several observations the speaker has made.) Choice (D) has a preposition to indicate relationship between "problem" and "people."

5. **C**

   "Allowed as how" is used sometimes in speaking, but the proper expression should be "allowed that." "Accommodated with," choice (A), is an idiom used to indicate "to supply with." Choice (B) is an infinitive phrase followed by a subordinate clause as the direct object. Choice (D), "had expected," is the past perfect tense to indicate previous past action: Mr. Burgess's estimate of the cost was made before the actual event.

6. **A**

    As this sentence reads, it is a fragment. "Having" should be eliminated, leaving "turned out" as the main verb in the proper tense. Choice (D), "so," is a coordinating conjunction relating two events of cause-and-effect; therefore, both main clauses should be independent. Choice (B) is the adverb form modifying the verb "turned out," and choice (C), "who," is the nominative form serving as the subject of "knows."

7. **B**

    "Protested against" is redundant; "protested" is sufficient. "Ago" in choice (A) is an adjective used following the noun "years" or as an adverb following "long." Choice (C) is a correct idiom. Choice (D), "any," is an adjective.

8. **D**

    Two subjects joined by "and" require a plural verb; "public opinion and government policy" should be completed by "have." Choice (A), "called," is a participle modifying "journalists." Choice (B), "rapidly," is an adverb modifying choice (C), which is a correct idiom.

9. **D**

    The expression should read, "renting (or buying) a tuxedo," in order to complete the parallelism following choice (B) "included": "hiring a limousine" and "buying gifts," choice (C). Choice (A) is a correct expression which can also be phrased, "more than he expected," if greater clarity is desired.

10. **C**

    The object pronoun "us" should follow the preposition "of." In choice (A), "viewing" is a gerund used as the subject and therefore requires the possessive adjective "our." Choice (B) is the verb. Choice (D) is a correct idiom.

11. **B**

    The modifier "only" is misplaced. To place this word before "stole" indicates that stealing is a minor problem; also, the meaning of the sentence clearly indicates Jules has stolen money one time, so the sentence should read, "stole money only once." Choice (A) is a correct preposition; choice (C) is a possessive pronoun modifying "conscience"; and choice (D) is an object pronoun as the object of "allow."

12. **C**

There is no antecedent for "it." Choice (A), "a person," is the subject to which "he" in choice (B) refers. "Never" in choice (D) is a correctly placed adverb. The sentence should include a phrase such as "a crime" to serve as the antecedent of "it," or the phrase "for it" could be deleted.

13. **B**

The adverb "daily" is misplaced and should be placed with "is bringing," choice (A), or with "habit." Choice (C) is a prepositional phrase, and choice (D) is a subject pronoun for the subordinate clause.

14. **A**

The adverb form, "frequently," should be used to modify the verb. Choices (B) and (C) are a correct subject-verb combination. The adjective form, "possible," of choice (D) follows the linking verb "is."

15. **C**

The antecedent for "it" is unclear because "it" can refer to the grass or to the branch. Choice (A), "growing over," and choice (B), "to," are correct pronouns. Choice (D) is a correct idiom because we become "annoyed with" people but "annoyed at" things or situations.

16. **E**

The sentence is correct as written. Choices (A) and (B) are a compound structure and are in proper parallel form. Choice (C) has a clear reference to "system." Choice (D) is a correct idiom.

17. **D**

The preposition "in" has three objects: "submarines," "missiles," and choice (D) which must be made parallel to the previous two nouns. Choice (A) is a participle modifying "navigation." Choice (B) is a part of a subordinate clause modifying "submarines." Choice (C) is a correct preposition.

18. **D**

This sentence is a fragment made by the conjunction "and" linking "enjoying" with "known," the participial adjective of choice (B); "and" should be eliminated and "enjoying" changed to "enjoys" to be the subject of "president." Choice (A) is an idiom. Choice (B) is the correct possessive form to complete the idiom.

19. **A**

There is no antecedent for this pronoun, although it is implied that the elderly and the handicapped are the logical ones to be grateful. Choice (B) and (D) are elliptical constructions, "grateful [that] the city" and "helps [to] pay." Choice (C) is a verb.

20. **B**

This sentence is not parallel. Two actions are mentioned, connected by "not only" and "but also." The sentence should read, "not only are Americans . . . but also they are." Choices (A) and (C) contain properly used infinitives. Choice (D), "particularly," is the adverb form modifying the adjective, "arid."

21. **D**

Sentences should not end with a preposition; the sentence should read, "an opinion with which everyone agreed." Choice (A) is a gerund as the object of a preposition. Choice (B) is an appropriate conjunction; and choice (C), "good," is the positive form of the adjective to follow the linking verb "tasted."

22. **A**

The expression should read, "as prevalent as" for the proper comparison. Choice (B) is a noun used as an adjective. Choice (C), "some of which," has clear reference to "ornaments." Choice (D), "such as," is correct to mean, "for example."

23. **E**

Choice (A) is subjunctive mood to indicate a condition contrary to fact. Choice (B) is a correct idiom. Choice (C) uses the adverb "politely" to modify "speaking," and choice (D) uses the adjective "angry" to follow the linking verb "becoming."

24. **C**

"Irregardless," an incorrect expression, is a combination of "irrespective" and "regardless." (Taking into account the prefix and the suffix of "irregardless," the combination would mean, "not, not regarding," and so would be redundant.) Usually, "regardless" is used, although "irrespective" is also correct. The idioms in choices (A) and (D) are correct. Choice (B) is an adjective.

25. **A**

The idiom should be "capable of winning." The verb in choice (B) indicates the prior action of two past actions; the prepositions in choices (C) and (D) are correct.

26. **D**

The conjunction "not only ... but also" must be properly placed to indicate which qualities are being discussed and to maintain proper parallelism. Choice (D) contains three adjectives to follow the verb "to be": "capable and efficient" and "adept." Choices (A), (B), (C), and (E) are not parallel. In addition, choices (B) and (C) have "to be" after the conjunction, and this construction would require another verb after the second conjunction, "but also."

27. **A**

This sentence contains two concepts, proper management and careful control. In choice (A) these two concepts are concisely worded and appear in parallel form. Choice (B) has no noun for "Managing" to modify. Choice (C) would be acceptable with the addition of commas to set off the introductory phrase. Choice (D) mangles the concepts, and the wording in choice (E) is poor.

28. **C**

Choice (A) is a "squinting" modifier: it is unclear if "on the next day" tells when "I agreed" or when "to put up." Choice (B) does not clarify this problem. Choice (D) unnecessarily splits the subject and the verb, and choice (E) unnecessarily splits an infinitive.

29. **B**

The interrupter, "though not nearly all," should be placed so as not to split important parts of the sentence. Choices (A), (D), and (E) are incorrect because the interrupter splits a preposition and its object. Choices (C) and (D) will produce a fragment because the subject "we" is missing.

30. **E**

To mean "for example," the expression "like" is incorrect; the correct usage is "such as." Therefore, choices (A) and (B) are incorrect. Choices (C) and (D) incorrectly use "likes" as a verb, thereby changing the intent of the sentence.

31. **A**

Choice (A) correctly uses the object pronoun "whom" to follow the preposition "of." Choice (B) uses the wrong pronoun. Choice (C) inserts an extraneous preposition "about" that has no object. Choice (D) is awkward wording; choice (E) is also poor wording, especially with the pronoun "him" so far away from its antecedent.

32. **C**

Choice (C) clearly and simply deals with the location and the fame of the Dead Sea. It is incorrect to use a preposition with no object in order to end a sentence. Choices (A), (D), and (E) are incorrect because they end with "famous for." Also, in the phrase, "where the Dead Sea is at," the word at is redundant; it is sufficient to write "where the Dead Sea is." Therefore, choices (A) and (B) are incorrect. Finally, since the Dead Sea still exists, the verbs must be in the present tense.

33. **C**

   The phrase "cannot help" should be followed by a gerund, not by "but." Choice (C) follows "cannot help" with the gerund "admitting." Choices (A) and (D) are incorrect because they follow "cannot help" with "but." The wording of choice (B), "cannot admit," and choice (E), "cannot know," twists the meaning of the sentence.

34. **B**

   The correct idiom is to have an insight into a situation or person. While "to" in choice (A) is close in meaning, it is not exact; "for" and "with" of choices (C), (D), and (E) are unacceptable. The location of "often" in choice (D) is poor, and the location of "often" in choice (E) makes no significant change in the meaning.

35. **D**

   It is obvious that the Greenes have just purchased plants: "Upon leaving the nursery." The location of the modifying phrase, "they had just bought," should be carefully placed in the sentence so it clearly modifies "plants" and not "car." Choice (D) has the modifying phrase immediately following "plants," and the meaning is clear. The wording of choices (A), (B), and (C) makes the reader think the car has just been purchased. Choice (E) omits the concept "they had just bought."

36. **E**

   Choice (E) retains the central idea while eliminating the wording problems of the other choices. There is no antecedent for "we" in choices (A) and (B). Also, the phrase "end up" is redundant; "up" should be eliminated. Therefore, choice (C) is incorrect. Choice (D) introduces a new concept of "war may end over there," an idea clearly not intended by the original.

37. **B**

   Choice (B) clearly and precisely states the issue of debate. Choice (C) is eliminated because it is too wordy and not the precise issue under debate. The correlative conjunctions, "whether...or," should be followed by parallel structures. Choice (A) follows "Whether" with a subject-verb combination not seen after "not." Choice (D) is parallel but in the wrong tense. Choice (E) has "Whether or not" run together and uses poor wording in the rest of the sentence.

38. **A**

Choice (A) has both correct agreement and clear reference. Choice (B) has a subject-verb agreement problem, "charging…are." Choice (C) produces a fragment. It is unclear in choice (D) who will have the bad credit rating, and the wording of choice (E) has the obvious subject, "people," in a prepositional phrase.

39. **D**

Choice (D) correctly presents the fifth grade field trip in a subordinate clause modifying "exhibit." Choices (A) and (B) have the coordinating conjunction "and," but the first part of the sentence is not equal in meaning or importance to the second part of the sentence. Choice (C) introduces "when" with no antecedent. Choice (E) uses "where" as the subordinating conjunction, but it is too far from its antecedent and is not the important idea of the sentence.

40. **E**

In choice (E) the present infinitive is correctly used to express an action following another action: "plans to appeal." Choices (A) and (B) use the wrong form, "appealing." Choice (C) uses the wrong tense, "is appealing." Choice (D) sounds as if the same person is deciding the case and appealing the case.

41. **A**

Choice (A) has clear wording. Choice (B) is a fragment because it puts the verb in the nonessential phrase. Choices (C), (D), and (E) produce twisted wording. Choice (C) has no object for the verb "allowed" and sounds as if the speakers were allowed to stay up later. Choice (E) needs commas and sounds as if the speakers decided to stay up later.

42. **B**

Choice (B) plainly states the subject and the verb, "I find." Choices (A) and (E) have the subject in a prepositional phrase, "for me." Choice (E) produces a fragment. Choice (C), a fragment, has no subject because both potential subjects are in prepositional phases: "agreement" and "plan." Choices (C) and (D) imply "everyone" as the main subject.

43. **B**

Choice (B) avoids the split infinitive and the incorrect expression, "inside of." Choices (A) and (D) split the infinitive "to finish" with the adverb "completely." Choice (C) uses "inside of," an expression that is incorrect to use because it is redundant ("of" should be deleted) and because it should not be used with measuring time. Choice (E) erroneously changes the idea and would employ two verbs in simple past tense: "hired" and "finished."

44. **B**

The original involves a needless voice shift from first person to third person. Choice (B) correctly uses third person for both. Choices (C), (D), and (E) all retain the voice shift; each is awkwardly wordy as well.

PPST Essay Scoring Guide

The PPST essay sections are scored by two writing experts on the basis of the criteria outlined below. In addition to comparing your essay to those included in our practice tests, you may use these guidelines to estimate your score on this section. Remember that your score is the sum of the scores of two writing experts, so provided you respond to the assigned topic, your score will fall somewhere between two and twelve. Scores will be assigned based on the following guidelines:

6   An essay receiving a score of 6 may contain one or two spelling or punctuation errors, but overall it exhibits a high degree of proficiency and thought on the assigned topic.

An essay scoring a 6

- is both well organized and well developed
- engages important concepts and explains them clearly
- varies expression and language
- demonstrates deft use of language
- is virtually free from errors involving syntax and structure

5   An essay receiving a score of 5 exhibits a high degree of proficiency and thought on the assigned topic, however it contains a number of minor mistakes.

An essay scoring a 5

- is both well organized and well developed
- engages important concepts and explains them
- varies expression and language somewhat
- demonstrates deft use of language
- is virtually free from errors involving syntax and structure

4   An essay receiving a score of 4 responds to the assignment and exhibits some degree of deeper understanding.

An essay scoring a 4

- demonstrates adequate organization and development

- engages and explains some important concepts, but not all that are necessary to demonstrate full understanding

- exhibits adequate use of language

- contains some syntactical and structural errors, without excessive repetition of those errors

3   An essay receiving a score of 3 exhibits some degree of understanding, but its response to the topic is obviously deficient.

An essay scoring a 3 is deficient in one or more of the following areas:

- insufficient organization or development

- insufficient engagement or explanation of important concepts

- consistent repetition of syntactical or structural errors

- redundant or unsuitable word choice

2   An essay receiving a score of 2 exhibits limited understanding and its response to the topic is seriously deficient.

An essay scoring a 2 is deficient in one or more of the following areas:

- weak organization or development

- very few pertinent details

- consistent and serious errors in syntax, structure

- consistent and serious errors in word choice

1   An essay receiving a score of 1 exhibits a lack of basic writing skills.

An essay scoring a 1 is disorganized, undeveloped, contains consistent repetition of errors, or is incomprehensible.

SAMPLE SCORED ESSAYS WITH EXPLANATIONS

Essay #1—(Score = 5–6)

In the past thirty years, television has become a very popular pastime for almost everyone. From the time the mother places the baby in his jumpseat in front of the television so that she can relax and have a sec-ond cup of coffee until the time the senior citizen in the retirement home watches Vanna White turn the letters on "Wheel of Fortune," Americans spend endless hours in front of the "boob tube." I believe that television can become an addiction that provides an escape from the problems of the world and from facing responsibility for your own life.

When my mother was a little girl, what did children do to entertain themselves? They played. Their games usually involved social interaction with other children as well as imaginatively creating entertainment for themselves. They also developed hobbies like woodworking and sewing. Today, few children really know how to play with each other or entertain themselves. Instead, they sit in front of the television, glued to cartoons that are senseless and often violent. Even if they watch educational pro-grams like "Sesame Street," they don't really have to do anything but watch and listen to what the answer to the question is.

Teenagers, also, use television as a way of avoiding doing things that will help them mature. How many kids do much homework anymore? Why not? Because they come home from work tired and relax in front of the television. Even if they watch a controversial pro-gram about some problem in the world like AIDS or the war in the Middle East, they don't usually do anything about it.

In addition, young mothers use television to escape their problems. The terrible woes of the people on the soap operas make their problems seem less important. This means that they don't need to solve their own problems.

Although it may seem as if television is really great for older people, I think even my grandma would have more fun if she had more interests rather than just watching quiz shows. I know she has blotted out the "real world" when she expects us to act like the Cosby kids when she comes to visit.

In conclusion, I believe that television really can become an addiction that allows people of all ages to avoid facing their own problems and lose themselves in the problems of other people.

ANALYSIS

Essay I has a score range of 5–6. It has a traditional structure; the first paragraph introduces the topic, even suggesting the chronological organization of the essay. Each of the next four paragraphs has a clear topic sentence and details that develop it. The concluding paragraph, although only one sentence in length, restates the main idea. The essay is, therefore, clearly unified around the writer's opinion, which the writer tries to prove in a logical fashion. The writer effectively employs transitional words to relate the main ideas, varied sentence structure, and controlled vocabulary. Although the writer misspells pastime, uses the colloquial word kids, and has some problem with parallelism, repetition, and pronoun usage, the essay is well written considering the 30-minute time limit.

ESSAY II (Score: 4–5)

I do not agree with the given statement. I think that instead of being bad for people, television not only does not blot out the real world but, instead, gives the person watching it a chance to experience the real world, even places he can't possibly go and may never get a chance to go.

For instance, I've learned a lot about history, like the Vietnam War, by watching TV. I heard things about it, about how some of the veterans didn't feel as if they were welcomed right when they came back from that war. I didn't understand what was the matter. Then they built a special memorial in Washington for the veterans that didn't come back. Since then, I have seen a lot of programs that showed what went on in Vietnam, and I've heard Vietnam vets talk about what happened to them. I think that that war became very real to me because of TV.

Television educates us about the dangers of growing up in America today. I've seen good programs about the dangers of using drugs, about teenage pregnancy and what happens if you try to keep the baby, about eating too much cholesterol (That doesn't matter to me yet, but my dad needs to watch that!), and also anorexia. These are things we all need to know about, and TV has told about them so we know what to do.

I really am convinced that television brings the real world into your house. I think us kids today know a lot more about the real world than our grandparents did who grew up without television.

ANALYSIS

Essay II has a score range of 4–5. It is competently written. The writer takes one position and develops it. The first paragraph provides a clear introduction, and paragraphs two and three develop the thesis. Generalized examples are provided. The final paragraph concludes the essay. The essay contains some problems in correct usage, colloquial words like *kids,* and a lack of specific, concrete examples. (What, specifically, did the writer learn about the Vietnam War?) Sentences lack variety in length and construction, with many beginning with the pronoun "I." Ideas are not always clearly related to each other. The theme contains unnecessary repetition and errors in pronoun use.

ESSAY III (Score: 3–4)

On the one hand, I think television is bad, But it also does some good things for all of us. For instants, my little sister thought she wanted to be a policeman until she saw police shows on TV. Then she learned how dangerous it is and now she wants to be an astronaut. I guess she was too young to watch the Challenger explode to scare her out of that.

But the bad thing about television programs are the ideas it puts in kids heads. Like violent things happen on television, and little kids see it and don't know that other people hurt when they are hit, battered up, beat, shot, ect. Then the kids go out and try to knock their friends around and think if they are strong and handsome that they can get their own way whatever happens. Even parents sometimes have trouble controling their own kids because of too much TV. Of course that's partly because the parents watch too much too when they should of been taking care of the kids they necklected them watching television.

So I think that television has both it's good and it's bad points. I'd hate to see us get rid of it all together, but I wonder if I'll let my kids watch it when I have them. It sometimes puts bad ideas in their heads.

ANALYSIS

Essay III has a score range of 3–4. The failure of the writer of this essay, to take one opinion and clearly develop it, weakens the essay. The writer does try to give specific examples, but the details in the introductory paragraph would be more appropriate later in the essay. The apparent topic sentence of the second paragraph suggests a discussion of the results of children's watching television, but the writer discusses the parents' viewing in the same paragraph. The last sentence of the conclusion repeats the idea of the topic sentence of the second paragraph. The writer does not express his ideas in precise fashion ("Even parents sometimes have trouble controling (sic) their own kids because of too much TV.") or provide clear relationships between them. The essay also contains colloquialisms and errors in pronoun use, spelling, use of the apostrophe, and sentence construction.

Essay #4—(Score 1–2)

I get really upset when someone says they don't think we should watch television. Us students learn a lot more from television than whats in a lot of our classes in school. I've even learned stuff from the comertials they show the best way to clean house or the best kinds of car to buy right now I wouldn't have no idea what to get my sister for her birthday if I hadn't of seen it on television and said to myself, "Sally'd love one of those!"

If no one watched television, can you just think about how much crime there would be because kids would be board and would have to get excitment somewheres else than in his own living room where the TV set is.

There's also educational television with shows that ask questions and see if you know any answers. That's where I learned a lot of stuff about the world and everything.

ANALYSIS

Essay IV has a score range of 1–2. The writer of this essay digresses from the emphasis of the assigned topic in his effort to defend the watching of television. Although he has a clearly stated opinion, he falls to develop it in a logical, united fashion. There is no clear introduction; the second paragraph, only one sentence in length, is not properly developed; and the paper is lacking a conclusion. In addition, the language of this essay is not exact, and the ideas are not developed with specific examples. The essay contains serious problems in grammar and usage such as double negatives, run-on sentences, errors in pronoun reference and case, misspelled words, and errors in idiom.

Practice Test 1

Reading Comprehension

1. Ⓐ Ⓑ Ⓒ Ⓓ Ⓔ
2. Ⓐ Ⓑ Ⓒ Ⓓ Ⓔ
3. Ⓐ Ⓑ Ⓒ Ⓓ Ⓔ
4. Ⓐ Ⓑ Ⓒ Ⓓ Ⓔ
5. Ⓐ Ⓑ Ⓒ Ⓓ Ⓔ
6. Ⓐ Ⓑ Ⓒ Ⓓ Ⓔ
7. Ⓐ Ⓑ Ⓒ Ⓓ Ⓔ
8. Ⓐ Ⓑ Ⓒ Ⓓ Ⓔ
9. Ⓐ Ⓑ Ⓒ Ⓓ Ⓔ
10. Ⓐ Ⓑ Ⓒ Ⓓ Ⓔ
11. Ⓐ Ⓑ Ⓒ Ⓓ Ⓔ
12. Ⓐ Ⓑ Ⓒ Ⓓ Ⓔ
13. Ⓐ Ⓑ Ⓒ Ⓓ Ⓔ
14. Ⓐ Ⓑ Ⓒ Ⓓ Ⓔ
15. Ⓐ Ⓑ Ⓒ Ⓓ Ⓔ
16. Ⓐ Ⓑ Ⓒ Ⓓ Ⓔ
17. Ⓐ Ⓑ Ⓒ Ⓓ Ⓔ
18. Ⓐ Ⓑ Ⓒ Ⓓ Ⓔ
19. Ⓐ Ⓑ Ⓒ Ⓓ Ⓔ
20. Ⓐ Ⓑ Ⓒ Ⓓ Ⓔ
21. Ⓐ Ⓑ Ⓒ Ⓓ Ⓔ
22. Ⓐ Ⓑ Ⓒ Ⓓ Ⓔ
23. Ⓐ Ⓑ Ⓒ Ⓓ Ⓔ
24. Ⓐ Ⓑ Ⓒ Ⓓ Ⓔ
25. Ⓐ Ⓑ Ⓒ Ⓓ Ⓔ
26. Ⓐ Ⓑ Ⓒ Ⓓ Ⓔ
27. Ⓐ Ⓑ Ⓒ Ⓓ Ⓔ
28. Ⓐ Ⓑ Ⓒ Ⓓ Ⓔ
29. Ⓐ Ⓑ Ⓒ Ⓓ Ⓔ
30. Ⓐ Ⓑ Ⓒ Ⓓ Ⓔ
31. Ⓐ Ⓑ Ⓒ Ⓓ Ⓔ
32. Ⓐ Ⓑ Ⓒ Ⓓ Ⓔ
33. Ⓐ Ⓑ Ⓒ Ⓓ Ⓔ
34. Ⓐ Ⓑ Ⓒ Ⓓ Ⓔ
35. Ⓐ Ⓑ Ⓒ Ⓓ Ⓔ
36. Ⓐ Ⓑ Ⓒ Ⓓ Ⓔ
37. Ⓐ Ⓑ Ⓒ Ⓓ Ⓔ
38. Ⓐ Ⓑ Ⓒ Ⓓ Ⓔ
39. Ⓐ Ⓑ Ⓒ Ⓓ Ⓔ
40. Ⓐ Ⓑ Ⓒ Ⓓ Ⓔ

Mathematics

1. Ⓐ Ⓑ Ⓒ Ⓓ Ⓔ
2. Ⓐ Ⓑ Ⓒ Ⓓ Ⓔ
3. Ⓐ Ⓑ Ⓒ Ⓓ Ⓔ
4. Ⓐ Ⓑ Ⓒ Ⓓ Ⓔ
5. Ⓐ Ⓑ Ⓒ Ⓓ Ⓔ
6. Ⓐ Ⓑ Ⓒ Ⓓ Ⓔ
7. Ⓐ Ⓑ Ⓒ Ⓓ Ⓔ
8. Ⓐ Ⓑ Ⓒ Ⓓ Ⓔ
9. Ⓐ Ⓑ Ⓒ Ⓓ Ⓔ
10. Ⓐ Ⓑ Ⓒ Ⓓ Ⓔ
11. Ⓐ Ⓑ Ⓒ Ⓓ Ⓔ
12. Ⓐ Ⓑ Ⓒ Ⓓ Ⓔ
13. Ⓐ Ⓑ Ⓒ Ⓓ Ⓔ
14. Ⓐ Ⓑ Ⓒ Ⓓ Ⓔ
15. Ⓐ Ⓑ Ⓒ Ⓓ Ⓔ
16. Ⓐ Ⓑ Ⓒ Ⓓ Ⓔ
17. Ⓐ Ⓑ Ⓒ Ⓓ Ⓔ
18. Ⓐ Ⓑ Ⓒ Ⓓ Ⓔ
19. Ⓐ Ⓑ Ⓒ Ⓓ Ⓔ
20. Ⓐ Ⓑ Ⓒ Ⓓ Ⓔ
21. Ⓐ Ⓑ Ⓒ Ⓓ Ⓔ
22. Ⓐ Ⓑ Ⓒ Ⓓ Ⓔ
23. Ⓐ Ⓑ Ⓒ Ⓓ Ⓔ
24. Ⓐ Ⓑ Ⓒ Ⓓ Ⓔ
25. Ⓐ Ⓑ Ⓒ Ⓓ Ⓔ
26. Ⓐ Ⓑ Ⓒ Ⓓ Ⓔ
27. Ⓐ Ⓑ Ⓒ Ⓓ Ⓔ
28. Ⓐ Ⓑ Ⓒ Ⓓ Ⓔ
29. Ⓐ Ⓑ Ⓒ Ⓓ Ⓔ
30. Ⓐ Ⓑ Ⓒ Ⓓ Ⓔ
31. Ⓐ Ⓑ Ⓒ Ⓓ Ⓔ
32. Ⓐ Ⓑ Ⓒ Ⓓ Ⓔ
33. Ⓐ Ⓑ Ⓒ Ⓓ Ⓔ
34. Ⓐ Ⓑ Ⓒ Ⓓ Ⓔ
35. Ⓐ Ⓑ Ⓒ Ⓓ Ⓔ
36. Ⓐ Ⓑ Ⓒ Ⓓ Ⓔ
37. Ⓐ Ⓑ Ⓒ Ⓓ Ⓔ

38. Ⓐ Ⓑ Ⓒ Ⓓ Ⓔ
39. Ⓐ Ⓑ Ⓒ Ⓓ Ⓔ
40. Ⓐ Ⓑ Ⓒ Ⓓ Ⓔ

Writing

1. Ⓐ Ⓑ Ⓒ Ⓓ Ⓔ
2. Ⓐ Ⓑ Ⓒ Ⓓ Ⓔ
3. Ⓐ Ⓑ Ⓒ Ⓓ Ⓔ
4. Ⓐ Ⓑ Ⓒ Ⓓ Ⓔ
5. Ⓐ Ⓑ Ⓒ Ⓓ Ⓔ
6. Ⓐ Ⓑ Ⓒ Ⓓ Ⓔ
7. Ⓐ Ⓑ Ⓒ Ⓓ Ⓔ
8. Ⓐ Ⓑ Ⓒ Ⓓ Ⓔ
9. Ⓐ Ⓑ Ⓒ Ⓓ Ⓔ
10. Ⓐ Ⓑ Ⓒ Ⓓ Ⓔ

11. Ⓐ Ⓑ Ⓒ Ⓓ Ⓔ
12. Ⓐ Ⓑ Ⓒ Ⓓ Ⓔ
13. Ⓐ Ⓑ Ⓒ Ⓓ Ⓔ
14. Ⓐ Ⓑ Ⓒ Ⓓ Ⓔ
15. Ⓐ Ⓑ Ⓒ Ⓓ Ⓔ
16. Ⓐ Ⓑ Ⓒ Ⓓ Ⓔ
17. Ⓐ Ⓑ Ⓒ Ⓓ Ⓔ
18. Ⓐ Ⓑ Ⓒ Ⓓ Ⓔ
19. Ⓐ Ⓑ Ⓒ Ⓓ Ⓔ
20. Ⓐ Ⓑ Ⓒ Ⓓ Ⓔ
21. Ⓐ Ⓑ Ⓒ Ⓓ Ⓔ
22. Ⓐ Ⓑ Ⓒ Ⓓ Ⓔ
23. Ⓐ Ⓑ Ⓒ Ⓓ Ⓔ
24. Ⓐ Ⓑ Ⓒ Ⓓ Ⓔ
25. Ⓐ Ⓑ Ⓒ Ⓓ Ⓔ

26. Ⓐ Ⓑ Ⓒ Ⓓ Ⓔ
27. Ⓐ Ⓑ Ⓒ Ⓓ Ⓔ
28. Ⓐ Ⓑ Ⓒ Ⓓ Ⓔ
29. Ⓐ Ⓑ Ⓒ Ⓓ Ⓔ
30. Ⓐ Ⓑ Ⓒ Ⓓ Ⓔ
31. Ⓐ Ⓑ Ⓒ Ⓓ Ⓔ
32. Ⓐ Ⓑ Ⓒ Ⓓ Ⓔ
33. Ⓐ Ⓑ Ⓒ Ⓓ Ⓔ
34. Ⓐ Ⓑ Ⓒ Ⓓ Ⓔ
35. Ⓐ Ⓑ Ⓒ Ⓓ Ⓔ
36. Ⓐ Ⓑ Ⓒ Ⓓ Ⓔ
37. Ⓐ Ⓑ Ⓒ Ⓓ Ⓔ
38. Ⓐ Ⓑ Ⓒ Ⓓ Ⓔ

Practice Test 2

Reading Comprehension

1. Ⓐ Ⓑ Ⓒ Ⓓ Ⓔ
2. Ⓐ Ⓑ Ⓒ Ⓓ Ⓔ
3. Ⓐ Ⓑ Ⓒ Ⓓ Ⓔ
4. Ⓐ Ⓑ Ⓒ Ⓓ Ⓔ
5. Ⓐ Ⓑ Ⓒ Ⓓ Ⓔ
6. Ⓐ Ⓑ Ⓒ Ⓓ Ⓔ
7. Ⓐ Ⓑ Ⓒ Ⓓ Ⓔ
8. Ⓐ Ⓑ Ⓒ Ⓓ Ⓔ
9. Ⓐ Ⓑ Ⓒ Ⓓ Ⓔ
10. Ⓐ Ⓑ Ⓒ Ⓓ Ⓔ
11. Ⓐ Ⓑ Ⓒ Ⓓ Ⓔ
12. Ⓐ Ⓑ Ⓒ Ⓓ Ⓔ
13. Ⓐ Ⓑ Ⓒ Ⓓ Ⓔ
14. Ⓐ Ⓑ Ⓒ Ⓓ Ⓔ
15. Ⓐ Ⓑ Ⓒ Ⓓ Ⓔ
16. Ⓐ Ⓑ Ⓒ Ⓓ Ⓔ
17. Ⓐ Ⓑ Ⓒ Ⓓ Ⓔ
18. Ⓐ Ⓑ Ⓒ Ⓓ Ⓔ
19. Ⓐ Ⓑ Ⓒ Ⓓ Ⓔ
20. Ⓐ Ⓑ Ⓒ Ⓓ Ⓔ
21. Ⓐ Ⓑ Ⓒ Ⓓ Ⓔ
22. Ⓐ Ⓑ Ⓒ Ⓓ Ⓔ
23. Ⓐ Ⓑ Ⓒ Ⓓ Ⓔ
24. Ⓐ Ⓑ Ⓒ Ⓓ Ⓔ
25. Ⓐ Ⓑ Ⓒ Ⓓ Ⓔ

26. Ⓐ Ⓑ Ⓒ Ⓓ Ⓔ
27. Ⓐ Ⓑ Ⓒ Ⓓ Ⓔ
28. Ⓐ Ⓑ Ⓒ Ⓓ Ⓔ
29. Ⓐ Ⓑ Ⓒ Ⓓ Ⓔ
30. Ⓐ Ⓑ Ⓒ Ⓓ Ⓔ
31. Ⓐ Ⓑ Ⓒ Ⓓ Ⓔ
32. Ⓐ Ⓑ Ⓒ Ⓓ Ⓔ
33. Ⓐ Ⓑ Ⓒ Ⓓ Ⓔ
34. Ⓐ Ⓑ Ⓒ Ⓓ Ⓔ
35. Ⓐ Ⓑ Ⓒ Ⓓ Ⓔ
36. Ⓐ Ⓑ Ⓒ Ⓓ Ⓔ
37. Ⓐ Ⓑ Ⓒ Ⓓ Ⓔ
38. Ⓐ Ⓑ Ⓒ Ⓓ Ⓔ
39. Ⓐ Ⓑ Ⓒ Ⓓ Ⓔ
40. Ⓐ Ⓑ Ⓒ Ⓓ Ⓔ

Mathematics

1. Ⓐ Ⓑ Ⓒ Ⓓ Ⓔ
2. Ⓐ Ⓑ Ⓒ Ⓓ Ⓔ
3. Ⓐ Ⓑ Ⓒ Ⓓ Ⓔ
4. Ⓐ Ⓑ Ⓒ Ⓓ Ⓔ
5. Ⓐ Ⓑ Ⓒ Ⓓ Ⓔ
6. Ⓐ Ⓑ Ⓒ Ⓓ Ⓔ
7. Ⓐ Ⓑ Ⓒ Ⓓ Ⓔ
8. Ⓐ Ⓑ Ⓒ Ⓓ Ⓔ
9. Ⓐ Ⓑ Ⓒ Ⓓ Ⓔ
10. Ⓐ Ⓑ Ⓒ Ⓓ Ⓔ

11. Ⓐ Ⓑ Ⓒ Ⓓ Ⓔ
12. Ⓐ Ⓑ Ⓒ Ⓓ Ⓔ
13. Ⓐ Ⓑ Ⓒ Ⓓ Ⓔ
14. Ⓐ Ⓑ Ⓒ Ⓓ Ⓔ
15. Ⓐ Ⓑ Ⓒ Ⓓ Ⓔ
16. Ⓐ Ⓑ Ⓒ Ⓓ Ⓔ
17. Ⓐ Ⓑ Ⓒ Ⓓ Ⓔ
18. Ⓐ Ⓑ Ⓒ Ⓓ Ⓔ
19. Ⓐ Ⓑ Ⓒ Ⓓ Ⓔ
20. Ⓐ Ⓑ Ⓒ Ⓓ Ⓔ
21. Ⓐ Ⓑ Ⓒ Ⓓ Ⓔ
22. Ⓐ Ⓑ Ⓒ Ⓓ Ⓔ
23. Ⓐ Ⓑ Ⓒ Ⓓ Ⓔ
24. Ⓐ Ⓑ Ⓒ Ⓓ Ⓔ
25. Ⓐ Ⓑ Ⓒ Ⓓ Ⓔ
26. Ⓐ Ⓑ Ⓒ Ⓓ Ⓔ
27. Ⓐ Ⓑ Ⓒ Ⓓ Ⓔ
28. Ⓐ Ⓑ Ⓒ Ⓓ Ⓔ
29. Ⓐ Ⓑ Ⓒ Ⓓ Ⓔ
30. Ⓐ Ⓑ Ⓒ Ⓓ Ⓔ
31. Ⓐ Ⓑ Ⓒ Ⓓ Ⓔ
32. Ⓐ Ⓑ Ⓒ Ⓓ Ⓔ
33. Ⓐ Ⓑ Ⓒ Ⓓ Ⓔ
34. Ⓐ Ⓑ Ⓒ Ⓓ Ⓔ
35. Ⓐ Ⓑ Ⓒ Ⓓ Ⓔ
36. Ⓐ Ⓑ Ⓒ Ⓓ Ⓔ
37. Ⓐ Ⓑ Ⓒ Ⓓ Ⓔ

38. (A) (B) (C) (D) (E)

39. (A) (B) (C) (D) (E)

40. (A) (B) (C) (D) (E)

Writing

1. (A) (B) (C) (D) (E)

2. (A) (B) (C) (D) (E)

3. (A) (B) (C) (D) (E)

4. (A) (B) (C) (D) (E)

5. (A) (B) (C) (D) (E)

6. (A) (B) (C) (D) (E)

7. (A) (B) (C) (D) (E)

8. (A) (B) (C) (D) (E)

9. (A) (B) (C) (D) (E)

10. (A) (B) (C) (D) (E)

11. (A) (B) (C) (D) (E)

12. (A) (B) (C) (D) (E)

13. (A) (B) (C) (D) (E)

14. (A) (B) (C) (D) (E)

15. (A) (B) (C) (D) (E)

16. (A) (B) (C) (D) (E)

17. (A) (B) (C) (D) (E)

18. (A) (B) (C) (D) (E)

19. (A) (B) (C) (D) (E)

20. (A) (B) (C) (D) (E)

21. (A) (B) (C) (D) (E)

22. (A) (B) (C) (D) (E)

23. (A) (B) (C) (D) (E)

24. (A) (B) (C) (D) (E)

25. (A) (B) (C) (D) (E)

26. (A) (B) (C) (D) (E)

27. (A) (B) (C) (D) (E)

28. (A) (B) (C) (D) (E)

29. (A) (B) (C) (D) (E)

30. (A) (B) (C) (D) (E)

31. (A) (B) (C) (D) (E)

32. (A) (B) (C) (D) (E)

33. (A) (B) (C) (D) (E)

34. (A) (B) (C) (D) (E)

35. (A) (B) (C) (D) (E)

36. (A) (B) (C) (D) (E)

37. (A) (B) (C) (D) (E)

38. (A) (B) (C) (D) (E)

Practice Test 3

Reading Comprehension

1. Ⓐ Ⓑ Ⓒ Ⓓ Ⓔ
2. Ⓐ Ⓑ Ⓒ Ⓓ Ⓔ
3. Ⓐ Ⓑ Ⓒ Ⓓ Ⓔ
4. Ⓐ Ⓑ Ⓒ Ⓓ Ⓔ
5. Ⓐ Ⓑ Ⓒ Ⓓ Ⓔ
6. Ⓐ Ⓑ Ⓒ Ⓓ Ⓔ
7. Ⓐ Ⓑ Ⓒ Ⓓ Ⓔ
8. Ⓐ Ⓑ Ⓒ Ⓓ Ⓔ
9. Ⓐ Ⓑ Ⓒ Ⓓ Ⓔ
10. Ⓐ Ⓑ Ⓒ Ⓓ Ⓔ
11. Ⓐ Ⓑ Ⓒ Ⓓ Ⓔ
12. Ⓐ Ⓑ Ⓒ Ⓓ Ⓔ
13. Ⓐ Ⓑ Ⓒ Ⓓ Ⓔ
14. Ⓐ Ⓑ Ⓒ Ⓓ Ⓔ
15. Ⓐ Ⓑ Ⓒ Ⓓ Ⓔ
16. Ⓐ Ⓑ Ⓒ Ⓓ Ⓔ
17. Ⓐ Ⓑ Ⓒ Ⓓ Ⓔ
18. Ⓐ Ⓑ Ⓒ Ⓓ Ⓔ
19. Ⓐ Ⓑ Ⓒ Ⓓ Ⓔ
20. Ⓐ Ⓑ Ⓒ Ⓓ Ⓔ
21. Ⓐ Ⓑ Ⓒ Ⓓ Ⓔ
22. Ⓐ Ⓑ Ⓒ Ⓓ Ⓔ
23. Ⓐ Ⓑ Ⓒ Ⓓ Ⓔ
24. Ⓐ Ⓑ Ⓒ Ⓓ Ⓔ
25. Ⓐ Ⓑ Ⓒ Ⓓ Ⓔ

26. Ⓐ Ⓑ Ⓒ Ⓓ Ⓔ
27. Ⓐ Ⓑ Ⓒ Ⓓ Ⓔ
28. Ⓐ Ⓑ Ⓒ Ⓓ Ⓔ
29. Ⓐ Ⓑ Ⓒ Ⓓ Ⓔ
30. Ⓐ Ⓑ Ⓒ Ⓓ Ⓔ
31. Ⓐ Ⓑ Ⓒ Ⓓ Ⓔ
32. Ⓐ Ⓑ Ⓒ Ⓓ Ⓔ
33. Ⓐ Ⓑ Ⓒ Ⓓ Ⓔ
34. Ⓐ Ⓑ Ⓒ Ⓓ Ⓔ
35. Ⓐ Ⓑ Ⓒ Ⓓ Ⓔ
36. Ⓐ Ⓑ Ⓒ Ⓓ Ⓔ
37. Ⓐ Ⓑ Ⓒ Ⓓ Ⓔ
38. Ⓐ Ⓑ Ⓒ Ⓓ Ⓔ
39. Ⓐ Ⓑ Ⓒ Ⓓ Ⓔ
40. Ⓐ Ⓑ Ⓒ Ⓓ Ⓔ
41. Ⓐ Ⓑ Ⓒ Ⓓ Ⓔ
42. Ⓐ Ⓑ Ⓒ Ⓓ Ⓔ
43. Ⓐ Ⓑ Ⓒ Ⓓ Ⓔ
44. Ⓐ Ⓑ Ⓒ Ⓓ Ⓔ
45. Ⓐ Ⓑ Ⓒ Ⓓ Ⓔ
46. Ⓐ Ⓑ Ⓒ Ⓓ Ⓔ

Mathematics

1. Ⓐ Ⓑ Ⓒ Ⓓ Ⓔ
2. Ⓐ Ⓑ Ⓒ Ⓓ Ⓔ
3. Ⓐ Ⓑ Ⓒ Ⓓ Ⓔ
4. Ⓐ Ⓑ Ⓒ Ⓓ Ⓔ

5. Ⓐ Ⓑ Ⓒ Ⓓ Ⓔ
6. Ⓐ Ⓑ Ⓒ Ⓓ Ⓔ
7. Ⓐ Ⓑ Ⓒ Ⓓ Ⓔ
8. Ⓐ Ⓑ Ⓒ Ⓓ Ⓔ
9. Ⓐ Ⓑ Ⓒ Ⓓ Ⓔ
10. Ⓐ Ⓑ Ⓒ Ⓓ Ⓔ
11. Ⓐ Ⓑ Ⓒ Ⓓ Ⓔ
12. Ⓐ Ⓑ Ⓒ Ⓓ Ⓔ
13. Ⓐ Ⓑ Ⓒ Ⓓ Ⓔ
14. Ⓐ Ⓑ Ⓒ Ⓓ Ⓔ
15. Ⓐ Ⓑ Ⓒ Ⓓ Ⓔ
16. Ⓐ Ⓑ Ⓒ Ⓓ Ⓔ
17. Ⓐ Ⓑ Ⓒ Ⓓ Ⓔ
18. Ⓐ Ⓑ Ⓒ Ⓓ Ⓔ
19. Ⓐ Ⓑ Ⓒ Ⓓ Ⓔ
20. Ⓐ Ⓑ Ⓒ Ⓓ Ⓔ
21. Ⓐ Ⓑ Ⓒ Ⓓ Ⓔ
22. Ⓐ Ⓑ Ⓒ Ⓓ Ⓔ
23. Ⓐ Ⓑ Ⓒ Ⓓ Ⓔ
24. Ⓐ Ⓑ Ⓒ Ⓓ Ⓔ
25. Ⓐ Ⓑ Ⓒ Ⓓ Ⓔ
26. Ⓐ Ⓑ Ⓒ Ⓓ Ⓔ
27. Ⓐ Ⓑ Ⓒ Ⓓ Ⓔ
28. Ⓐ Ⓑ Ⓒ Ⓓ Ⓔ
29. Ⓐ Ⓑ Ⓒ Ⓓ Ⓔ
30. Ⓐ Ⓑ Ⓒ Ⓓ Ⓔ
31. Ⓐ Ⓑ Ⓒ Ⓓ Ⓔ

32. Ⓐ Ⓑ Ⓒ Ⓓ Ⓔ

33. Ⓐ Ⓑ Ⓒ Ⓓ Ⓔ

34. Ⓐ Ⓑ Ⓒ Ⓓ Ⓔ

35. Ⓐ Ⓑ Ⓒ Ⓓ Ⓔ

36. Ⓐ Ⓑ Ⓒ Ⓓ Ⓔ

37. Ⓐ Ⓑ Ⓒ Ⓓ Ⓔ

38. Ⓐ Ⓑ Ⓒ Ⓓ Ⓔ

39. Ⓐ Ⓑ Ⓒ Ⓓ Ⓔ

40. Ⓐ Ⓑ Ⓒ Ⓓ Ⓔ

41. Ⓐ Ⓑ Ⓒ Ⓓ Ⓔ

42. Ⓐ Ⓑ Ⓒ Ⓓ Ⓔ

43. Ⓐ Ⓑ Ⓒ Ⓓ Ⓔ

44. Ⓐ Ⓑ Ⓒ Ⓓ Ⓔ

45. Ⓐ Ⓑ Ⓒ Ⓓ Ⓔ

46. Ⓐ Ⓑ Ⓒ Ⓓ Ⓔ

Writing

1. Ⓐ Ⓑ Ⓒ Ⓓ Ⓔ

2. Ⓐ Ⓑ Ⓒ Ⓓ Ⓔ

3. Ⓐ Ⓑ Ⓒ Ⓓ Ⓔ

4. Ⓐ Ⓑ Ⓒ Ⓓ Ⓔ

5. Ⓐ Ⓑ Ⓒ Ⓓ Ⓔ

6. Ⓐ Ⓑ Ⓒ Ⓓ Ⓔ

7. Ⓐ Ⓑ Ⓒ Ⓓ Ⓔ

8. Ⓐ Ⓑ Ⓒ Ⓓ Ⓔ

9. Ⓐ Ⓑ Ⓒ Ⓓ Ⓔ

10. Ⓐ Ⓑ Ⓒ Ⓓ Ⓔ

11. Ⓐ Ⓑ Ⓒ Ⓓ Ⓔ

12. Ⓐ Ⓑ Ⓒ Ⓓ Ⓔ

13. Ⓐ Ⓑ Ⓒ Ⓓ Ⓔ

14. Ⓐ Ⓑ Ⓒ Ⓓ Ⓔ

15. Ⓐ Ⓑ Ⓒ Ⓓ Ⓔ

16. Ⓐ Ⓑ Ⓒ Ⓓ Ⓔ

17. Ⓐ Ⓑ Ⓒ Ⓓ Ⓔ

18. Ⓐ Ⓑ Ⓒ Ⓓ Ⓔ

19. Ⓐ Ⓑ Ⓒ Ⓓ Ⓔ

20. Ⓐ Ⓑ Ⓒ Ⓓ Ⓔ

21. Ⓐ Ⓑ Ⓒ Ⓓ Ⓔ

22. Ⓐ Ⓑ Ⓒ Ⓓ Ⓔ

23. Ⓐ Ⓑ Ⓒ Ⓓ Ⓔ

24. Ⓐ Ⓑ Ⓒ Ⓓ Ⓔ

25. Ⓐ Ⓑ Ⓒ Ⓓ Ⓔ

26. Ⓐ Ⓑ Ⓒ Ⓓ Ⓔ

27. Ⓐ Ⓑ Ⓒ Ⓓ Ⓔ

28. Ⓐ Ⓑ Ⓒ Ⓓ Ⓔ

29. Ⓐ Ⓑ Ⓒ Ⓓ Ⓔ

30. Ⓐ Ⓑ Ⓒ Ⓓ Ⓔ

31. Ⓐ Ⓑ Ⓒ Ⓓ Ⓔ

32. Ⓐ Ⓑ Ⓒ Ⓓ Ⓔ

33. Ⓐ Ⓑ Ⓒ Ⓓ Ⓔ

34. Ⓐ Ⓑ Ⓒ Ⓓ Ⓔ

35. Ⓐ Ⓑ Ⓒ Ⓓ Ⓔ

36. Ⓐ Ⓑ Ⓒ Ⓓ Ⓔ

37. Ⓐ Ⓑ Ⓒ Ⓓ Ⓔ

38. Ⓐ Ⓑ Ⓒ Ⓓ Ⓔ

39. Ⓐ Ⓑ Ⓒ Ⓓ Ⓔ

40. Ⓐ Ⓑ Ⓒ Ⓓ Ⓔ

41. Ⓐ Ⓑ Ⓒ Ⓓ Ⓔ

42. Ⓐ Ⓑ Ⓒ Ⓓ Ⓔ

43. Ⓐ Ⓑ Ⓒ Ⓓ Ⓔ

44. Ⓐ Ⓑ Ⓒ Ⓓ Ⓔ

Practice Test 4

Reading Comprehension

1. (A) (B) (C) (D) (E)
2. (A) (B) (C) (D) (E)
3. (A) (B) (C) (D) (E)
4. (A) (B) (C) (D) (E)
5. (A) (B) (C) (D) (E)
6. (A) (B) (C) (D) (E)
7. (A) (B) (C) (D) (E)
8. (A) (B) (C) (D) (E)
9. (A) (B) (C) (D) (E)
10. (A) (B) (C) (D) (E)
11. (A) (B) (C) (D) (E)
12. (A) (B) (C) (D) (E)
13. (A) (B) (C) (D) (E)
14. (A) (B) (C) (D) (E)
15. (A) (B) (C) (D) (E)
16. (A) (B) (C) (D) (E)
17. (A) (B) (C) (D) (E)
18. (A) (B) (C) (D) (E)
19. (A) (B) (C) (D) (E)
20. (A) (B) (C) (D) (E)
21. (A) (B) (C) (D) (E)
22. (A) (B) (C) (D) (E)
23. (A) (B) (C) (D) (E)
24. (A) (B) (C) (D) (E)
25. (A) (B) (C) (D) (E)

26. (A) (B) (C) (D) (E)
27. (A) (B) (C) (D) (E)
28. (A) (B) (C) (D) (E)
29. (A) (B) (C) (D) (E)
30. (A) (B) (C) (D) (E)
31. (A) (B) (C) (D) (E)
32. (A) (B) (C) (D) (E)
33. (A) (B) (C) (D) (E)
34. (A) (B) (C) (D) (E)
35. (A) (B) (C) (D) (E)
36. (A) (B) (C) (D) (E)
37. (A) (B) (C) (D) (E)
38. (A) (B) (C) (D) (E)
39. (A) (B) (C) (D) (E)
40. (A) (B) (C) (D) (E)
41. (A) (B) (C) (D) (E)
42. (A) (B) (C) (D) (E)
43. (A) (B) (C) (D) (E)
44. (A) (B) (C) (D) (E)
45. (A) (B) (C) (D) (E)
46. (A) (B) (C) (D) (E)

Mathematics

1. (A) (B) (C) (D) (E)
2. (A) (B) (C) (D) (E)
3. (A) (B) (C) (D) (E)
4. (A) (B) (C) (D) (E)
5. (A) (B) (C) (D) (E)
6. (A) (B) (C) (D) (E)
7. (A) (B) (C) (D) (E)
8. (A) (B) (C) (D) (E)
9. (A) (B) (C) (D) (E)
10. (A) (B) (C) (D) (E)
11. (A) (B) (C) (D) (E)
12. (A) (B) (C) (D) (E)
13. (A) (B) (C) (D) (E)
14. (A) (B) (C) (D) (E)
15. (A) (B) (C) (D) (E)
16. (A) (B) (C) (D) (E)
17. (A) (B) (C) (D) (E)
18. (A) (B) (C) (D) (E)
19. (A) (B) (C) (D) (E)
20. (A) (B) (C) (D) (E)
21. (A) (B) (C) (D) (E)
22. (A) (B) (C) (D) (E)
23. (A) (B) (C) (D) (E)
24. (A) (B) (C) (D) (E)
25. (A) (B) (C) (D) (E)
26. (A) (B) (C) (D) (E)
27. (A) (B) (C) (D) (E)
28. (A) (B) (C) (D) (E)
29. (A) (B) (C) (D) (E)
30. (A) (B) (C) (D) (E)
31. (A) (B) (C) (D) (E)

32. Ⓐ Ⓑ Ⓒ Ⓓ Ⓔ

33. Ⓐ Ⓑ Ⓒ Ⓓ Ⓔ

34. Ⓐ Ⓑ Ⓒ Ⓓ Ⓔ

35. Ⓐ Ⓑ Ⓒ Ⓓ Ⓔ

36. Ⓐ Ⓑ Ⓒ Ⓓ Ⓔ

37. Ⓐ Ⓑ Ⓒ Ⓓ Ⓔ

38. Ⓐ Ⓑ Ⓒ Ⓓ Ⓔ

39. Ⓐ Ⓑ Ⓒ Ⓓ Ⓔ

40. Ⓐ Ⓑ Ⓒ Ⓓ Ⓔ

41. Ⓐ Ⓑ Ⓒ Ⓓ Ⓔ

42. Ⓐ Ⓑ Ⓒ Ⓓ Ⓔ

43. Ⓐ Ⓑ Ⓒ Ⓓ Ⓔ

44. Ⓐ Ⓑ Ⓒ Ⓓ Ⓔ

45. Ⓐ Ⓑ Ⓒ Ⓓ Ⓔ

46. Ⓐ Ⓑ Ⓒ Ⓓ Ⓔ

Writing

1. Ⓐ Ⓑ Ⓒ Ⓓ Ⓔ

2. Ⓐ Ⓑ Ⓒ Ⓓ Ⓔ

3. Ⓐ Ⓑ Ⓒ Ⓓ Ⓔ

4. Ⓐ Ⓑ Ⓒ Ⓓ Ⓔ

5. Ⓐ Ⓑ Ⓒ Ⓓ Ⓔ

6. Ⓐ Ⓑ Ⓒ Ⓓ Ⓔ

7. Ⓐ Ⓑ Ⓒ Ⓓ Ⓔ

8. Ⓐ Ⓑ Ⓒ Ⓓ Ⓔ

9. Ⓐ Ⓑ Ⓒ Ⓓ Ⓔ

10. Ⓐ Ⓑ Ⓒ Ⓓ Ⓔ

11. Ⓐ Ⓑ Ⓒ Ⓓ Ⓔ

12. Ⓐ Ⓑ Ⓒ Ⓓ Ⓔ

13. Ⓐ Ⓑ Ⓒ Ⓓ Ⓔ

14. Ⓐ Ⓑ Ⓒ Ⓓ Ⓔ

15. Ⓐ Ⓑ Ⓒ Ⓓ Ⓔ

16. Ⓐ Ⓑ Ⓒ Ⓓ Ⓔ

17. Ⓐ Ⓑ Ⓒ Ⓓ Ⓔ

18. Ⓐ Ⓑ Ⓒ Ⓓ Ⓔ

19. Ⓐ Ⓑ Ⓒ Ⓓ Ⓔ

20. Ⓐ Ⓑ Ⓒ Ⓓ Ⓔ

21. Ⓐ Ⓑ Ⓒ Ⓓ Ⓔ

22. Ⓐ Ⓑ Ⓒ Ⓓ Ⓔ

23. Ⓐ Ⓑ Ⓒ Ⓓ Ⓔ

24. Ⓐ Ⓑ Ⓒ Ⓓ Ⓔ

25. Ⓐ Ⓑ Ⓒ Ⓓ Ⓔ

26. Ⓐ Ⓑ Ⓒ Ⓓ Ⓔ

27. Ⓐ Ⓑ Ⓒ Ⓓ Ⓔ

28. Ⓐ Ⓑ Ⓒ Ⓓ Ⓔ

29. Ⓐ Ⓑ Ⓒ Ⓓ Ⓔ

30. Ⓐ Ⓑ Ⓒ Ⓓ Ⓔ

31. Ⓐ Ⓑ Ⓒ Ⓓ Ⓔ

32. Ⓐ Ⓑ Ⓒ Ⓓ Ⓔ

33. Ⓐ Ⓑ Ⓒ Ⓓ Ⓔ

34. Ⓐ Ⓑ Ⓒ Ⓓ Ⓔ

35. Ⓐ Ⓑ Ⓒ Ⓓ Ⓔ

36. Ⓐ Ⓑ Ⓒ Ⓓ Ⓔ

37. Ⓐ Ⓑ Ⓒ Ⓓ Ⓔ

38. Ⓐ Ⓑ Ⓒ Ⓓ Ⓔ

39. Ⓐ Ⓑ Ⓒ Ⓓ Ⓔ

40. Ⓐ Ⓑ Ⓒ Ⓓ Ⓔ

41. Ⓐ Ⓑ Ⓒ Ⓓ Ⓔ

42. Ⓐ Ⓑ Ⓒ Ⓓ Ⓔ

43. Ⓐ Ⓑ Ⓒ Ⓓ Ⓔ

44. Ⓐ Ⓑ Ⓒ Ⓓ Ⓔ

Practice Test – Additional Answer Sheet

Reading Comprehension

1. Ⓐ Ⓑ Ⓒ Ⓓ Ⓔ
2. Ⓐ Ⓑ Ⓒ Ⓓ Ⓔ
3. Ⓐ Ⓑ Ⓒ Ⓓ Ⓔ
4. Ⓐ Ⓑ Ⓒ Ⓓ Ⓔ
5. Ⓐ Ⓑ Ⓒ Ⓓ Ⓔ
6. Ⓐ Ⓑ Ⓒ Ⓓ Ⓔ
7. Ⓐ Ⓑ Ⓒ Ⓓ Ⓔ
8. Ⓐ Ⓑ Ⓒ Ⓓ Ⓔ
9. Ⓐ Ⓑ Ⓒ Ⓓ Ⓔ
10. Ⓐ Ⓑ Ⓒ Ⓓ Ⓔ
11. Ⓐ Ⓑ Ⓒ Ⓓ Ⓔ
12. Ⓐ Ⓑ Ⓒ Ⓓ Ⓔ
13. Ⓐ Ⓑ Ⓒ Ⓓ Ⓔ
14. Ⓐ Ⓑ Ⓒ Ⓓ Ⓔ
15. Ⓐ Ⓑ Ⓒ Ⓓ Ⓔ
16. Ⓐ Ⓑ Ⓒ Ⓓ Ⓔ
17. Ⓐ Ⓑ Ⓒ Ⓓ Ⓔ
18. Ⓐ Ⓑ Ⓒ Ⓓ Ⓔ
19. Ⓐ Ⓑ Ⓒ Ⓓ Ⓔ
20. Ⓐ Ⓑ Ⓒ Ⓓ Ⓔ
21. Ⓐ Ⓑ Ⓒ Ⓓ Ⓔ
22. Ⓐ Ⓑ Ⓒ Ⓓ Ⓔ
23. Ⓐ Ⓑ Ⓒ Ⓓ Ⓔ
24. Ⓐ Ⓑ Ⓒ Ⓓ Ⓔ
25. Ⓐ Ⓑ Ⓒ Ⓓ Ⓔ
26. Ⓐ Ⓑ Ⓒ Ⓓ Ⓔ
27. Ⓐ Ⓑ Ⓒ Ⓓ Ⓔ
28. Ⓐ Ⓑ Ⓒ Ⓓ Ⓔ
29. Ⓐ Ⓑ Ⓒ Ⓓ Ⓔ
30. Ⓐ Ⓑ Ⓒ Ⓓ Ⓔ
31. Ⓐ Ⓑ Ⓒ Ⓓ Ⓔ
32. Ⓐ Ⓑ Ⓒ Ⓓ Ⓔ
33. Ⓐ Ⓑ Ⓒ Ⓓ Ⓔ
34. Ⓐ Ⓑ Ⓒ Ⓓ Ⓔ
35. Ⓐ Ⓑ Ⓒ Ⓓ Ⓔ
36. Ⓐ Ⓑ Ⓒ Ⓓ Ⓔ
37. Ⓐ Ⓑ Ⓒ Ⓓ Ⓔ
38. Ⓐ Ⓑ Ⓒ Ⓓ Ⓔ
39. Ⓐ Ⓑ Ⓒ Ⓓ Ⓔ
40. Ⓐ Ⓑ Ⓒ Ⓓ Ⓔ

Mathematics

1. Ⓐ Ⓑ Ⓒ Ⓓ Ⓔ
2. Ⓐ Ⓑ Ⓒ Ⓓ Ⓔ
3. Ⓐ Ⓑ Ⓒ Ⓓ Ⓔ
4. Ⓐ Ⓑ Ⓒ Ⓓ Ⓔ
5. Ⓐ Ⓑ Ⓒ Ⓓ Ⓔ
6. Ⓐ Ⓑ Ⓒ Ⓓ Ⓔ
7. Ⓐ Ⓑ Ⓒ Ⓓ Ⓔ
8. Ⓐ Ⓑ Ⓒ Ⓓ Ⓔ
9. Ⓐ Ⓑ Ⓒ Ⓓ Ⓔ
10. Ⓐ Ⓑ Ⓒ Ⓓ Ⓔ
11. Ⓐ Ⓑ Ⓒ Ⓓ Ⓔ
12. Ⓐ Ⓑ Ⓒ Ⓓ Ⓔ
13. Ⓐ Ⓑ Ⓒ Ⓓ Ⓔ
14. Ⓐ Ⓑ Ⓒ Ⓓ Ⓔ
15. Ⓐ Ⓑ Ⓒ Ⓓ Ⓔ
16. Ⓐ Ⓑ Ⓒ Ⓓ Ⓔ
17. Ⓐ Ⓑ Ⓒ Ⓓ Ⓔ
18. Ⓐ Ⓑ Ⓒ Ⓓ Ⓔ
19. Ⓐ Ⓑ Ⓒ Ⓓ Ⓔ
20. Ⓐ Ⓑ Ⓒ Ⓓ Ⓔ
21. Ⓐ Ⓑ Ⓒ Ⓓ Ⓔ
22. Ⓐ Ⓑ Ⓒ Ⓓ Ⓔ
23. Ⓐ Ⓑ Ⓒ Ⓓ Ⓔ
24. Ⓐ Ⓑ Ⓒ Ⓓ Ⓔ
25. Ⓐ Ⓑ Ⓒ Ⓓ Ⓔ
26. Ⓐ Ⓑ Ⓒ Ⓓ Ⓔ
27. Ⓐ Ⓑ Ⓒ Ⓓ Ⓔ
28. Ⓐ Ⓑ Ⓒ Ⓓ Ⓔ
29. Ⓐ Ⓑ Ⓒ Ⓓ Ⓔ
30. Ⓐ Ⓑ Ⓒ Ⓓ Ⓔ
31. Ⓐ Ⓑ Ⓒ Ⓓ Ⓔ
32. Ⓐ Ⓑ Ⓒ Ⓓ Ⓔ
33. Ⓐ Ⓑ Ⓒ Ⓓ Ⓔ
34. Ⓐ Ⓑ Ⓒ Ⓓ Ⓔ
35. Ⓐ Ⓑ Ⓒ Ⓓ Ⓔ
36. Ⓐ Ⓑ Ⓒ Ⓓ Ⓔ
37. Ⓐ Ⓑ Ⓒ Ⓓ Ⓔ

Practice Test – Additional Answer Sheet

38. (A) (B) (C) (D) (E)

39. (A) (B) (C) (D) (E)

40. (A) (B) (C) (D) (E)

Writing

1. (A) (B) (C) (D) (E)

2. (A) (B) (C) (D) (E)

3. (A) (B) (C) (D) (E)

4. (A) (B) (C) (D) (E)

5. (A) (B) (C) (D) (E)

6. (A) (B) (C) (D) (E)

7. (A) (B) (C) (D) (E)

8. (A) (B) (C) (D) (E)

9. (A) (B) (C) (D) (E)

10. (A) (B) (C) (D) (E)

11. (A) (B) (C) (D) (E)

12. (A) (B) (C) (D) (E)

13. (A) (B) (C) (D) (E)

14. (A) (B) (C) (D) (E)

15. (A) (B) (C) (D) (E)

16. (A) (B) (C) (D) (E)

17. (A) (B) (C) (D) (E)

18. (A) (B) (C) (D) (E)

19. (A) (B) (C) (D) (E)

20. (A) (B) (C) (D) (E)

21. (A) (B) (C) (D) (E)

22. (A) (B) (C) (D) (E)

23. (A) (B) (C) (D) (E)

24. (A) (B) (C) (D) (E)

25. (A) (B) (C) (D) (E)

26. (A) (B) (C) (D) (E)

27. (A) (B) (C) (D) (E)

28. (A) (B) (C) (D) (E)

29. (A) (B) (C) (D) (E)

30. (A) (B) (C) (D) (E)

31. (A) (B) (C) (D) (E)

32. (A) (B) (C) (D) (E)

33. (A) (B) (C) (D) (E)

34. (A) (B) (C) (D) (E)

35. (A) (B) (C) (D) (E)

36. (A) (B) (C) (D) (E)

37. (A) (B) (C) (D) (E)

38. (A) (B) (C) (D) (E)

Practice Test – Additional Answer Sheet

Reading Comprehension

1. (A) (B) (C) (D) (E)
2. (A) (B) (C) (D) (E)
3. (A) (B) (C) (D) (E)
4. (A) (B) (C) (D) (E)
5. (A) (B) (C) (D) (E)
6. (A) (B) (C) (D) (E)
7. (A) (B) (C) (D) (E)
8. (A) (B) (C) (D) (E)
9. (A) (B) (C) (D) (E)
10. (A) (B) (C) (D) (E)
11. (A) (B) (C) (D) (E)
12. (A) (B) (C) (D) (E)
13. (A) (B) (C) (D) (E)
14. (A) (B) (C) (D) (E)
15. (A) (B) (C) (D) (E)
16. (A) (B) (C) (D) (E)
17. (A) (B) (C) (D) (E)
18. (A) (B) (C) (D) (E)
19. (A) (B) (C) (D) (E)
20. (A) (B) (C) (D) (E)
21. (A) (B) (C) (D) (E)
22. (A) (B) (C) (D) (E)
23. (A) (B) (C) (D) (E)
24. (A) (B) (C) (D) (E)
25. (A) (B) (C) (D) (E)

26. (A) (B) (C) (D) (E)
27. (A) (B) (C) (D) (E)
28. (A) (B) (C) (D) (E)
29. (A) (B) (C) (D) (E)
30. (A) (B) (C) (D) (E)
31. (A) (B) (C) (D) (E)
32. (A) (B) (C) (D) (E)
33. (A) (B) (C) (D) (E)
34. (A) (B) (C) (D) (E)
35. (A) (B) (C) (D) (E)
36. (A) (B) (C) (D) (E)
37. (A) (B) (C) (D) (E)
38. (A) (B) (C) (D) (E)
39. (A) (B) (C) (D) (E)
40. (A) (B) (C) (D) (E)

Mathematics

1. (A) (B) (C) (D) (E)
2. (A) (B) (C) (D) (E)
3. (A) (B) (C) (D) (E)
4. (A) (B) (C) (D) (E)
5. (A) (B) (C) (D) (E)
6. (A) (B) (C) (D) (E)
7. (A) (B) (C) (D) (E)
8. (A) (B) (C) (D) (E)
9. (A) (B) (C) (D) (E)
10. (A) (B) (C) (D) (E)

11. (A) (B) (C) (D) (E)
12. (A) (B) (C) (D) (E)
13. (A) (B) (C) (D) (E)
14. (A) (B) (C) (D) (E)
15. (A) (B) (C) (D) (E)
16. (A) (B) (C) (D) (E)
17. (A) (B) (C) (D) (E)
18. (A) (B) (C) (D) (E)
19. (A) (B) (C) (D) (E)
20. (A) (B) (C) (D) (E)
21. (A) (B) (C) (D) (E)
22. (A) (B) (C) (D) (E)
23. (A) (B) (C) (D) (E)
24. (A) (B) (C) (D) (E)
25. (A) (B) (C) (D) (E)
26. (A) (B) (C) (D) (E)
27. (A) (B) (C) (D) (E)
28. (A) (B) (C) (D) (E)
29. (A) (B) (C) (D) (E)
30. (A) (B) (C) (D) (E)
31. (A) (B) (C) (D) (E)
32. (A) (B) (C) (D) (E)
33. (A) (B) (C) (D) (E)
34. (A) (B) (C) (D) (E)
35. (A) (B) (C) (D) (E)
36. (A) (B) (C) (D) (E)
37. (A) (B) (C) (D) (E)

38. Ⓐ Ⓑ Ⓒ Ⓓ Ⓔ

39. Ⓐ Ⓑ Ⓒ Ⓓ Ⓔ

40. Ⓐ Ⓑ Ⓒ Ⓓ Ⓔ

Writing

1. Ⓐ Ⓑ Ⓒ Ⓓ Ⓔ

2. Ⓐ Ⓑ Ⓒ Ⓓ Ⓔ

3. Ⓐ Ⓑ Ⓒ Ⓓ Ⓔ

4. Ⓐ Ⓑ Ⓒ Ⓓ Ⓔ

5. Ⓐ Ⓑ Ⓒ Ⓓ Ⓔ

6. Ⓐ Ⓑ Ⓒ Ⓓ Ⓔ

7. Ⓐ Ⓑ Ⓒ Ⓓ Ⓔ

8. Ⓐ Ⓑ Ⓒ Ⓓ Ⓔ

9. Ⓐ Ⓑ Ⓒ Ⓓ Ⓔ

10. Ⓐ Ⓑ Ⓒ Ⓓ Ⓔ

11. Ⓐ Ⓑ Ⓒ Ⓓ Ⓔ

12. Ⓐ Ⓑ Ⓒ Ⓓ Ⓔ

13. Ⓐ Ⓑ Ⓒ Ⓓ Ⓔ

14. Ⓐ Ⓑ Ⓒ Ⓓ Ⓔ

15. Ⓐ Ⓑ Ⓒ Ⓓ Ⓔ

16. Ⓐ Ⓑ Ⓒ Ⓓ Ⓔ

17. Ⓐ Ⓑ Ⓒ Ⓓ Ⓔ

18. Ⓐ Ⓑ Ⓒ Ⓓ Ⓔ

19. Ⓐ Ⓑ Ⓒ Ⓓ Ⓔ

20. Ⓐ Ⓑ Ⓒ Ⓓ Ⓔ

21. Ⓐ Ⓑ Ⓒ Ⓓ Ⓔ

22. Ⓐ Ⓑ Ⓒ Ⓓ Ⓔ

23. Ⓐ Ⓑ Ⓒ Ⓓ Ⓔ

24. Ⓐ Ⓑ Ⓒ Ⓓ Ⓔ

25. Ⓐ Ⓑ Ⓒ Ⓓ Ⓔ

26. Ⓐ Ⓑ Ⓒ Ⓓ Ⓔ

27. Ⓐ Ⓑ Ⓒ Ⓓ Ⓔ

28. Ⓐ Ⓑ Ⓒ Ⓓ Ⓔ

29. Ⓐ Ⓑ Ⓒ Ⓓ Ⓔ

30. Ⓐ Ⓑ Ⓒ Ⓓ Ⓔ

31. Ⓐ Ⓑ Ⓒ Ⓓ Ⓔ

32. Ⓐ Ⓑ Ⓒ Ⓓ Ⓔ

33. Ⓐ Ⓑ Ⓒ Ⓓ Ⓔ

34. Ⓐ Ⓑ Ⓒ Ⓓ Ⓔ

35. Ⓐ Ⓑ Ⓒ Ⓓ Ⓔ

36. Ⓐ Ⓑ Ⓒ Ⓓ Ⓔ

37. Ⓐ Ⓑ Ⓒ Ⓓ Ⓔ

38. Ⓐ Ⓑ Ⓒ Ⓓ Ⓔ

Practice Test Essay Section
(use additional paper as necessary)

Practice Test Essay Section
(use additional paper as necessary)

_____

_____

_____

_____

_____

_____

_____

_____

_____

_____

_____

_____

_____

_____

_____

_____

_____

_____

_____

_____

_____

_____

_____

_____

_____

Practice Test Essay Section
(use additional paper as necessary)

_____

_____

_____

_____

_____

_____

_____

_____

_____

_____

_____

_____

_____

_____

_____

_____

_____

_____

_____

_____

_____

_____

_____

_____

Practice Test Essay Section
(use additional paper as necessary)

_____

_____

_____

_____

_____

_____

_____

_____

_____

_____

_____

_____

_____

_____

_____

_____

_____

_____

_____

_____

_____

_____

_____

_____

_____

Practice Test Essay Section
(use additional paper as necessary)

Practice Test Essay Section
(use additional paper as necessary)

Practice Test Essay Section
(use additional paper as necessary)

Practice Test Essay Section
(use additional paper as necessary)

Practice Test Essay Section
(use additional paper as necessary)

Practice Test Essay Section
(use additional paper as necessary)